The CAMPUS RAPE FRENZY

THE ATTACK ON DUE PROCESS AT AMERICA'S UNIVERSITIES

KC JOHNSON & STUART TAYLOR JR.

First American edition published in 2017 by Encounter Books,
an activity of Encounter for Culture and Education, Inc.,
a nonprofit, tax exempt corporation.
Encounter Books website address: www.encounterbooks.com

Manufactured in the United States and printed on
acid-free paper. The paper used in this publication meets
the minimum requirements of ANSI/NISO Z39.48–1992
(R 1997) (*Permanence of Paper*).

FIRST AMERICAN EDITION

LIBRARY OF CONGRESS CATALOGING-IN-PUBLICATION DATA

Names: Johnson, Robert David, 1967– author. | Taylor, Stuart, 1948– author.
Title: The campus rape frenzy : the attack on due process at America's
universities / by KC Johnson and Stuart Taylor, Jr.
Description: New York : Encounter Books, 2017. | Includes
bibliographical references and index.
Identifiers: LCCN 2016019693 (print) | LCCN 2016033441 (ebook) |
ISBN 9781594038853 (hardback) | ISBN 9781594038860 (Ebook)
Subjects: LCSH: Rape in universities and colleges—United States. | Rape in
universities and colleges—Political aspects—United States. | Presumption
of innocence—United States. | Due process of law—United States. | BISAC:
HISTORY / United States / 21st Century. | LAW / Civil Rights. | LAW /
Educational Law & Legislation.
Classification: LCC LB2345.3.R37 J65 2017 (print) | LCC LB2345.3.R37 (ebook)
| DDC 371.7/82—dc23
LC record available at https://lccn.loc.gov/2016019693

Interior page design and composition: BooksByBruce.com

DEDICATIONS

*To my sisters Gwennie and Clare, my wife Sally,
and our daughters Sarah and Molly*
—Stuart Taylor Jr.

In memory of my mother, Susan McNamara Johnson
—KC Johnson

CONTENTS

PREFACE

A decade ago, once our book *Until Proven Innocent: Political Correctness and the Shameful Injustices of the Duke Lacrosse Rape Case* had been published, we hoped that politicians, journalists, and academics alike would come to grips with a central lesson of the Duke lacrosse case: that for institutional, ideological, and pedagogical reasons, college faculties and administrations had become dangerously hostile to due process whenever students were accused of sexual assault. But instead, a powerful movement has made it even less likely that colleges and universities—and their students—will judge sexual assault allegations fairly.

We do not seek to minimize the scourge of sexual assault. But amid massive attention to the plight of students who are victims of sexual assault, the fate of students who have been wrongfully accused of sexual assault has been virtually ignored. This book seeks to remedy the problem, by bringing readers inside a system on our nation's campuses in which accused students effectively have to prove their innocence, often under procedures that deny them any meaningful opportunity to do so.

INTRODUCTION

In the early morning of February 5, 2012, a student named Alice Stanton* met Michael Cheng,* her roommate's boyfriend, in a dormitory common area of Massachusetts' Amherst College.[1] After the two started making out, another student remarked that they should "get a room." Cheng, who was extremely intoxicated, went with Stanton (who later said she had been "tipsy") back to her room, where Stanton performed oral sex on him. Her roommate, Cheng's girlfriend, was out of town for the weekend.[2]

As soon as Cheng left her room, a panicked Stanton texted a male friend (her dorm's resident counselor): "Ohmygod I jus did something so fuckig stupid." In subsequent texts to this friend, she implied that she had initiated the sexual contact with Cheng and was worried about the fallout. Fellow students who had seen Cheng and her leave the dorm common area, she complained, were "not gonna believe that we left to NOT fuck." She floated a cover story about their reason for leaving but worried that Cheng was "too drunk to make a good lie out of shit."

Stanton soon turned her attention to other matters. Earlier that evening, before her encounter with Cheng, she had been flirtatiously texting another male student. Praising his "military trained bod," she had advised him that she had her room to herself for the weekend "if you wanted to come over and entertain me." Now she texted him

---

1 Throughout this book, we have used parties' real names when those parties previously identified themselves, by giving interviews or filing a lawsuit. In one additional case (University of Virginia), multiple media outlets reported the accuser's identity, which subsequent legal filings confirmed. In all other cases, the use of an asterisk indicates a pseudonym.

again. He asked her why her texts had stopped for 45 minutes (the time during which she had been with Cheng). She replied that she had been engaged in "sophomore floor bonding," since "I thought you were a lost cause."

At 2:30 a.m., the male student texted Stanton to say that he was coming over. Stanton relayed this information to her friend, who responded encouragingly: "Double your pleasure, double your fun." Shortly after her new guest arrived, Stanton texted the same friend again, complaining, "OK. Why is he just talking to me?...Like, hot girl in a slutty dress. Make. Your. Move. YEAH." She followed up with the results: "Ohmygod action did not happen til 5 in the fucking morning."

The next morning, Stanton realized her mistake: "I am a shitty friend," she conceded. After her texting pal promised not to tell anyone about the episode with Cheng, Stanton resolved that "no one can know," because if anybody knew, her roommate "would literally never speak to me again." She tried to rationalize her behavior: "We didn't technicallyyyy have sex. So that's not quiteeee as bad?" Her friend wasn't convinced. "Hahahaha. Technically?" When Stanton countered that she wanted the madness to stop, her friend—far more presciently than he ever could have known—responded, "The madness hasn't even begun."

Stanton's behavior soon was no secret at Amherst, a residential college with fewer than 2,000 students. As a result, Cheng and his girlfriend broke up. And Stanton "lost her group of friends," as one of the former friends later recalled.

There are countless such casual hookups on college campuses every year. If this one had occurred a few years before, few people would have heard about it. But Alice Stanton's view of her adventures that night would become swept up in a chain of events that the Obama administration had set in motion—a chain that would, almost two years after Stanton's encounter with Cheng, upend his life.

In an unprecedented initiative, in 2011 the federal government ordered almost all universities to institute revolutionary changes in their disciplinary policies in order to counter what the Obama administration described as an epidemic of rape and other sexual assaults on college campuses. (We henceforth use "sexual assault" as inclusive of rape.) These changes dramatically weakened accused students' rights to fair proceedings.

As the initial effects of these commands swept across the country, Amherst, like many other colleges, was in the grip of a moral panic about students' sexual behavior. What would previously have been a regrettable sexual encounter transformed into actionable sexual misconduct. In this frenzy, Michael Cheng would become a victim.

In October 2012, eight months after Stanton and Cheng had oral sex, a former Amherst undergraduate named Angie Epifano penned a column in the campus newspaper, *The Amherst Student*. She alleged that college employees had treated her callously after she told them that a fellow student had raped her.[3] She had neither complained to police nor asked Amherst to discipline the alleged rapist. Nor did she make public any evidence supporting her accusation. But she painted a damning portrait of how three Amherst officials reacted to her assertions that she had been raped.

She claimed that the college's sexual assault counselor, Gretchen Krull, had told her, "You have to forgive and forget." And that—after she threatened to kill herself, and had been involuntarily committed to an on-campus psychiatric facility for observation—an Amherst doctor had said, "I really don't think that a school like Amherst would allow you to be raped." And that a dean had told her, after her request to study in South Africa had been denied (apparently due to her mental state), that she would be better off avoiding "those horrible third-world conditions: diseases...huts...lions!"[4]

Were these things actually said? That seems unlikely, but there was no indication that *The Amherst Student* gave Krull, the doctor, or the dean the chance to respond to Epifano's narrative.

The Amherst administration and faculty accepted Epifano's October 2012 account on faith. The college canceled a full day's classes for a "teach-in" about Epifano's complaints. President Biddy Martin proclaimed that "the administration's responses to reports have left survivors feeling that they were badly served" and must "change immediately."[5] Krull left her job the next day; officials would not say whether she had resigned or been fired. Campus activists expressed regret at Krull's departure, noting her past sympathy for rape victims. No one, it seems, explored whether Epifano's out-of-character portrayal of Krull should figure in determining Epifano's overall credibility.

In response to the controversy, Martin created a panel to recommend changes in Amherst's disciplinary procedures for sexual assault, to focus on "empowering victims."[6] Chaired by Margaret Hunt, a professor of women's and gender studies, the eight-member committee included the school's Title IX coordinator, other administrators, and one lawyer—an Amherst trustee with no apparent criminal law experience. One of the two student members, Liya Rechtman, described herself as a sexual assault victim. All procedural changes adopted on the committee's recommendation increased the likelihood of guilty findings.[7]

By then, Alice Stanton had a new circle of friends. They included Liya Rechtman and Dana Bolger, another self-described sexual assault victim who would later help found the campus accusers' rights group Know Your IX. Stanton joined the duo in contributing regularly to a website frequented by Amherst's victims' rights advocates. On October 25, 2012, Stanton penned an essay reinterpreting her encounter with Cheng (whom she did not name in the essay). She now claimed that she "was raped," though in the essay she focused on the pain of seeing friends turn on her after disbelieving her story.

Months passed. Then, in April 2013, at Rechtman's urging, Stanton spoke with Amherst's deputy Title IX coordinator, Susie Mitton Shannon. Shifting her story from her October article, she told Mitton Shannon that Cheng had sexually assaulted—but not raped—her. Mitton Shannon notified both campus security and the Amherst Police but allowed Stanton to defer any adjudication process for as long as she wanted. She did not inform Cheng of Stanton's allegation.

Throughout the summer and early fall of 2013, Mitton Shannon repeatedly sent Stanton complaint forms, to remind her of the possibility of filing charges. On October 28, Stanton did so, though she did not involve the local police. In a written statement to the college, Stanton claimed that during the encounter with Cheng, she withdrew her consent because she was repulsed by Cheng's sexual innuendo referencing her roommate. Shortly after the encounter, however, Stanton had presented the issue much differently, texting her friend: "dirty talk comparing me to my roommate should NOT DO THINGS FOR ME." In addition, Stanton claimed to have been so terrified of Cheng after he left her room that she tossed his phone (which he had left behind) out into the hall and locked the door. Shortly after the encounter, however, Stanton told a friend that she had told Cheng to "go away" when he came back for his phone—because by then the student with the "military trained bod" was in her room. "I feel so baddddddd," she added.

Whether Amherst officials would see these and other credibility-destroying texts would emerge as the key issue in the case.

The college hired an employment attorney, Allyson Kurker, to investigate. It was her first job for Amherst, and she interviewed all but one of the witnesses in a single day. She then prepared a report stating that the accuser "did not email, text, or otherwise reduce what had happened with Mr. [Cheng] to writing." Amherst administrators reviewed, and suggested multiple edits to, the report. But the inaccurate statement about text messages remained in. Kurker, who received $10,080 for her brief investigation, did not respond to an interview request by us.

Reflecting Amherst's new sexual assault policy, Cheng's hearing on December 12, 2013, occurred not before a panel of his peers—his fellow students—but before three administrators drawn from the student life and diversity bureaucracies of nearby Smith College, the University of Massachusetts, and Mount Holyoke College. To prepare them for this role, each of the three had received secret "training" from his or her institution's Title IX office, along with additional guidance from Amherst.

This group represented an ideological fringe of the campus. Panel member Eric Hamako, for instance, who held a doctorate in social justice education, had produced academic work applying a "multi-issue social justice analysis" to such examples from popular culture as Harry Potter and zombies in his efforts at "anti-oppression education."[8] Stanton's advisor for the hearing, professor Rhonda Cobham-Sander, had served as Amherst's first special assistant to the president for diversity. She had also attracted attention on campus by delivering a passionate paean to victims' rights after the 2012 Epifano sexual assault controversy. Cheng's advisor, Torin Moore, was an Amherst administrator who shared Hamako's background in "social justice education." The college treated the two advisors differently: Cobham-Sander received a summary of Stanton's initial interview with the college, from the previous spring. Moore, and thus Cheng, did not.

During the hearing, Stanton struggled to tell a coherent story. When a panel member asked what she had done after the alleged assault, she claimed that she had texted a friend to come spend the night with her, because she had felt "very alone and confused." This text, a reference to the student with the "military trained bod" whom Stanton had invited to her room *before* she ever encountered Cheng that evening, was clearly relevant to the panel's inquiry. Stanton's acknowledgment that she had sent it contradicted her assurance to Kurker (the investigator) that she had sent no relevant electronic communications. But none of the panelists asked to see the text or seemed to notice the contradiction. Nor did they respond later to questions from us about their lack of curiosity about this critical evidence.

At Cheng's request, the panel chair asked Stanton whether she had voluntarily gone to her room to hook up with him. The response was: "Yes. Well—although I would like to say that I did feel some…like, well, pressure to do so." When a panel member asked Stanton to elaborate on this previously unmentioned "pressure," Stanton said, "So as we were making out in the common room, so some of the students there, so I think, so I think, so I think, [another student] included, were just like, well, chanting like, well, things about me."

Of what relevance was the claim to Stanton's allegations, since the "pressure" came neither from Cheng nor at his behest?

Despite Stanton's changing, bizarre story, the panel ruled in her favor. Although they noted that Cheng had probably been "blacked out" during the oral sex, the panel said that "[b]eing intoxicated or impaired by drugs or alcohol is never an excuse."

This finding only raised more questions about Amherst's fairness, since under the facts before it, the panel could have investigated *Stanton*. Her admitted behavior of leading Cheng to her room and initiating sex (before allegedly withdrawing consent) contradicted the college's sexual assault policy, which indicated that "an individual who is incapacitated"—as the disciplinary panel found Cheng to be— "is not able to make rational, reasonable judgments and therefore is incapable of giving consent."[9] Defending the board's decision not to fulfill its independent obligations to investigate a potential Title IX violation, Amherst blamed Cheng for not having filed a sexual assault complaint himself.

Without the opportunity to see Stanton's text messages, and despite her inconsistent testimony, the panel members treated Stanton as credible. Since Cheng, having been "blacked out," could not know whether Stanton had later said no, the panel assumed she had. They recommended expelling Cheng for sexual assault. The next day, one of the panelists had second thoughts and asked Amherst's Title IX office whether a less severe response was possible. No record exists of a response from Amherst.[10]

Cheng appealed. Three days after his hearing, under the headline "Amherst College Sexual Assault Policies Treat Alleged Rapists Better Than Laptop Thieves," *The Huffington Post* quoted Stanton—without identifying her connection to the case—as saying that at the college, "The typical laptop thief is suspended for five semesters.... Rapists are not suspended for that long, if at all.... No rapist... has been expelled from Amherst in 20 years. That's unacceptable and something Amherst has to change immediately."[11] Amherst administrators would have had good reason for seeing the article as an indication that the college would face another Epifano-like public relations disaster if it upheld Cheng's appeal. The appeal was rejected.

After his expulsion, Cheng hired a lawyer. He obtained the texts decimating Stanton's credibility, not in compulsory discovery but in the type of routine investigation that Allyson Kurker had failed to perform. His ex-girlfriend, having heard about the texts, asked Stanton's friend for a copy of them. As she read them, she realized that Stanton's allegations "were not truthful." Stanton's performance, her former roommate understood, had not only resulted in an "unjust disciplinary process" but "made it more difficult for victims of sexual abuse to come forward without fear of being accused of fabricating their allegations." Cheng also received a sworn affidavit from the student with the "military trained bod." On the evening of the episode, this student described Stanton as "friendly, flirtatious, and spirited"—just as her text messages showed—not "anxious, stressed, depressed, or otherwise in distress."

---

10 Colleges use words such as "culpable" and "responsible" instead of "guilty." On this issue, some also use words such as "sexual misconduct" instead of "sexual assault." Here we often use the colloquial "guilty" and words that best describe the specific alleged acts that become known to fellow students and others familiar with their cases.

When shown the new evidence in the spring of 2014, Amherst refused to reopen the case, saying it was too late to do so. The college's lawyers added that the investigator, Kurker, had not been "charged with seeking to obtain" exculpatory evidence; she had been charged only with determining "whether [Stanton] had communicated or recorded in writing that the Incident had been 'non-consensual.'" Documents that *corroborated* Stanton's claim of sexual assault, Kurker later testified, were "the only e-mails that I would have found material." In other words, according to Amherst's legal filings, the process in Michael Cheng's case had worked as the college intended.

This is not a fictional tale like *The Trial* by Franz Kafka. It happened at one of the nation's most prestigious colleges, thanks to policies approved by Amherst president Biddy Martin, under pressure from appointees of President Barack Obama. And with apparent support from Amherst's board of trustees.

Cheng filed a lawsuit, which remains pending as of September 2016, against Amherst and several of its administrators. Amherst's lawyer, Scott Roberts, said in a May hearing before U.S. District Judge Mark Mastroianni that he detected no inconsistency between the college having a "thorough, fair, and impartial" adjudication procedure and one that was "biased in favor of alleged victims."[12]

The facts of Cheng's case are unusually clear, because his lawsuit included copies of Stanton's text messages, the transcript of his disciplinary hearing, and the college investigator's full report. This type of material almost never sees the light of day, since all campus adjudications of sexual assault claims—unlike court proceedings—occur in secret. "Sunlight is said to be the best of disinfectants," Justice Louis Brandeis wrote more than a century ago. But colleges go to great lengths, even beyond the dictates of federal privacy law, to keep their sexual assault proceedings in the dark.[13]

Amherst's resolution of Alice Stanton's charges typifies how most colleges handle sexual assault allegations these days. Start with an alcohol-soaked set of facts that no state's criminal law would consider sexual assault. Add an incomplete "investigation," unfair procedures, and a disciplinary panel uninterested in evidence of innocence. Stir in a de facto presumption of guilt based on misguided Obama administration dictates, ideological zeal, and fear of bad publicity. It's a formula for judging innocent male students to be sex offenders. "I'm afraid...we are over-correcting," Harvard Law School professor Janet Halley recently remarked. "The procedures that are being adopted are taking us back to pre–Magna Carta, pre-due-process procedures."[14]

Ironically, even as colleges have engaged in such conduct, many sexual assault accusers and their champions have followed Angie Epifano's example by telling implausible tales of college officials coddling alleged rapists and mistreating alleged victims. Such narratives of alleged rape on college campuses have come from activists at the University of North Carolina, the University of Virginia, Los Angeles' Occidental College, and elsewhere. The main villains in such narratives are not the alleged rapists but rather college officials who have allegedly shown almost unspeakable cruelty to the victims they are supposed to protect. The media and many academics have parroted such tales as proof of a campus "rape culture."

A sympathetic emotional response to a vulnerable person who tells of being raped is only human. On a personal level, alleged victims deserve to be believed—unless evidence suggests otherwise. That reality helps explain the warm applause that erupted at the 2016 Academy Awards when Lady Gaga performed her Oscar-nominated song "Til It Happens to You" and when Vice President Joe Biden introduced a group of female college students who said they had been sexually assaulted.[15]

But Biden's appearance also furthered the Obama administration's effort to blur the critical distinction between the need for personal empathy toward victims and the need for a college disciplinary process that pursues even-handed justice in search of the truth. Few people who heard a friend, family member, or colleague tell of sexual assault would express skepticism or bring up burden of proof, the importance of cross-examination, or the need for fair adjudicatory procedures. But those conditions are vital to wise public policy.

Since 2011, when the Obama administration ordered colleges and universities to transform their disciplinary procedures for alleged sexual assault on college campuses, between 20,000 and 25,000 such allegations have been made to schools, according to figures compiled through the federal government's Clery Act database. Not all students who have been accused in such cases faced campus trials. Some accusers doubtless chose not to proceed with institutional charges. Others went to the police instead. And still others perhaps made allegations against non-students, people outside the purview of the college disciplinary process.

But at the least, many thousands of accused students have faced campus proceedings that were similar to—or even more one-sided than—what Michael Cheng experienced at Amherst. For accused college students—and only them—the federal government, joined by virtually all colleges and universities, has mounted a systematic attack on bedrock American principles including the presumption of innocence, access to exculpatory evidence, the right to cross-examine one's accuser, and due process.

The mere existence of rape instills fear in potential victims, especially women, in all segments of society. Rape victims suffer deep psychological, emotional, and physical harms, which can last for a lifetime.[16] The lengthy criminal sentences recommended by all states' criminal codes indicate societal recognition of the magnitude of these harms. Under certain circumstances, rape even constitutes a war crime.[17]

By creating a growing contingent of wrongfully punished students—almost all of them male—the anti–due process polices decreed since 2011 by the federal government are already harming the intended beneficiaries: sexual assault victims.[18] As more *accused* students, like Michael Cheng, become victims of deeply unfair processes, society will have reason to distrust *all* college decisions against accused students. In this respect, procedural fairness not only is critical to wrongly accused students but also serves the best interests of victims.

The idea that students accused of sexual assault are not entitled to due process has somehow taken hold, even though two of the last decade's three highest-profile campus rape accusations were hoaxes. The Duke lacrosse case of 2006–2007 featured a politically desperate district attorney, Mike Nifong, using the power of the state to try to railroad three innocent students. His allies in rushing to judgment included unscrupulous underlings and police officers, news media employees, and more than 100 professors and administrators led by Duke president . Richard Brodhead. They persisted in condemning the lacrosse players

18 Although universities' policies are gender-neutral, the most recent data available indicate that "nearly all" (99 percent) of accused students are male. United Educators, "Confronting Campus Sexual Assault: An Examination of Higher Education Claims," https://www.ue.org/uploadedFiles/Confronting%20Campus%20Sexual%20Assault.pdf.

even after evidence of their innocence appeared on the public record. (We discuss this case in depth in chapter 3.)

Then came *Rolling Stone*'s since-retracted story of a sadistic gang rape at the University of Virginia's Phi Kappa Psi fraternity.[19] *Rolling Stone* and its freelance reporter, Sabrina Rubin Erdely (who had been roaming campuses in several states in search of a sensational rape story), unquestioningly accepted the fictitious tale that a succession of fraternity brothers raped a first-year student atop shattered glass. So did most of the media, as well as the University of Virginia's president and faculty. Even more troubling, most UVA students rushed to judgment—unlike their Duke counterparts in 2006—and proved unwilling to reconsider, even as overwhelming evidence of the alleged victim's lies emerged.[20] (We discuss these issues in depth in chapter 10.)

The last decade's third high-profile campus sexual assault case was no hoax: after a campus party in 2015, former Stanford swimmer Brock Turner sexually assaulted—in a public area—an unconscious woman. Yet, albeit in different ways than the Duke and UVA cases, the Turner case undermined the narrative of campus accusers' rights activists. Despite their suggestions that local police and prosecutors didn't care about campus rape, Turner was arrested, tried, and convicted of sexual assault. Despite their insinuations of a nation awash in "rape culture," his lenient sentence—six months in jail, plus a requirement to register as a sex offender—was widely criticized, including by us.[21] And despite efforts by Stanford activists to portray Turner's crime as "typical" student behavior, the national outcry itself showed this case (which we discuss further in chapter 6) to be highly atypical.[22]

In this book, we explore around four dozen of the many cases since 2011 in which innocent or almost certainly innocent students have been branded as sex criminals by their colleges. We have studied tens of thousands of pages of legal documents (many of which have not previously been publicly disseminated), along with information gleaned from university handbooks, statistical studies, and confidential "training" material created for colleges and universities nationwide.

We are not partisans. We are moderates who both voted for Barack Obama in 2008 and again, though with much less enthusiasm, in 2012. One of us (KC Johnson) donated to the Obama campaign in both 2008 and 2012.

The campus witch hunts of the past five years recall the day-care abuse allegations of the 1980s, when shockingly implausible allegations were widely accepted as true. Dozens of innocent men and women around the country were sent to prison based on transparently absurd claims that child day-care centers were dens of pedophilia, murder, and Satanic ritual.

Then, as now, overhyped reports triggered a highly emotional response among the media and, subsequently, lawmakers and the general public. Then, as now, the myth was cultivated that anyone claiming to be a victim must be believed and the accused must be guilty. Then, as now, political figures changed procedures in light of what was perceived as an insufficient number of guilty findings, to degrade the presumption of innocence and make findings of guilt more likely. During the day-care panic, quack psychotherapists were paid to "recover" through hypnosis forgotten memories that they were, in fact, planting, and then to confirm these tales on the witness stand. In the current campus sexual assault panic, meaningful cross-examination of accusers is exceedingly rare—thereby dramatically increasing the chances of guilty findings.[23]

David Rudovsky, a University of Pennsylvania law professor and longtime civil rights lawyer, sees parallels with "other moral panics," such as the internment of Japanese Americans during World War II, the communist scares of the 1940s and 1950s, and elements of the response to terrorism after September 11, 2001—"where we lost our way because too many were convinced that the threat was too great to be countered with normal due-process protections."[24] After a hearing in a case challenging a university's handling of a sexual assault complaint, U.S. District Judge F. Dennis Saylor had to reach even farther back in time for an appropriate historical analogy: "It's closer to Salem, 1692 than Boston, 2015."[25]

This book will touch only briefly (if at all) on several related topics that are distinct from the campus rape frenzy. Most closely related are federal and academic efforts to punish free expression of views that they mischaracterize as sexual (or racial) harassment, as well as a developing body of sexual harassment law and theory of which federal policies on campus sexual assault are an extension. Then comes universities' zeal to stifle intellectual diversity in their pursuit of racial, gender, and ethnic diversity.

At the high school level, in a much-discussed 2015 article revealing closed-mindedness about gender questions at a prestigious prep school, New York University professor Jonathan Haidt explored the inculcation of politically correct ideology by many elite prep schools.[26] The last several years have also witnessed a handful of widely publicized high school rape cases. One was the rape trial of a recent graduate of the elite St. Paul's School, in Concord, New Hampshire. The former student was convicted of the statutory rape of a 15-year-old schoolmate, motivated by a degenerate tradition called the "senior salute." Another case was the gang rape of a passed-out-drunk 16-year-old student at Steubenville High School, in Ohio, by two 16-year-old football players. Onlookers had recorded the crimes on their cell phones and celebrated them in social media and text messages.

In the last five years, sexual assault on college campuses has received unprecedented attention from politicians, academics, and the media. The conventional narrative goes something like this:

An astonishing 20 to 25 percent of female undergraduates will be sexually assaulted before they graduate. This epidemic[27] has been sustained by a "rape culture" that permeates university administrations as well as fraternities and other groups of male students.[28] "Women are at a greater risk of sexual assault as soon as they step onto a college campus," asserts New York senator Kirsten Gillibrand (the foremost congressional opponent of campus due process). Ignoring this emergency, colleges have been indifferent and even hostile to the millions of sexual assault victims in their student bodies.[29] The federal

------

27 A term popularized by, among others, Valerie Jarrett, President Obama's most influential advisor.
29 This claim is odd in an era in which 58 percent of the nation's undergraduate students are female. "Table 310. Degrees Conferred by Degree-Granting Institutions, by Level of Degree and Sex of Student: Selected Years, 1869–70 through 2021–22," National Center for Education Statistics, June 2012, https://nces.ed.gov/programs/digest/d12/tables/dt12_310.asp.

government thus ordered almost all universities to change their disciplinary rules in order to ferret out more sex criminals. Complaints about the presumption of innocence and due process should be disregarded because the crisis is so urgent and because 90 to 98 percent of accused males are guilty. The few falsely accused innocents will suffer no great injustice or harm, because campus tribunals have no prisons; if expelled, these students can move on to other colleges.

These claims are all untrue or unsubstantiated.

Far from a "rape culture" dominating campus discourse, those who seek due process for the accused are assailed as rape apologists, no matter how strong the evidence of innocence. For an example of this mind-set, one of the new campus regime's stoutest defenders is Brett Sokolow, founder of the National Center for Higher Education Risk Management (NCHERM), a firm that helps colleges investigate sexual assaults. He accused the nation's preeminent campus civil liberties organization, the Foundation for Individual Rights in Education (FIRE), of "sticking up for penises everywhere."[30]

This kind of environment presents due process as an obstacle to justice on college campuses. The political appointees leading the Education Department's Office for Civil Rights (OCR) issued a statement in 2014 that colleges must "ensure that steps to accord any due process rights do not restrict or unnecessarily delay the protections provided by Title IX to the complainant." At least in some circumstances, the administration maintained that its newfound interpretation of Title IX should trump constitutional protections, even for students at public universities.[31]

Harvard Law School professor Jeannie Suk Gersen explained the thinking behind such sentiments in a 2015 New Yorker essay. "It is a near-religious teaching among many people today," Suk Gersen noted, "that if you are against sexual assault, then you must always believe individuals who say they have been assaulted.... Examining evidence and concluding that a particular accuser is not indeed a survivor, or a particular accused is not an assailant, is a sin that reveals that one is a rape denier, or biased in favor of perpetrators.... Fair process for investigating sexual-misconduct cases, for which I, along with many of my colleagues, have fought, in effect violates the tenet that you must always believe the accuser."[32]

"It is better that ten guilty persons escape than that one innocent suffer."[33] That often-quoted wisdom comes from William Blackstone's *Commentaries on the Laws of England*, first published more than 250 years ago. In today's environment, the issue of sexual assault on college campuses appears to reflect the opposite premise: better that ten innocents suffer than that one guilty student escape punishment.

In a 2015 congressional hearing on policies toward campus sexual assault, Rep. Jared Polis (D-Colorado) mused, "If there are ten people who have been accused, and under a reasonable likelihood standard maybe one or two did it, it seems better to get rid of all ten people." Breaking into sarcastic laughter, and showing his ignorance of the impact of being expelled as a rapist, he went on: "We're not talking about depriving them of life or liberty, we're talking about them being transferred to another university, for crying out loud."[34]

In a moment that captured the witch-hunt atmosphere surrounding discussions of campus sexual assault, the audience, packed with accusers' rights activists, burst into applause.

1

THE FOUNDATIONS
OF THE FRENZY

For years, the leadership of Michigan State University has been very concerned with sexual assault on campus. In 2013, the university initiated a "No Excuse for Sexual Assault" campaign, designed to do "whatever we can to raise awareness to prevent sexual assault on Michigan State University's campus!"[1] MSU required all incoming students to attend two training sessions on sexual assault, with additional training for student-athletes. It distributed posters intended to dispel "myths." It handed out shirts, stickers, buttons, and brochures with the "No Excuse" slogan at university events. It developed a "No Excuse" Facebook page. It created a special help line for students to report sexual assault. And it translated all of these materials into Korean, Arabic, and Chinese.

This activity had not been inspired by an explosion of sex crimes on the 50,000-student MSU campus. From 2012 through 2015—the four most recent years for which data are available at the time of writing—the number of sexual assault accusations per year averaged 21, fewer than one for every 2,250 students.[2]

And far from dispelling "myths" about sexual assault, MSU's training *inculcated* misinformation into many students. In a university survey of all duly trained first-year and transfer students, for example, 74.9 percent of the students incorrectly identified as "false" a statement that "someone can still give consent for sex if they are using alcohol or drugs." In fact the statement was true: under Michigan law, only extreme intoxication—sufficient to render the victim "physically helpless"—can negate consent.[3]

Even as this campaign was occurring, two alleged victims of sexual assault filed a Title IX complaint against the university. As the Education Department's Office for Civil Rights (OCR) launched its investigation, MSU preemptively changed its disciplinary process to empower a single official not only to investigate and prosecute all claims of student-on-student sexual assault but also to pass judgment on the alleged perpetrators.

Under this "single investigator-adjudicator system" (which the Obama administration urged colleges to adopt), a single person effectively serves as not only detective and prosecutor but also judge and jury. An alleged perpetrator cannot see all the evidence to be used against him, defend himself before a panel of peers or faculty members, have a lawyer meaningfully represent him in the process, or cross-examine his accuser or any other witness.

With these limitations, for more than three and a half years all appeals in sexual assault cases at MSU were unsuccessful.

Despite these policies, in September 2015 OCR ruled that MSU had created a "sexually hostile environment" for women. The university, OCR claimed, took too long to investigate the sexual assault allegations of the two students who had filed the Title IX complaint. (One of these allegations, even OCR conceded, proved to be unsubstantiated.) The agency also faulted MSU for not using adequate "interim measures" during the investigation to "minimize the burden on the victim." (Again, in one of these cases, there was no "victim.") OCR's use of the word "victim," unqualified by "alleged," was one of countless occasions on which the agency has seemed to assume that all accusations of sexual assault are legitimate.

OCR's 42-page "resolution letter"—the university's legally binding agreement to resolve an OCR investigation—also criticized MSU for being insufficiently zealous to punish students accused of sexual assault. OCR expressed concern about campus surveys indicating that students were more likely to report rape and other sexual assault to law enforcement than to the university—as if reporting an alleged crime to the police should be frowned upon. The letter noted with displeasure that a campus walkway was nicknamed the "rape trail"—a name dating to the 1970s, before current undergraduates had been born. And it complained that only 7.4 percent of students could name the school's Title IX coordinator—a bureaucrat endowed by OCR with vast powers over student discipline—yet 71.5 percent could name "the University's head basketball coach."[4]

This chapter will trace how a federal office and a president lost their way, twisting Title IX—the 1972 law that seemed to be a crowning achievement for gender equity in education—into a tool for weakening civil liberties on college campuses.

Title IX built on both the Civil Rights Act of 1964 and the proposed Equal Rights Amendment of 1972. The 1964 Act established the principle of ending most forms of discrimination based on race, color, religion, sex, or national origin, but it did not ban sex discrimination by private schools or colleges. The ERA never acquired force of law because it was not ratified by enough states. But it evidenced the broad congressional support for gender equality behind Title IX, which sought to advance gender equality in education by leveraging the dependence of almost all universities on federal funds.

Title IX's key provision states that "no person in the United States shall, on the basis of sex, be excluded from participation in, be denied the benefits of, or be subjected to discrimination under any education program or activity receiving federal financial assistance."[5] In 1970, President Nixon's Task Force on Women's Rights and Responsibilities had stated that "discrimination in education is one of the most damaging injustices women suffer."[6] Nixon's domestic policy chief, John Ehrlichman, sensed a political "golden opportunity" and recommended that the president "should, whenever possible, champion female equality."[7] As a result, Title IX received easy, bipartisan approval.[8]

At no point during the 1972 debate did any member of Congress suggest that Title IX would apply to college disciplinary issues of any kind, much less to sexual assault.[9] In the following years, despite widespread attention to sexual assault—thanks to feminist activism and books such as Susan Brownmiller's *Against Our Will* (Simon and Schuster, 1975), which portrayed rape as "nothing more or less than a conscious process of intimidation by which all men keep all women in a state of fear"[10]— the regulatory guidance for Title IX did not touch on college discipline or sexual assault either.

At the time, Title IX was known mainly as a force for gender equality in athletics. But the new law did come up in a lawsuit by five female students at Yale University in New Haven, Connecticut. The students claimed that Yale had offered them no redress after male professors had sexually harassed them, in two cases by coercing sex. A 1977 court decision, *Alexander v. Yale*, dismissed most of the claims for procedural reasons, but the U.S. District Court in New Haven set a limited precedent by holding that it was "perfectly reasonable to maintain that academic advancement conditioned upon submission to sexual demands [by professors] constitutes sex discrimination in education."[11] Neither Judge Jon Newman nor the 2nd Circuit panel that affirmed his judgment suggested that isolated student-on-student sexual assault could render a university liable under Title IX.

The intellectual architect of the *Alexander* complaint was Catharine MacKinnon, a 1977 graduate of Yale Law School, who later (in the 1980s and 1990s) pushed for a vastly expanded definition of rape. "Politically," MacKinnon wrote in 1981, "I call it rape whenever a woman has sex and feels violated."[12] In her major work, *Toward a Feminist Theory of the State* (1989), MacKinnon maintained that "the similarity between the patterns, rhythms, roles and emotions, not to mention acts, which make up rape (and battery) on one hand and intercourse on the other...makes it difficult to sustain the customary distinctions between violence and sex [and casts doubt on] whether consent is a meaningful concept."[13] She even implied that all sex is akin to rape: "Perhaps the wrong of rape has proved so difficult to define because the unquestionable starting point has been that rape is defined as distinct from intercourse, while for women it is difficult to distinguish the two under conditions of male dominance."[14]

As such ideas metastasized in the academy, MacKinnon allied with the radical activist Andrea Dworkin, who declared the act of penetration by a male of a female to be a form of "occupation," a "violation of female boundaries," and a "means of physiologically making a woman inferior."[15] She also asserted that "romance...is rape embellished with meaningful looks."[16]

MacKinnon and Dworkin also took on sexual harassment, pornography, and, in the process, freedom of speech, which was also under assault from activists eager to suppress "hate speech." The duo championed a model anti-pornography law on the theory that some sexually explicit materials were by definition violence against women. The best-known law based on their model, a 1984 Indianapolis ordinance, was struck down by the U.S. Court of Appeals for the 7th Circuit, in *American Booksellers Association v. Hudnut* (1985). Judge Frank Easterbrook, quoting the Supreme Court, held that "'the First Amendment means that government has no power to restrict expression because of its message [or] its ideas.'"[17]

Not only the courts but also many mainstream liberals, for whom free speech was then a transcendently important value, rejected these sorts of policies. In 1993, American Civil Liberties Union president Nadine Strossen warned against "two influential movements to limit First Amendment protection for certain words and images, both spearheaded by law professors: the movement among some feminists [including MacKinnon] to suppress certain sexually oriented expression, which they label 'pornography'; and the movement to restrict racist and other forms of 'hate speech' through such measures as 'speech codes' on university campuses." Such "revisionist" approaches to the First Amendment were, Strossen worried, dominating "faculty appointments and promotions, law journal publications and certain law school courses."[18]

Meanwhile, starting with the work of Mary Koss, a psychology professor at Kent State University in Ohio, MacKinnon and Dworkin's campaign to expand definitions of rape became focused on sexual assault on college campuses. Pioneering a tactic that recent surveys have made into a ritual, Koss refrained from asking her subjects whether they had been sexually assaulted. Instead, she explored particular behaviors, which she treated as evidence of sexual assault even when the law (or her subjects) did not. Although her questions about specific behaviors were not inherently misleading, Koss infused the answers with her own ideological biases. She classified as "sexual assault" incidents that 73 percent of her subjects did not consider to be sexual assault. This technique enabled her to declare that 25 percent of college women were victims of sexual assault.[19]

Thirty years later, Koss asserted: "I have never believed that it was useful to restrict our research to rape. Universities still have to deal with acts that may not be crimes, but they're still violations."[20] In other words, in order to identify a rape epidemic, Koss—like MacKinnon and Dworkin—had changed the meaning of "rape" to include many noncrimes.[21]

A simple but effective rhetorical trick.

Koss' claims came under sustained attack in the 1980s from commentators including University of California professor Neil Gilbert, self-described feminist Christina Hoff Sommers, and Princeton graduate student Katie Roiphe. Gilbert said that the roughly 60-fold difference between the rape rate in contemporaneous government statistics and Koss' figure "is the difference between the view that male-female relations are normally enjoyable for most people and the view that they are inherently antagonistic and dangerous."[22] Roiphe's critique of Koss, in a lengthy *New York Times Magazine* essay and then in a book, attracted enough attention to draw an accusation from Koss that Roiphe was making women not "feel free" to report rapes.[23]

Still, by 1991, the ideas of MacKinnon, Dworkin, Koss, and their allies had become so influential as to prompt *Washington Post* columnist Richard Cohen to write that although rape had long been underreported, "the pendulum seems to have swung in the other direction," so that "at least in some surveys, rape is now overreported."[24]

Far from such intellectual debates, the criminal justice system, much maligned by many rape victims and their champions, had made important progress toward treating rape victims with greater sensitivity. For example, the percentage of female police officers in the United States increased from 2 percent in 1970 to nearly 12 percent by 2007, and the percentage of women in some law-enforcement departments was as high as 18 percent in 2007.[25] Police culture became less sexist and more professional. Prosecutors also improved their handling of rape cases.

In 1976, Manhattan became one of the first jurisdictions with a sex crimes unit, which Linda Fairstein headed until her retirement in 2002.[26] District attorneys working with feminist groups established specially trained sex crimes units in the 1990s, and almost all large and most medium-sized cities have such units today.[27] Lawmakers and judges enacted rape shield and other laws to make the criminal justice process easier on rape victims and harder on alleged perpetrators.[28] In 1993, Oklahoma and North Carolina became the last states to eliminate exemptions for spousal rape. Finally, sexual assault nurse and examiners (SANEs) professionalized victim care and evidence collection.[29]

There remain police departments that are indifferent or even hostile to rape victims, hospitals that botch the evidence collection process, and prosecutors who are overworked, overcautious, biased, or incompetent.[30] Certainly too many jurisdictions allow rape kits to go untested for too long.[31] But it's clear that the criminal justice system handles allegations, and treats victims, of sexual assault far better now than it did in 1970.

Yet many protagonists in the current debate assume law enforcement to be frozen in time. Echoing accusers' rights activists, Sen. Claire McCaskill (D-Missouri) claimed in 2015 that "the criminal justice system has been very bad . . . in terms of addressing victims and supporting victims and pursuing prosecutions."[32] On September 30, 2015, the activist group Know Your IX (@knowyourIX), which was created in 2013 with the goal of "empowering students to stop sexual violence,"[33] tweeted that requiring victims of sexual assault to report their *own* crimes to authorities "force[s] survivors into a violent criminal legal system" and may lead to "deportation, police brutality, [or] arrest of the victim." But those who say law enforcement is no better for victims today than it was 45 years ago are blind to reality. And even if they were right, that condition would not justify eviscerating the due-process rights of college students.

In the late 1980s and early 1990s, the law enforcement pendulum sometimes started to swing too far. Consider an incident from Brandeis University, in a wealthy liberal enclave of suburban Boston. The ideological and procedural biases displayed in this case foreshadowed how colleges and universities would soon handle the overwhelming majority of sexual assault complaints.

In April 1988, a male and a female Brandeis student who had been friends but never romantic partners had sex. Months later—after she broke up with her boyfriend, suffered an emotional breakdown, and invited the friend she would later accuse of rape to her family's house for a weekend getaway—the female student told police she had been raped. She also told another friend that her attacker had been someone other than the student whom she had accused.

The case was referred to feminist lawyer Nancy Gertner, later a federal judge and Harvard Law School professor. Given the obvious weaknesses in the accuser's story, Gertner believed that the male student was innocent, but she declined to take the case due to her feminist credentials. She handed it off to a partner and then watched in horror as the process went awry. "The atmosphere surrounding date rape had changed more dramatically than I had appreciated, at least in Massachusetts," she recalled.

The district attorney brought charges despite the case's weakness, Gertner wrote, "lest he face political repercussions, for being yet another politician ignoring a woman's pain." A member of the grand jury that returned the indictment later told Gertner that the members had "assumed [the male student] would be acquitted." The defendant waived a jury trial because the opening of the case coincided with a television broadcast about date rape. In December 1989, Judge John Paul Sullivan, who had seemed skeptical during the proceedings, nonetheless pronounced the defendant guilty. Although Sullivan "did not say so explicitly," Gertner wrote, "the message seemed clear. If he acquitted [the defendant], he would be pilloried in the press. 'Judge acquits rapist,' the headlines would scream. But if he convicted [him], no one would notice."[34]

Fortunately for the accused student, the guilty verdict was reversed in 1991, in an appeal handled by Gertner. The Massachusetts Supreme Judicial Court ruled unanimously that the trial judge had committed several reversible errors. It also noted that "the evidence in many ways was contradictory, and, even looking only at the complainant's testimony, in some respects was inconsistent with an allegation of rape."[35]

This new environment inevitably affected the political process. In 1980, OCR, the enforcement agency for Title IX, became part of the new Department of Education, created by Congress' division of the Department of Health, Education, and Welfare. A 1981 memorandum from OCR's director of litigation confined the office's definition of sexual harassment to acts committed "by an employee or agent" of the school, not peer-on-peer behavior.[36] Terry Pell, who headed the agency from 1985 through 1988, said in a 2014 interview that OCR never did "anything on the topic of sexual assault." "While schools were thought to be liable for offensive classroom behavior by professors," Pell recalled, "they were not thought to be liable for offensive behavior by male students outside of the classroom."[37]

In the early 1990s, however, responding to popular and media pressure, Congress increased the federal government's role in campus discipline. In 1990, Congress required universities to report all crimes (including sex crimes) on campus to the Education Department, which made each university's numbers public. The law was named after Jeanne Clery, a Lehigh University student who had been raped and murdered (by another student) in her dorm room in 1986. Clery's parents maintained that they would not have enrolled their daughter at the school if they had known of Lehigh's "slipshod" security and reports of recent violent crimes.

Although the Clery Act established the precedent of congressional oversight of campus discipline, its goals were initially limited to transparency. The measure explicitly denied the Education Department any authority "to require particular policies, procedures, or practices by institutions of higher education with respect to campus crimes or campus security."[38]

A little-noticed provision of the 1992 Higher Education Amendments weakened that restriction. The statute required all federally funded colleges and universities to "develop and distribute a statement of policy regarding [both] campus sexual assault programs, which shall be aimed at prevention of sex offenses; and procedures followed once a sex offense has occurred."[39] This law distinguished for the first time between sexual assault and all other felonies, such as attempted murder, aggravated assault and battery, armed robbery, and drug dealing.

Neither the floor debates nor the committee hearings offered a clear explanation of why Congress chose to require colleges and universities—in cases of sexual assault, and only in cases of sexual assault—to end their traditional reliance on law enforcement and implement a quasi-criminal process of their own. But the most plausible explanation for the move is media and public pressure.

In the late 1980s, thanks in part to *Ms.* magazine cofounder Gloria Steinem, the writings of Mary Koss attracted considerable national attention. At a handful of campuses, most notably Brown University in Providence, Rhode Island, student protests urged schools to more aggressively address the issue of sexual assault on college campuses.[40] In a 1989 *New York Times* interview, campus crime expert Michael Clay Smith argued that "rape is of course the single growing problem on campus. What has been so surprising is the failure to recognize the offense."[41]

Although it created an important precedent, the 1992 law attracted little notice. Colleges and universities were changing in other important ways, however. The 1980s and 1990s brought a surge in new administrative positions in the areas of "student life" and "diversity." Some of these new staffers focused on the day-to-day experiences of students, but many were ideologues who thought that racial minorities and women had always been and still were systematically oppressed.

One such figure was Catherine Comins, an assistant dean of student life at Vassar College in Arlington, New York. In a 1991 interview, Comins, who oversaw all student rape complaints at Vassar, made the appalling suggestion that male students could benefit from being falsely accused of sex crimes. "[Accused male students] have a lot of pain," she noted, "but it is not a pain that I would necessarily have spared them. I think it ideally initiates a process of self-exploration. 'How do I see women?' 'If I didn't violate her, could I have?' 'Do I have the potential to do to her what they say I did?' Those are good questions."[42] A spokesperson for Vassar later claimed, without explaining how, that Comins had been quoted out of context.[43]

A seminal book on due process, free speech, and campus discipline showed how higher education's obsession with certain types of diversity had subjected scores of students, staffers, and professors to unfair treatment for allegedly violating "speech code" and "anti-harassment" provisions.[44] That book was *The Shadow University: The Betrayal of Liberty on America's Campuses* (Free Press, 1998), by Alan Charles Kors and Harvey Silverglate. Kors was a history professor at Penn, and Silverglate was a Boston lawyer specializing in civil rights and civil liberties.

Kors and Silverglate noted that college disciplinary processes had *always* been unfair, as well as often rigged to privilege the well-connected.

They pointed out how, in the 1960s and 1970s, students from prosperous families had gotten away with criminal harassment. In one horrifying incident in the 1960s, for example, Princeton University only trivially punished a group of athletes and senior-class officers who had vandalized the room of two gay socialists.[45]

By the 1990s, there had been a reversal of power. Zealous "diversity" advocates who had achieved substantial influence in universities used the disciplinary process to punish students whose speech offended the administrators' favored groups. As a result, at many colleges the disciplinary process started to tilt in favor of the accuser's perspective in sexual harassment cases.

For example, in the mid-1990s, the University of Maryland classified "comments about a person's clothing, body, and/or sexual activities," "sexual teasing," and "telephone calls of a sexual nature" as sexual harassment. At West Virginia University, a student could face sexual harassment charges for "insults, humor, jokes and/or anecdotes that belittle or demean an individual's or a group's sexuality or sex" or "inappropriate displays of sexually suggestive objects or pictures which may include but not limited to [sic] posters, pin-ups, and calendars." Montana State University defined "sexual intimidation" as "any unreasonable behavior that is verbal or non-verbal, which subjects members of either sex to humiliation, embarrassment, or discomfort because of their gender"—such as "using sexist cartoons to illustrate concepts" or "making stereotypical remarks about the abilities of men or women."[46]

Rules like these led to complaints by students and lawyers about unfair disciplinary actions and procedures. In 1994, after representing a student charged in a sexual harassment case, Pennsylvania lawyer Donald Russo lamented that "college professors and administrators who undoubtedly view themselves as enlightened progressives are engendering a roughshod style of 'kangaroo-court' justice that would make a 1950s Southern sheriff blush."[47]

Campus administrators in the 1990s went along with a zero-tolerance-for-due-process posture more because of careerism, Kors and Silverglate wrote, than because of the kind of ideological zealotry displayed by Vassar's Catherine Comins. "The primary goal of modern academic administrators," Kors and Silverglate argued, "is to buy peace during their tenure and to preserve the appearance of competence on their watch—an appearance essential to their careers. Administrators ask one question above all: Who can disrupt my campus and tarnish my reputation?" And that question answers itself: "The willingness of militants of the cultural Left to disrupt a university" is simply greater than that of civil libertarians.[48] Defenders of campus due process don't stage sit-ins in the university president's office, shout down speakers whose views they dislike, or get the news media to paint campuses as sexist and racist and therefore morally depraved.

In 1999, Kors and Silverglate formed a new civil liberties group, the Foundation for Individual Rights in Education (FIRE). It has become the nation's most energetic and effective defender of campus civil liberties, especially because the American Civil Liberties Union has done little to defend victims of campus witch hunts.

Gender (and racial) issues on college campuses loomed large on the national political stage during Bill Clinton's presidency, from 1993 until 2001. The federal courts emerged as the bulwark for protecting students' rights: Several judges struck down campus speech codes as inconsistent with the First Amendment.[49] In 1996, the 5th Circuit, in *Rowinsky v. Bryan Independent School District*, held that Title IX applied only to the "conduct of grant recipients" (in this instance, the school). Accordingly, the appellate court ruled that "a school district might violate title IX if it treated sexual harassment of boys more seriously than sexual harassment of girls, or even if it turned a blind eye toward sexual harassment of girls while addressing assaults that harmed boys." Allegations of sexual misconduct by students, in and of themselves, would not qualify as a violation.[50]

Clinton's OCR, stacked with advocates of identity politics, moved in a different direction. OCR has 12 local branches; its California office proved particularly aggressive in trampling students' civil liberties. In 1994, it held that sexist criticism in an online forum hosted by Santa Rosa Junior College created "a sexually hostile educational environment" for two of its female students. OCR added (incorrectly) that the forum participants who made sexist remarks were unprotected by the First Amendment because "the Supreme Court has repeatedly asserted that the First Amendment does not protect expression that is invidious private discrimination."[51] The same year, in a case at Sonoma State University, the California OCR branch claimed that allegations of sexual assault by one student against another fell within the agency's jurisdiction, even though no legal or regulatory guidance justified this stance.[52]

OCR remedied that problem in 1997. A "Sexual Harassment Guidance" document pressured institutions to discipline students for any speech that could even arguably be considered sexist. The agency also, for the first time, linked Title IX to allegations of student-on-student sexual assault. In a section on interim measures in harassment cases, the agency said that if "a student alleges that he or she has been sexually assaulted by another student, the school may decide to immediately place the students in separate classes or in different housing arrangements on a campus, pending the results of the school's investigation." The guidance document also directly commented on adjudication procedures, holding that "[i]n some cases, such as alleged sexual assaults, mediation will not be appropriate even on a voluntary basis."[53]

Title IX reached the Supreme Court in 1999, in an ambiguous decision, *Davis v. Monroe County Board of Education*.[54] Overturning the *Rowinsky* standard, Justice Sandra Day O'Connor wrote for a five-justice majority that educational institutions "are properly held liable in damages only where they are deliberately indifferent to sexual harassment, of which they have actual knowledge, that is so severe, pervasive, and objectively offensive that it can be said to deprive the victims of access to the educational opportunities or benefits provided by the school."

Dissenting justice Anthony Kennedy said he worried about applying this standard, derived from a case involving the harassment of a fifth-grader, to college students. But he reassured himself with the "small concession" that O'Connor's wording excluded "the possibility that a single act of harassment perpetrated by one student on one other student can form the basis for an actionable claim."[55]

OCR, on the other hand, discerned no such limitation. Guidance issued on the final full day of Clinton's term, January 19, 2001, distinguished between the facts of *Davis*, which involved a claim for monetary damages against the school district, and the office's investigatory role. (*Davis* did not set "severe and pervasive" as the standard to open an investigation.) The new guidance wholly ignored the "pervasive" element of *Davis*, maintaining that "a single or isolated incident of sexual harassment may, if sufficiently severe, create a hostile environment." In a commitment that future OCR guidance would seek to undermine, however, the 2001 letter did affirm that "the rights established under Title IX must be interpreted consistent with any federally guaranteed due process rights involved in a complaint proceeding."[56]

In both 1997 and 2001, the Clinton administration complied with the provisions of the Administrative Procedure Act, publishing the proposed guidance in *The Federal Register* and soliciting public comment before issuing the guidance.

During the eight years of George W. Bush's presidency, OCR mostly avoided the aggressive interpretations of Title IX that it had pursued under President Clinton. Some regional compliance documents reflected a quite limited scope of the institution's Title IX obligations. In 2004, an OCR regional office informed Oklahoma State University that "a university does not have a duty under Title IX to address an incidence of alleged harassment where the incident occurs off-campus and does not involve a university-related event."[57] A 2005 letter to Buffalo State University confirmed that the university "was under no obligation to conduct an independent investigation" of sexual assault allegations that "involved a possible violation of the penal law, the determination of which is the exclusive province of the police and the office of the district attorney."[58]

There was, however, one particularly troubling federal court ruling during the Bush years: in 2002, U.S. District Judge Janet Hall, a Clinton nominee, held that a single alleged sexual assault, plus the accuser's complaints about the university's response, could create Title IX liability.

Hall's decision grew out of a complaint to Yale University, in New Haven, Connecticut, by a divinity student named Kathryn Kelly.[59] In October 1999, Kelly claimed that a fellow student, Robert Nolan, had raped her. She reported the incident to police, but the local prosecutor declined to press charges. Yale's Sexual Harassment Committee nonetheless conducted its own investigation. The committee delayed the initial hearing because its usual chair, Kristin Leslie, a doctoral candidate specializing in acquaintance rape, recused herself after providing pastoral care to Kelly. Kelly, by contrast, interpreted this delay as a scheme to sweep her complaint under the rug. Despite provisions of Yale's disciplinary code requiring both parties to keep all matters relating to a complaint confidential, details about her allegations were leaked to her friends, who blanketed the campus with flyers denouncing Yale and Nolan. Nolan tried to defend himself by filing a counter-complaint about Kelly's flouting of the rules, but Yale refused to consider *his* complaint.

Once the university reassembled its disciplinary panel, a hearing commenced. The university's policies forbade Nolan from having a lawyer represent him at the hearing, and he could not cross-examine Kelly or any other witness. Thirty-eight days after Kelly filed her initial complaint, Yale determined that Nolan had committed sexual misconduct, on grounds that Kelly had been too intoxicated to have consented to intercourse. Divinity School Dean Richard Wood required Nolan to take a leave of absence until after Kelly's expected graduation. Student protests nonetheless continued; Wood tried to pacify one of these gatherings by citing the authorities' decision not to prosecute, noting that what had happened to Kelly did not, therefore, constitute "legal rape."

To the extent that Yale's process treated anyone unfairly, it was Nolan, not Kelly. But *Kelly* sued Yale, under Title IX (among other claims). She alleged that Yale had failed her because it "allowed the accused to go to class & be on campus" and that the university should have adjudicated her complaint more promptly. She also faulted Yale for not allowing Kristin Leslie to serve as her advocate during the hearing, despite the conflict of interest of the committee's usual chairperson appearing in an advocacy role for a complainant. And she charged that Wood had defamed her by describing her case as one of university misconduct rather than "legal rape."

Yale countered by pointing out that Kelly's desired accommodation would have required suspending Nolan on the basis of an accusation, and that the 38-day process could hardly be termed dilatory. Moreover, the university noted that although Kelly claimed to have experienced harassment after she filed her complaint, she had offered no evidence of any harassing behavior or even an "explanation as to what harassment is alleged to have occurred." Citing *Davis*, Yale argued that the Supreme Court had "rejected the idea that Title IX requires schools to 'remedy' peer harassment or to 'ensure that students conform their conduct to certain rules.'"

Hall disagreed, and in 2002 she denied Yale's motion for summary judgment. "[T]here is no question," she held, "that a rape, as alleged by Kelly, constitutes severe and objectively offensive sexual harassment." But she did not find that Nolan's one act of alleged sexual misconduct proved sexual assaults to be *pervasive* at Yale—as they clearly were not. She thus ignored the Supreme Court's *Davis* holding that educational institutions could be held liable under Title IX for student-on-student conduct only if it was "severe, *pervasive, and* objectively offensive" (emphasis added).[60]

Hall provided contradictory advice for how universities could avoid liability under Title IX. She did "not find that Yale's refusal to bar Nolan from attending classes was clearly unreasonable," chastising the university only for taking too long to accommodate Kelly's concerns. But Hall also ruled that "a reasonable jury could conclude that further encounters, of any sort, between a rape victim and her attacker could create an environment sufficiently hostile to deprive the victim of access to educational opportunities provided by a university." By this standard, universities would not be safe unless they immediately suspended any accused student, lest he have an encounter "of any sort" with his accuser.

Hall also wrote (incorrectly) as if Nolan were guilty of a criminal offense, observing that Kelly "was sexually assaulted by Robert Nolan" and was "a rape victim"—even though New Haven authorities, after a criminal investigation, had declined even to file charges.[61] The federal government would soon adopt the same guilt-presuming language about unproven allegations.

The *Kelly* decision attracted scant public attention. But during George W. Bush's presidency, a handful of cases (at the University of Georgia, the University of Colorado, and Arizona State University) involving highly credible sexual assault allegations against college football and basketball players kept the issue in the public eye. In each case, the accuser filed a Title IX lawsuit against her school, alleging that it had knowingly recruited potentially violent felons solely because they were talented athletes and it had thereby shown deliberate indifference to the well-being of female students. Each case ended with a denial of the university's motion to dismiss, followed by a settlement, driven by a hailstorm of negative publicity, in which the university apologized for not doing enough to protect women on campus.[62] The American Civil Liberties Union filed *amicus* briefs supporting the Arizona State and Colorado plaintiffs.[63]

These three cases established judicial precedents stronger than Hall's for holding universities liable for sexual assaults by their students. But these precedents were limited by the undisputed facts that the universities had known of past alleged sexual misconduct by the male athletes before recruiting them. As the 11th Circuit repeatedly explained in the University of Georgia case, the team's basketball coach knew that the accused student had "had disciplinary and criminal problems, particularly those involving harassment of women, while attending other colleges." This background, along with the accuser's allegations of multiple instances of harassment by these student-athletes, overcame what the court recognized as the limits on universities' Title IX obligations from *Davis*. At most, then, the Georgia, Arizona State, and Colorado decisions suggested that admitting students previously implicated in alleged sexual assaults could expose a school to a Title IX complaint down the road.[64]

As President Bush's time in office drew to a close, few could have predicted what was to come from the nation's next chief executive. During his 2008 presidential campaign, Barack Obama appears never to have commented on the use of Title IX to accuse universities of sex discrimination for failing to punish or prevent alleged student-on-student sexual assaults.[65] His only remarks about sexual assault on college campuses were in defense of the rights of *accused* students. He was the second member of the Senate to (unsuccessfully) urge the Justice Department to open a criminal investigation of Mike Nifong, the Durham County district attorney notorious for violating myriad ethics rules in targeting three Duke lacrosse players falsely accused of a brutal gang rape.[66] In late 2008, Obama's transition team's 25-item document outlining its agenda for women continued to reference sexual assault only in the criminal law context.[67]

Twenty-eight months later, in April 2011, the federal government issued to thousands of universities the directives that led to the evisceration of the due-process rights of accused students across the nation.

The first indication of a change from the perspective on campus discipline that Obama had offered during his campaign—even as data from the FBI's Uniform Crime Reports and the Bureau of Justice Statistics showed that the rate of rape was declining both on college campuses and overall—came in early 2010, with the publication of what was described as a nine-month Center for Public Integrity (CPI) investigation of issues surrounding sexual assault on college campuses.[68]

OCR's new leader, Russlynn Ali, implicitly repudiated the work of the Bush-era OCR. "I certainly can't speak to the decisions made in the past," Ali remarked to CPI reporter Kristen Lombardi. "I can, though, commit to you that where universities or school systems don't comply with civil rights laws, where they are unwilling to look to find a resolution... we will use all of the tools at our disposal including referring to Justice or withholding federal funds or going to adjudication to ensure that women are free from sexual violence." Lombardi later boasted that "since the Center for Public Integrity series ran, OCR is much more aggressive."[69]

In an interview with NPR, Ali previewed the agency's efforts to encourage students to file Title IX complaints as a way to heighten pressure on universities. "We want them to get training, we want to provide some help," the OCR head asserted, "so that the adults and the students alike can ensure that this plague—it's [sic] really has become a plague in this country—begins to diminish."[70] Ali did not respond to our request for an interview during the writing of this book; she also did not respond to written questions in lieu of an interview.

Ali, a Northwestern Law School graduate, had been appointed the Education Department's Assistant Secretary for Civil Rights, in charge of OCR, by President Obama in May 2009. Before that, she had spent nearly a decade at the Educational Trust, devoted to "educational justice" for students "from low-income families or who are black, Latino, or American Indian."[71] Democratic presidential administrations have long imported activists from the civil rights establishment. But that establishment's ideology has drifted to the left over the years, putting it at odds with the more inclusive vision that Obama had outlined in his 2008 campaign.

Many actors in the campus environment encouraged Ali in her efforts—including some who stood to benefit from changes in federal policy. Perhaps the most prominent such organization has been the National Center for Higher Education Risk Management (NCHERM), which sells sexual-assault-related policy and legal advice to more than 2,000 clients. The organization conducts two-day on-campus seminars, drafts college sexual assault policies, and sometimes serves as a college's "special counsel" or provides expert testimony in lawsuits.[72] NCHERM's founder, Brett Sokolow, is hardly neutral on these questions. A source for the CPI series, he argued for new sexual assault procedures that would shift the burden of proof, ending a presumption of innocence by forcing the accused student to (as the CPI's Kristin Jones paraphrased) "demonstrate that consent was given."[73]

A few months after the CPI publication, in October 2010, campus activists gave Ali a chance to act by filing a Title IX complaint against Yale University. The complaint described how Delta Kappa Epsilon fraternity pledges had stood blindfolded on campus shouting, "No means yes, yes means anal." The resulting backlash led fraternity members to apologize and led Yale administrators to punish some of the pledges, thereby abandoning Yale's tradition of free-speech absolutism.[74] And when faced with a Title IX investigation by OCR, the university's leaders quickly caved, whether for fear of losing federal funds, for fear of legal expenses, for fear of bad publicity, or out of ideological sympathy with the protesters.

In a "voluntary" resolution agreement with OCR, dated June 11, 2012, Yale agreed to hire more Title IX bureaucrats and rework its sexual assault policy so as to enhance the likelihood of guilty findings.[75] The humbling of Yale was just a start. Ali and her colleagues at OCR had much bigger designs.

The 2010 midterm congressional election gave Ali an unexpected opportunity. A disaster for Democrats, especially for moderate members of Congress in swing districts and states, the election had the effect of driving the Obama administration farther to the left, with special attention to its identity politics base.

The Democrats lost more House seats in 2010 than in any contest since 1938. Senate seats in deep-blue states such as Illinois, Wisconsin, and Pennsylvania fell to the Republicans. A rare bright spot for the party was Colorado, where Michael Bennet, an appointed senator who had never before run for public office, narrowly prevailed.

In a campaign that Obama's chief political strategist, David Axelrod, later described as a "particularly instructive" model for 2012, Bennet upset Republican Ken Buck by assembling a coalition of minorities, younger voters, and well-educated suburbanites, especially women.[76] Driven by social issues, this coalition overcame a huge anti-Bennet vote among white working-class voters. Buck made Bennet's job easier by aggressively opposing abortion and, on national television, likening homosexuality to alcoholism.[77]

Over the next 20 months, the federal government emphasized the types of gender, sexuality, and ethnic issues that had worked so well for Bennet. The biggest were marriage for same-sex couples, Obama's executive order permitting the undocumented immigrants known as DREAMers to remain in the United States, the Obamacare contraceptive mandate, and Planned Parenthood funding.

The same logic would pave the way for the federal government to suddenly adopt a hard line against students accused of sexual assault. The move energized two key constituencies that had moved heavily to the Democrats during Obama's 2008 campaign: (1) female college students and (2) women with college and especially postgraduate degrees. Republicans—while opposing all of Obama's other identity politics initiatives—initially were either silent about or supportive of the new policy regarding sexual assault on college campuses. This alignment of political forces lent Ali's OCR almost complete freedom of action.[78]

And so it was that on April 4, 2011, the day that Obama announced his reelection bid, the Office for Civil Rights issued its 19-page "Dear Colleague letter." The document commanded the more than 7,000 universities that receive federal funds to adopt federally specified procedures to investigate and adjudicate sexual assault accusations.[79]

No other presidential administration had ever asserted the power to dictate specific disciplinary procedures to universities, under Title IX or any other statute. Title IX itself includes nothing that even hints at such a power. Not until 2016 did OCR cite the specific precedents for its decision: two obscure "voluntary" resolution agreements, with Georgetown and Evergreen State University.[80] Yet the 1995 Evergreen State case involved an allegation of *faculty* misconduct. And although the 2004 Georgetown agreement did include a preponderance requirement, it did so without explanation, buried in the middle of a paragraph on the third page of a 17-page letter—hardly what would be expected of a letter announcing a revolutionary change in policy.[81]

In the words of a May 2016 open letter signed by more than 20 law professors, "Through a series of directives and compliance enforcement actions, OCR has brazenly nullified the Supreme Court definition [in *Davis*] of campus sexual harassment," thereby "exerting a direct and deleterious effect on campus free speech and due process. These unlawful actions have led to pervasive and severe infringements of free speech rights and due process protections at colleges and universities across the country."[82]

Each of the Dear Colleague letter's mandates increased the likelihood that students accused of sexual assault would be found guilty.

First, the letter ordered universities to use no higher standard of proof than a bare "preponderance of the evidence"—meaning 50.01 percent—to find students guilty of sexual assault. Many colleges at that time, including most in the Ivy League, were using a higher standard of proof—the "clear and convincing" standard.[83]

OCR and its allies have claimed that lowering the standard of proof levels the playing field between accuser and accused. As author Jon Krakauer has argued, "The harm done to a rape victim who is disbelieved can be at least as devastating as the harm done to an innocent man who is unjustly accused of [and expelled for] rape." But the implications of Krakauer's assertion, and similar statements by many others, in the college disciplinary process means that letting a guilty man go unpunished is as bad as punishing an innocent one. This standard turns civil liberties and centuries of common law upside down.

Second, the letter strongly discouraged—and in effect, at least as implemented by nearly all colleges, all but forbade—what the Supreme Court has called "beyond any doubt the greatest legal engine ever invented for the discovery of truth": direct cross-examination of accusers.

Other provisions ordered colleges to (a) speed up investigations, making it harder for the accused to prepare a defense; (b) allow accusers to appeal not-guilty findings, exposing accused students to a form of double jeopardy that would be unconstitutional in the criminal justice system; and (c) implement "interim" punishments, such as removing an accused student from his dorm or his classes, or limiting his library access, prior to any investigation.

Ali's justification for OCR's revolutionizing of the college disciplinary process for alleged rape was that "we've had hundreds of institutions across the country that just didn't know what to do."[84] Many college administrators disagreed. One wrote anonymously, "I do not appreciate having my hands tied by the presumption of guilt the Dear Colleague Letter portrays."[85] To Lee Burdette Williams, who spent nine years as dean of students at Wheaton College, it felt as though "misinformed interlopers"—lawyers and policy specialists—"had shown up to tell me how to do a job I had done for years...[a]bsent any input from people in jobs like mine."[86]

The agency was indifferent to such pleas. But others welcomed the move. "The 'Dear Colleague' letter was one of the most important moments of my professional life," NCHERM's Sokolow gushed. In an interview with *Philadelphia* magazine a few months after the letter's issuance, Sokolow said he looked forward to the changes, since "the number of expelled students is going to go way up." The unsettled bureaucratic environment also benefited his firm's profit margin: an August 2011 NCHERM conference grossed $425,000 for the organization, as 1,700 campus administrators sought guidance on the new legal terrain from a figure who admitted he entered his profession as an activist on the issue.[87]

However, there is no evidence that shifting felony investigations away from law enforcement and into colleges will reduce the number of sexual assaults. As Adam Goldstein, a lawyer for the Student Press Law Center, observed, the "best case scenario" of a university's disciplinary process is that a rapist is expelled and out "walking the streets." Since that's also "the worst case outcome of the criminal justice process," Goldstein said pointedly, "you have to ask, 'What is this process for?'"[88]

Obviously, lowering the standard of proof from approximately 75 percent to 50.01 percent will in and of itself increase the number of accused students found guilty. But the shift likely has had an intangible effect as well. "Under the stronger standards," *Atlantic* columnist Conor Friedersdorf noted, "it's possible to find against an accuser without implying or seeming to imply that he or she is a liar. After all, a 'not guilty' finding could mean that there was strong evidence, but that it did not meet the high standard of proof that the institution imposed as a safeguard against wrongly punishing innocents."

Under the preponderance standard, by contrast, "an adjudicator who finds against an accuser is arguably saying that it's more likely than not that he or she is lying." Friedersdorf suspected that the reality of the current campus environment "will cause many adjudicators to feel some pressure, if only self-imposed, to render verdicts that validate the claims of accusers."[89]

In issuing the new guidance, OCR flouted the Administrative Procedure Act's requirement that federal agencies provide substantial public notice and allow comment before issuing new substantive rules.[90] (Although the 1997 and 2001 Dear Colleague letters had complied with the APA, going through notice and comment in this instance likely would have delayed release of the document until after the 2012 presidential election, minimizing its political benefit.) "This kind of policy-making process—or, rather, policy-making without process—is unlawful and wrong," Harvard Law School professor Jacob Gersen wrote in January 2016.[91] OCR contended it could ignore the notice-and-comment requirement because the letter only provided "guidance" on current law—it did not impose new mandates. But as Samantha Harris and Greg Lukianoff have pointed out, "court decisions and even guidance from the executive branch's own Office of Management and Budget belie that argument."[92] And Catherine Lhamon, who succeeded Ali in 2013 as head of OCR, testified in 2014 that the agency expected universities to obey its directives.[93]

OCR justified its new standards by comparing campus sexual assault hearings to civil litigation, which also uses a "preponderance of the evidence" standard and lets either side appeal. But civil litigation, unlike the campus proceedings overseen by OCR, operates under a panoply of rules to ensure fairness. It allows all parties representation by legal counsel; it has procedures to ensure discovery of relevant evidence; it requires witnesses to testify under oath; and, barring a settlement, it concludes with a public trial, often by jury, in which both parties testify subject to cross-examination. As Sen. James Lankford (R-Oklahoma) informed the Education Department in early 2016, "on its own terms, the Dear Colleague letter does not provide many essential protections defendants in a court of law enjoy."[94]

To be sure, due process does not require that college proceedings be as rigorous as criminal proceedings. But Supreme Court precedent holds that effective due-process protections are most critical when official actions affect important private interests and "the risk of an erroneous deprivation" is great.[95]

"[This is] a major societal issue and a major threat to the academic integrity of our institutions of higher learning," a distinguished former high-level official of a major university (who declined to be identified) explained in an email interview with one of us. "One friend, a long-time faculty member, thinks that it's all beyond hope, having observed the situation for five decades."

This former university official explained: "No academic leader (and no association of such worthies) is willing to engage in litigation on the subjects, largely because litigation is invariably prolonged and one is exposed to the intense heat of university constituencies...that are prepared to be quoted in the media on a daily basis and happy to accuse the administration of varieties of thought crimes ('sexism,' 'racism' etc.) while the academic leaders are effectively required to remain mute. The other concern is that going to the mat with OCR... invites the classic bureaucratic responses that one associates with corrupt municipal governments who are out to 'get' a businessman or property owner— namely, a variety of inquiries and worse, designed to remind you who is in charge. It's all quite disgusting."

The effect of OCR's commands and the accusers' rights crusade they have helped inspire was described by two Harvard law professors. In a 2015 *New Yorker* article, professor Jeannie Suk Gersen, a former David Souter clerk, wrote, "Far-fetched at the time, Catharine MacKinnon's 1981 statement, 'Politically, I call it rape whenever a woman has sex and feels violated,' is effectively becoming closer to law, even if it is not on the books."[96] And in an email to *The Wall Street Journal*, professor Elizabeth Bartholet, director of Harvard's Child Advocacy Program, predicted that "history will demonstrate the federal government's position to be wrong [and] our society will look back on this time as a moment of madness."[97]

The Obama administration based its radical policy on a dubious set of assumptions regarding sexual assault on college campuses: (a) hundreds of thousands of female undergraduates are sexually assaulted each year, and virtually no one noticed until very recently; (b) the number of sexual assaults is increasing; (c) the overwhelming majority of claims of sexual assault are true, therefore rendering irrelevant concerns about due process; and (d) students who are victims of sexual assault are treated with such hostility by the institutions they attend that only unprecedented federal intervention can protect them. The next two chapters will expose the falsity of each of these assumptions.

2

MISLEADING
THROUGH
STATISTICS

Five myths provide the basis for the federal government, many universities, and activists to claim that an epidemic of sexual assault on college campuses must be met with draconian punishments unimpeded by due process for the accused:

1. One in five female college students will be sexually assaulted.
2. The number of rapes on college campuses has grown alarmingly.
3. A college campus is a more dangerous place for female students than the off-campus environment is.
4. A relatively small number of serial predators commit 90 percent of rapes on college campuses.
5. Between 90 and 98 percent of accused students are guilty, so a cursory disciplinary process with minimal due process is good enough.

To the contrary:

1. By far the most reliable (though still far from perfect) statistical crime surveys, conducted every six months by the Justice Department, suggest that roughly one in 40 (not one in five) female college students is sexually assaulted over four years. No

data specify how many of the perpetrators are fellow college students.

2. The same surveys also suggest that the number of rapes and other sexual assaults of female college students dropped by more than half between 1997 and 2013.

3. The same surveys further suggest that young women in college are less likely to be sexually assaulted than young women not in college.[1]

4. There are no data suggesting that campuses are stalked by serial rapists, and the so-called scholarship underlying the serial-predator claim has been discredited.

5. Suggestions that between 90 and 98 percent of accused students are guilty come from misreadings of studies about the rate of false rape reports.

The first myth listed above is, more than any other, at the heart of the federal government's anti-rape crusade. "An estimated one in five women has been sexually assaulted during her college years—one in five," President Obama asserted in September 2014 at a White House event announcing a campaign against sexual violence on college campuses.[2] In September 2015, his would-be successor, Hillary Clinton, echoed the sentiment, claiming there was an "epidemic" of sexual assault on college campuses.[3] Citing the same claim, OCR head Catherine Lhamon said the nation did not "treat rape and sexual assault as seriously as we should" and praised Obama's as the "first administration to call sexual violence a civil rights issue."[4]

The National Crime Victimization Survey (NCVS), conducted every six months by the U.S. Census Bureau for the Justice Department's Bureau of Justice Statistics (BJS), has long been regarded as the gold standard of crime surveys. In 2014, BJS estimated that 0.61 percent of female college (and trade school) students, of whom 0.2 percent are raped, are sexually assaulted per year. Nonrape sexual assaults include unwanted sexual touching, attempted rape, and threats.[5]

The BJS numbers doubtless would have been much lower if the surveys had focused on students whose attackers could have been subjected to campus discipline—that is, whose attackers were students at the same college or university. That's because neither the BJS (nor any other) data tell us *where* the alleged offense occurred or whether the alleged perpetrator was a student at the alleged victim's school. One finding of a 2015 survey by the Association of American Universities (AAU) was suggestive. It revealed that 17.6 percent of those female respondents who said they had been "penetrated by force" also indicated that either the alleged rapes had occurred off campus or the alleged rapists had not been fellow students.[6] The women who had been surveyed were enrolled at mostly or entirely residential institutions. Millions of female undergraduates live off campus; millions more attend nonresidential schools; and 3.82 million attend college part-time.[7] For students at these schools, the rate of nonstudent perpetrators would likely be much higher than in the AAU survey.

The BJS numbers show sexual assaults on female college students to be a serious problem, worthy of attention from the local police in all college and university communities. But they provide no basis for recent efforts to create a separate, quasi-judicial process for accused college students. Nor do they suggest a rationale for weakening the due-process protections of accused college students.

Activists claim that the BJS numbers understate the number of sexual assaults. Their most plausible arguments are that, as the BJS Special Report itself noted, some victims "may not be willing to reveal or share their experience with an interviewer," especially if family members are present.[8] This line of argument was also a key point in a lengthy report by a National Research Council panel claiming that "it is likely that the NCVS is undercounting rape and sexual assault victimization." The report emphasized three other factors: (1) a supposedly inefficient sample design; (2) the survey's focus on crimes, which might "inhibit reporting of incidents that the respondent does not think of as criminal [or] does not want to report to police"; and (3) the use of "ambiguous" words such as "rape" in the survey questions.[9]

But the NRC panel shed little light on the extent to which such supposed NCVS undercounting is offset by the *overcounting* suggested by other parts of the panel's report. For example, according to the report, in 2011, BJS changed its process for counting series victimizations, by starting to count as 10 separate sex crimes a single respondent's claim to have been victimized 10 times in a year. "The effect of the change was substantial for estimates of rape and sexual assault: these victimizations were undercounted in the past, but series victimizations (based on only a few reports) now account for almost 40 percent of the national estimates of rape and sexual assault."[10] In addition, the NRC panel's report, which discusses NCVS sex-crime estimates for the entire U.S. population, is of limited relevance to the BJS Special Report's sex-crime estimates for female college students.

The BJS estimates are about as good as any, given the inherent difficulty of accurately assessing the number of sexual assaults. Such crimes usually happen behind closed doors, with no unbiased witnesses. Many victims do not report the incidents to police or campus authorities. Victims may fear reprisal, may wish to avoid the trauma of police investigations or reliving the event, or simply may not expect to be believed.

The BJS methodology compares favorably with those used in each of the many surveys that purport to find much higher rates of sexual assault. The BJS survey interviews very large population samples twice a year—90,630 households and 160,040 persons 12 years or older in 2013. The response rate is very high—88 percent for eligible persons in 2013, for example.[11]

A second reality check: The most recent data from the Department of Education indicate that approximately 10 million women are enrolled (full- or part-time) as undergraduates. The one-in-five figure would indicate that 2 million of them will be sexually assaulted at college. That's 400,000 to 500,000 sexual assaults *per year*, depending on how many schools are classified as four-year and how many are classified as five-year. For comparison's sake, under the expanded definition of rape used in the FBI's Uniform Crime Reports, in 2014 there were 116,645 rapes in the entire United States, a nation of 160 million females, one-sixteenth of whom are in college.[12]

The 1990 Clery Act requires all colleges to report the total number of student sexual assaults. According to the most recent aggregate reports, universities reported an annual average of between 4,558 and 5,335 sexual assaults for the period 2012 through 2014.[13]

How to explain the ratio of almost 100 to one between the White House's claims (400,000 to 500,000 incidents of sexual assault annually) and the recent Clery Act reports (4,558 to 5,335 incidents of sexual assault annually)?

Activists offer two implausible explanations. First, they suggest that university administrators suppress their numbers in order to make their schools look safer. But little recent evidence of such suppression exists. It's true that college administrators in decades past likely discouraged some alleged victims of sexual assault from making formal accusations, out of either self-interest or indifference. But with very few exceptions, mostly involving athletes at schools in the nation's leading athletics conferences, administrators today—like their faculties and their government overseers—have become so concerned with the issue that many seem, if anything, eager to exaggerate the incidence of sexual violence.

Second, activists say, accurately, that sexual assault is the most underreported crime in the United States. Non-reporting percentages are by definition difficult to estimate.[14] The Obama administration claimed that "[r]eporting rates for campus sexual assault are also very low: on average only 12% of student victims report the assault to law enforcement," based on a 2007 academic study.[15] Yet if the separate federal government claim that one in five female college students are raped and the Clery Act data were both true, then the reporting rate could be no more than 1.3 percent—far below even the White House's estimate of 12 percent.[16] And although the reporting rate is, by definition, speculative, the Obama administration had every incentive to *understate* it.

The one-in-five claim might receive undeserved credence due to the comparatively high numbers of sex-related complaints filed by female students at elite residential colleges and universities. Those institutions, with their frenzied campus environments, receive disproportionate attention in American society. It is no coincidence that Ivy League schools, top liberal arts colleges, and other top-tier research universities are also far more steeped than other institutions in activism driven by the influence of identity-politics faculty members.[17]

Though only a handful of schools have a reporting rate that comes close to the one-in-five claim, recent Clery Act reports suggest that by far the highest sexual assault rates are at elite institutions. This dramatic reporting increase comes at a time when *national* violent crime and sexual assault rates have plunged, with sexual assaults dropping by more than 60 percent from 1995 to 2010.[18]

For instance, in 2014, one in every 181 female Ivy League undergraduates reported to their university that they had been raped, according to the Clery Act database. That's well over three times the rate—one in 665—at nearby non-elite institutions. Dartmouth College, in Hanover, New Hampshire, had the highest percentage among the Ivy League schools, with 1.41 percent of female undergraduates reporting they had been raped. According to that figure, a female undergraduate at Dartmouth is more likely than a resident of Memphis, Tennessee—which (according to the FBI's Uniform Crime Reports) is the nation's second most dangerous city—to be a victim of violent crime. Dartmouth's president has responded to this alleged crime epidemic not by urging more police on campus but by suggesting that students shun hard liquor.[19]

Among the 11 elite liberal arts colleges in the New England Small College Athletic Conference—Amherst College, Bates College, Bowdoin College, Colby College, Connecticut College, Hamilton College, Middlebury College, Trinity College, Tufts University, Wesleyan College, and Williams College—one in 85 female undergraduates reported being raped in 2014, according to the Clery Act database. That's more than six times the rate—one in 546—at a group of far less elite liberal arts colleges in the South. Wesleyan College, in Middletown, Connecticut, had the highest percentage, 2.41 percent. That means a female undergraduate at Wesleyan is substantially more at risk of being a victim of violent crime than is a resident of Detroit, which (FBI reports indicate) is the nation's most dangerous city. Yet Wesleyan's president has not urged any increase, at all, in the presence of law enforcement on campus.[20]

If American college campuses really were facing a sexual assault epidemic, why would there be far fewer reported sexual assaults at the University of Northern Iowa or the University of Northern Colorado than at Wesleyan or Dartmouth? The answer is that there wouldn't. The difference in reporting rates is due to the fact that moral panic about sexual assault is most feverish at institutions where identity-politics activism is most prevalent.

Occidental College in Los Angeles, for instance, reported 10 "sex offenses" in 2012. The next year, after a handful of faculty members and student activists portrayed the elite liberal arts college as dominated by a "rape culture," the number of reports of sex offenses skyrocketed, to 60.

This figure suggested that as many as 5.1 *percent* of Occidental's around 1,200 female undergraduates were victims of violent crime, making the upscale campus one of the most dangerous places in the country. Yet none of these claims appears to have resulted in a criminal charge, much less conviction. In 2014, the Occidental activist coalition fell apart due to ideological infighting. With the witch hunt over, the number of rape reports plummeted to eight.[21] The apparent surge in violent crime had been ephemeral.

The currently prevalent claim that one in five female college students will be sexually assaulted dates to the 2007 "Campus Sexual Assault Study," or CSA, funded (but not conducted) by the National Institute of Justice.[22] The random, anonymous, self-reported, online sample of 5,446 women found that 19 percent of respondents at two large, unnamed universities, one in the Midwest and one in the South, had been sexually assaulted.

There are several problems with this survey. First, the respondents did not say (because they were not asked) whether they had been sexually assaulted. Second, the low response rate—fewer than half of the 14,000 women invited to participate—probably inflated the percentage found to have been assaulted. Women who think of themselves or their friends as victims of sexual assault are possibly more motivated than others to respond to such surveys. The lower the response rate, the more this bias skews the result.[23] Third, the survey included incidents that had not occurred on campus and had not involved other students, rendering them irrelevant to the debate over college adjudication processes.[24] Fourth, and perhaps most important, CSA used an overbroad definition of sexual assault: respondents were counted as sexual assault victims if, for example, they had experienced "rubbing up against you in a sexual way" or had intimate encounters while even a little bit intoxicated. As defense lawyer and civil libertarian blogger Scott Greenfield has observed, "[t]erms like 'unwanted' focused the respondents on how they felt about the conduct rather than whether they communicated to the other party involved that it was unwanted."[25]

Even the CSA study's authors have criticized attempts to apply its findings about two schools to all college students nationwide. "We don't think that 1-in-5 is a nationally representative statistic," Christopher Krebs, the lead author, told journalist Emily Yoffe.[26]

Other compelling examples of misleading statistics come from the reemergence of the one-in-five claim in two large surveys in 2015.[27]

In September 2015, the Association of American Universities released a survey of students at 27 public and private universities across the country. Though it inspired apocalyptic headlines in both *The Washington Post* and *The New York Times*, even the association had warned that "estimates such as '1 in 5' or '1 in 4' as a global rate across all [universities] is [*sic*] at least oversimplistic, if not misleading. None of the studies...are nationally representative."[28]

The survey, which had cost $2.34 million, concluded that almost 25 percent of female college students had been sexually assaulted by sexual touching, and 20 percent of those (and 5 percent of all respondents) had been raped—that is, sexually penetrated either by force or when incapacitated or both. The survey's response rate of 19.3 percent was low, and even the AAU admitted that "estimates may be too high because non-victims may have been less likely to participate."[29] Female respondents outnumbered males three to two.[30]

Of these female respondents, 2.17 percent said they had reported to their schools that they had been penetrated without consent since entering college.[31] In a nation with 10 million female undergraduates, over five years there would have been 217,000 student reports of penetration without consent, plus many more reports derived from the survey's other categories of sexual assault.

But 217,000 is *between 10 and 11 times* the number of students (between 20,282 and 22,513) who actually did report sexual assaults to their universities from 2010 through 2014, the five years in which nearly all respondents to the AAU survey were in college, according to the relevant Clery Act reports. Either the AAU data were enormously unrepresentative, or many of the women who told researchers that they had reported assaults to their universities were lying. The AAU's 288-page report failed to address this flaw in its findings.[32]

In a manner typical of such surveys, the AAU classified as "sexual assault" a far broader range of behaviors than defined by criminal law or according to common understanding. In an interview with Emily Yoffe, the survey's designers admitted that they, at the behest of participating universities, specifically avoided asking about "rape" or "sexual assault." Instead, the AAU counted it as "sexual assault" or "sexual misconduct" every time a respondent answered yes to any of the following questions (and others like them): Have you experienced "forced kissing"? Unwanted sexual "touching," which could include attempted close dancing while fully clothed? "Promised rewards" for sex? Threats to "share damaging information about you" with friends? In addition, the survey's failure to define "incapacitated" in one key question invited respondents to assume that the answer should be yes if they had been even only a little bit drunk.[33]

The AAU acknowledged that—for the majority of respondents who said they had not reported to campus authorities the events that the AAU classified as sexual assault—"*the dominant reason was it was not considered serious enough*" (emphasis added). Seventy-five percent of the respondents who told researchers that they had been "penetrated using physical force" said they had never reported any incident to campus authorities. And 58.6 percent of that group said they "did not consider [the rape] serious enough" to report to their colleges' confidential rape hotlines, or their sexual assault resource centers, or their burgeoning Title IX bureaucracies, or their campus or city police.[34]

There are only two possible explanations for this data. The first is that a large percentage of female students at some of the nation's leading universities (such as Harvard, Yale, and Columbia) do not consider rape to be a "serious" offense. The second—which is far more plausible—is that these same female students did not, unlike the survey designers, classify what happened to them as sexual assault.

As scholar and journalist Heather Mac Donald wryly noted, "The rate of nonreporting climbs as the sexual assault categories ginned up by the AAU grow ever more distant from the common understanding of rape. . . . If only college administrators devoted the same passion to discovering what their students knew about the origins of the French and American revolutions as they do to soliciting and classifying data on whose digit has penetrated or rubbed which orifice belonging to which variant of gender identity."[35]

Notwithstanding these flaws, college presidents competed to claim that the survey showed sexual assault to be rampant on their watch. Harvard president Drew Gilpin Faust announced that her institution's students experienced sexual assault with "alarming frequency," and she thus called for an "even more intent focus on the problem of sexual assault." Harvard claimed that 16 percent of female seniors had been raped and nearly 40 percent had experienced a wider range of nonconsensual sexual contact.[36]

"But if these heads of institutions of higher education truly believe the survey results," Emily Yoffe observed, "their collective response constitutes a dereliction of duty. What the AAU survey describes is an epic criminal justice calamity that should prompt emergency action. If 1 in 4 women on their campuses can expect to be victimized each year, college presidents should reinstate the long-abandoned sexual segregation of dorms; there should be a strictly enforced ban on underage drinking; and a large and visible law enforcement presence should prowl campus as a deterrent to sexual predators. But no college president would suggest such things. I suspect that's in part because they recognize that there is a fundamental problem with sexual assault surveys."[37]

Three months before the AAU survey, in June 2015, there had been a similar *Washington Post*–Kaiser Family Foundation poll, as part of a package of articles on the campus sexual assault issue.[38] The package featured both the results of the poll and detailed interviews of some respondents. The main heading: "1 in 5 Women Say They Were Violated."

The survey had a very low (8 to 10 percent) response rate.[39] Respondents were not directly asked whether they had been sexually assaulted or raped. Some of the questions addressed conduct that wasn't sexual assault (for example, having sex while "drunk") or that addressed issues that could be handled through mediation or better education (for example, unsolicited "rubbing up against you in a sexual way, even if it is over your clothes"). The newspaper itself acknowledged, albeit inconspicuously, that the questions were *designed* to elicit "dramatically" higher positive answers than would "terms like sexual assault and rape."

The Washington Post asserted that "in recent years the number of reports of forcible sexual offenses on campus has surged," without mentioning that BJS data indicated that the number of sexual assaults on college campuses actually had *plunged by more than half* between 1997 and 2013.[40] One *Post* article classified as sexual assault "survivors" women who "say they were coerced into sex through verbal . . . promises." Such conduct would not constitute rape anywhere in the country.

The paper's follow-up interviews showed that some respondents *had* been victimized, but not on campus or by fellow students. Several said they had been raped hundreds or even thousands of miles from campus. An Eastern Michigan University student, for example, said a stranger raped her in a bathroom after she became separated from her friends while on vacation in New York City. Incidents like these have nothing to do with the debate over how colleges should handle matters of sexual assault on campus.

In an article headlined "Sex Assault in College," the lead story was about Michigan State University student Rachel Sienkowski, "a survivor" who had blacked out from drinking at a football tailgate party and ended up with "a man she didn't recognize" in her bed. The next morning, "her head was bleeding" from a gash, prompting her to go to the police. Thousands of words later, the article disclosed that Sienkowski "doesn't know for sure whether she had wanted sex in the moment." The police report quoted her alleged attacker as saying that she "was very into everything that was happening." It also contained photographs of the hickeys that he said Sienkowski had put on his neck. The bloody gash on her head appears to have been a result of her falling out of bed on her own.

This is a "survivor"? If rape were rampant on college campuses, why would the *Post* article feature an apparent non-rape that neither participant remembered very well? Perhaps because a conscientious editor or reporter noticed that it was the only case that included an accused student's side of the story—albeit only by incorporating details of the police report. As mentioned in this book's introduction and discussed in chapter 10, the dangers of this one-sided approach had already become apparent in 2014, after a failure to even *try* to contact an alleged rapist had prevented *Rolling Stone* reporter Sabrina Rubin Erdely from discovering that the alleged rapist did not, in fact, exist.[41]

Of course, the overwhelming evidence that the White House and its allies have exaggerated the number of sex crimes on our nation's college campuses does not negate the danger of sexual assault of college students. All reliable data indicate that women between 18 and 24—a range that includes most college and university students—are those most likely to be sexually assaulted. But there is also ample evidence that college victims, like all other victims of crime, can obtain far more effective redress from the criminal justice system than from campus kangaroo courts. In addition to the Brock Turner case at Stanford that we mentioned in the introduction:

- At a 2008 fraternity party, an intoxicated Oregon State University student named Gregory Sako so violently assaulted a female party guest that both her underwear and his were left bloodied. Instead of going to the campus Title IX office, the victim filed a police report. After Sako made inconsistent statements to the police, he was arrested. A jury convicted him of first-degree rape and first-degree sexual abuse. He was sentenced to eight years in prison and 11 years of probation and was required to register as a sex offender.[42]

- In 2012, a first-year University of Massachusetts student was partying when four male teenagers signed into her dorm. She let them into her room, where the four—Justin King, Alex Liccardi, Emmanuel Bile, and Caleb Womack—raped her. She filed a police report. The four were arrested, convicted of rape, sentenced by a judge to prison terms ranging from five to 12 years, and required to register as sex offenders.[43]

- In 2014, a University of Wisconsin student named Douglas Gill got high on cocaine, entered a female acquaintance's dorm room, started kissing her, and digitally assaulted her without consent. (She then said "stop" and he did.) He later texted an apology to her, including this: "I'm just gonna take a lot of drugs n pass out, sorry for literally raping you that was so not cool."[44] Instead of going to her campus Title IX office, the victim went to the police, who arrested Gill. He pleaded guilty to false imprisonment and two counts of fourth-degree sexual assault.[45]

- Also in 2014, a Pennsylvania State University student named Christopher Ender had sex with an incapacitated woman. Instead of going to her campus Title IX office, she filed a police report. Under police questioning, Ender said that he had been drinking so heavily as to be unsure what "no" meant. He was arrested; after a plea bargain in 2016, he was sentenced to between 9 and 23.5 months in jail.[46]

- Again in 2014, Manuel Mario Vega, a student at the University of Minnesota–Moorhead, bought alcohol for an 18-year-old female fellow student. After she became drunk, he videotaped himself sexually assaulting her. Instead of going to her campus Title IX office, the victim filed a police report. Vega was arrested. In a plea bargain, he was sentenced to four months in prison and ordered to register as a sex offender.[47]

Because the victims in these cases went to the police, their attackers were locked up—like other criminals—rather than merely removed from campus and left free to rape again. Even the six-month sentence in the Brock Turner case carried a significant penalty (i.e., the need to register as a sex offender) and came at the end of a trial in whose outcome the public could have faith. If the case had been handled exclusively by Stanford's manifestly unfair judicial process, the outcome would have warranted no public confidence, and the worst punishment Turner could have received would have been expulsion.[48]

Accusers' rights activists and their political supporters have all but conceded in candid moments that they don't really care whether the one-in-five claim is true. Sen. Bob Casey (D-Pennsylvania), for example, told *USA Today* in October 2015 that "even if the argument proves true that it's not [valid]—that [the rate is] 1 in 6, 1 in 7, 1 in 10, 1 in 20—that is still way too high.... We could spend all day debating numbers.... What I worry about isn't whether the 1-in-5 statistic is accurate, but about underreporting."[49]

The second and third elements of conventional wisdom about rape on college campuses—that the number of such rapes has grown alarmingly and that campuses are especially dangerous places for young women—are also false. The number of sexual assaults and rapes on college campuses *decreased*, by more than half, between 1997 and 2013, as the BJS Special Report shows. This result is in line with the overall drop in violent crime across the nation during those same years.[50]

The third myth was summarized in 2014 by Sen. Kirsten Gillibrand: "We should never accept the fact that women are at a greater risk of sexual assault as soon as they step onto a college campus. But today they are."[51] Yet the rate of rape and sexual assault was 20 percent *higher* for nonstudents of college age (7.6 per 1,000 per year) than for college students (6.1 per 1,000 per year), according to the BJS Special Report. There were twice as many alleged sexual assaults on nonstudents (65,700) as on students (31,300) and half again as many rapes of non-students (3.1 per 1,000) as of students (2.0 per 1,000).[52]

Even if BJS surveys understate the number of sexual assaults, as activists and some others claim, that does not affect the validity of rape rate comparisons from year to year or from on campus to off campus.[53]

Class bias provides the most convincing explanation for the vastly greater concern about *on-campus* sexual assault among bureaucrats, politicians, activists, journalists, and academics. The founders of key campus accusers' rights groups, such as Know Your IX, SurvJustice, End Rape on Campus, and No Red Tape, all hail from elite residential institutions: Yale, Amherst, the University of Wisconsin, the University of North Carolina, and Columbia. They often have seemed interested in activism for its own sake. Members of Know Your IX, for instance, deem activism a chance to "validate our traumas."[54]

Off-campus rape victims, by contrast, are disproportionately poor or lower-middle class. "Women in the lowest income bracket, with annual household incomes of less than $7,500, are sexually victimized at...about six times the rate of women in the highest income bracket (households earning $75,000 or more annually)," criminologist Callie Marie Rennison wrote in 2014. "The focus on sexual violence against some of our most privileged young people has distracted us from the victimization of those enjoying less social and economic advantage."[55]

The crusade to eliminate due-process protections through a campus judicial process does nothing for the majority of female college students.[56] They go to college part-time (3.82 million) or to nonresidential colleges that enroll millions more, like the online University of Phoenix and the overwhelmingly nonresidential City University of New York. CUNY, the nation's largest public educational institution, enrolls around 150,000 female students.[57] Since these students overwhelmingly live off campus, they largely rely on police in cases of rape or other assault. If President Obama's statistical claims were true, more than 100,000 of these off-campus college women are being sexually assaulted per year, absent any concern from the federal government.

The fourth myth centers on the research of a retired University of Massachusetts psychologist, David Lisak. In a 12-page paper published in 2002, Lisak theorized that a relatively small number of serial predators commit 90 percent of campus rapes. Averaging six rapes apiece, these sociopaths select their victims ahead of time and carefully plan how to get them drunk or otherwise vulnerable.[58]

This 12-page paper is virtually the only basis for the decisions by the federal government and countless universities to focus college disciplinary procedures largely on the notion that serial rapists predominate and must be expelled to protect female students.[59] Tyler Kingkade, *The Huffington Post*'s campus sex crimes reporter, tweeted that "virtually all the Title IX/prevention field accepted it [Lisak's serial-predator theory] as definitive.... I saw Lisak treated like a celeb at conferences" (@ tylerkingkade, November 23, 2015). A 2014 federal report cited Lisak's theory several times.

In 2015, Lisak's research was discredited in four *Reason* magazine exposés by Linda LeFauve (Associate Vice President for Planning and Institutional Research at Davidson College) and Robby Soave (*Reason* staff writer). They showed that Lisak's admirers seem not to have read his 2002 paper (with Paul Miller as coauthor) but only to have repeated what Lisak now describes as its conclusions.

LeFauve's article noted that Lisak's paper contains no data supporting his many claims that serial predators commit 90 percent of campus rapes. It does not refer to assaults on college students or even to assaults on or near a campus. It was based on a small subset of data collected between 1991 and 1998 by doctoral students for dissertations, none pertaining to sexual assault on college campuses. The data consisted of surveys completed by just over 1,800 subjects, 120 of whom Lisak defined as rapists or attempted rapists, and 76 of whom he defined as repeat offenders. Aged 18 to 71, none of the subjects lived on a college campus. None of the dissertations could identify whether the subjects were students when they committed the assaults. Lisak himself, when questioned by LeFauve in a phone interview, admitted that "a number of these cases were domestic violence situations." When LeFauve's questions became too specific and probing for Lisak's taste, he terminated the interview.[60]

Lisak also refused to answer questions about his methodology from Soave, who exposed as almost certainly false Lisak's claim that follow-up interviews had been conducted with most of the alleged serial rapists.

Soave then turned to James Hopper, one of the former graduate students whose work Lisak had repurposed for his 2002 paper, to confirm the claim. Hopper would not, or could not, do so. He did tell Soave that the researchers had made no attempt to exclude non-students from their studies, which were not about students. Still, Hopper speculated that college students "if anything... might be at higher risk for committing sexual assault" because "they think they can get away with it." They are, Hopper sneered, "entitled!"[61]

A second article by LeFauve, in November 2015, undermined the main illustration of Lisak's serial-predator theory: a video featuring a hired actor reading a purportedly unedited, verbatim interview of an unidentified serial rapist, to whom Lisak gave the pseudonym Frank.[62] As told by Lisak acolyte Jon Krakauer in his book *Missoula: Rape and the Justice System in a College Town* (Doubleday, 2015), "Frank" explained his technique as follows: "We'd be on the lookout for the good-looking girls, especially the freshmen, the really young ones. They were the easiest.... Then we'd get them drinking right away.... They'd be guzzling it, you know, because they were freshmen, kind of nervous." When "she was so plastered that she probably didn't know what was going on," Frank added, he would hold a female student down and rape her.[63]

But as LeFauve learned through careful investigation, this "Frank interview" was actually a compilation of 12 interviews with 12 different men. These interviews had taken place in the mid-1980s—ages ago in terms of attitudes about sexual assault. And, contrary to Lisak's implication, the "Frank interview" had no connection to his 2002 serial-predator paper.

In short, the *Reason* articles wholly undermined Lisak's serial-predator theory. Lisak has not responded substantively to the criticisms. A large-scale statistical critique, published in *The Journal of the American Medical Association* (JAMA) in 2015, also concluded that the serial-predator theory had led to "misguided" rape-prevention policies.[64] Lisak and Hopper demanded that JAMA retract the paper; JAMA refused, after conducting a thorough review and deeming their complaint unjustified. So the duo filed a research misconduct complaint of dubious merit against the study's lead author, Kevin Swartout.[65]

The last of the five myths identified at the start of this chapter was highlighted by a 2014 White House Task Force document asserting that "in reality, only 2-10 percent of reported rapes are false." The task force cited a 2010 study, "False Allegations of Sexual Assault," principally authored by none other than David Lisak.[66] The resulting insinuation that there are few innocents among the accused allowed the Obama administration and its allies to rationalize the unfair college disciplinary systems they had endorsed.

Ironically, in a paper published in 2009, Lisak had claimed that "estimates for the percentage of false reports begin to converge around 2-8 percent."[67] Later, in the 2015 documentary film *The Hunting Ground*, his estimate jumped to "more likely 95 to 98 percent of [campus] rape reports are not false." So, over a six-year period and based on the same data, Lisak cited an upper range of false rape claims as 5 percent (2015), 8 percent (2009), and 10 percent (2010). These discrepancies came without explanation from someone purporting to be a careful scholar.

The best-known source of the claim that only 2 percent of rape accusations are false is Susan Brownmiller's 1975 book *Against Our Will: Men, Women, and Rape*. For this fact, Brownmiller cited not a study but rather a speech, by a New York judge, who mentioned unpublished alleged findings by the "NYC Rape Analysis Squad."

Lisak, for his part, counted as false only those claims that had been *both* thoroughly investigated *and* proven false under restrictive definitions of that word. His 2010 study of a unnamed "major Northeastern university" came up with a false-accusation rate of only 5.9 percent by counting accusations as "false" only if a "thorough investigation" had determined that "key elements of a victim's [sic] account of an assault were internally inconsistent *and* directly contradicted by multiple witnesses *and* if the victim [sic] then altered those key elements of his or her account" (emphasis added).

Quite beyond the very tight description of falsity, Lisak's finding did not mean that 94 percent of reports were true. In fact, the study indicated that only 35.3 percent of the 136 allegations were credible enough to be adjudicated. Those that fell in between—the majority of those analyzed by Lisak and his team—had either no evidence or conflicting evidence or there was insufficient information even to classify them. For instance, Lisak classified as *not* false accusations in which "the victim [sic] mislabeled the incident (e.g., gave a truthful account of the incident, but the incident did not meet the legal elements of the crime of sexual assault)"—which law enforcement would treat as unfounded.[68]

The reductio ad absurdum of Lisak's see-no-false-accusations approach came during a November 2007 speech at Rutgers University in New Brunswick, New Jersey, in which he indicated that he would not classify as "false" the previous year's Duke lacrosse case. "I don't know what happened at Duke," he said. "No one knows."[69]

To the contrary, everyone who had followed the widely publicized case—as surely a specialist such as Lisak should have done—understood that the mentally unbalanced accuser had not been raped by anyone. The evidence of innocence included DNA tests showing that none of the three defendants had sex with the accuser despite her tale of a violent, 30-minute, condom-free attack; a timed ATM video showing one of the alleged rapists to be more than a mile away from the accuser at the time of the alleged attack; and an extraordinarily thorough investigation by North Carolina Attorney General Roy Cooper that led him to declare all three defendants innocent.[70]

A 2007 study authored by Kimberly Lonsway and Joanne Archambault, published by a victims' activist group, used methodology similar to Lisak's to produce a false-accusation rate of 7 percent.[71] This study counted a rape accusation as false only if it was proven false after a "thorough" police investigation. At the same time, the authors indicated that it was "probably not the best use of limited resources" for police departments to thoroughly investigate rape claims for falsity.[72] If police detectives follow the authors' recommendation to not spend time investigating rape claims for falsity, and the only way to prove a claim false is by thorough investigation, this leads to a situation in which no rape accusation can ever be classified as false.[73]

Lonsway and Archambault added that even to "alter or exaggerate the details of what happened [in order] to create a case that seems more believable," or to "report that the suspect used a weapon when this is not really true," or to "describe threats of physical violence that were not really made," did not render a claim false.

Only 20 percent of the accusations in Lonsway and Archambault's study proceeded to any kind of adjudication, and the study did not disclose how many of the accused were found guilty.

Given the inherently subjective nature of the research, and the differing definitions of "false" used by individual researchers, University of Nottingham law professor Candida Saunders concluded in 2012 that "the only thing we know with any certainty about the prevalence of false allegations of rape is that we do not know how prevalent they are."[74]

In contrast to the spectrum offered by Lisak, a 2016 dissertation by Benjamin Baughman, examining 351 confidential investigative files from a police department in the southeastern United States, concluded that 17 percent of the allegations were "fabricated," with another 66 percent uncertain.[75] A 2014 report by the Defense Department's Sexual Assault Prevention and Response Office (SAPRO) analyzing the disposition of the previous year's sexual assault allegations in the military found that 19.1 percent of the 2,586 cases were classified as "unfounded."[76] A 2012 Urban Institute study estimated that of 227 men convicted of rape for whom DNA evidence was available and usable, 15 percent were eliminated as the source of the evidence, which "was supportive of exoneration."[77] A 1994 study by Purdue professor Eugene Kanin, using data from an unidentified Midwestern city, found that between 1978 and 1987 the police department concluded that 41 percent of rape allegations were false.[78]

In the campus context, Cynthia Garrett, a lawyer and board member of Families Advocating for Campus Equality, a group formed to combat wrongful allegations of sexual assault on college campuses, stressed that "it is very likely that the prevalence of false allegations of sexual misconduct on campuses has risen in recent years, not only due to expanded definitions of sexual assault," but also due to limitations on cross-examination of accusers, due to the use of hearsay, and due to the lack of any meaningful deterrent in the campus context against false allegations.[79]

Debates over statistics, however important, obscure a critical point: none of the surveys help identify what percentage of people accused of sexual assault actually committed the offense. But campus activists and their media allies often have cited the surveys as proving that almost all alleged perpetrators are guilty. Examples:

- "Only 2 to 8 percent of reports of sexual assault are actually false. That means 92 to 98 percent are not false," asserted Kirby Dick, director of the documentary film *The Hunting Ground*, at the 2015 Sundance Film Festival. "Another way to look at it is, on average, 19 out of 20 reports of sexual assault that you hear are true. That's where you should start."[80]

- "It's important to keep in mind what the flip side of these numbers reveal: Between 90 percent and 98 percent of rape allegations are true," Jon Krakauer wrote in *The New York Times* in 2015.[81]

- "2–8% of rape reports turn out to be false. Meaning out of 100 women, 92–98 are truthful," *Rolling Stone* contributing editor Sabrina Rubin Erdely (@SabrinaRErdely) asserted on Twitter on October 22, 2013, just over a year before her UVA travesty.

- The "best research" shows that "2-10% [of] rape allegations [are] false," meaning that "90–98% [are] real," former *Daily Beast* and *American Prospect* journalist Dana Goldstein (@DanaGoldstein) tweeted on December 5, 2014.

- "[T]ry writing '92–98% of rape allegations are true' rather than '2–8 of all rape allegations are fabricated or unfounded,'" *WIRED* science reporter Nick Stockton (@StocktonSays) tweeted, also on December 5, 2014.

- "Instead of saying 2–8% of rape reports are false to weigh in on the issue, why not say at least 92–98% are true?" feminist writer and activist Wagatwe Wanjuki (@wagatwe) tweeted on May 7, 2015.

- "[F]or every false accusation of rape, there are up to 100 actual rapes that take place," wrote Daniel Roberts, of the sports website Deadspin, in December 2014.[82]

Dylan Matthews, then at *The Washington Post*'s data-driven "WonkBlog," topped them all. Under the heading "The saddest graph you'll see today,"[83] he shared a graph prepared by activist group the Enliven Project, suggesting that only 2 out of every 1,000 men (0.2 percent) accused of rape were innocent.[84]

A game of telephone winding up with results so far from the truth would be hard to imagine.

Consider how the claim that "all allegations not proven false must be true" would apply to the following case, from Miami University in Oxford, Ohio.

On August 31, 2013, Matthew Sahm, a sophomore, met fellow student Mary Kaptur* at a fraternity party. Both were drinking alcohol, both were underage, and, after flirting, Kaptur suggested they go back to his room, where they had sexual contact. Sahm said that he stopped when Kaptur asked him to stop because, she told him, she was worried about cheating on her boyfriend. She then left his room and, with some friends, left the party.

Drunken hookups like this have been commonplace on college campuses for many years. Between 2005 and 2011, the Online College Social Life Survey, designed by New York University sociologist Paula England, asked some 25,000 students on 21 four-year campuses, "How much alcohol did you drink before or during the date/hookup?" Male respondents averaged 5.46 drinks, and female respondents averaged 3.73 drinks. More than 30 percent of the female respondents and 40 percent of the male respondents said they had had six or more drinks before hooking up.[85]

A few days after the fraternity party, Kaptur filed a complaint with the university, alleging that she had been too intoxicated to consent. She also told the Oxford Police Department that she had been sexually assaulted by an unknown assailant.[86] The university "investigated" and tried Sahm in three weeks. When he was brought before the disciplinary board, it was unclear who had the burden of proof, according to Sahm. In addition, he was prohibited from being represented by a lawyer.

Kimberly Lau, a New York lawyer who has represented several accused students, described the terror of unrepresented students facing such disciplinary tribunals: "These are, like, 19-, 20-year-old kids who've probably never been grilled about sex, they probably don't even talk about it with their own parents yet, and quite frankly, these students are scared shitless. Their entire education is on the line. They could possibly be marked as a sexual predator and be exiled from this school and also persona non grata [at] other schools, because who wants to take that kind of student?...They're deathly afraid."[87]

Only after the disciplinary board had found him guilty of sexual misconduct did Sahm, now with the help of a lawyer, uncover information that should have exonerated him.

One student, a member of Kaptur's sorority, reported that after filing the sexual assault claim, Kaptur had coached her sorority sisters—two of whom she had told the night of the party that she had cheated on her boyfriend—on how to respond to the investigator's questions. Worse, this student witness revealed that the school's Title IX investigator, Susan Tobergte, had discouraged her from testifying at the hearing. Tobergte advised the student that, according to Google, "less than 2 percent of sexual assault cases were wrongful convictions." The student, thus discouraged, did not testify at Sahm's campus hearing, though she later provided an affidavit to his lawyer.

It would seem, then, that the Title IX investigator had abetted a cover-up of exculpatory evidence. Tobergte, in addition to being an eight-year veteran of the university police force, was a veteran of the university's sexual assault task force, which had produced a report claiming, with no hard evidence, that "as many as eight to nine women per week may be victims of sexual assault" on the Miami University campus. (According to Clery Act data, the university actually averaged 0.2 sexual assault reports per week in the three years prior to Sahm's case.[88]) The task force also asserted that many "college date rapists...did not see themselves as 'real criminals'" and that "some men may purposely get drunk when they want to act sexually aggressive, knowing that intoxication will provide them with an excuse for their socially inappropriate behavior."[89]

In any fair process, an investigator who had endorsed such guilt-presuming views would have been recused from Sahm's case, especially because Sahm and Kaptur had consumed alcohol. But Tobergte sat in judgment of Sahm. She did not respond to a request from us for comment during the writing of this book. Miami later defended Tobergte's conduct as, at worst, due to a "lack of experience in handling such investigations." The university did not attempt to reconcile this assertion with its earlier decision to acknowledge Tobergte's lengthy experience by naming her to the school's sexual assault task force.

Three other witnesses filed affidavits on Sahm's behalf after the disciplinary board had ruled against him. One of these witnesses passed along a text she had received on the night of the party from a sorority sister: "Please help. [Mary] just cheated on her boyfriend and is literally a mess." Another witness said she saw Kaptur, shortly after the sexual encounter, acting distraught—not because she had been assaulted, but because, she was saying, "I can't believe I cheated on my boyfriend."

One of Kaptur's sorority sisters swore in an affidavit that she recalled Kaptur telling several friends that she had initiated the sexual contact with Sahm, in order to test her feelings for her boyfriend. This witness added that she had come forward because "as a woman and a woman in a sorority, I think that making false accusations and presenting oneself as weak and a victim is extremely insulting."

The police never filed charges against Sahm. But the university upheld its disciplinary board's judgment, on the ground that Sahm could have found this exonerating evidence "at the time of the original hearing." In other words, a 20-year-old sophomore should have been able to ferret out exculpatory evidence that the university's own Title IX investigator helped keep buried.

After his expulsion, Sahm applied to Allegheny College in Pennsylvania but was rejected when he had to explain the details of why he had left Miami. In a lawsuit by Sahm against Miami, Clinton appointee Judge Susan Dlott, of the U.S. District Court in Cincinnati, said she found Tobergte's conduct "troubling," admitting that it suggested bias "against students accused of sexual assault." But Dlott implied that this conduct at a public institution was not the sort of thing about which a federal judge should be bothered. She dismissed the lawsuit, and Sahm elected not to appeal.

Now consider how advocacy researchers might still avoid classifying as "false" Mary Kaptur's allegation that Matthew Sahm sexually assaulted her. Because of Miami's deficient investigation, and because local police concluded that there was no probable cause to have filed charges against Sahm, and therefore had no grounds to fully investigate *Kaptur's* truthfulness, under the methodologies of Lisak and Lonsway the accusation would be classified as "not false." And that result would open the way for the likes of Kirby Dick, Jon Krakauer, and Sabrina Rubin Erdely to, fantastically, classify the allegation as true.

3

THE REALITIES OF "RAPE CULTURE"

Carrying the Weight Together, one of the many activist groups that has sprung up on college campuses in recent years (and now part of the larger group Know Your IX), defined "rape culture" as "the normalization of behaviors including sexual objectification, victim blaming, trivialization and denial of sexual violence, and the refusal to recognize sexual violence that does not adhere to stereotypes such as being...only committed by strangers, and/or always being extremely physically violent."[1] In an extreme manifestation of these ideas, a 2016 document from Southern Connecticut State University held that "teaching women to avoid getting raped" exemplified "rape culture."[2]

After reviewing the literature, libertarian journalist Cathy Young identified four key tenets behind the "rape culture" concept: "1) Women almost never lie when they report a sex crime, and to doubt them is to perpetuate rape culture; 2) rape is any sexual act in which the woman feels violated—unless she suffers from false consciousness and needs to be educated about her violation; 3) rape includes situations in which the woman agrees to sex because of persistent advances, 'emotional coercion,' or intoxication—or because she doesn't have the nerve to say no; 4) no matter how willing the woman appears to be, it is the man's responsibility to ensure explicit consent—or he may be guilty of rape."[3]

As Young's summary implies, the anti-"rape culture" movement proceeds from a patronizing view of women—portraying them as weak or ignorant, incapable of making their own choices, and untrustworthy if they fail to accept the activists' assumptions. The movement, of course, has an even more negative view of male students—as, on average, more malicious and dishonest than their female counterparts.

The belief in a college "rape culture" is shared by campus activists and powerful politicians alike. President Obama, for one, explained that "we need to encourage young people, both men and women, to realize that sexual assault is unacceptable."[4] By thus implying that lots of young people consider sexual assault *acceptable*, the president all but embraced the "rape culture" myth. Later in 2014, Claire McCaskill, in a forum on "campus rape culture" in her home state, gave a telling reply to a male student who pressed her on the danger of vagueness in defining "consent": "[M]aybe this has gotten so blurred because of the sexual culture that you've grown up in that a victim doesn't even know if they're a victim."[5] The Missouri senator did not respond to a request for comment from us during the writing of this book.

In 2014, without defining "rape culture," the National Association of Student Personnel Administrators urged signatories to pledge to challenge "negative gender stereotypes, sexism, and rape culture on campus" and promise to "listen to, believe, and assist victims of gender-based violence."[6]

The media have done little better. A 2014 article in *The Christian Science Monitor* painted Harvard's efforts to weaken due process for students accused of sexual assault as "another indication that institutions are responding to the growing chorus of concerns about a 'rape culture' on college campuses."[7] Late the same year, a *New York Times* article scoffed at "conservatives [who] bristle at the concept of a rape culture that permeates the discussion of sexual assault on campuses."[8]

"Like many radical theories, the idea of rape culture contains plausible elements of truth," as Cathy Young has noted.[9] Some of our nation's millions of college students make horrifying statements—and on gender issues, fraternity members have made more than their share. In 2013, the social chair of Georgia Tech's Phi Kappa Tau fraternity emailed members about getting female party guests drunk to turn them into "rapebait."[10] In 2014, American University's Epsilon Iota fraternity members callously discussed rape-related themes.[11] In 2015, on moving-in day at Old Dominion, Sigma Nu fraternity members taunted female students and their parents with banners saying "Rowdy and fun. Hope your baby girl is ready for a good time."[12]

There is scant evidence, however, that such isolated remarks reflect broad student opinion. Indeed, each of these instances provoked widespread revulsion, and both Georgia Tech and Old Dominion suspended the fraternities. As *The Atlantic*'s Caitlin Flanagan—no apologist for fraternities—argued in 2013, such "patently vile" fraternity conduct also can be seen as an "obvious," if immature, reaction to an oppressive campus atmosphere of political correctness.[13]

By implying that widely condemned behavior reflects common beliefs, the "rape culture" myth is divorced from reality. Few if any institutions in contemporary American society are *less* inclined than colleges to tolerate rapists in their midst or even to presume the innocence of accused students. The dominant view on college campuses is that all those who make accusations of sexual assault are "victims"—or "survivors."

For the classic example of how entrenched the "rape culture" narrative has become, and how the campus reality so differs from what "rape culture" advocates claim, consider events at Duke University since 2006.

On March 13, 2006, members of the Duke men's lacrosse team, along with a few friends, threw a spring break party at a home rented by three of the team's captains. Late in the evening, a pair of hired female strippers arrived and began to perform for the party attendees. One of the strippers, a woman named Crystal Mangum, appeared incapacitated, and within minutes the performance ended in anger. One of the few students who lingered culminated a racially charged exchange by responding with the N-word after the other dancer, Kim Roberts, called them "limp-dick white boys."

There the story might have ended. But while Roberts was driving away with an incoherent Mangum in tow, the latter feigned passing out.

Roberts stopped at a 24-hour grocery store and got a security guard to call the police. They roused Mangum and took her to a mental health intake facility, in a condition that might well have led to her being institutionalized and losing custody of her children, as had happened temporarily the year before. But when a nurse asked the barely responsive Mangum whether she had been raped, she nodded yes. She then went to the Duke University Hospital for a rape exam.

Over the next few weeks, Mangum said variously that zero, two, three, four, five, six, and twenty white lacrosse players had raped her. Eventually, she settled on a story in which three members of the team assaulted and penetrated her in a bathroom without using condoms. But when shown photos of the players, she couldn't identify any of them as her attackers.

So District Attorney Mike Nifong told police to ignore departmental guidelines and show her another photo array, this time telling Mangum that she would be shown all 46 white Duke lacrosse players and no one else. The implicit message: pick any three.

Nifong, a longtime assistant DA, had been temporarily appointed to the top spot after his predecessor became a judge. At the time of the alleged rape, he was running in a primary election for a full term. Behind both in polls and in campaign contributions, he appeared likely to lose to a longtime rival who would fire him rather than allow him to return as an assistant DA.

Then came a case that was tailor-made for posturing as champion of a downtrodden black woman to a primary electorate that was nearly half black, with an ultra-progressive white contingent. Nifong seized the opportunity. In a pre-primary publicity blitz, he gave dozens of interviews peppered with race-baiting rhetoric portraying the lacrosse players as clearly guilty of both the rape and a cover-up. Despite the ethically dubious nature of these statements, they probably were the only thing that would keep Nifong from losing his job.[14]

In a better world, Nifong's conduct would have galvanized Duke faculty members and administrators to defend their students' civil liberties. Instead, Duke's leadership and many of its most prominent professors did the opposite. As news of Mangum's implausible allegations spread, they raced, without waiting for evidence, to join Nifong in condemning the lacrosse players.

The reaction began on March 25, 2006, when the Raleigh *News & Observer* published an interview of Mangum describing the alleged assault. Duke president Richard Brodhead abruptly canceled that afternoon's lacrosse game. That decision was all but unprecedented for an elite Division I program in any sport.

In an announcement of the cancellation that was generally hostile to the lacrosse players, Brodhead also mentioned the presumption of innocence—the most hallowed tradition of Anglo-American law. He was pilloried for the assertion at a March 29 faculty meeting. Among his advisors, Larry Moneta, vice president for student affairs, told a defense lawyer he didn't believe the players were innocent.[15]

On the ground, professor Tim Tyson, joining a protest outside the lacrosse captains' home hours after the canceled game, proclaimed that "the spirit of the lynch mob lived in that house" and that the refusal of most players to submit to police interrogation without lawyers present "may be illegal."[16] A few days later, Houston Baker, a professor of English and African-American Studies, fumed that unless Duke ordered "immediate dismissals" of all 46 white team members, it would be guilty of "a tepid and pious legalism with respect to the disaster of recent days: the actual harm to the body, soul, mind, and spirit of black women."[17]

Several professors brought their anti-rape crusade into the classroom. History professor John Thompson told the lacrosse players in his class that they needed to be "men" and turn in their rapist teammates. Another history professor, Reeve Huston, declared in class that he believed Mangum had been raped. Professor Kim Curtis lowered the grades of two lacrosse players in her political science class. (One later won a lawsuit against Duke over his grade.) Curtis also marched in anti–lacrosse team protests in the neighborhood where many team members lived.[18]

The student government and the student newspaper waited to see the evidence before passing judgment. But student activists, calling themselves "potbangers," protested outside the captains' house; one sign urged that the lacrosse players be castrated. "We are having a 'Cacerolazo,' or a pots & pans protest, because it is a tool women all over the world use to call out sexual assaulters," declared a flyer. One potbanger cautioned fellow protesters: "IF YOU ARE A MAN: Please be mindful of the energy you bring and space you take up in the conversation. Keep in mind that assertion of male domination and violence, even in a well intended response, is part and parcel of this whole thing."

Another campus protest featured a sign saying "If lacrosse players are 'innocent until proven guilty,' why are survivors of sexual assault 'guilty until proven innocent'?"[19] Yet another group of protesters blanketed the campus with "wanted" posters featuring photographs of the players.[20]

Meanwhile, journalists participated in their own rush to judgment. On March 31, 2006, *New York Times* sportswriter Selena Roberts asserted that "something happened" to Mangum. She hailed the potbangers for their "heartening" protest. Ignoring or perhaps ignorant of the three captains' eyewitness accounts to police, Roberts castigated the players for not coming "forward to reveal an eyewitness account." She added that Mangum's unproven claims threatened "to belie [the players'] social standing as human beings."[21]

The attacks on the team intensified on April 5, 2006, when the Durham *Herald-Sun* published a disgusting email that lacrosse player Ryan McFadyen had sent to his teammates after the party, in which he parodied a scene from *American Psycho* about raping and killing women. (How the Durham Police obtained the email remains unknown.) Brodhead immediately canceled the season and forced Mike Pressler, the blameless lacrosse coach, to resign.

Brodhead accompanied these moves with a public statement excusing the guilt-presuming protests and falsely implying that the lacrosse team was permeated with racism. "We can't be surprised at the outpouring of outrage," he said, given "concerns of women about sexual coercion and assault." Brodhead associated the lacrosse players with rape and "dehumanization," with "memories of the systematic racial oppression we had hoped to have left behind us," with "inequalities of wealth, privilege, and opportunity...and the attitudes of superiority those inequalities breed."[22]

Brodhead's 2,397-word statement never mentioned the presumption of innocence. It barely suggested the *possibility* of innocence. In a confidential email a few days later to top aides, the Duke president said that "we can't do anything to side with [the lacrosse players], or even, if they are exonerated, to imply that they have behaved with honor." In another email later that month, Brodhead drew a damning parallel between the lacrosse players and the film *Primal Fear*, in which Ed Norton plays a cold-blooded killer who fools his lawyer into believing him innocent.[23]

Meanwhile, on April 6, 2006, 88 Duke professors, using university funds, bought a full-page advertisement in the student newspaper. Sponsored by the African-American Studies Department, the "Group of 88" statement, authored by professor Wahneema Lubiano, asserted that something had "happened" to Mangum and promised that the Group of 88's crusade "won't end with what the police say or the court decides." The Group of 88 also sent a message "to the protestors making collective noise," thanking them "for not waiting and for making yourselves heard."[24]

The Group of 88's guilt-presuming assault on innocent students was a culmination of three decades of elevating gender and racial grievances through a range of academic disciplines. Duke, like other universities across the nation, had aggressively filled newly created race, class, and gender subdisciplines of humanities and social sciences departments. These professors preached that American society was beset by racial oppression, pervasive sex discrimination, "rape culture," and hostility to the poor. Less politicized faculty members mostly kept silent.

On April 10, 2006, the lacrosse players' lawyers publicized nearly conclusive proof of their innocence. As they had predicted, and as Nifong had known for almost two weeks, the state crime lab's official test results showed no DNA matches between the evidence from Mangum's rape kit and any member of the team. This finding would have been almost impossible had there been any truth to Mangum's story.

Faculty members and the media were not much interested in this evidence. And Nifong plowed forward. In a desperate effort to find something that the state lab might have missed, Nifong hired Brian Meehan, director of a private lab. He would soon become Nifong's co-conspirator in covering up still more evidence of the lacrosse players' innocence.

Nifong obtained indictments of two lacrosse players, Reade Seligmann and Collin Finnerty, on April 17, 2006. He proceeded despite Seligmann's lawyer's release of a bank ATM video showing him more than a mile from the scene at the time of the alleged rape. The indictments apparently inspired Brodhead to give Nifong an assist two days after the arrests by verbally attacking the two sophomores, who were now facing decades in prison.

"If our students did what is alleged, it is appalling to the worst degree," Brodhead stated during an appearance before the Durham Chamber of Commerce. "If they didn't do it, whatever they did is bad enough."[25] He ignored the exculpatory DNA results, the ATM video, and other proof of innocence. David Evans, one of the captains, was indicted almost a month later, based on DNA distortions by Meehan and Nifong.

Higher education had once valued impartiality and courage in its leaders. But Brodhead's traducing of his own innocent students appears to have cost him nothing except some public ridicule. Duke's board of trustees unequivocally supported him. He was rewarded with two new five-year terms as president, in 2009 and again in 2014. Beyond Duke, his star rose in the national hierarchy of academic prestige. In 2011, he was named co-chair of an American Academy of Arts and Sciences commission to bolster teaching and research in the humanities and social sciences. In 2013, the Carnegie Corporation of New York gave him an Academic Leadership Award and called him one of the "exceptional leaders in higher education." In 2016, while reflecting on his performance, Brodhead remarked, "I don't spend my time looking back on [the lacrosse scandal]." When he did reflect on that case, however, he had a simple response: "I am certainly at ease in my conscience with the role that I played."[26]

While Brodhead was fanning the flames of hatred that threatened to consume the lacrosse players, Duke faculty members became harder and harder to distinguish from wacky guests on cable news. For example, on May 1, 2006, the same day that local TV news programs broadcasted Seligmann's airtight alibi, 10 Duke sociology professors and 27 sociology graduate students released yet another guilt-presuming open letter. "At Duke and many campuses," they declared, citing no evidence, "sexual assault is endemic." The professors demanded that Duke's judicial code recognize "actions that inflict, threaten, or cause injuries that may be corporal, psychological, material, or social, in which victims are presumed representatives of a bias-related classification (i.e., race, gender and sexuality)." They said that Duke must become a "proactively anti-racist, anti-sexist, non-homophobic, non-heteronormative, and anti-classist" place in order to explode the "myth of the meritocratic ideal... [that] allows individuals to justify the continuation of racial and gender inequality."[27]

Duke professors such as these were kindred spirits of Wendy Murphy, a former Massachusetts prosecutor and adjunct professor at the New England School of Law. In dozens of interviews, Murphy made unsubstantiated, misleading, and outright false statements smearing the lacrosse players as rapists. (For example, she asserted that exculpatory, time-stamped photos taken by one player at the stripper party had been "doctored.") "I bet one or more of the players was, you know, molested or something as a child," she mused to CNN. When, after the lacrosse players' innocence had become clear, she was asked to justify such statements, Murphy shrugged them off by saying, "My role as a pundit is to draw inferences and make arguments on behalf of the side which I'm assigned."[28]

In the late spring of 2006, the voices of integrity on the Duke campus came almost exclusively from the student body. Perhaps the highest-profile action came during the women's lacrosse national semifinals. During their game against Northwestern, members of the Duke women's lacrosse team made a statement of solidarity, wearing wristbands with the numbers 6, 13, and 45 (those of Evans, Finnerty, and Seligmann). Duke administrators did not comment on the move, which generated furious attacks in the media. *The New York Times'* Harvey Araton chastised the women he described as "lacrosse gals" for showing how "cross-team friendship and university pride [could] negate common sense at a college as difficult to gain admission to as Duke." They were, he scoffed, "staking their own reputations" on the case's outcome.[29]

Through the summer and into the early fall of 2006, proof of Nifong's dishonesty and unethical conduct mounted. Local and national media outlets began to dismantle key aspects of the prosecutor's tale and note some of his misconduct.

The New York Times, however, clung to the presumption of guilt into which both its news and opinion pieces had settled. As the evidence of innocence mounted higher, the integrity of the paper's coverage sank lower. The culmination of this embarrassing journalism was a 5,600-word front-page story in August 2006 that backed Nifong by claiming there was "a body of evidence to support his decision to take the matter to a jury." The authors of the piece, Duff Wilson and Jonathan Glater, omitted key pieces of exculpatory evidence, tried to explain away others, and made several factual errors, which the *Times* never corrected. Unsurprisingly, by fall 2006, Nifong later recalled, the *Times* was the only newspaper he read.[30]

Voters returned Nifong to office in November 2006. But his case soon fell apart. In a December 15, 2006, hearing, Brian Meehan, the private consultant he had hired to test DNA, admitted that he and Nifong had colluded to spin his lab's DNA test results as "non-probative" even though in fact they exonerated the players—again.[31] With Nifong under investigation by the state bar, North Carolina Attorney General Roy Cooper took over the case and assigned two top prosecutors to do a thorough reinvestigation. They concluded that the charges "were [the] result of a tragic rush to accuse" and should never have been brought.

At a climactic press conference on April 11, 2007, the attorney general announced, "We believe these three individuals are innocent."[32] Such admissions by prosecutors are almost unheard of. Nifong was disbarred a few months later, after a public hearing, for multiple violations of the North Carolina State Bar ethics code. He was also sentenced by Judge Osmond Smith to a symbolic day in jail for lying to the judge about the exculpatory DNA evidence.

Meanwhile, Duke began negotiating with the three indicted lacrosse players' lawyers, who were gearing up to sue the university and the many individual administrators and professors who had publicly rushed to judgment. A settlement was announced in June 2007. It included cash payments to Seligmann, Finnerty, and Evans that were later revealed to total about $20 million—a sum large enough to amount to an admission that Duke's smears had done the three grave harm. Seligmann, Finnerty, and Evans, in exchange, agreed not to sue Duke or any of its employees. Brodhead issued a halfhearted apology in September 2007: he expressed regret over "ill-judged" and "divisive" comments by Duke faculty members but mentioned none of his own such utterances.[33]

Some faculty members remained unrepentant toward the lacrosse players and even to other students who had defended them. In a January 2007 op-ed, English professor Cathy Davidson, one of the Group of 88's most prominent members, charged that the campus had been polluted with "racist and sexist remarks" in the spring of 2006. She claimed that campus defenders of the players had resorted to "rampant" and "pernicious stereotypes about African-Americans, especially poor black women." Davidson cited not a single example.[34] In our own exhaustive review of the case, we found none.

Despite the behavior of the Group of 88, none of its members was penalized, and some were seemingly rewarded for leading the rush-to-judgment mob. In the spring of 2007, Paula McClain, an outspoken member of the Group of 88, was elected chairperson of Duke's Academic Council, the highest-ranking elected position for faculty at Duke; in 2012, she was named dean of the Duke Graduate School and vice provost for graduate education, the university's second highest-ranking academic position. Duke hailed her as an "outstanding university citizen" and praised "her concern for the well-being of individual students."[35]

These encomiums were a sad commentary on the state of Duke. No reason exists to believe that other elite universities have a better condition. Indeed, Houston Baker, Grant Farred, and at least eight other Group of 88 members were hired away to prestigious positions at schools including Vanderbilt, Cornell, the University of Chicago, and the CUNY Graduate Center.[36]

Duke administrators, too, saw their careers advance without obstruction, despite their conduct in the lacrosse case. Donna Lisker, Ada Gregory's predecessor as director of the Duke Women's Center, taught women's studies and gender and sport before taking an administrative job at Duke. Commenting on the DNA evidence that had proved the lacrosse players' innocence in April 2006, she said, "I don't want it to deter anyone from reporting [a sexual assault]."[37] And she stressed that it was "weird" to see people cheering for the reconstituted 2007 team, because "we know to be true [that] [t]hey had a party, hired women to strip, the women were (verbally) threatened and there was underage drinking."[38] Lisker presented no evidence to corroborate the charge that both women had been threatened.[39] She also claimed falsely that Mangum had been "raked over the coals" by the media.[40] In fact, for months, the mainstream media had inaccurately portrayed Mangum—who doubled as a prostitute—in *glowing* terms, as an honors student and demure working mother who had reluctantly become a stripper in order to spend more time with her children. Lisker was promoted to associate dean of undergraduate education in late 2007.[41]

Meanwhile, kindred spirits of the Group of 88 at other universities and in the media did their best to reinterpret events at Duke to confirm their preexisting beliefs. In May 2010, Stony Brook University sociology professor Michael Kimmel opined in *The Huffington Post* that the real story, as told to him by unidentified Duke professors, was that friends of the lacrosse players thought the rape allegations were "utterly plausible."[42] Former MSNBC host Melissa Harris-Perry portrayed the Duke professors who championed the false accuser as the real victims, because they had been pressured to feel "ashamed of ever believing that their own experiences, beliefs, and feelings were valid."[43]

Angela Hattery, director of George Mason University's Center for Women and Gender Studies, claimed that "one of the [players'] fathers indicated that he didn't see what the issue was, [because] he and his Wall Street colleagues routinely unwind together at the end of the day at strip clubs." She cited as authority a *Washington Post* article that said nothing consistent with her claim. Confronted by one of her readers about this contradiction, Hattery refused to retract her smear, sniffing, "I am a scholar and do not 'make things up.'"[44]

The effort to rehabilitate the original mob presumption of guilt peaked with the publication of William D. Cohan's book *The Price of Silence: The Duke Lacrosse Scandal, the Power of the Elite, and the Corruption of the Great Universities* (Scribner, 2014). In order to embrace the fashionable dogma that standards of proof should yield to categorical bias, Cohan framed the lacrosse case as part of an epidemic of sexual assault on college campuses. A Duke graduate who had written best-selling purported exposés of the financial industry, Cohan based his reinvention of the fraud on unpublished interviews (by a friend) with the disbarred Nifong, a proven liar.[45]

Cohan said on CNN, "There is an incredible amount of evidence that something untoward happened in that bathroom."[46] He never specified what that evidence was. Nor did he even try to interview the defense lawyers, the veteran prosecutors who had taken over from Nifong and exonerated the lacrosse players, the state bar officials who had stripped Nifong of his law license, or the judge to whom Nifong had lied.

Illustrating the urge in the news media to rehabilitate the original rape narrative, Cohan's revisionist mendacity won glowing reviews in *The New York Times Sunday Book Review*, *The Daily News*, *Newsday*, *The Pittsburgh Post-Gazette*, *Salon*, *The Daily Beast*, and even the usually less politically correct *Wall Street Journal*, *The Economist*, and *FT Magazine*. Cohan basked in puffball interviews on MSNBC's *Morning Joe* and *The*

Cycle; by *New York* and *Cosmopolitan* magazine; and by Diane Rehm and other public radio broadcasters. Civil libertarian Radley Balko noted that Cohan's book won "airy praise in elite outlets from reviewers who have little prior working knowledge of Durham, [while] getting panned by people who have specialized knowledge of Nifong, and of the lacrosse case in particular."[47]

Because Mangum was not a Duke student and Nifong had seized control of the case, Duke's formal disciplinary system never went after the lacrosse players. But in 2009, the university—still run by the same administration that had rushed to judgment in 2006—adopted a "zero tolerance" sexual assault policy that tilted its disciplinary process in favor of alleged victims.

The new policy included a breathtakingly broad concept of rape. "Real or perceived power differentials between individuals may create an unintentional atmosphere of coercion," Duke maintained—and that condition alone could turn consensual sex into rape, regardless of anyone's intent.[48] This provision implied that a male student could be guilty (under Duke's rules) if a woman with whom he had consensual sex later complained that she went along with it only because he was a big man on campus.

Duke's new policy also provided that even a student's enthusiastic agreement to have sex was not "consent" if she was "intoxicated," and it classified *all* intercourse as rape unless both parties had given "affirmative" consent "in each instance of sexual activity."

While giving lip service to the presumption of innocence, the new policy denied to accused students any rights to have a lawyer present, to confront their accuser, or to examine witnesses. Accused students could only suggest questions for members of the hearing panel to ask. They were guaranteed only five days' notice before their hearings. They were denied the rights, which the new policy gave to accusers, to be treated with "sensitivity," to "make opening and closing statements to a hearing panel," and to receive "a copy of the written information given to a hearing panel."

The head of the Duke Women's Center, Ada Gregory, defended the new policy's almost unlimited definition of rape by saying: "[T]he higher IQ, the more manipulative they are, the more cunning they are. Imagine the sex offenders we have here at Duke—cream of the crop."[49]

Later, in a letter to the Duke *Chronicle* claiming that she had been quoted out of context, Gregory made the same assertion in slightly less inflammatory language. She cited David Lisak as her authority.[50] But despite the many flaws in his research, even Lisak had never suggested a link between high IQ and sexual assault. Shortly after the article appeared, one of us asked Gregory to identify any such claim by Lisak.[51] She did not respond.

Gregory also dismissed the concerns of some Duke administrators that the new policy would encourage more false claims of sexual misconduct. "We're creating an environment that says, 'This is not tolerated in our community,' and when you create that environment, victims are more likely to come forward and seek help," she said.[52] To Gregory, it appears, there was no such thing as a false claim. She was promoted to executive director of the Office of Interdisciplinary Program Management in 2012.

Sheila Broderick, Duke's gender violence intervention services coordinator, was even more explicit than Gregory in condemning all alleged perpetrators of sexual assault, regardless of the evidence. If campus disciplinary panels "say he's not responsible," even under Duke's guilt-presuming rules, asserted Broderick, "you and I know that he's responsible, and that's at the end of the day what really matters."[53]

That's worth reading twice. This high-ranking Duke bureaucrat declared that *all* students accused of sexual misconduct are guilty. Period.

In today's campus culture, such pronouncements are immune from correction or rebuke. Broderick also asserted that the university was mired in a "rape culture." This condition was neither apparent from the school's reported sexual assault rate of 0.03 percent in the previous calendar year nor supported by any other evidence. Broderick cited as evidence only a fictional character—"Party Boy Chad"—invented by Broderick herself, Ada Gregory, and other Women's Center colleagues. All first-year students were required to watch a Party Boy Chad skit. Shortly after news of the skit emerged, one of us asked Broderick to define "rape culture" and asked her whether she had any evidence for its existence other than her own skit. She did not respond.[54]

Duke's approach to sexual assault allegations typifies that of universities around the country. Sensitivity to alleged victims was the rule at most schools long before the federal government imposed it.

But the 2011 Dear Colleague letter gave Duke a pretext to tighten its de facto presumption of guilt. The university lowered the standard of proof in sexual assault cases to "preponderance of the evidence"—even as it still judged Duke students accused of plagiarism or other less serious offenses under the more stringent standard of "clear and convincing evidence."[55] In addition to following OCR's orders, Duke adopted other onerous new provisions that OCR had not mentioned. The university "trained" panel members to believe that fewer than 2 percent of all sexual assault allegations are false. (Even David Lisak has never made such a claim.) Duke made expulsion the standard sanction for sexual assault, now so broadly defined as to include kissing ("however slight") without an "affirmative decision to engage" by both parties. Still another provision accommodated witnesses who preferred not to appear before a hearing panel, allowing them to instead be interviewed by an investigator.

Duke also retained unfair elements of its previous policy, such as barring alleged perpetrators from asking questions of their accusers or other witnesses and denying them any right to have a question asked by panel members unless the latter choose to ask it. Indeed, Sheila Broderick suggested that panelists were under orders not to ask accusers any hard questions at all. "Nobody gets slut-shamed in that room, nobody gets disrespectfully spoken to," Broderick explained. "The conduct panel members are exceedingly pleasant."[56]

It was meager consolation for innocent accused students that Duke also removed the most egregious provisions of its 2009 policy—the ones classifying as "sexual misconduct" sex between students with "perceived power differentials" and denying to the accused (while giving to accusers) the rights to "sensitivity," opening and closing statements, and the written information given to the panel.[57] The Duke *Chronicle*, in an increasingly rare sign of independent thinking at a college newspaper, nonetheless worried that the new policies might "increas[e] the risk of false positives and wrongful expulsion of innocent students for nonexistent crimes."[58]

The first test of the new policies, the case of Duke senior Lewis McLeod, proved the *Chronicle* right.

On November 13, 2013, McLeod went out to Shooters, a local bar, for drinks with friends. While there, he met a first-year student,

Sarah Wilson,* who was also drinking, despite her underage status. The bartender saw them together before they took a taxi back to a house that McLeod was renting with friends, where, according to McLeod, he and Wilson had a drunken hookup. The next day, Wilson told Duke and the Durham Police Department that she had not consented to the sex and had wanted to be driven home. McLeod denied the allegation.

The police found no basis for criminal charges.[59] Duke, however, hired a clinical psychologist named Celia Irvine to look into the allegation. Irvine had no experience investigating alleged sexual assaults and nowhere near the 3,000 hours of training required by North Carolina law to qualify as a private investigator. Her practice focused on "the healing relationship," working "holistically" by "incorporating ideas from philosophy, eastern and western spiritual traditions, and various psychological theories."[60]

The sole issue in the McLeod case was Wilson's level of intoxication. Irvine never contacted neutral witnesses who could have shed light on this critical fact, such as Shooters employees who had seen the two students together or the cabbie who had driven them to McLeod's off-campus residence. The latter would have been a critical evaluator of Wilson's claim that she had wanted to be taken home. When we asked Irvine by email why she did not try to interview these witnesses, she did not reply.

Irvine spent most of her limited inquiry time speaking to Duke students. Wilson consented to Irvine interviewing only one of the students whom she could have named as witnesses—and the investigator accepted this severe limitation on her inquiry. Three of McLeod's housemates said that Wilson had been neither intoxicated, nor exhibiting slurred speech, nor acting irrational. In her report, Irvine chose to disbelieve these three identified witnesses and to credit an anonymous witness who claimed that Wilson had been incapacitated. This witness appears to have contacted Irvine at Wilson's request.

Although based in Chapel Hill, a short drive from Durham, Irvine interviewed witnesses by telephone, thus blinding herself to the visual cues and body language that serious investigators consider vital when assessing credibility.[61] She made no recordings or transcripts of witnesses' statements.

At McLeod's campus hearing in April 2014, the three-person disciplinary tribunal, "trained" to believe that fewer than 2 percent of sexual assault claims are false, blocked all cross-examination of the accuser, who was the only witness to testify against McLeod. The critical anonymous witness and other students were presented only through Irvine's summaries—so they could not be cross-examined.

McLeod later said that Dean of Students Stephen Bryan had advised him that "an attorney would not be useful or necessary." McLeod had been given a non-attorney "advocate," who seemed well-intentioned but incapable of helping much. "There's not one central body that works with students who are accused," Bryan explained to the *Chronicle*. "We have disciplinary advisers who are trained by our office to offer support and guidance, but it's not like the Women's Center setup" for accusers.[62]

The panel found McLeod more likely than not to be a rapist because, it claimed, his accuser "had reached an incapacitating level of intoxication that rendered her unable to give consent to sex." The panel recommended expulsion, as per Duke's newest guidelines. According to McLeod, when he asked Bryan for a copy of Duke's as yet unpublished policy making expulsion the presumed punishment for sexual assault, the reply was "You can get it when you sue us."

McLeod did just that, filing suit in North Carolina state court. He requested orders that Duke not expel him and the school award him his undergraduate degree, since he had completed all his course work. The case went before Judge Osmond Smith, the same jurist who had found Nifong in contempt for lying to him.

Duke sent Associate Vice President for Student Affairs and Dean of Students Sue Wasiolek to defend its handling of the case. She admitted that Duke traditionally had not expelled students found guilty of sexual assault and that it had not yet published its new policy in the student handbook. "It is an understood practice," she explained. "We didn't feel the need to make it public." McLeod's lawyer, Rachel Fitch, asked Wasiolek whether—if both accuser and accused had been drunk—they would "have raped *each other* [emphasis added] and [both be] subject to expulsion" under the logic of Duke's policy. No, said Wasiolek: "Assuming it is a male and female, it is the responsibility in the case of the male to gain consent before proceeding with sex."[63]

That puts the Duke policy, as explained by its dean of students, in violation of Title IX, which bans anti-male as well as anti-female discrimination.

Smith, unimpressed by Wasiolek's testimony, ordered Duke on June 2, 2014, not to finalize any expulsion before a trial and final ruling. But he also declined McLeod's request for an order that Duke give him his degree immediately, and, as of the writing of this book, the case remains stalled in state court. McLeod, an Australian in the United States on a student visa, has had to leave the country, because when his degree was withheld he lost both his visa and the job he had lined up.

As occurred after the lacrosse case, the record of procedurally dubious actions in the McLeod case prompted no critical self-examination at Duke. Quite the reverse. In a 2015 interview with *The Wall Street Journal*, Larry Moneta, the same Duke administrator who pronounced the lacrosse players guilty in 2006, rejoiced at how, in the aftermath of the Dear Colleague letter, "the pendulum has swung" even farther in favor of alleged sexual assault victims.[64]

It might be argued that Duke's hostility to due process for accused students, as well as the willingness to believe even non-credible sexual assault accusers, is an exception to the "rape culture" that dominates all other campuses. The next chapter, however, shows how administrators at many institutions have been as eager as Duke's Larry Moneta to use federal marching orders to undermine meaningful fairness in campus sexual assault adjudications.

4

DENYING DUE PROCESS

I n fall 2011, two male students at Brandeis University, in Waltham, Massachusetts, first met. One, Joseph Babeu, was open about his homosexuality; the other, Matt Francis,* was still in the closet. They soon started dating. Francis came out, and the two began a monogamous relationship, which lasted for 21 months. But as often occurs in college romances, the two drifted apart. They broke up in the summer of 2013.[1]

Though they remained friendly immediately after the breakup, the friendship deteriorated later that fall. Then, in January 2014, Babeu informed Brandeis: "Starting in the month of September, 2011, the Alleged Violator of Policy had numerous inappropriate, nonconsensual sexual interactions with me. These interactions continued to occur until around May 2013." Based solely on this nonspecific, two-sentence accusation, Brandeis placed Francis on "emergency suspension."

Even though the university possessed a functioning disciplinary hearing process, Brandeis investigated Babeu's complaint through a single investigator, a former OCR lawyer named Elizabeth Sanghavi. OCR has urged colleges to employ a process in which the investigator effectively serves as police, prosecutor, judge, and jury. Sanghavi interviewed both parties—in a subsequent interview, Babeu described her as "very sensitive"—and a handful of others.[2] She did not record these interviews. Francis had no right to counsel, and he couldn't even see his accuser's testimony, much less cross-examine him.

After these interviews, Sanghavi produced a report that rejected some of Babeu's claims but accepted others. Sanghavi evaluated the allegations not in the context of a long-term, ongoing romantic relationship but rather in isolation, as if Francis and Babeu had been complete strangers until immediately before each alleged sexual encounter. For instance, Sanghavi concluded that Francis had committed his first sexual assault when he made a pass at Babeu the night before the two students first slept together, without first obtaining affirmative, verbal consent. As Francis' lawyer, Patricia Hamill, observed, it "defies reason" to conclude that that "'first move' leading to a 21-month consensual relationship was a sexual assault"—especially since the alleged initiator was closeted and thus hardly in a position to advertise his sexual orientation.

Though the two students had regularly slept together thereafter, Sanghavi also found Francis guilty of nonconsensual sexual conduct because he sometimes awoke Babeu with kisses and sometimes looked at Babeu without obtaining prior consent when both were nude in a communal bathroom—routine events in many long-term relationships.

The right to appeal was no more than token, since the university refused to allow Francis to see Sanghavi's 25-page report until the appeals process concluded. The guilty finding was upheld, but a panel convened by Brandeis' dean of academic services, Lisa Boes, implicitly recognized the trivial nature of the allegations by punishing Francis only through a written reprimand in his student file.

But that mark on his record was enough to lose Francis an internship for a local politician and to threaten his career prospects, after coverage in left-leaning outlets portrayed him as a predator. In *The Huffington Post*, Tyler Kingkade reported that Francis (whom Kingkade labeled the "attacker") had been found guilty of "all charges," including "sexual assault, taking advantage of one's incapacitation, sexual harassment, physical harm and invasion of personal privacy."[3] An article on the case from Abigail Bessler of *ThinkProgress* was entitled "Universities Keep Failing to Actually Punish Rapists."[4]

In response, Francis sued Brandeis. In defending its actions, the university's lawyers contended that no federal law prohibited "discrimination based on a student's status as the accused." They added that the process had worked as the school intended. In other words, Brandeis had every right to be as biased as it wanted to be.

U.S. District Judge F. Dennis Saylor appeared baffled by the school's notion of justice. "I don't understand how a university, much less one named after Louis Brandeis, could possibly think that that was a fair procedure to not allow the accused to see the accusation," the judge said during November 2015 oral argument on the university's motion to dismiss. "Our Constitution provides for a right of confrontation, a public proceeding in which you confront your accuser, the right of cross-examination. It's carved on the walls of this building how important the right of cross-examination is, and part of that, of course, is knowing the charge, knowing precisely what it is you're responding to....Most of these schools have this one-sided procedure. I don't understand how a college could set this up. I don't understand it."

In March 2016, Saylor allowed the case to proceed. His 89-page ruling was the most comprehensive to date by any judge in a campus due-process case. Saylor understood the political environment in which Brandeis had acted. He noted the pressure from the federal government, and he interpreted the Dear Colleague letter's lower evidentiary standard "as part of an effort to tilt the playing field against accused students, which is particularly troublesome in light of the elimination of other basic rights of the accused." But inappropriate federal pressure could not, in his opinion, justify the university's behavior. Brandeis, Saylor wrote, "appears to have substantially impaired, if not eliminated, an accused student's right to a fair and impartial process. And it is not enough simply to say that such changes are appropriate because victims of sexual assault have not always achieved justice in the past. Whether someone is a 'victim' is a conclusion to be reached at the end of a fair process, not an assumption to be made at the beginning....If a college student is to be marked for life as a sexual predator, it is reasonable to require that he be provided a fair opportunity to defend himself and an impartial arbiter to make that decision." Viewing himself as vindicated by Saylor's ruling, Francis then withdrew his lawsuit.

Fair-minded people tend to recoil when they learn how universities handle claims such as the one in the Brandeis case. Consider the reaction of Robin Steinberg, a feminist who works as a public defender at a Bronx legal-aid clinic. After reading Columbia University's sexual assault procedures (sent to her by journalist Judith Shulevitz), she vowed, "We are never sending our boys to college."

"Steinberg, like most people, hadn't realized how far the rules governing sexual conduct on campus have strayed from any commonsense understanding of justice," Shulevitz observed in a *New Republic* article. She added that the Obama administration had essentially embraced "the notion popularized in the 1970s and '80s by Andrea Dworkin and Catharine MacKinnon that male domination is so pervasive that women need special protection from the rigors of the law." This stance, Shulevitz stressed, contradicted American liberalism's fundamental tenet that rights may not be curtailed "even for a noble cause."[5]

The fundamental unfairness seen in the Brandeis case was hardly unique. Other cases handled through a college disciplinary process reflect a similar pattern.

Vassar College, Poughkeepsie, New York

At a February 2012 Vassar crew team party, Peter Yu and Judy Slaughter* flirted. Both were drinking. They left the party and stopped by a bar; Yu later recalled Slaughter telephoning her roommate to ask whether their room was free. It wasn't, so they went to Yu's room, where they had mutual oral sex.[6] The hookup ended when Yu's roommate came in. Slaughter said she did not want to go any further because she had just broken up with her boyfriend and had changed her mind about wanting "anything new."

The next day, Slaughter sent Yu a Facebook message saying she "had a wonderful time" and was "really sorry I led you on last night." In one of several further exchanges that spring, Slaughter confessed to Yu, without prompting, that "I did not treat you very well" and said that she "apologiz[ed] for that night about two months ago." In another message, she invited Yu to dinner at the home of her father, a Vassar professor.

Three hundred sixty-four days after their encounter, on the final day that she was allowed to file a complaint under Vassar's rules, Slaughter accused Yu of sexually assaulting her because her intoxication on the night of the party meant she could not have consented to sex. Vassar suspended Yu from the crew team the next day. Under Vassar's definition of "consent," Yu could have filed a sexual assault claim of his own against Slaughter, since he too had been drunk that night. But, in a catch-22, by the time Yu was notified by Vassar's Title IX office of Slaughter's complaint, it was (in Vassar's view) too late for him to file a complaint of his own. A lawyer might have challenged the timing issue, but in Vassar's process, Yu was not allowed a lawyer.

An investigator from Vassar's Title IX office interviewed a handful of witnesses and prepared a summary of the case. Yu received only three days to examine the school's evidence and prepare a defense. The case proceeded to a disciplinary panel, which heard from five unsworn witnesses, more than a year after the incident. That list did not include the last people to see Yu and Slaughter together on the night of the party—Yu's roommate and witnesses who encountered the two students at the bar. Nor could the panel subpoena Slaughter's phone records to determine whether she had phoned her roommate before the two headed to Yu's room, as Yu had claimed. The panel dismissed Slaughter's friendly, non-accusatory messages to Yu after the episode and concluded that Slaughter had been, more likely than not, too drunk to consent to sex. Implementing that finding, the dean of students ordered the harshest penalty the college could impose: expulsion. The investigation, hearing, and punishment process took only eight days.

In a 58-page opinion dismissing Yu's subsequent lawsuit against Vassar, Judge Ronnie Abrams, of the U.S. District Court for the Southern District of New York, celebrated the "thriving national debate" about due process for students accused of sexual assault. She suggested that federal courts should defer to college disciplinary procedures. Yu elected not to appeal.

University of Cincinnati

In March 2014, two female students accused a male Cincinnati undergraduate of sexual assault after what he said was a consensual three-way sexual encounter in a dorm room. The two women, who claimed they had been too intoxicated to consent, also went to the police, who uncovered significant discrepancies in their stories and declined to pursue charges.

One of the detectives investigating the case testified that his colleague believed that the university had "obstructed" the police investigation, seemingly to minimize the accusers' credibility problems, and that the university's general counsel "was trying to impede our train of thought and our investigation." Cincinnati nonetheless moved forward with its own hearing, at which its officials incorrectly told the accused student that "neither party has any burden of proof."

The "training" of the university's disciplinary panel, which misstated the university's own written policy on sobriety and consent, consisted of implausible assertions such as "the average rapist rapes 14 people before he ever spends a night in jail." Although the key issue was how intoxicated the two accusers had been, the hearing panel refused to examine contemporaneous text messages from the accusers' phones and a surveillance video of the three walking into the dorm. The guilty finding seemed so preordained that the university allowed one accuser to make a "victim impact" statement before the panel had even reached its decision. The accused student was expelled.

In another case at Cincinnati, the accuser was allowed to present her version of events and then leave the hearing without being asked any of the questions submitted by the accused student. That panel, too, returned a guilty finding.

Both students sued, and their case went before U.S. District Court Judge Sandra Beckwith, a graduate of both the University of Cincinnati and the University of Cincinnati Law School, who had served as a board member of the U.C. Friends of Women's Studies and the U.C. College of Law Board of Visitors.[7] In March 2016, Beckwith dismissed the lawsuits, interpreting the relevant circuit precedent (which involved a student expelled from medical school after pleading guilty to a drug felony) as not having "clearly established that [the accused students] were entitled to the presumption of innocence." She even suggested that it might be acceptable for a university to force accused students to bear "the burden of proof." Because Cincinnati had assigned an experienced administrator, not a lawyer, to prosecute the two cases before the panel, Beckwith concluded the university was free to force the accused students to defend themselves, without legal assistance. She also saw no constitutional problem with banning all cross-examination, which was the effect of the panel's guilty finding against a student whose accuser fled the room after her direct testimony. And Beckwith ruled that it could not be anti-male gender discrimination for a university to comply "with Title IX guidance issued by the Department of Education."

In a June 2016 filing before the 6th Circuit, the public university's lawyers maintained that even if Cincinnati required an accused student to prove his innocence, "that would not constitute a due process violation."[8]

On September 29, 2016, the two sides appeared before a panel consisting of Judges Martha Daughtrey, Deborah Cook, and Julia Gibbons. Daughtrey, who had penned a high-profile 2014 dissent championing the judiciary's role in ensuring that individual "rights, liberties, and duties need not be held hostage by popular whims," seemed like an ideal draw for the accused students.[9] But the longtime feminist—who dominated questioning throughout the oral argument—suggested that on this issue, judicial protection of civil liberties needed to take a back seat to federal dictates and university decisions. College disciplinary tribunals, Daughtrey reasoned, best resembled not a trial or other adversial proceeding but a board of inquiry. Boards of inquiry are commonly associated with military justice. Even OCR has never suggested that colleges should imitate military discipline in order to weaken accused students' rights.

Joshua Engel, whe represented the accused students, had to explain to the panel why due process matters, because the judges seemed oblivious to its critical role in truth-finding. "The due process protections that exist in the civil system and in the criminal system," Engel observed, "did not spring out of the earth and are imposed on parties for an arbitary reason. They're there because we believe that they're valuable in the truth-finding process. So every time that you move away from one of these ideas—one of these protections—that are considered . . . a core due process protection, you lose some truth-finding process,"[10] A decision remains pending at the time of this writing (September 2016).

St. Joseph's University, Philadelphia

A night of flirtatious text messages on November 17, 2012, ended with St. Joe's student Jenny Bentley* inviting a fellow undergraduate, Brian Harris, to "come cuddle with me" and "sleep over!!!!" in her room. He arrived, and they had intercourse. But later they disagreed on whether Bentley had consented.

St. Joe's turned the matter over to a public safety investigator, Joe Kalin, a retired Pennsylvania State Police officer. Kalin's subsequent report did not include any of the text messages, such as Bentley's invitation. He did not reply to a request from us as to why he chose not to pass along this exculpatory information.

After a proceeding in which, as the university's guidelines put it, "civil or criminal rules of procedure and evidence do not apply,"[11] a St. Joe's panel found Harris guilty.

St. Joe's responded in a later lawsuit that "the process worked," since Harris got "what the University promises; no more, no less," and it never promised due process to anyone accused of sexual assault. It also argued that its procedures did not require its investigator to refer any exculpatory evidence to the disciplinary panel. U.S. District Judge Felipe Restrepo, of Philadelphia, disagreed. In May 2014, he allowed Harris' lawsuit against St. Joe's, Kalin, and Bentley to proceed. Soon thereafter, Kalin stopped working at St. Joe's, and the parties reached a confidential settlement.[12]

Columbia University, New York City

A drunken hookup at Columbia has led to what may be the most important federal appeals court decision ever supporting the rights of an accused student in campus disciplinary proceedings. All the more striking was the fact that the unanimous decision, in July 2016, by the 2nd Circuit U.S. Court of Appeals, was written by a Clinton appointee (Judge Pierre Leval) and joined by another Clinton appointee (John Koeltl) and an Obama appointee (Christopher Droney).

The incident dated from May 2013, when a female student texted a male member of the Columbia crew team, Mark Ottinger,* expressing concern about how the drunken hookup they had had might affect their social standing.[13] When word of the hookup got out at the start of the following semester, she filed a complaint with the university. (She never went to the police.) The charge arrived amid a frenzied campus atmosphere—both the Columbia Democrats and op-ed columns in the Columbia *Spectator* portrayed the university as soft on sexual assault, and Columbia president Lee Bollinger promised a town hall to discuss the issue.

The university conducted what appears to have been a desultory investigation. Ottinger later stated that Columbia officials hadn't informed him of his right to a non-attorney advocate or his ability to submit an opening statement to the hearing panel. More problematically, the university's investigator, Jilleian Sessions-Stackhouse, didn't interview several witnesses who had seen the two students together on the night of the encounter and could testify that the accuser had appeared able to consent. These witnesses were eventually deemed irrelevant, on grounds that Ottinger's offense had occurred much earlier—that he had "directed unreasonable pressure for sexual activity toward the [the female student] over a period of weeks." This extraordinarily vague standard could apply to many college (and non-college) sexual encounters.

When Columbia suspended Ottinger for 1.5 years, even the *accuser* deemed the punishment too harsh. Then, despite the promised confidentiality of the disciplinary process, Ottinger's identity was leaked (the source was never discovered) and his name was scrawled on walls at the school, as among the "sexual assault violators on campus."[14]

Ottinger sued. His case was assigned to Judge Jesse Furman, who had a number of personal connections to the matter (his wife was a Columbia Law professor at the time the university's disciplinary hearing occurred; his brother was a high-ranking Obama administration official as he evaluated a lawsuit that strongly criticized Obama policies). Furman, even as he conceded that "Columbia may well have treated [the accuser] more favorably than [Ottinger] during the disciplinary process," dismissed the complaint, in April 2015. The judge scoured for lawful excuses—fear of negative publicity, or fear of an OCR investigation—for the university's unfair treatment of its student. Though only a district court opinion and thus not a very important precedent, the opinion was extraordinarily influential. Virtually every institution facing a due-process or Title IX lawsuit from an accused student cited it; a January 2016 brief from Yale, seeking to dismiss a complaint filed by an accused student, favorably referenced Furman nine times.

Ottinger appealed to the 2nd Circuit, which has jurisdiction over cases from Connecticut, New York, and Vermont. The three-judge panel overturned Furman's opinion, criticizing the lower court's restrictive definition of what might constitute gender discrimination. A university "that adopts, even temporarily," Judge Pierre Leval wrote in July 2016, "a policy of bias favoring one sex over the other in a disciplinary dispute, doing so in order to avoid liability or bad publicity, has practiced sex discrimination, notwithstanding that the motive for the discrimination did not come from ingrained or permanent bias against that particular sex." The case was sent back to Furman's court, where it remains as of this writing (September 2016).

Pennsylvania State University–University Park

Through 2016, Penn State guidelines required a guilty finding for sexual assault even if the "board may not be completely convinced, and may still may have considerable reservation" about the alleged victim's veracity. All decisions were based on evidence presented in an investigator's report.

After attending a fall 2015 fraternity party at the school's University Park campus, a female Penn State student claimed to have had non-consensual sex with an engineering student of Syrian and Kuwaiti descent. The school's investigator concluded that because the accuser had engaged in "unusual and/or outrageous" behavior at the time of the alleged assault, she could be considered drunk, and the accused student guilty; Penn State sought to suspend him for a year. He sued, arguing that the lack of an opportunity to confront his accuser denied his constitutional rights and that the suspension would invalidate his student visa and possibly compel his return to war-torn Syria. The university countered that a student accused of sexual assault was entitled to no more constitutional protection than a worker seeking unemployment benefits, adding that any danger he might face as a result of returning to Syria was "speculative."

U.S. District Judge Matthew Brann issued a restraining order, which blocked the accused student's deportation. The day before a hearing to determine whether the injunction would be made permanent, Penn State vacated its decision, allowing the accused student to re-enroll. The university promised Brann that it would institute "material changes to its disciplinary system" to ensure fairer treatment of all accused students.[15]

There are dozens of such cases, an outgrowth of the Obama administration's approach to campus sexual assault. They involve credible allegations of bias against accused students at DePauw University, the University of Massachusetts, Holy Cross, the University of Vermont, Wesleyan, Cornell, Brown, Philadelphia University, Drew University, Rider University, Hobart & William Smith, Case Western Reserve, James Madison, the University of Kentucky, George Mason, Washington

& Lee, Denison, IUPUI, Lynn University, the University of St. Thomas, Augustana (South Dakota), Clemson, the University of Houston, Southern Methodist, the University of Colorado, Western State (Colorado), Colorado State–Pueblo, the University of California–Santa Barbara, the University of California–Berkeley, USC, Georgia Tech, Colgate, Clark, and Marlboro College, among others.

Even NCHERM head Brett Sokolow, whose firm has profited from the frenzy over campus sexual assault, has admitted that the witch hunt is out of control. In an April 2012 newsletter, he noted that "a lot of colleges now are expelling and suspending people they shouldn't, for fear they'll get nailed on Title IX."[16] In 2014, after working on five cases involving "drunken hook-ups" in which each accused male student was found guilty, he concluded that "in each case, I thought the college got it completely wrong.... Finding each of the accused in violation of sexual misconduct is sex discrimination. We are making Title IX plaintiffs out of them.... Some boards and panels still can't tell the difference between drunk sex and a policy violation.... Surely, every drunken sexual hookup is not a punishable offense, especially if the parties know what they did and liked it."[17]

Alcohol alone did not seem to explain the problem, Sokolow noted in May 2014. "Millennial sexual mores are clouding the evidence," he lamented. *"We see complainants who genuinely believe they have been assaulted, despite overwhelming proof that it did not happen* [emphasis added].... We hate even more that another victim-blaming trope—victim mental health—continues to have legs, but how do you not question the reality contact where case-after-case involves sincere victims who believe something has happened to them that evidence shows absolutely did not?"[18]

As for the more than 100 lawsuits filed by students who say they were wrongfully punished by their colleges after being accused of sexual assault, Harvard Law School professor Elizabeth Bartholet has observed, "When you get things like the federal government pressuring universities to create a sexual assault process that lacks adequate due process for those accused, you're going to get students trying to protect themselves."[19]

A system in which filing a lawsuit is a wrongly accused student's best chance of achieving justice has gone badly astray. Lawsuits take a great deal of time, and they often cost tens or hundreds of thousands of dollars.

For this reason, Sokolow, hardly a defender of accused students' rights, recognized that "almost all" of the due-process lawsuits must have been "filed by 1 percenters [in terms of income]."[20] If that's true, there likely have been thousands of cases of unfair campus decisions against students accused of sexual assault in which the accused student's family lacked the resources to sue and the secret nature of campus tribunals shielded dubious university decisions from public scrutiny.

For students whose families *can* afford to enter the court system, lawsuits are hard to win, even for those who clearly were punished wrongfully. Abrams' decision in the Vassar case reflected a long—although outdated—tradition of judicial deference to the college disciplinary process. It was forged at a time when colleges almost always left sexual assault accusations to law enforcement and the stakes in campus discipline were small or involved exclusively academic matters such as plagiarism or other forms of academic misconduct.

Universities also have grown more aggressive in anticipation of lawsuits from accused students. In May 2016, the National Association of College and University Attorneys published a research note urging colleges and universities to "approach each allegation of sexual misconduct with an eye toward eventual litigation." Along these lines, the authors noted: "Many e-mails—as well as staff notes that precede an investigation report, notes of hearing participants during a disciplinary hearing, drafts of hearing outcome reports, and other such working papers—might actually prove very useful to a plaintiff's lawyer who may wish to argue that the institution acted in an inconsistent manner or that assertions of institutional witnesses are inconsistent with contemporaneous working drafts. For that reason, it would be prudent to retain a 'master set' of all final reports, proceedings, and outcome documents, and promptly destroy the various preliminary and personal documents. That way, the institution will have a single, consistent record that is not contradicted or undermined by the institution's own files."[21]

Activists and their political and media allies often trivialize the harm done when universities make mistakes (at least mistakes involving accused students). Take Georgetown Law School research fellow Nancy Cantalupo, whom Sen. Claire McCaskill and Sen. Richard Blumenthal (D-Connecticut) invited to participate in a June 2014 roundtable sponsored by Senate Democrats. Cantalupo told the senators that in order "to put the complaining student and the responding student on an even playing field," colleges should provide only "quite minimal" due process for accused students—no more than "notice and a right to be heard."[22] In a subsequent interview, she questioned the idea that having a sexual misconduct finding "on your permanent record is going to destroy your life forever because there are many students whose lives do not appear destroyed."[23]

Such sentiments would sound strange to the parents at meetings of Families Advocating for Campus Equality (FACE), which was founded to support hundreds of students who say they have been unfairly treated by campus tribunals. Most FACE adherents are, says a lawyer who represents some of them, "angry and hurt parents (mostly mothers) who can't believe what they've seen their sons go through and feel helpless to do anything." In interviews with a few accused students and more than a dozen parents (mostly mothers), one of us (Stuart Taylor) heard heartbreaking stories of lasting trauma, suicidal thoughts, suicide attempts, and ruined lives.[24]

Len Reddan* and his mother recalled the life-changing harms he suffered after he was accused of rape in October 2012, as a first-year student at a university in the South.

It all started after Reddan and some new friends went drinking at a bar near his older brother's apartment. The only woman there, Jessie Armstrong,* arrived with one of the new friends. According to Reddan, she soon shifted her attentions to him, and they ended up going to Reddan's brother's room, where they briefly had sex. Three days later, Armstrong told police that Reddan had used force to rape her. Later— according to Reddan's testimony and other documents—she added new claims, claiming that she had slapped Reddan and run out of the bar. (Still later, while testifying in university proceedings, she would modify her story to allege that she had passed out while he was raping her.) But three polygraph tests—the second and third necessitated by Armstrong's shifting stories—found Reddan truthful. After the grand jury rejected Armstrong's claims—a rare phenomenon in cases of alleged sexual assault—she filed a rape accusation with the university.

As Reddan recalled, "The school disallowed 90 percent of my evidence.... The administrators were pretty nasty about it. [One female bureaucrat] looked at me like, 'Tough shit, kid, you're getting screwed either way.' That's the look I got from her face.... Every single administrator [at the university] assumed I was guilty." Even after Armstrong's lack of credible evidence forced the university to clear Reddan, he was shunned by his friends, and he dropped out of school in 2015. "He called me sobbing in mid-semester and said, 'I can't take this anymore. I'm so tired. I can't do this anymore,'" his mother recalled. "It broke my heart. It still does. As a mom, it's impossible to hear."

Now, at 22, Reddan suffers from severe anxiety, depression, and post-traumatic stress disorder, which have harmed his physical health. "I get to college," Reddan recalled, "and then all of my dreams and aspirations and everything just go out the window a month after I get there. You feel like you're on top of the world, and then someone just makes up something about you that completely destroys you. . . . It destroyed my reputation. . . . And [in his home town], I'll be at a bar, and some girl's like, 'What's your name?' and I tell her, [and then she says], 'Oh, I've heard stories about you.'"

"His life has been destroyed by what the process did to him emotionally," Reddan's mother added. "He feels like he'll never be normal again. [He has said,] 'I wouldn't commit suicide, but I think a lot about killing myself.'" As of March 2016, Reddan was still taking medications and receiving counseling but was having trouble completing courses at another college.

James Hays,* who also suffers from post-traumatic stress disorder, was accused of rape and other sex crimes by a fellow student whose story kept changing, according to his mother. Hays was attending a university in the mid-Atlantic region when he was accused by a fellow student, Mary Gill,* of an unwanted kiss attempt in the spring of 2014. Hays was a shy, withdrawn, socially awkward, 20-year-old given to video games and wearing costumes to comic book conventions. He had previously had some sexual contact, but not intercourse, with Gill. She was white and fairly wealthy; he was half black. She had told him to keep their relationship secret.

Asked whether there might have been a racial element in the case, Hays' mother said, "As Black Americans, we have always been cautioned about white women wanting to entrap black men, especially in the South, where interracial dating was taboo. When my son and this girl first started 'fooling around,' he told me reluctantly [that] she didn't want anyone to know. Especially her ex. That's a big red flag for me."

Hays said Gill consented to what they did and there was no intercourse. But, with the school following OCR's mandate to implement an "interim" punishment, Hays was taken by campus security from his dormitory suite to a single room in a senior dorm, because his accuser had said she feared for her safety. Afterward, his mother recalled, Hays "just stayed in his room and was severely depressed, never left his bed. He couldn't eat or sleep. Every night at home he had horrible screaming nightmares. [They] lasted about four months.... He said he thought about suicide all the time, and he tried once." Then he started seeing psychologist Cecil C. Byrd II twice a week. "Cecil saved my son's life and my life as well," his mother recalled. "He saved our family."

Byrd is the executive director of the National Association of Concerned Veterans. After attaining more than 40 years of experience treating veterans, students, and other patients of all ages who suffer from post-traumatic stress disorder and other chronic maladies, he began counseling college students who told him they had been wrongfully accused of sex crimes.

While the stories of *victims* of sexual assault and other horrors are often covered in the media, Byrd told one of us (Stuart Taylor): "The stories and plights of falsely accused and wrongly punished young men are not. The trauma *they* go through is its own hell and horror. Their lives are in many cases wrecked, with little hope of healing or return to normalcy.

"While there is little data on this," continued Byrd, "we do know that it is horribly destructive and...life changing. These young students have little maturity, few defense mechanisms. [Their plight] goes against everything society has drilled into us—'the truth will out,' 'justice is fair.' The trauma, pain, devastation, and heart-wrenching upheaval quickly turn these students' lives upside down with no mercy, no compassion, no empathy, no gentleness.

"Overnight, everything the accused knows and has is taken from him: his friends, his familiar and friendly environment. He loses his name, his reputation. Life as he knows it disintegrates before his eyes. He is terminated from school and barred from other schools, jobs, careers, pursuits, options.... Worse, he is falsely labeled a sexual predator; a pervert; a sick, evil bastard. He has no idea what to do, to whom he can turn. And the financial costs to [him] and [his] family are astronomical, [leaving him] no hope of ever achieving any of his hopes and dreams."

Another student, Josh Adams,* went from being a high-achieving, hardworking scholar and team captain in high school to being hospital-ized as suicidal after facing allegations of sexual assault at a university in California.

. Adams' two drunken hookups, which both occurred in the post–Dear Colleague letter environment, were hardly unusual at his univer-sity. However, the two women he hooked up with were friends with each other. The news of their one-night stands with Adams became socially awkward, and one of them lost a potential boyfriend. Months later, they jointly filed reports with the university, claiming that, because of their alcohol intake, their sex with Adams had been nonconsensual. They did not go to the police.

Naively, Adams did not even inform his parents about the campus proceeding. A university official told him he did not need a lawyer, while a single investigator-adjudicator oversaw his fate. Less than two weeks prior to the investigator-adjudicator's decision came a highly publicized filing of Title IX complaints against the school in unrelated cases, as well as protests attacking the Title IX administrator—the same person who would decide Adams' fate—as being soft on sexual assault. Both events received national attention. "They needed a scalp for the OCR," Adams' mother said. "My son was it." He was expelled, even though by then he had all the credits required for a degree. Adams' parents learned of his dire situation from a phone call when he was hospitalized as suicidal after the decision against him. They hired an attorney, but it was too late. All the lawyer had to work with on appeal were the notes of the investigator-adjudicator, who had not recorded her interviews. There was nothing that could be done.

With the disciplinary mark on his transcript, Adams was unable to transfer to another college. He developed depression, anxiety, and post-traumatic stress disorder.

Looking back on the case that got her son thrown out of college, Adams' mother said: "If drinking and having sex is sexual assault, then most sex on campus is sexual assault. It's a game of Russian roulette. Who will be accused? How long after the fact? Without alcohol, 99 percent of 'sexual assault' would not occur. Yet universities do nothing to curb underage drinking."

An even odder process victimized Bobby Glenn,* whose problems, he told one of us (Stuart Taylor), began after a make-out session with a female classmate that led to oral sex. (After her roommate came into the room while they were making out, the female student suggested to Glenn that they move to his room. He agreed but told her he was not ready for intercourse. She then performed oral sex on him.) In subsequent encounters with Glenn on their small Midwestern campus, the female student was first standoffish, then hostile.

Three weeks later, Glenn was told there had been an anonymous accusation of sexual assault against him. He was ordered to move from his dorm to a hotel. In advance of his hearing, he was assigned as a "hearing counselor" a fourth-year female student with no relevant experience. Without asking Glenn for his side of the story, Glenn recalled, she told him that he would have to plead guilty to letting things get out of control and "show remorse."

At the hearing, according to Glenn, his accuser said she had felt pressured—seemingly by the general college environment, but not, critically, by Glenn—to have oral sex. "When I asked her about her asking to go to my room after her roommate came in, she looked like she was about to cry," Glenn recalled. He testified that he was "certain that she consented," verbally and by conduct.

The next day, Glenn was called into the dean's office. The dean handed him a four-page letter finding him guilty and ordering "immediate expulsion." A copy of this letter is in our possession. A muddle of confusing verbiage, it fails to specify what Glenn supposedly did. It also fails to mention anything his accuser said or did to show she did not consent. It implies that Glenn was "guilty" of unspecified sexual contact without consent; of an unspecified "threat"; of unspecified "sexual harassment"; and of failing to show "concern for [another student's] feelings" and to "offer assistance to others whose behavior appears harmful to themselves."

"He was devastated to leave [the school]," his mother recalled. "His life was destroyed, and he may never be the same." Glenn added, "I had horrible nightmares," and he told of daytime flashbacks: "Even years later, like when my phone rings, I go back to being called in and told I have to pack my bag and get off of campus. And nightmares about the hearing where they yelled questions at me."

Speaking of such accused students, Byrd explained: "Many do not even know how to talk to their friends, significant others, families, or anyone about this. [The wrongfully accused student] feels guilty, dirty, and ashamed. He has no will to fight and sees no way out. Some succumb to severe, deep, clinical depression, losing all motivation, all drive, all confidence, all belief in themselves and all hope of finding a way out. They begin questioning everything they have ever believed or known. Some turn to self-harm and contemplate suicide. Parents are helpless and don't have a clue what to do and where to go for help and how to get their child through this nightmare."

Byrd added that "over and over again, families of the accused report how unfair and lacking the [college's] process is for the finding the truth and allowing their sons to tell their side of the story." He lamented that "the court of public opinion rushes to judgment, [driven by] the media, the movies, the music world. There is clearly the need for a more humane, safe, and fair process and mechanism."

Some commentators who are concerned about the unfair treatment of accused students like Byrd's patients nonetheless want to expiate for sexism in previous generations. In a July 2015 editorial, the *Los Angeles Times* editorial board noted that while "the rights of the accused cannot be sacrificed to make their accusers feel comfortable," they must be balanced against the long history of colleges having "ignored or mishandled students' allegations of sexual assault—in some cases belittling those students or unfairly doubting their claims."[25]

Although schools may have been reluctant to deal with rape allegations in the past, only in special circumstances—usually involving football or basketball players at top athletic schools, or students at religious institutions—do we find the same reluctance today. In most cases, alleged victims are heavily favored. Specialized bureaucrats—figures such as Larry Moneta and Ada Gregory at Duke, Susan Tobergte at Miami, and Joe Kalin at St. Joe's—demonstrate an ideological predisposition to presume the truth of sexual assault allegations.

Peter Paquette is the investigator who, until early 2016, decided the fate of alleged perpetrators at Georgia Tech. In one 2015 case, the alleged victim posted on Facebook that she had "worked very closely" with Paquette. Yet he declined to recuse himself from her case; he later testified that he actually had *not* worked closely with her, without explaining why she would have made such a claim or how it harmed her credibility to assert she had worked closely with him if it were not true. His investigative report in the case repeated unsubstantiated negative comments about the accused student; one unidentified witness called the student "unpleasant and creepy." The student sued, and eventually a confidential settlement with the university was reached. In a second 2015 case, Paquette found the accused student guilty despite admitting that "it is reasonable to believe that based on the nonverbal action of [the accuser] that [the accused student] believed he had consent." The university's regents found the decision so unfair that they overturned it—one day before a federal court hearing challenging the action. They also paid the accused student $125,000, to settle a related civil suit.[26]

Mae Marsh is director of diversity and equal opportunity at the University of Alaska–Fairbanks, where she coordinates sexual assault investigations. In April 2015, she learned that a female student had gone to the police to press rape charges against Nolan Youngmun, a graduating senior who played for the UAF hockey team. Oblivious to the rank unfairness of planning a student's expulsion before anyone from UAF had spoken to either party in the case, Marsh emailed one of her deputies, informing him that because "the alleged perp graduates in 3 weeks," they needed to "get the administrative investigation concluded so we can make a preponderance call and expel prior to graduation." But the accuser didn't cooperate, and Youngmun was placed on an interim suspension, even though he had finished all his course work.

A jury eventually found Youngmun not guilty in his criminal case; he currently is suing UAF, seeking his degree. The university claimed that the suit was premature because the investigation theoretically was still open—even though, some 15 months after the accuser filed her complaint, the school still hadn't interviewed Youngmun. UAF's lawyers also blandly denied that Marsh's stated intention to "expel prior to graduation" indicated that she had prejudged the case.[27]

Colgate University, in Hamilton, New York, exemplifies how college investigators operate in the current frenzied campus atmosphere. There is (at the time of this writing, in September 2016) a pending federal investigation into whether Colgate has discriminated against black and Asian students (all of them male) in its investigations of alleged sexual misconduct.

In an unusual twist on the arbitrary treatment of accused students by many colleges, a now-settled federal lawsuit plausibly alleged that Lyn Rugg, Colgate's associate provost for equity and diversity (and Title IX coordinator), and Kim Taylor, the associate dean for conduct, unlawfully *imprisoned* a student for a day and a half. In an episode initially reported by Peter Berkowitz, the student, Abrar Faiaz, was accused of dating violence in February 2013. He first was locked in the back of a campus safety vehicle and then was confined in the basement of Colgate's Curtis Hall before he even knew the charges against him, after he refused a one-way ticket to his native Bangladesh. Colgate later expelled Faiaz, over the objection of his alleged victim, after a hearing during which there was no complainant or witness against him. His subsequent lawsuit alleged that Colgate and individual defendants including Rugg and Taylor had subjected him to racial and gender discrimination as well as false imprisonment.[28]

Rugg acknowledged at a September 2014 faculty meeting that four of the seven "Equity Grievance Process" (EGP) proceedings for alleged sexual misconduct had been brought against minority men. "This is a worrying percentage given that men of color comprise only about 6% of the student body," an anonymous person commented on a faculty blog on February 26, 2015. Rugg also acknowledged that no fewer than half of the students expelled for sexual misconduct had been international students of color.[29] A December 8, 2014, blog post by "Concerned Minority Faculty" said that "we should all be clear that the university is arguably building its reputation for making the campus safer on the backs of black and international males."[30]

Accused students have not been the only students mistreated by Colgate's Title IX staffers. A junior feminist professor at the school told one of us (Stuart Taylor), "I've watched students, both men and women, completely devastated by this process."

At a March 2014 meeting of Colgate's chapter of the American Association of University Professors, a faculty member expressed her concerns that the EGP had had "unintended, devastating impacts on those involved, both complainants and respondents." She described the anxiety and PTSD symptoms of male students who had been put through the EGP—whether they ultimately prevailed or not—emphasizing that the treatment that Faiaz received at the hands of Title IX officials, especially illegal imprisonment, had resulted in fear and despair on the part of men of color who subsequently found themselves subject to an EGP.

She also shared the negative impacts on female students as a result of their involvement with the EGP. The alleged victim in the Faiaz case claimed in her letter in support of his appeal that she had had to request extensions in all of her classes and seek counseling as a result of being traumatized by the college's response to his case. This faculty member recounted that another student, a childhood sexual assault survivor, had been pressured by the Title IX investigator to participate in an EGP hearing. This student had subsequently reported she was sleeping in her car, a strategy she had developed as a child to escape her unbearable home situation. This time she was running not from an abuser, but from the ordeal her own university was putting her through.

Students have also been concerned about the way the EGP functions. An anonymous female student, calling herself "OP," described in a remarkable succession of Yik Yak posts how bureaucrats had pressured her into testifying falsely against a student accused of sexual assault. Her January 2016 exchange with other students provides a window into the way colleges sometimes push for guilty findings by pressuring witnesses, including accusers, to testify falsely.

> STUDENT NO. 1: OP you realize this isn't a game right? This kids life is on the line. I'm not saying he's right or wrong, but falsifying or misrepresenting facts in such a situation is fucking horrendous...
>
> STUDENT NO. 2: Op, I hope you find help from friends or family in sorting through the logic that [led] you to lie in such a formal and important situation. What you did is despicable, as shown by the reaction here.
>
> OP: Before you judge me, you need to go through it. I really was pressured to say certain things. It wore me down. It wasn't like I was trying to lie, but they call you in for questioning, it's intimidat[io]n
>
> STUDENT NO. 2: I don't need to go through it to judge you, what it takes to stand up to that pressure is moral direction, of which you seem to have little or none.
>
> OP: I'm trying to help other people who find themselves in this situation...
>
> STUDENT NO. 3: You literally fucking ruined someone's life by lying...
>
> OP: Actually I didn't report the guy, but that's enough to have to be part of the lawsuit.... I was a witness.

STUDENT NO. 4: While I think what you did was despicable, this also does point to some SERIOUS problems in how Colgate is dealing with (and has dealt with) these types of cases. (Look up Faiaz v. Colgate University)

OP: that's why I posted. I don't want anyone else put in my position. People are paying the price for the pressure Colgate uses to get a conviction. Even if the guy didn't do anything....I didn't argue when the investigator said things I knew weren't true. I did at first, but eventually I got too confused and intimidated. It's like being interrogated by the police.

STUDENT NO. 5: So say "that's not true" is it really that difficult?

OP: Yes,...it was actually...I just want to convince others not to let themselves get into my position...

STUDENT NO. 4: ...if many people are being pressured into giving false testimony in the EGP, while it is terrible for them to actually do so, the problem will not go away until it is dealt

OP: We need a process that is unbiased and doesn't put pressure on people...I'm sure other people are better/stronger than me. But I agree...that the problem is bigger than the individuals. But if people are aware of the implications of saying things you don't 100% mean under pressure, it might help change things.

Despite events such as those at Colgate and Georgia Tech, people might interpret the more than 340 Title IX complaints since the Dear Colleague letter's issuance in 2011 to mean that many college administrators are insensitive to alleged victims of sexual assault. And there are examples of such insensitivity. Brigham Young University, for instance, charged alleged victims of sexual assault with violating the university's stringent honor code for details that came out in reports the accusers made to local police.[31] The problem, according to a *Salt Lake Tribune* exposé, was particularly acute for gay students; the university's prohibition on any type of same-sex sexual experience all but required them to admit honor code violation in reporting an assault.[32] An investigation by ESPN, meanwhile, raised suspicion that employees from Baylor

University had colluded with local police to shield football players from sexual assault claims (discussed in chapter 7).[33]

Beyond such indefensible policies, many allegations made in Title IX complaints are entirely plausible. But the administrators' behavior outlined in many of these complaints (at least the portions made public) seem to reflect not gender discrimination of the type prohibited by Title IX so much as incompetence and arrogance of the type found in many large bureaucracies. Frustratingly, but perhaps expectedly, OCR makes robust public discussion about the issue difficult; the office has regularly fulfilled Freedom of Information Act requests by redacting all information about the specifics of complaints against universities.[34]

In any case, the answer to the problem of universities allegedly mistreating alleged victims of sexual assault cannot be to eviscerate other students' due-process rights. Yet some Title IX complaints have come close to making such a demand. In 2012, for example, after a disciplinary hearing at the University of Virginia found an accused student not guilty of sexual assault, the accuser filed a Title IX complaint. Her lawyer, the same Wendy Murphy who had disgraced herself in her Duke lacrosse case commentary, maintained that the "preponderance standard is simple. When her accusations are deemed credible, and his denials are not described with the same glowing terminology, she wins." Under this interpretation of Title IX, once UVA *charged* a student with sexual assault, the school needed to find him guilty. Even OCR has never gone this far.[35]

Perhaps the highest-profile questionable Title IX claim was filed against the University of North Carolina. Former UNC student Andrea Pino's story begins in 2012, when, she says, she was raped at an off-campus party—leaving her bloodied—by another UNC student, whose identity she didn't know and whom she never saw again. (How she knew that her attacker was a UNC student is thus unclear.) None of her fellow partygoers witnessed the event. Although Pino claims to have then left the party, run across campus (still bleeding), and "woke up in a pool of blood that dripped over onto the cracks of the wooden floor," nobody reported seeing her in distress. She did not report the attack to Chapel Hill police or to UNC. She said that her friends discouraged her from reporting it to UNC.[36]

The villain of Pino's narratives was an unidentified UNC academic who called her "lazy" in a conversation after the alleged assault. In an essay for *The Huffington Post*, Pino implied it was an academic advisor who didn't know she had been raped but whom she had asked to meet with because a class she was taking that term had "triggered" her. Sympathetic reporters from *Inside Higher Ed* and *BuzzFeed* paraphrased her as saying the academic advisor *did* know she had been raped but was indifferent. Later still, in an interview with *ESPNW*, Pino told a different story. She attributed the "lazy" comment not to an academic advisor but to a "professor," who knew not only of her victim status but also of her activism. "When I went public" as an activist, Pino said, "I was told I was creating a hostile environment at UNC. When I explained to a professor what was happening and how it was affecting my grades, I was told I was lazy." Pino also told *ESPNW* that she had dropped not one but *12* classes. No reporter identified or interviewed the person who supposedly accused Pino of being lazy.[37]

But Pino's claims triggered a movement at UNC. In 2013, she joined three students, a former student, and former assistant dean of students Melinda Manning to file a Title IX complaint against UNC. North Carolina's McClatchy newspapers described the 34-page complaint (which was not made public) as follows: "The students say they are sexual-assault victims and that the university mishandled their cases by not believing or supporting them or by accusing them of being at fault in their attacks."[38]

The proliferation of Title IX complaints has resulted from the efforts of a handful of organizations that allied with the Obama administration to weaken campus due process. The most prominent such group is Know Your IX. One Know Your IX founder, self-described rape survivor Dana Bolger, had worked with Alice Stanton (see the introduction) at the Amherst College online publication *AC Voice*. Bolger had rejoiced at the expulsion of Michael Cheng, the Amherst student whose experience opened this book—adding, without citing evidence, that many more "perpetrators...will be crossing the stage at graduation this May."[39]

Know Your IX's other founder, Yale law student Alexandra Brodsky, gushed about vocal feminist Catharine MacKinnon. The MacKinnon philosophy, said Brodsky, "feels very real to students. It's not abstract when you're failing out of school because you have to share a library with your rapist." Returning the compliment, MacKinnon told Emily Bazelon of *The New York Times*: "I'm flat-out inspired by these girls."[40] Know Your IX's ambitious attack on due process implies that a fair process is one that effectively presumes all accused campus students guilty. The group also seeks to revolutionize the criminal law by denying basic procedural protections to people accused of sex crimes.

"The criminal justice process revictimizes rape survivors," Bolger has argued, because "police disbelieve victims" and "juries buy into the rape myths that saturate our society and acquit perpetrators."[41] In a May 2016 appearance, she asserted that for "many victims, particularly those who are of color...going to the cops can be really dangerous, and often results for them being criminalized." (She provided no evidence for this claim.) Bolger additionally claimed to possess "lots of evidence of...people perpetrating rape and being allowed to stay on campus." How a student found guilty of rape could remain out of jail, much less enrolled at his college, she did not explain. She identified no such case.[42]

Know Your IX has shown little interest in considering recent evidence that might disprove their dogmas. In early 2016, for example, the organization continued to use "training materials" based in part on the "seminal work" of the by-then-discredited David Lisak. These training materials also recommended that schools provide accusers with "protections against cross-examination" and "questions regarding irrelevant sexual history"—while denying the same protections to accused students.[43]

Some Title IX complaints seem unlikely to survive legal scrutiny, at least to the extent that the facts are publicly available. Examples:

- In 2013, a handful of accusers led by 19-year-old Sarah Tedesco filed a Title IX complaint against Emerson College, in Boston. Tedesco said she had been raped three times, by two different students. She had reported at least two of these incidents to police. But she had ceased cooperating with authorities—in part, it appears, because she hadn't liked the questions that police officers were asking her, and in part (she claimed) because an Emerson official urged her to file a complaint with the college instead. But even under Emerson's accuser-friendly rules, the student whom Tedesco accused was found not guilty. That result led her to file her Title IX complaint.[44]
- In 2014, the mother of University of Michigan student Emily Campbell filed a Title IX complaint after Campbell accused two male students of raping her. A local judge had dismissed the rape charges as lacking probable cause, and the university had ruled

for the accused students in a disciplinary proceeding. The basis of the mother's Title IX filing was that the university had allowed the accused to present expert testimony and had taken too long to reach a decision.[45]

- In 2013, accusers' rights activists at Dartmouth, at the urging of UNC's Andrea Pino, alleged that the college's procedures violated Title IX, citing no evidence. To the contrary, Dartmouth's rules denied meaningful due process to *accused* students. The school prohibited accused students from having lawyers at their hearings unless criminal charges were pending; denied any right to cross-examine accusers; disavowed "formal rules of evidence and courtroom procedures"; and found accused students guilty if a majority of the five-member panel thought they were "more likely than not" guilty, even if two panelists found the opposite.[46]

- In 2013, a USC student named Tucker Reed told *The Huffington Post* that a USC administrator had informed her that the disciplinary process was "educative," not designed to "punish." Reed apparently did not understand that this "educative" spin was the key rationale for denying due process to *accused* students. She filed a Title IX complaint against the school.[47]

- In 2015, a student filed a Title IX complaint against Duke, despite the university's assiduous efforts over the years to rig and re-rig its process in favor of accusers. The basis for the complaint has not been disclosed. But Duke's former spokesperson, John Burness, captured the lessons of experience when he said, "There is a sense that no matter where the institution is, it will be found [by OCR] to have violated something."[48]

Even implausible Title IX complaints, in the hands of OCR, trigger investigations that consume universities' financial and human resources for years. "[N]o matter what [colleges and universities] try to do, or what facts they present, OCR is going to come out with a findings letter that says they violated the law," observed Robb Jones, senior vice president at United Educators, an insurance and risk-management firm, in a 2015 interview with *The Chronicle of Higher Education*. Terry Hartle, senior vice president at the American Council on Education, echoed the analysis; in a 2016 interview with *The Washington Post*, he called OCR "a Court of Star Chamber, with arbitrary rulings, no rights for those under investigation and a secret process."[49] And the office wants to intensify its efforts; in 2015, OCR head Catherine Lhamon demanded that Congress fund the hiring of 500 more OCR investigators.[50]

For a university interested in finding the truth, fairly handling a sexual assault complaint while facing an OCR investigation is extremely difficult. For a university with scant interest in fairness, OCR's pressure can make an unfair process even worse. It was the misfortune of Ohio State University medical student Tom Hall* that his university was in the middle of a four-year OCR compliance review when a fellow student accused him of rape.

Hall, who was working toward degrees in medicine and business, received a phone call in July 2014 from Mary Hopkins,* a fellow medical school student with whom he had been flirting for a few weeks. She invited him to join her and some friends at a local bar.[51] He did so. The two later had sex in his apartment. They went on a couple of dates after that, but they did not sleep together again.

Ten months later, OSU asked Hopkins, who was already on academic probation due to failing grades, to leave the medical program. Two days after that, Hopkins told the university's Title IX coordinator that Hall had sexually assaulted and possibly drugged her. She claimed to remember no details of the alleged assault. She had never reported the incident to police or, it appears, to anyone else before learning that she was about to be expelled. But she used the rape accusation to avoid expulsion. Citing Title IX and OCR guidance, and backed by the university's Title IX office, Hopkins successfully demanded an "academic accommodation": permission to remain at the medical school.

OSU turned over Hopkins' complaint to an investigator named Jeff Majarian. His perfunctory probe consisted of interviews with Hopkins and Hall and a handful of people they suggested. He declined to do a follow-up interview with Hopkins to confront her with new information gathered during his investigation. He also refused to ask the bar where the two had met that evening for its videotape, which might have provided valuable evidence as to Hopkins' level of intoxication.

Most troublingly, neither OSU's Title IX officials nor the accuser ever told the investigator about the suspicious timing of the accuser's rape complaint: just in time to avoid being expelled. In other words, Hopkins had a very powerful motive to lie. But this exculpatory evidence did not make it into Majarian's report, which found "reasonable cause" to proceed to a hearing. Nor did the disciplinary panel learn of the close timing between Hopkins' academic difficulties and her decision to file a complaint against Hall.

Despite OSU's denying him critical evidence about his accuser's possible motive to lie, at the hearing Hall tried to prove his innocence by showing that Hopkins had not been severely intoxicated when they had sex. He testified that neither of them had any alcoholic drinks after he arrived at the bar. He also obtained an expert report from an OSU professor of pharmacology expressing his "opinion to a reasonable degree of scientific certainty that based upon [Hopkins'] calculated blood-alcohol concentrations and the supporting eyewitness observations," she had "not [been] substantially impaired by alcohol at the time of the events in question." But the panel chair, Matthew Page, held that accused students were barred from presenting expert testimony, citing an ambiguously worded university rule. Under another rule, this decision could not be appealed.

To ensure a speedy resolution of the case, in July 2015, OSU even paid accuser Hopkins $500 to fly back to Columbus to testify against Hall. The accused, denied the opportunity to present the very strong evidence of his innocence, could only hope that the panelists would believe his testimony.

But they had been "trained" by OSU to adopt a "victim centered approach"; that questioning how much alcohol the accuser had ingested "becomes a vehicle for blaming the victim"; that sex offenders "are overwhelmingly white males" (Hall is white); that "sex offenders are experts in rationalizing their behavior"; and that as many as 57 percent of college men "report perpetrating a form of sexually aggressive behavior." The training material also told panelists to find Hall guilty if the evidence tipped against him by "50% and a feather," even if there was no "damning evidence." The panelists did as they were encouraged and returned a guilty finding. The school then expelled the almost certainly innocent Hall, who was just four months shy of earning his medical degree.

Hall filed a federal lawsuit. After three OSU officials refused to give a simple "yes" when asked under oath whether they had been obliged to get the decision correct, Senior U.S. District Judge James Graham, of Columbus, allowed the lawsuit to proceed. "The right to some form of cross-examination in university expulsion hearings is a clearly established due process right . . . in a case that turns on 'a choice between believing an accuser and an accused,'" Graham wrote. "it is plausible that [Hall's] right to cross examine was effectively denied by the Administrators' failure to turn over critical impeachment evidence," the judge continued, expecially if "the Administrators knew that [Hopkins] lied about the timing of her accommodation at the hearing and permitted her testimony to stand unrebutted."

The OSU administrators appeared to have a different conception of due process. Sexual Violence Support Coordinator Natalie Spiert was especially blunt. When asked by Hall's lawyer whether her admitted duty to "support students at Ohio State" included "an obligation to make sure that the hearing panel gets it right," her answer was "no." When asked whether she had an obligation to correct a false statement at the hearing, she replied, "I do not know." When investigator Majarian was asked whether the Title IX coordinator's job was to ensure that the process was fair, he, too, said, "I don't know."

Meanwhile, OSU resolved matters with OCR by agreeing to more than 100 demands ranging from new reporting requirements to undertaking "campus climate" surveys to increasing the powers of the Title IX coordinator.[52] In an interview with Sabrina Rubin Erdely, OCR's Catherine Lhamon pronounced herself "thrilled" with a "terrific agreement" that represented a "significant step forward to correct Title IX compliance."[53]

Though her highest-profile critique of universities' handling of sexual assault matters was published a few months before Hopkins filed her charges, Harvard Law School professor Janet Halley could have been speaking of the OSU case: "[N]o one participates in the management of high-conflict divorces without taking into account the role of spite in some spouses' negotiation and litigation," Halley wrote, "but somehow we have imagined sexual harassment charges to be pure of distorting motives like these . . . morphed into the form of a sexual misconduct charge."[54]

Such nuances did not concern OSU officials. Nor have activists seemed to worry about championing weak accusations. Radley Balko offers the most plausible explanation: "It may be that [they] deliberately seek out and champion the ambiguous cases to demonstrate their commitment to the cause."[55] That theory explains the credulous attention lavished by a U.S. senator and many others on the highest-profile Title

IX complainant to date: Emma Sulkowicz—widely known as the "mattress girl"—a 2015 graduate of New York's Columbia University.

Beginning in September 2014, Sulkowicz told her story in interviews with *The New York Times*, *New York*, *The New York Daily News*, *Mic*, a New York City radio station, *The Guardian*, *Democracy Now*, the Columbia *Spectator*, MTV, and other news outlets. By her account, in August 2012, after she had twice had casual sex with a fellow student named Paul Nungesser, he choked her, hit her, and penetrated her anally without consent, leaving her near death. But it took her some time, by her account, to understand that this behavior constituted a criminal sexual assault.

Months later, in April 2013, Sulkowicz accused Nungesser of rape in complaints to both Columbia and (the following year) the New York City Police Department. In myriad subsequent interviews, she claimed that Columbia's disciplinary panelists asked her inappropriate questions before finding Nungesser not guilty. She later dropped the criminal complaint, saying the process would be too draining.

Sulkowicz filed a complaint with OCR accusing Columbia of violating Title IX. She also launched a successful publicity campaign, for which she received academic credit as a visual arts project, of carrying a mattress around campus until Columbia expelled Nungesser or they both graduated. Activists on more than 150 campuses nationwide conducted imitation "carry that weight" events to draw even more attention to the plight of college sexual assault victims. Many asked Sulkowicz to share her wisdom. She told an audience at Brown that "if we use proof in rape cases, we fall into the patterns of rape deniers."[56] Sen. Kirsten Gillibrand invited her to the 2015 State of the Union address, where Sulkowicz met Secretary of State John Kerry. "He didn't really know who I was, and even when Senator Gillibrand introduced me no one seemed to know who I was," a seemingly disappointed Sulkowicz later noted.[57]

The Sulkowicz coverage reflected a typical media acceptance of the accuser's version of events, with little or no effort to obtain information from the other side. But a handful of first-rate journalists have broken from this pattern. One is columnist Cathy Young, who publishes in *Newsday*, *The Daily Beast*, and *Real Clear Politics*. Her investigative reporting showed that Sulkowicz's story was riddled with inaccuracies and concealment of exculpatory facts.

Young was the only journalist who interviewed the male graduate student who had served as Nungesser's disciplinary advocate. (Under the procedures it used at the time, Columbia did not allow Nungesser to have a lawyer.) He told Young that he initially had no opinion of Nungesser's guilt or innocence but, after listening to all the evidence at the Columbia hearing, concluded that Sulkowicz's allegations were false. He also asserted that Sulkowicz's description of the hearing was a fantasy. "[T]he panel were asking sensitive questions; they were equally asked of Paul, and had been asked of Paul through the entire process," the graduate student said. "The questions were extremely personal because they had to be . . . the questions were asked with the utmost sensitivity." He asked Young for anonymity lest he be blackballed in the academy for telling inconvenient truths.

Even more devastating to Sulkowicz's credibility, Young obtained numerous private Facebook messages between Sulkowicz and Nungesser. They showed that—for months *after* an alleged brutal, near-fatal assault—Sulkowicz had eagerly sought a romantic relationship with Nungesser but had been spurned. "I love you Paul. Where are you?!?!?!?!," she had said in a typical message in early October 2012, two months after the alleged assault. Nungesser also told Young that after Sulkowicz went to the police, he had been interviewed by New York City prosecutors, and they had found no basis for charging him criminally. This information contradicted Sulkowicz's previous assertion that *she* had pulled the plug on the police inquiry.[58]

Sulkowicz responded to Young's exposé on the Gawker website *Jezebel*. She implausibly claimed that she had said "I love you Paul" to get Nungesser to confess that he had raped her. Despite having shared intimate tales with many ideologically sympathetic reporters, Sulkowicz also expressed outrage that Young would "violate" her privacy—by reporting the obviously newsworthy Facebook messages that she had sent to Nungesser months after he had (by her account) violently raped her.

The more Sulkowicz talked, the more she struggled to keep her story straight. Her rationale for dropping her complaint to the NYPD, for instance, shifted dramatically, from "too draining" to a new claim that the police had started visiting her apartment unexpectedly. She also claimed for the first time to have told an unidentified friend about the alleged rape the day after it happened. (She didn't explain why she failed to invite this crucial witness to testify on her behalf in the Columbia hearing or why she hadn't mentioned this key information to the myriad reporters who previously interviewed her.) Meanwhile, a lawsuit by Nungesser against Columbia for indulging Sulkowicz's harassment of him revealed still more Facebook messages discrediting Sulkowicz.[59]

These hammer blows to Sulkowicz's credibility took a toll on her media and academic support. Even Columbia president Lee Bollinger made a show of turning his back when she carried her famous mattress across the stage at her May 2015 graduation, with Nungesser present. Then Sulkowicz starred in and released a pornographic film reenacting the alleged rape—which she had initially prepared through her Columbia visual arts project.

Perhaps the most remarkable—although, in these times, not surprising—aspect of "the mattress girl's" case is that until Cathy Young showed what real journalism looks like, almost all previous coverage had uncritically embraced Sulkowicz's version of events. The next chapter will discuss many more such examples, from some of the nation's most prominent news outlets.

5

MEDIA
MALPRACTICE

Tom Jolly, *New York Times* sports editor, confessed in February 2008 that he regretted aspects of his paper's much-criticized coverage of the Duke lacrosse case. He vowed to do better. "Knowledge gained by hindsight has informed our approach to other stories since then," said Jolly, who later became an associate managing editor.[1]

But the *Times* did not do better. Its handling of recent campus sexual assault cases has been pervaded by the same biases that drove its Duke lacrosse coverage. The paper has continued to unquestioningly accept alleged victims' stories while omitting evidence that might harm their credibility. Like almost all other mainstream media, the *Times* also has glossed over how university procedures stack the deck against accused students.

With the *Times* setting the tone, the mainstream media have presented a misleading picture of almost every aspect of the campus sexual assault problem. The coverage has had three critical flaws.

The first is the "believe-the-survivor" dogma, which presumes the guilt of accused students—a sentiment that Harvard Law School professor Jeannie Suk Gersen has identified as a "near-religious teaching."[2]

Second, most journalists have embraced without skepticism or context surveys purporting to show that 20 percent of female college students are sexually assaulted—thereby portraying campuses as awash in an unprecedented wave of violent crime. Third, most media coverage of alleged sexual assault on college campuses fails to report in any meaningful way (if at all) the actual procedures that colleges employ in sexual assault cases.

Richard Pérez-Peña, a veteran reporter who joined the *Times* in 1992, wrote most of its stories on alleged campus sexual assault between January 2012 and December 2014. He debuted on the beat with a long article suggesting that Yale quarterback Patrick Witt was a liar and a rapist. Pérez-Peña implied that Witt and Yale officials had misled the public when they said that Witt had withdrawn from the Rhodes Scholarship competition because of a conflict between the Yale-Harvard game and his scheduled interview. The real reason for Witt's withdrawal, Pérez-Peña asserted, was a mysterious sexual misconduct allegation.

Even if true, this information would hardly have been worthy of aggressive treatment by the nation's most powerful newspaper. In addition, the reporter relied on an undisclosed number of anonymous sources. Indeed, he never figured out who Witt's accuser was. He never learned what the accuser alleged Witt had done. (Neither did Witt.) He insinuated that Yale had suspended Witt. (In fact, Witt was finishing his senior thesis off campus while preparing for the NFL draft.) In his article, Pérez-Peña never described the "informal complaint" process that Yale used against Witt, a process that denied him any right to present evidence of his innocence. Witt, like all students accused under the "informal" process since 2011, was found guilty and given a reprimand.[3]

The Yale Daily News almost immediately raised doubts about the article, citing contemporaneous emails from Witt that conflicted with Pérez-Peña's account. Shortly thereafter, several people outside the traditional media, including one of us (KC Johnson), raised questions about Pérez-Peña's work. The cheeky sports website Deadspin published a comprehensive takedown of Pérez-Peña's timeline. *Worth* editor-in-chief Richard Bradley, writing on his personal blog *Shots in the Dark*, concluded that "*The Times*—and, yes, Richard Pérez-Peña—owe Patrick

Witt an apology. Then Pérez-Peña and the editor who green lighted this story should be fired."[4]

Pérez-Peña was not fired. But the problems with his work spurred the *Times'* public editor, Arthur Brisbane, to do the reporting that Pérez-Peña should have done. Brisbane spoke to Witt's agent, uncovered emails Pérez-Peña hadn't found, and described Yale's "informal" complaint process. "Maybe you just can't publish this story, not with the facts known now," Brisbane concluded, because "when something as serious as a person's reputation is at stake, it's not enough to rely on anonymous sourcing, effectively saying 'trust us.'"[5]

Such criticism appears to have had little or no effect inside the *Times* newsroom. Indeed, in a November 4, 2014, tweet, *Times* reporter Vivian Yee (@VivianHYee) defended Pérez-Peña's work, gloating that despite the public editor's devastating criticism, "for the record, there was no 'retraction' on our story" about Witt. Meanwhile, Yale's actions, compounded by *Times* errors, "nearly ruined my life," Witt wrote in November 2014.[6]

Most of Pérez-Peña's nearly 20 articles (a few with joint bylines) on campus sexual assault allegations exhibited the same problems as his Witt coverage. In an October 2012 piece, he uncritically presented Angie Epifano's "wrenching account" of her supposed mistreatment by Amherst. Pérez-Peña made no effort to contact either the student Epifano accused of rape or the Amherst employees she portrayed as uncaring. In what was billed as a straight news article, the reporter celebrated Amherst president Biddy Martin's adoption of draconian disciplinary procedures—the same procedures that paved the way for Amherst's expulsion of Michael Cheng.[7] In another article, Pérez-Peña gushed that "it may be that no college leader in the country was as well prepared to face this controversy than [sic] Biddy Martin."[8]

In a March 2013 article, Pérez-Peña wrote inaccurately that the Dear Colleague letter "did not markedly change interpretation of the law; instead, it reminded colleges of obligations that many of them had ignored, and signaled that there was a new seriousness in Washington about enforcing them." Hours later, an editor seems to have noticed the error, and the first clause quoted above was changed to say that "[t]he letter [did] change[] interpretation of parts of the law."[9] But with the rest of the sentence unaltered, the new version was an absurd assertion that OCR had "reminded" colleges of *nonexistent* "obligations" that they had previously "ignored."

In 2014, an article by Pérez-Peña and Kate Taylor asserted that "there is scant evidence that sexual assault is more or less prevalent than in the past"—a claim contradicted by Bureau of Justice Statistics data concluding that sexual assault rates had plunged since 1996. FBI crime statistics show a similar pattern.[10]

The spring and summer of 2014 also featured two in-depth pieces on alleged campus sexual assault by *Times* investigative journalist Walt Bogdanich, a three-time Pulitzer Prize winner and acclaimed investigative reporter. Unlike Pérez-Peña's articles, Bogdanich's two articles presented cases in which the allegations were plausible. The acknowledged conduct in both cases was deeply disturbing, and the accused students were extremely unsympathetic. But, still, both pieces omitted critical evidence.

Bogdanich's comments in a 2015 interview may help explain why. Discussing his approach to campus sexual assault allegations, he remarked that investigative reporters like him "get upset...when we see powerful people unfairly taking advantage of the less powerful."[11] But in the typical campus context (if not in one and perhaps both of Bogdanich's cases), the *accused* student is more often the party treated unfairly by "powerful people." Bogdanich's emotionalism and apparent presumption of guilt in cases involving campus sexual assault accusations served his readers poorly.

Bogdanich's first showcase article was a 5,200-word front-pager in April 2014. It left the clear impression that Jameis Winston—the Heisman Trophy–winning, NFL first draft choice, former Florida State University quarterback—had raped a fellow first-year student named Erica Kinsman. Whether or not a rapist, Winston was a singularly unappealing character—"an embarrassment in a lot of ways to the university," as former FSU coach Bobby Bowden put it. He seemed a perfect fit for the media narrative of coddled star athletes raping fellow students and getting away with it.[12] Perhaps it was for this reason that in almost all of the paper's more than 20 articles about the case, Bogdanich and other *Times* reporters omitted virtually all the evidence that cast doubt on the alleged victim's credibility.

Shortly into his magnum opus, Bogdanich implied that Kinsman had been drugged. She claimed that someone at a bar had given her a drink, apparently spiked with a date-rape drug, which caused her to black out. He did not mention that two toxicology reports had shown no trace of any known drug in her system.

Bogdanich added, "After partially blacking out, . . . she found herself in an apartment with a man on top of her, sexually assaulting her." That portrayal, and Kinsman's various suggestions to police to the same effect, was contradicted not only by other witnesses but also, later, by Kinsman's own December 2014 testimony admitting that she went voluntarily with Winston into his bedroom.[13]

Kinsman's initial, recorded phone report (through a friend) to campus police was that after leaving an off-campus bar, she had been hit on the back of the head, blacked out, and found herself being raped by a stranger. Yet a medical exam detected no sign of a blow to the head. Kinsman never repeated the claim. The Times never mentioned it and therefore did not explore how the accuser changed her story.

Finally, Winston's lawyers have alleged that Kinsman's aunt (also her first lawyer) introduced an ugly racial element to the case, when she said in a phone call that Kinsman (who is white) would never voluntarily sleep with a "black boy." The aunt never responded to an email from one of us asking whether she had made such a remark. The possibility of racial bias in the accuser's family has never been mentioned in the Times.[14]

The two most plausible views of the encounter are that after Kinsman went voluntarily into Winston's bedroom, (1) she made it clear at some point that she did not consent to sex but he proceeded anyway or (2) she consented to sex and never clearly withdrew her consent but later alleged rape because she felt she had been badly treated by Winston during the encounter—as she clearly was, according to *his* version of events (for example, he let his roommate enter the room while he was in bed with Kinsman before taking her into the bathroom to have sex on the hard floor). The evidence in the case remains ambiguous, and Kinsman's shifting stories significantly undermine her credibility. State Attorney William Meggs concluded that the evidence did not show probable guilt. Former Florida Supreme Court Justice Major Harding, who presided over FSU's two-day disciplinary hearing, cited conflicts between Kinsman's testimony and other, undisputed evidence, to reach the same conclusion.

One of us (Stuart Taylor) exposed the *Times'* mistreatment of Winston at length in February 2015, in *Real Clear Sports*. An official *Times* response stressed that the point of the Bogdanich article had been to critique shoddy work on the case by Tallahassee police.[15] But the *Times* did not challenge any of the exposé's factual assertions. None of this record prevented the Pulitzer Prize Board from naming Bogdanich in April 2015 as a finalist, for "stories exposing preferential police treatment for Florida State University football players who are accused of sexual assault and other criminal offenses."[16]

In his next piece for the *Times*, this one focusing on Hobart and William Smith (HWS), a small school in upstate New York, Bogdanich displayed a similarly one-sided approach.

According to Bogdanich, at a party in September 2013, a first-year student called "Anna" had had sex with several football players in a row. Bogdanich's work clearly conveyed the impression that this was a rape, because Anna had been incapacitated by alcohol. But neither the police nor an HWS disciplinary hearing found sufficient evidence to make that determination, even (in the latter case) under the low standard of proof decreed by OCR. Bogdanich waved away these findings by claiming, again, that the police work had been shoddy. He also asserted that at HWS, the absence of "the usual courtroom checks and balances" had been unfair to the *accuser*.

On top of such claims, Bogdanich committed acts of careless journalism. He did not explore (until after *The Finger Lakes Times* had reported) the accuser's refusal, on the advice of her lawyer, to give police access to her rape kit, which hampered their investigation. Bogdanich appears not even to have attempted to speak with the accused students or their lawyers. Worse, he glossed over the refusal of the accuser's only corroborating witness to testify in the HWS disciplinary process. The reporter wrote that this critical witness "stands by his account, according to Anna."

"According to Anna"? A careful reporter would have asked the witness himself, whom Bogdanich quoted on other points.[17]

The Finger Lakes Times reported claims by both the district attorney and HWS's president that Bogdanich had taken out of context material from the college disciplinary board's hearing transcript. If these assertions were unfair, *The New York Times* could have disproved them by posting the transcript on its website.[18] It did not do so. (All available materials from cases mentioned in this book are posted on https://kc-johnson.com.)

The New York Times' coverage of alleged sexual assault on college campuses "seems of a piece with the leftist bias I noticed within the *Times* newsroom regarding climate change, gay marriage, abortion, affirmative action, labor, and other hot-button issues," former *Times* editor Tom Kuntz told us via email. Kuntz, a self-described libertarian, had worked for the newspaper since 1987 but left in early 2016, in part because he no longer felt comfortable with its generally slanted coverage and lack of balance.

"This bias can no longer be chalked up as simply a function of too many lefty reporters and editors in the newsroom," Kuntz added. "The *Times* has geared its survival strategy to preaching to the liberal converted. Although no one in authority at the *Times* says so explicitly in public, you can read between the lines of such statements as the October 2015 announcement by CEO Mark Thompson. He said that the *Times* plans to 'double the number of [its] most loyal readers,' and 'double its digital revenue,' by 2020, by catering to those who most reliably part with money for *Times* content."

A company statement quoted by Kuntz said the *Times* planned to develop loyal readers "increasingly from younger demographics and international audiences"—groups with predominantly liberal views.[19] Indeed, said Kuntz, "I noticed in many corporate strategy briefings over recent years that the *Times* seems to care little about bringing conservative readers into the fold. In PowerPoint presentations and the like, competitors listed as ones that mattered were liberal outfits like the *Huffington Post* and the *Guardian*—not conservative outlets, with the exception of the *Wall Street Journal*. The Drudge Report, Fox News, and the *Daily Mail*, for example, were ignored despite their enormous audiences."

This corporate strategy was consistent with a much-noted 2014 newsroom innovation study led by Arthur Gregg Sulzberger, son and possible successor of the current publisher, according to Kuntz. The junior Sulzberger soon became senior editor for strategy (before rising even further in the company), and his "first task," according to Executive Editor Dean Baquet's memo about the appointment, was "to help the newsroom's leaders and [editorial page editor] Andy Rosenthal build a joint newsroom-editorial page audience development operation that can pull all the levers and build readership."[20]

Another longtime and respected *Times* journalist with whom we spoke has a very different view of the newspaper's motivations. This insider says that "the notion that there is a decision to feed red meat to the liberal base is just nonsense. It's horseshit. We write a lot about climate change, and we do it with a point of view that accepts the scientific consensus and 'liberal' worldview. Is that an attempt to attract eyeballs by throwing red meat to liberal readers or is it coverage of something important we and our readers care about? We write a lot about police violence, Black Lives Matter and the post-Ferguson law enforcement environment. We write a lot about women's issues such as access to abortion and contraception. You can argue with the coverage, if you like, but it's complete nonsense to think there's a sudden strategy to drive digital readership on campus sex issues by throwing out liberal swill to drive up pageviews.

"There's a complicated and fair discussion you could have about bias, conscious and unconscious in what we do," the *Times* journalist continued. "On campus rape, I think you can argue both that it's a hugely important issue we need to address and that our coverage has tended to disproportionately reflect the 'liberal' world view of feminist activists, and that it has been slow to adequately address the rights of accused males. That's a worthy discussion. But seeing some kind of cabal to crank out liberal catnip to get clicks reflects a complete failure to understand how this place works."

Whether the reason is groupthink or a strategy of firing up the newspaper's liberal base, the *Times'* coverage of alleged sexual assault on college campuses has represented a journalistic failure—and a particularly troubling one, given the paper's earlier failure on this issue in the Duke lacrosse case. And, as in the lacrosse case, the *Times* blanket coverage has legitimized similarly biased coverage elsewhere. In the most spectacular example of the pattern, *Rolling Stone* reporter Sabrina Rubin Erdely cited the *Times'* handling of campus sexual assault as precedent for her disastrous decision not to contact the (nonexistent, as it turned out) accused student in her November 2014 story of sexual assault at the University of Virginia (an issue we discuss in chapter 10).[21]

In 2013 and 2014, *Los Angeles Times* investigative reporter Jason Felch accused Occidental College of covering up numerous campus sexual assaults. The trigger point for Felch's articles came in 2013, when professors Danielle Dirks and Caroline Heldman, along with several students, formed a group called the Oxy Sexual Assault Coalition. They presented a 12-point list of demands for new procedures to increase the likelihood of accused students being expelled.[22] They made these demands despite Occidental's already accuser-friendly campus sexual assault policy, which decreed that "'Yes' may not always mean 'Yes'" and that "burden of proof" and other legal terms "are not applicable" in campus proceedings.[23]

Felch published unproven sexual assault accusations by Occidental students and their faculty allies as though they were established facts. Then, in a December 2013 article, he accused Occidental of violating the Clery Act by hiding 27 campus sexual assault complaints in 2012 alone. Felch noted in passing that Occidental had reported seven such complaints to the federal government.

Felch asserted that in order to protect the school's image, administrators had "actively discouraged victims" (note the absence of "alleged") from filing reports.[24] The reporter based his claims on "documents, interviews and a *Times* review of two confidential federal complaints against the school." Protests predictably ensued, California legislators talked about changing state law, and the college promised to reexamine its procedures to ensure even more favorable treatment of alleged sexual assault victims. In a follow-up article, Felch quoted an Occidental spokesperson as saying that "the challenge for the college is not false reports."[25]

But Felch's story itself was a false report. As *The Los Angeles Times* admitted in a March 2014 editor's note, the college had done nothing wrong in any of the 27 cases that prompted the reporter's attack. Some were not covered at all by the Clery Act because they had occurred off campus and the alleged perpetrators were not Occidental students. All the others, the editor's note said, "involved sexual harassment, inappropriate text messages or other conduct not covered by the act." Felch had counted them as sexual assaults based solely on characterizations by campus activists.

How could an experienced reporter have made such blunders? The editor's note offered an explanation: Felch "had engaged in an inappropriate relationship with someone who was a source for the December 7 story and others Felch had written about Occidental's handling of sexual assault allegations." The paper then fired Felch.[26]

Others, however, fanned the flames of the Occidental scandal. The online publication *BuzzFeed*—which had assigned two reporters to what it called the campus "rape culture" beat[27]—sent reporter Jessica Testa to Occidental. She produced a piece that could have passed for an *Onion* parody.

One of the faculty members involved in the Title IX fight, Caroline Heldman, claimed that Occidental administrators were tracking her emails, and she implied that someone in cahoots with the administration had broken into her faculty office, but she offered no evidence. The other faculty member involved was Felch's unnamed lover. She, too, claimed—while citing no evidence—that her faculty workspace "was broken into," adding that "pages from her journal that referenced her relationship with Felch were laid out on her desk." Felch's lover added that because her iPhone "had been acting strangely," she thought someone had been listening in on her conversations. "Whether or not you're actually being surveilled, if you think you are, it's still destructive," she told Testa.[28]

Meanwhile, professor Danielle Dirks gave provocative interviews with *LA Weekly*, *The Los Angeles Times*, *LA Progressive*, *Marie Claire*, and others. She told *New York*, for instance, that most male college students "are calculated predators [who] seem like nice guys, but they're not nice guys."[29]

It costs Occidental parents more than $65,000 a year to have their children taught by professors such as these.

Self-appointed media watchdogs can be just as biased on the topic of sexual assault as the media they purport to police. For example, even in a lengthy essay on *Rolling Stone*'s buying wholesale a fabricated tale of gang rape at a University of Virginia fraternity (see chapter 10), *The Columbia Journalism Review* exuded pro-accuser bias. Sheila Coronel, dean of academic affairs at the Columbia School of Journalism, and Steve Coll, dean of the school, characterized accusers whose claims had not been adjudicated as "victims" and "survivors," correspondingly using the guilt-presuming label "perpetrators" to characterize accused males who had not been proven guilty. For example, they advised journalists on various ways to "persuade both victims and perpetrators to talk."

Citing the discredited David Lisak, Coronel and Coll parroted the claim that "[s]ocial scientists analyzing crime records report the rate of false rape allegations is 2 to 8 percent." *CJR* also advised reporters to "gain a deep understanding of...[the] directives from [OCR] and recommendations from the White House"—as though these were disinterested expert judgments. The magazine said nothing about how to cover colleges' unfair disciplinary proceedings or basic denial of due process.[30]

The Poynter Institute, which has billed itself as "the world's leading instructor, innovator, convener and resource" for educating journalists, has featured an even more extreme degree of bias. In 2012, Kelly McBride, whose Poynter biography describes her as "one of the country's leading voices when it comes to media ethics," touted as "one of the nation's leading experts on sexual abuse" none other than Wendy Murphy.[31]

Poynter even chose Murphy to teach journalists in seminars. In response to an emailed request by one of us for comment about how she could possibly have seen Murphy as credible, McBride stressed Murphy's "expertise" and characterized as "opinions" her stream of false assertions of fact about the Duke lacrosse case. McBride added that she hoped "to bring Wendy back to a Poynter seminar on sexual assault" to teach still *more* journalists.[32]

If a "men's rights" activist had smeared a rape victim with falsehoods like Murphy's, he would properly have been dismissed as a crank. But many media outlets have joined Poynter in presenting Murphy as a credible expert. She has recently been quoted by Fox News, *The Boston Globe*, *The Washington Post*, *The Kansas City Star*, *Business Insider*, *U.S. News & World Report*, *Rolling Stone*, *The Chronicle of Higher Education*, *The Philadelphia Inquirer*, *The Providence Journal*, *The Huffington Post*, and others. In the words of liberal commentator Alex Pareene, Murphy's career shows that "there are, in the mass media, absolutely no consequences for blatant, constant lying."[33]

The conventional wisdom—that there is a growing epidemic of rape on campus, that colleges tend to coddle rapists and deny justice to accusers, and that due process is a distraction—has bled into popular culture. The two highest-profile examples came in the 2015 book *Missoula* and the 2015 documentary film *The Hunting Ground*.

Glowing reviews from major publications greeted *Missoula*'s recounting of alleged sexual assaults by University of Montana students from 2010 to 2012, including three that involved members of the football team. Doubleday initially printed 500,000 copies.[34] Unlike William D. Cohan for his 2014 book on the Duke lacrosse case, *Missoula* author Jon Krakauer did some serious research, even obtaining the transcript of a University of Montana disciplinary hearing. But his biases—not only in favor of rape accusers but also, especially, against criminal defense lawyers, whom he accused of "chicanery, outright deceit, and other egregious misconduct"—blinded him to the significance of much of the material he uncovered. Krakauer's book also suffers from his total faith in the discredited work of psychologist David Lisak, whom the book mentions more than 100 times.[35]

Missoula, which contends that rape victims are badly treated by police, prosecutors, and universities, fails to prove that a single one of the alleged victims featured in the book was badly treated. Police and prosecutors treated them with sensitivity—although in one case, neither the police nor the prosecutor found the accuser credible. On the other hand, several of the *accused* students profiled in the book *were* treated unfairly—by the University of Montana.

One of the book's central villains is Montana quarterback Jordan Johnson, whom (much to the author's dismay) a jury acquitted, in a very short time, of rape charges. A tangled, unfair university process likewise eventually found him not guilty. A reader of Krakauer's book might experience whiplash to learn that Montana subsequently paid Johnson $245,000 in exchange for his agreement not to file a civil suit against the university and several administrators for their mistreatment of him.[36]

An even more telling indictment of the university came from a federal judge. Shortly before the university opened its disciplinary hearing against him, Johnson requested a temporary restraining order from the U.S. District Court in Missoula. Judge Dana Christensen decided against Johnson at that stage, on procedural grounds. But in the process, Christensen castigated Montana's handling of the case. "The process applied to Plaintiff [Johnson] and the behavior of University officials in investigating and prosecuting this matter," the judge wrote, "offends the Court's sense of fundamental fairness and appears to fall short of the minimal moral obligation of any tribunal to respect the rights and dignity of the accused."[37]

In *Missoula's* 349 pages, Krakauer never mentioned this devastating assessment—by an Obama-nominated judge—of how the university officials whom the author so praised actually handled a sexual assault case.

Johnson's lawyer, David Paoli, claimed that Dean of Students Charles Couture had acted "as a biased investigator, prosecutor and judge in spite of being required by all rules and regulations to be impartial and provide fairness and equal treatment in the process."[38] Krakauer made the same Charles Couture one of the heroes of *Missoula*, despite—or perhaps because of—his handling not only of Johnson's case but also of another. In that case, a junior named Kaitlyn Kelly accused a freshman whom Krakauer called "Calvin Smith" of raping her during a drunken hookup in October 2011. But both a police detective and Assistant District Attorney Kirsten Pabst found no justification for criminal charges.

Kelly got another bite at the apple through the university's disciplinary process. It was run by Couture, a specialist in university admissions with no legal experience and less access to evidence than the police and prosecutor. This administrator interviewed Kelly and Smith, then pronounced Smith a rapist, stressing that Smith had been "very, very drunk" and could not remember much.

When Smith appealed to the "University Court," the same Charles Couture who had already declared him guilty ran the show. Citing university policy, he prohibited both Smith's lawyer and the university's own general counsel, who was present, from speaking. In an unusual development, prosecutor Pabst testified for the defense at the hearing. She not only said that the authorities believed Smith innocent but that the evidence was relatively "clear-cut, in that, according to all of the witnesses, Mr. Smith and the alleged victim" agreed to have sex, and Kelly herself "in fact told the detective that that was her plan: to go back to her room and have sex" with Smith. Couture argued that these facts did not matter because Kelly had revoked any consent and Smith knew it.

The university's general counsel urged postponing the rest of the hearing to allow time to obtain from the police the potentially exculpatory witness statements and other evidence on which the prosecutor had based her testimony. But Couture rejected the request and silenced the general counsel, and the campus "court" ordered Smith's expulsion. Krakauer celebrated this ruling, suggesting that no matter how much proof of Smith's innocence the police might have, it should not "have any bearing on the university's disciplinary proceeding."[39]

This episode revealed an unfair campus disciplinary process at work. But Krakauer seemed satisfied with the outcome. His major complaint was that without a criminal prosecution, Kelly could not testify "in a court of law about how Smith violated her body and wounded her soul." Krakauer would have been happy, it seems, to see a student considered not guilty by law enforcement to be put through the ordeal of a criminal trial in order to give his accuser an emotional release.[40]

If there were any truth to the myth—embraced by Krakauer—that 20 percent of female students are sexually assaulted, then there must have been many hundreds of victims at the 15,000-student University of Montana. The fact that his book presented the story of only one proven victim—Alison Huguet, who was not hard to find, with her rapist sitting in prison—is telling.

Far more prejudiced than even Krakauer's book, *The Hunting Ground* is an emotionally powerful, critically acclaimed, but propagandistic documentary film on alleged campus sexual assault. Co-produced by CNN and created by Emmy-winning director Kirby Dick and Oscar-nominated producer Amy Ziering, the film was shown at the White House, at the Sundance Film Festival, on CNN, at many campuses, and in major cities.

The 103-minute film shows a parade of college women telling heartbreaking and terrifying stories of being raped by male students and then further victimized by callous college officials who, the film alleges, covered up the crimes to avoid bad publicity.

One of the film's producers candidly (if confidentially) confessed its avoidance of exculpatory facts. In a December 2013 email that later came to light in a lawsuit, "investigative producer" Amy Herdy assured one of the film's potential subjects: "[W]e don't operate the same way as journalists—this is a film project very much in the corner of advocacy for victims, so there would be no insensitive questions or the need to get the perpetrator's side."[41]

The film's claim that colleges discourage students from reporting rapes might remain true at a few schools, especially some religious institutions (like BYU) and universities that have sought to deflect plausible claims of sexual assault against star athletes in order to maintain the quality of their key sports teams (like Baylor). But this generalization is incongruent with the ample evidence that—both before and after OCR aggressively intervened—almost all universities have for many years been eager to help alleged victims of sexual assault.

The film's portrayals of the accounts of at least three of the five accusers who get the most airtime are, at best, misleading.

The section on the University of North Carolina presents as credible Andrea Pino—despite the inconsistencies in her central vignette, which involves alleged mistreatment by an unidentified UNC professor or administrator. Pino's credibility has continued to unravel since the film was released. For example, she asserted in a public appearance captured on YouTube that she had been carrying a Taser the night of her alleged rape.[42] She had not previously offered such a claim.

The film also joined *The New York Times* in framing Jameis Winston as an obviously guilty rapist by giving his accuser, Erica Kinsman, more airtime than any other in the film, by a full 15 minutes. An exposé in the blog *Real Clear Sports* showed that the film made a hash of the facts and ignored the copious evidence that Kinsman was not telling the truth about how she ended up in Winston's bedroom.[43]

While pursuing her public campaign against Winston in *The Hunting Ground*, Kinsman also sued Florida State University under Title IX. The case ended in a January 2016 settlement that some portrayed as an admission of fault by FSU. The university said that it cost less to settle—$950,000, of which $700,000 was designated for legal fees and $250,000 for Kinsman—than it would have cost to litigate and win. In addition, FSU was on notice that settling with Kinsman was the only way to appease OCR, which was investigating her Title IX complaint. By settling her lawsuit by January 25, Kinsman avoided giving sworn deposition testimony the next day. Had she gone forward and repeated any of her past stories, Winston's lawyers would no doubt have accused her of perjury.

Many of *The Hunting Ground*'s major storylines were discredited by Emily Yoffe, then a columnist at *Slate* (and now at *The Atlantic*). Yoffe examined the alleged victimization of Harvard University student Kamilah Willingham, first by fellow student Brandon Winston and then by Harvard. (Brandon Winston was named in promotional materials but not in the film.)

Yoffe showed in great detail that "the evidence (including Willingham's own testimony)...is often dramatically at odds with the account presented in the film." She raised serious questions about Willingham's credibility, noting that the "record shows that what happened that night was precisely the kind of spontaneous, drunken encounter that administrators who deal with campus sexual assault accusations say is typical....Nor is Willingham's story an example of official indifference. Harvard did not ignore her complaints; the school thoroughly investigated them." So did local prosecutors. Like Harvard, the grand jury that heard the case did not credit Willingham's rape claim, a claim that "almost destroyed the life of the accused, a young black man with no previous record of criminal behavior."[44]

When 19 Harvard Law School professors—people familiar with both the law and the facts of the Winston case, and including prominent feminists—castigated the film's misrepresentations of fact and hostility to due process, Dick and Ziering lashed out. They accused the professors of creating a hostile environment for alleged victims of sexual assault and attacked the Harvard Law faculty for defending "white male privilege."[45] (Brandon Winston is black, as are three of the 19 professors who defended him.)

A *Huffington Post* op-ed by Dick and Ziering contained no fewer than seven errors of fact, ranging from a false assertion that the Harvard Law School professors were involved with a website put together by Winston's defense lawyers to a false assertion that Winston had admitted guilt.[46] Dick and Ziering refused to acknowledge (much less correct) their errors. In a rare display of mainstream media common sense, *Variety*'s Ella Taylor dismissed the documentary as "a loaded piece of agitprop that plays fast and loose with statistics and our sympathy with victims of campus sexual assault." It was, she added, characterized by "death-defying leaps of logic on the basis of skimpy and distorted evidence."[47]

Yoffe's deconstruction of *The Hunting Ground* was consistent with her 2013 article advising college women to consider self-protection by avoiding excessive consumption of alcohol,[48] a piece that had provoked a tidal wave of vitriol from feminists in *The Huffington Post, The Atlantic,*

The New Republic, Salon, New York, The Daily Mail, Feministing, Jezebel, and elsewhere, especially social media. Columnist Jessica Valenti had tweeted that Yoffe's article had "made the world a little bit safer for rapists" (@JessicaValenti, October 16, 2013). Yale activist and Know Your IX cofounder Alexandra Brodsky had tweeted that "there is a special place in hell for women who are Emily Yoffe" (@azbrodsky, December 8, 2014).

Why? Because Yoffe's advice ran afoul of the consensus that focusing on self-protection would distract attention from the cause of punishing accused students.

The attacks on Yoffe help explain why so many journalists shy away from anything at which accusers' rights activists might take offense. But the attacks did not deter Yoffe from producing, in December 2014, what remains the single most impressive essay on the sexual assault panic, an 11,600-word article in *Slate*.[49]

"The College Rape Overcorrection" opened with an incident that had previously received no national attention: In March 2012, a University of Michigan engineering student named Drew Sterrett spent a night socializing and drinking with his floormates. A female acquaintance, Carol Betros,* asked whether she could spend the night in his room. He agreed, and she crawled into his bed; they soon started to have sex. Sterrett's roommate texted him from the top bunk, "Dude, you and [Betros] are being abnoxtiously [*sic*] loud and inconsiderate, so expect to pay back in full tomorrow."

Five months passed. When Betros went home for the summer, her mother found her diary, which discussed her drug and alcohol use and her sexual encounters. Betros phoned her roommate, claiming (for the first time) that the encounter with Sterrett about which her mother had learned was nonconsensual. She asked the roommate to back up her new story. Soon the mother filed a sexual assault complaint with the university.

In August, a university official named Heather Cowan arranged a Skype session with Sterrett, who was home for the summer and wholly unaware of Betros' allegation. When Cowan and another university official started interrogating Sterrett, he realized what Betros must have said, and he asked for time to consult a lawyer. He was told that he must submit to interrogation immediately or he would be faulted for noncooperation while the investigation continued without his input. Thus threatened, he answered the questions.

University officials chose to believe Betros, based in large part on two unidentified witnesses who said that she had told them that she had tried to "push the Respondent off her." But later—when Betros had to testify under oath, under penalty of perjury—she admitted that she had never said such a thing. Betros' roommate also later testified under oath that Betros' mother had telephoned the roommate to pressure her to say, falsely, that Betros' behavior had changed dramatically after the evening of the alleged rape.

University investigators not only missed these critical facts but also discounted the word of Sterrett's roommate, who swore in an affidavit about hearing the loud sexual encounter in the bunk below him and specified that Betros never said "no" or anything else suggesting lack of consent.

Sterrett sued the university for violating his constitutional due-process rights and Title IX's prohibition of gender discrimination. After part of the lawsuit survived a motion to dismiss, the case was settled, vacating the disciplinary ruling against him. Afterward, he transferred to another school.

Yoffe placed Sterrett's nightmarish experience in the context of "colleges, encouraged by federal officials, . . . instituting solutions to sexual violence against women that abrogate the civil rights of men." First, she dissected and discredited the statistical basis for the administration's view that college campuses are (in Yoffe's words) among "the most dangerous places for a young woman in America today." She added a dose of common sense: Could it be, she wondered, that "young American college women are raped at a rate similar to women in Congo, where rape has been used as a weapon of war"? The one-in-five claim implies that the answer to that question, absurdly, is yes.

"College students today are increasingly treated as a special sexual caste," observed Yoffe, "who unlike their peers out in the working world can't be relied upon to have sex without convoluted regulations that treat lovemaking as if it were a contract negotiation." Castigating the federal government for ignoring the role of alcohol in fueling campus sex, she suggested diminishing OCR's power, reestablishing a higher standard of proof in campus tribunals, recognizing the limits of academic studies before basing policy changes on them, and changing "the culture of discourse around sexual assault on campuses" to get people to understand that advocating due process is not the same as denying the reality of rape.[50]

Yoffe's article also discussed a case at Occidental College that came in the wake of the hysteria fanned by Richard Felch's work at *The Los Angeles Times*. In March 2015, in *Esquire*, Richard Dorment gave the same events some of the finest media coverage of any single case to date, a welcome but rare contrast to the record of the media as a whole.

As Dorment related, in September 2013, two first-year students who had just met had engaged in what the evidence showed to be very drunken but consensual sex. (*Esquire* did not identify either student, instead calling them "John" and "Jane.") In the run-up to the encounter, the eventual accuser texted a friend, "I'mgoingtohave sex now." She also texted the male student, John, to make sure he had a condom before she went to meet him in his room. The next day, the two twice bumped into each other and had a seemingly cordial discussion.[51]

But, upon reflection, the evening's events upset Jane. Eventually she found her way to the same professor Danielle Dirks who had told *New York* magazine that most male college students "are calculated predators." Dirks convinced Jane that she had been raped because she had been impaired by alcohol. According to Jane, Dirks also said that John "fit the profile of other rapists on campus in that he had a high GPA in high school, was his class valedictorian, was on a [sports] team, and was 'from a good family.'"

That's worth repeating: An Occidental professor, still in good standing, persuaded a first-year student who was upset about having had drunken sex that she had been raped—and that the male student with whom she had slept "fit the profile of other rapists on campus in that he had a high GPA in high school, was his class valedictorian, was on a [sports] team, and was 'from a good family.'" Dirks later claimed that Jane had misquoted her. But the professor did not indicate who, if not she, might have given Jane that idea.

Taking Dirks' advice, Jane filed charges with police. A female LAPD officer spoke with Jane and other witnesses (but not with John, who declined a police interview on advice of counsel). She wrote for her files that they "agreed that the [alleged] victim and suspect were both drunk, however, that they were both willing participants exercising bad judgment." The officer told Dorment that "these really bad text messages…supported a consensual encounter." A female prosecutor reviewed the file and agreed.

In the upside-down world of campus sexual assault, however, evidence and logic often do not prevail. Occidental, for reasons it has refused to explain, denied John a hearing before a panel and instead announced that his case would be heard by a single adjudicator, a local lawyer named Marilou Mirkovich. The college's policies prohibited the accused from having a lawyer present. The adjudicator concluded that Jane had been too drunk to give consent and, therefore, that John had committed sexual assault—despite the text-message evidence that Jane had planned sex and consented *in writing*. Mirkovich added that John's own intoxication was irrelevant. The college, which was facing an OCR investigation, expelled John. He tried to transfer to another school, but his acceptance was rescinded once that school learned of Occidental's decision.

John then filed a lawsuit against Occidental in state court. While still pending at the time of this writing (September 2016), the case has brought to light documents confirming Dorment's narrative. It turns out that in the disciplinary process, the college's adjudicator, Mirkovich, vetoed all but nine of the 38 questions requested by the accused, who was not allowed to cross-examine Jane himself. The same adjudicator concluded that the accuser must have been incapacitated because taking off her shirt was something "that she would not normally do," thereby proving that "her decision making was significantly impaired."[52]

Remarkably, OCR concluded its investigation of Occidental by endorsing its sexual assault procedures. A June 2016 resolution letter celebrated the college's decision "to eliminate the hearing panel" in cases of alleged sexual assault, even as John's case showed the dangers of that approach. OCR also upheld Occidental's refusal to vacate its findings branding two students as rapists even after it was forced to admit that their adjudications had been procedurally unfair. The office claimed that Occidental's expedient of lessening the original punishment successfully balanced "the due process rights of the respondent with the rights of the complainant."[53] But, as FIRE's Susan Kruth pointed out, "a reduction in punishment is not the correct solution," because the admitted procedural errors had cast doubt on "the accuracy of the outcome."[54]

A few other journalists have exposed the inner workings of campus tribunals. In December 2013, *The Wall Street Journal's* James Taranto examined the fate of Joshua Strange, a student at Alabama's Auburn University. After a bad breakup, a girlfriend with whom he had been living accused Strange of sexual assault in reports both to the police and to the university. A grand jury found no probable cause to prosecute for sexual assault, but the university's disciplinary process found Strange guilty.

Taranto obtained an audio recording of Strange's Auburn hearing, giving him the first detailed look inside a secret campus hearing since OCR revolutionized discipline for alleged sexual assault in 2011. "The most striking quality of the 99-minute proceeding is its abject lack of professionalism," Taranto wrote. A de facto presumption of guilt hung over the whole process. Not only was Strange barred from cross-examining his accuser, he was separated from her by a curtain. The presiding officer, an Auburn librarian, seemed uncertain of the rules. She deferred to assembled Auburn administrators such as Susan McCallister, who pronounced the accuser credible based on a previous discussion with her. At the same time, McCallister admitted in testimony that "I really don't need to know a lot of details, and so I didn't ask her to go into great detail. I don't really want survivors to have to tell their story over and over again."

Auburn's way of testing the accuser's credibility was to disregard evidence casting doubt on it. Sexual assault victims "frequently cry," and their "storytelling is sometimes disjointed, sometimes not," and "there's often a lot of emotion inserted into the story that is about being very upset or in disbelief or unsure what to do next, petrified," Title IX administrator Kelley Taylor told the panel. Since the latter two conditions apply to virtually any circumstance, true or false, Taranto recognized that Auburn's standards "amounted to a claim that in principle a woman's tears are sufficient to establish a man's guilt—an inane stereotype that infantilizes women in the interest of vilifying men."[55]

"This is the kind of story I became a journalist to write," Taranto tweeted when it was published (@jamestaranto, December 6, 2013). But the article enraged Andrea Gabor, of Baruch College's journalism department and formerly of *Business Week* and *U.S. News & World Report*. She dismissed Strange's story as an "anecdote" that did not reach "the level of 'importance.'" With "so much injustice," Gabor wondered, why was Taranto "focusing on this"? Taranto responded: "Because it's a hell of a good story, and important. I have to explain that to a journalism prof?" Gabor then sank to a sorry cliché—"Pity the poor men," she tweeted—and to twisting the truth, as in her insinuation that Taranto's "point is rapists sh[ou]ld NOT get expelled."[56]

The record since 2011 suggests that Gabor's approach to reporting on campus due process reflects the journalistic norm. In this environment, Yoffe's and Dorment's pieces were unusual in presenting the stories not only of accusers but also of the accused and painting them as real people with whom readers could empathize. Drew Sterrett at Michigan and "John" at Occidental could be anyone's son, or brother, or nephew. Their lives were irreparably damaged by witch-hunt justice for doing what countless college students have done: having consensual (if later regretted) sex fueled by alcohol.

Yoffe and Dorment also took care to paint the *accusers* in these two cases as real people whose actions readers could understand, if not respect. The writers showed that absent outside intervention—from the accuser's mother in the Michigan case, and from the ideologue Dirks at Occidental—it's likely that neither of these students would have become an accuser at all. In any event, a fair-minded disciplinary system respectful of basic decency would have prevented them from wreaking havoc on the lives of innocent fellow students. The primary villains in these cases, Yoffe and Dorment made quite clear, were the colleges, which victimized their own students.

In some other cases, however, accusers have made undeniably false claims. These cases have received scant attention from the mainstream media except when previously publicized claims of depravity have conspicuously collapsed, as at Duke.

One example occurred in September 2012, when a female student leveled an accusation against Praise Martin-Oguike, a football player at Temple University in Philadelphia. Acting on this information, the university arrested and suspended Martin-Oguike. But more than a year later, both police and Martin-Oguike's lawyer obtained text messages contradicting the accuser's original story—on matters ranging from when she last had sex, to when she had suffered the injuries that she attributed to Martin-Oguike, to her anger when Martin-Oguike showed his reluctance to have a sexual relationship.

These texts persuaded the prosecutors to drop all charges, after which Temple ended Martin-Oguike's suspension. But that fell far short of making the falsely accused student whole again. As Martin-Oguike's lawyer stated, "After being branded as a rapist for a crime he did not commit, he was ostracized, stripped of his athletic scholarship, kicked out of Temple University and vilified nationally and online. The stain on his reputation and the impact on his life will never be completely erased."[57]

These events might have been seen as a newsworthy caution-ary tale. But the case received no mention in *The New York Times*, *USA Today*, and *The Los Angeles Times* and only a passing mention on *Washingtonpost.com*. The campus rape–obsessed *Huffington Post* ran a 127-word wire-service story. *The Philadelphia Daily News*, which could not so easily ignore the collapse of a local rape claim that it had previ-ously publicized, continued to shield the accuser's identity, based on a policy of not publishing the names of "alleged victims" of sexual assault.

The media were similarly uninterested in the collapse of the May 2015 claim by a University of Minnesota student that two men had threatened her with a knife, forced their way into her dorm room, and raped her. University police reviewed surveillance video from the dorm, and three days later the accuser changed her story. The police announced that their investigation had shown there was "no immediate and ongoing threat to public safety." Rather than charging the accuser with lying to campus police, a university official, Katie Eichele, contin-ued to claim that "the victim-survivor" was "the most important person in all of this. The university therefore would be "supporting what it is they're going through and what they may want in the process." But this accuser was, of course, neither "victim" nor "survivor." The case received no mention in *The New York Times*, *The Washington Post*, or any of the other above-named news outlets. The campus newspaper, *The Minnesota Daily*, continued to describe the false accuser as "the victim."[58]

In 2002, Brian Banks, a high school senior, was headed to USC as a highly recruited linebacker—when a classmate, Wanetta Gibson, accused him of rape. He accepted a plea deal and went to prison for five years. But the allegation was false, and Gibson, who had received a $1.5 million settlement from the school district, eventually recanted. The story attracted national attention on the sports pages when Banks tried in 2012 to revive his interrupted football career. He won tryouts with the Seahawks, Falcons, and Bengals, but he didn't make a team.[59]

That's a big story for straight news coverage, one might think. But apart from publishing material from the AP wire, *The Huffington Post* confined the Banks case to its "Black Lives" section. The most prominent discussion in the *Times*, meanwhile, came in a May 2015 column by Nicholas Kristof. Kristof cited Jon Krakauer to claim that whatever sympathy people might feel toward Banks, "far more common is another kind of injustice: perpetrators of rape who get away with it again and again." Kristof used the falsely accused Banks' suffering to hail both David Lisak's serial-rapist theory and his "careful study" claiming that false accusations of rape are very rare.[60]

One of the most troubling false campus accusations came to light in February 2010, when a University of North Dakota student claimed (both to local police and to the university) that fellow undergraduate Caleb Warner had raped her two months previously. The university responded by putting Warner through a cursory investigation without interviewing any of the witnesses who supported him.

Two days later, while the Director of the Women's Center sat with a comforting arm around the weeping accuser, the 22-year-old Warner was prosecuted by the dean of students in front of the university's general counsel and a six-person panel. Warner's lawyer could not participate in the hearing (although he was present). The university's counsel dismissed Warner's witnesses by saying that fraternity brothers were known to lie for each other. He "was found guilty and immediately expelled upon pain of arrest if he was found on the campus," recalls his mother, Sherry Warner-Seefeld.[61]

Then, suddenly, Warner was vindicated by the police investigation, which concluded with criminal charges against his accuser for making a false report.

But Warner's exoneration by law enforcement did not sway the university to grant his request for a new disciplinary hearing. Instead, according to its associate general counsel, Julie Ann Evans, the criminal charges against the accuser for a false report did not constitute "substantial new evidence" because she had testified to the university's disciplinary panel.[62]

Despite the rare criminal charges against Warner's accuser, once again the case was ignored by *The New York Times* and the other above-named news outlets, excepting a brief summary in a long Associated Press story about Title IX. Although noting that police had charged the accuser with filing a false report, the AP reporter, Justin Pope, did not identify her, because the "AP's policy is not to identify alleged sexual assault victims."[63]

It took a major media campaign by Warner's mother, plus a threat to sue the university, to "shame UND into doing the right thing," Warner-Seefeld recalls. "This was a state of about 685,000 people in 2011, and I made some significant noise.... UND administrators were fielding calls from people they knew and received lots of pressure to resolve the case."[64] The campus civil liberties group FIRE and a *Wall Street Journal* op-ed by FIRE cofounder Harvey Silverglate helped bring national attention to the university's conduct.[65] Finally, in October 2011—*17 months* after the prosecutor's false report charge—the university vacated its decision against Warner.

But like other schools whose policies regarding sexual misconduct have led to injustices, the university showed no interest in providing more due-process protections to prevent future injustices. Nor did UND appear to have changed the view expressed by Julie Ann Evans, in her May 2011 letter, that the university's process had worked as intended.

Rather than allow the experience to embitter her, Warner-Seefeld joined Judith Grossman, Jean Barish, and Allison Strange in founding Families Advocating for Campus Equality (FACE). FACE has advocated in Congress and elsewhere for legal and other reforms to achieve a semblance of justice for wrongly accused students.

The next chapter will take a closer look at how other colleges have outstripped in unfairness even the guilt-presuming commands of OCR's 2011 Dear Colleague letter.

6

THE WITCH-HUNT
MENTALITY

I n a July 2015 ruling, San Diego County Superior Court Judge Joel
Pressman made clear how far one university—hardly atypically—
had gone even beyond the demands of the Obama administration
and state law. Vacating a University of California–San Diego decision
finding an almost certainly innocent student to be guilty of sexual
assault, Pressman, who had been appointed by Democratic governor
Gray Davis, denounced the "fundamental unfairness" of UCSD's
procedures.[1]

The background: In late January 2014, a UCSD junior, Brian
Cohen,* and fellow student Mary Burke* got together after an event
on "Spirit Night," the culmination of a weeklong celebration of campus
spirit. They exchanged flirtatious texts and had sex several times. On the
afternoon of January 31, the 19-year-old Burke texted Cohen, who was
a year older, to make plans for the evening. She had only "a third of a
fifth of Captain" because "the guy who usually buys us alcohol is out of
town," but "as long as I don't get in trouble you can do what you want
haha." They had intercourse that night. The next evening, they went
to a formal at Burke's sorority and had intercourse again. That marked
the end of the sexual relationship, though they texted cordially over

the next few months about their grades in a common course and about attending a pregame party.

During the spring of 2014, Burke, a Mormon, began having personal problems. In March, she was arrested for underage drinking. Her cousin then told her family about her having slept with Cohen. When her parents found out that she had thus deviated from Mormon doctrine, they ordered her to come home on weekends. The tipping point came on May 14, after Cohen showed up at a social event at Burke's sorority on the arm of one of her sorority sisters. Burke was displeased, and she let Cohen know it. Others at the party told him that Burke had said he had raped her. In an angry text message to Burke, he said "that's a serious accusation to make and it's not okay," adding, "far from the truth."

Three weeks later, Burke filed a written complaint with UCSD alleging that Cohen had sexually assaulted her. She never went to the police, although she claimed in her statement to UCSD that Cohen "broke the law and he has to pay the consequences for it." Elena Acevedo Dalcourt, a UCSD investigator, interviewed her. In a second written statement, she asserted that although she had "brought a change of clothes to his place" with the expectation of sleeping over, the sex on January 31 had been involuntary because she had been too intoxicated to consent. She was "inexperienced" with alcohol, and this occasion was only "the second or third time I had drank," she wrote, despite her previous reference to "the guy who usually buys us alcohol."

Burke's new statement added an allegation that the morning after the alleged rape, Cohen "kept trying to move my underwear and touch me but I kept telling him that it hurt really badly and asked him to stop." It was weeks later, Burke added, that she decided—after researching "rape and consent" online—that she had been raped that night and assaulted by touching the next morning. She admitted that her sex with Cohen after the formal had been voluntary.

After interviewing 14 witnesses, Dalcourt rejected Burke's claim that she had been raped, finding that Burke had been sober enough to consent. But Dalcourt did find it more likely than not that Burke had not given "effective consent" the next morning for Cohen to touch her sexually. In Dalcourt's view, in interviews four months later, Burke exhibited "signs of a trauma victim." The investigator did not indicate what those signs were, and she never produced any notes of these interviews. Dalcourt refused to disclose Burke's specific allegations to Cohen or to his lawyer, Mark Hathaway.

Hathaway soon discovered that the UCSD investigative file that had been provided to Cohen contained neither Burke's initial statement nor the notes of Dalcourt's initial interview of Burke or the 14 witness interviews. The university contended that it did not need to provide these materials to Cohen because it had not shared them with the UCSD disciplinary panel either. UCSD added that the investigator's interview notes made no mention of Cohen's alleged morning-after sexual assault by touching, the sole basis for the charges that Cohen now faced.

Cohen's disciplinary hearing took place on December 12, 2014, before a panel of two UCSD administrators and a graduate student.

Shielded behind a partition, her demeanor invisible, was Burke. She had a victims' advocate at her side. UCSD official Anthony Jakubisin presented her case. Cohen's lawyer, Hathaway, was prohibited from speaking. Jakubisin opened by arguing that Cohen's "prior sexual misconduct"—Burke's claim of rape, which the UCSD investigator *had found no evidence to substantiate*—"seriously undermines" his claim of innocence. Jakubisin then asked Burke to describe how intoxicated she had been that night.

Burke, the sole witness, said five times that Cohen had been "trying" to digitally penetrate her without her consent. In her report, however, Dalcourt had written that Burke told her Cohen *had* digitally penetrated her without her consent. Jakubisin did not explore this contradiction.

Cohen and his lawyer were prohibited from cross-examining Burke, and Dalcourt did not even appear before the panel. In his defense, Cohen could only submit questions for the panel to ask. As criminal defense lawyer and civil libertarian blogger Scott Greenfield has pointed out, "Questions beget answers, and answers beget more questions.... No one can effectively confront an accuser without hearing her answers and following up."[2]

Panel chair Rebecca Otten, UCSD's director of housing allocations, refused to ask 23 of the 32 questions that Cohen submitted. She omitted those concerning Burke's text messages, her claim of sexual assault and inexperience with alcohol, whether she had "been honest and forthright," and whether she had turned over "all relevant text messages" to

UCSD. The university later claimed that "due process" justified these omissions. Otten did not respond to our request for comment.

Cohen denied having had any sexual contact on the morning that Burke claimed he was "trying" to touch her. In his closing statement, Jakubisin twisted this testimony into an admission by Cohen that contact had occurred but that Burke had consented. The panel members let this misrepresentation pass unremarked, and Cohen's lawyer was unable to object.

The panel found that Burke "stated that she physically wanted to have sex with [Cohen] but mentally wouldn't." On this theory, the panel found Cohen guilty of sexual assault and recommended a suspension for one academic quarter. When he appealed, Dean Sherry Mallory ratcheted up the penalty to a one-year suspension, plus additional sanctions. When he appealed again, to a council of the university's provosts, they increased the penalty to a year and a quarter, without explanation.

Nothing in UCSD's legal filings or public statements explained why the university had chosen to go beyond even OCR's mandates for sexual assault hearings. OCR did not require concealing an investigator's notes from the accused, or gagging the accused's lawyer as evidence was misrepresented, or having accusers testify only from behind a partition. Or suppressing fair questions undermining an accusation, or penalizing the accused for questioning the process and exercising his rights.

Although Pressman respected "the university's determination to address sexual abuse and violence on its campus," he found that UCSD had violated Cohen's fundamental rights: "The limiting of the questions in this case curtailed the right of confrontation crucial to any definition of a fair hearing." Pressman noted that UCSD's investigator never testified, could not be cross-examined, and had her notes of witness interviews concealed from the accused. He faulted the panel for treating the alleged assault by touching on the morning of February 1, 2015, as though it were an isolated event rather than part of the "entire narrative" of the relationship. Pressman added that Burke's "own mental reservations alone cannot be imputed to petitioner [Cohen], particularly if she is indicating physically she wants to have sex." Finally, he found that "the university abused its discretion in increasing sanctions after appeal without explanation."

Less than three weeks after the decision, UC chancellor Janet Napolitano, the former Arizona governor who served as Barack Obama's first Homeland Security Secretary, testified about campus sexual assault before the Senate Health, Education, Labor, and Pensions Committee. Sen. Lamar Alexander (R-Tennessee) asked her what schools could do to protect the due-process rights of the accuser *and* the accused. For several seconds, Napolitano didn't respond. Then she admitted that UC was "now" looking into this "difficult" matter. She *did* express confidence, however, that students accused of sexual assault on campus shouldn't have the same right to confront their accusers in campus disciplinary proceedings as in criminal trials.[3]

The university went on to appeal Pressman's decision, arguing that Cohen had "received the process he was due." It even claimed that the student had "had ample opportunity to present his defenses"—in a process that barred his lawyer from speaking, blocked most of the questions that he requested, and concealed the exculpatory evidence possessed by the university's investigator. At oral argument, the three appellate judges sounded unconvinced. One remarked, "When I...finished reading all the briefs in this case, my comment was, 'Where's the kangaroo?'" But the appeals court's written opinion, incredibly, sided with the university, allowing a kangaroo court for accused students.

College discipline has stinted on due process for decades, in part because schools tended not to adjudicate felony charges such as sexual assault, so the issue was not as pressing. And universities across the country had started to weaken due process for students accused of sexual assault even before the Dear Colleague letter ordered them to do so. Duke's policies, which we previously discussed, are one example.

In 2010, Stanford president John Hennessey approved a three-year pilot program called the "Alternate Review Process" (ARP) to adjudicate sexual assault claims, choosing law professor Michele Dauber to oversee the new procedures. She was of the activist view that the criminal justice system was intractably misogynist and thus not the best venue to deal with sexual assault cases. Complaining that rape prosecutions were "extremely rare," she castigated local prosecutors in 2013 for not bringing enough charges in "college acquaintance rape cases." The university needed to "handle sensitive complaints" in a manner specifically "tailored" to address the "unique aspects" of the campus environment, she argued. "Talking about rape is scary" at universities, she told *The San Jose Mercury-News*—even though universities are perhaps the most welcoming institutions in the country for discussion of the issue in recent years.[4]

Before the adoption of ARP, Stanford's policy was already tilted against accused students. It held students "legally incapable of giving consent" if they were "intoxicated" by alcohol. To be even "friendlier to victims," Dauber eliminated the disciplinary hearing, which she dismissed as a "mock trial."[5] Instead, a disciplinary panel would meet "with each party separately" in a comfortable, living room–like setting. "Having the 18-year-old rape victim be cross-examined by the guy who raped her? That's just wrong, wrong, wrong," Dauber said in a 2014 interview in which she made clear she believed that all or most students accused of sexual assault were guilty as charged.[6]

Dauber's committee further tilted Stanford's scales against alleged perpetrators by allowing a finding of guilt without disciplinary panel unanimity. Rather than six months, alleged victims now had 24 months to file a sexual assault complaint. Investigations into complaints were accelerated, and punishments such as "removal from a position of trust or removing a student from housing" were meted out even for students who were found not guilty.[7]

Stanford provided special, guilt-presuming training for disciplinary panelists. The 2010–2011 training manual advised that "act[ing] persuasive and logical" or being "vague about events and omit[ting] details" should be considered signs of guilt in the accused. Panelists were told to be "very, very cautious in accepting a man's claim that he has been wrongly accused of abuse or violence." This guidance was put together by the Center for Relationship Abuse Awareness, which Stanford had hired as a consultant. The organization's founder, Nicole Beran, recalled in a 2014 essay that she wanted all ARP panelists "to stop blaming victims and start holding people who choose to rape accountable," as if the Stanford student body or staff members commonly felt otherwise.[8]

In 2013, one ARP student panelist so trained told the student government not to worry about due-process issues raised by Stanford Law

School professor and former federal appellate judge Michael McConnell. The student said his training had enabled him to perceive that every accused student he had encountered was guilty.[9]

These new procedures produced dramatic results: Stanford more than tripled its findings of guilt in sexual assault cases between 2010 and 2013. Yet outside observers were hard-pressed to see what many of the punished students had done wrong. In 2014, Dauber declared that all students found guilty under the ARP should be expelled. Citing the discredited work of David Lisak, she suggested that most were calculated serial rapists.[10]

Stanford made minor changes to its policies in 2016: it required a unanimous finding of guilt, reduced the number of panelists to three, and tightened its definition of sexual assault to more closely track California law. Dauber assailed the modifications, saying they would make Stanford "one of the most, if not the most, unfriendly schools for sexual violence survivors in the country."[11]

By this time, in any event, Dauber had diverted her attention to the Brock Turner case. A friend of the victim's family, Dauber sent a letter urging the court to impose a lengthy sentence on Turner, to deter other assaults on campus. "[A]t Stanford, assaults that are very similar to this case are unfortunately all too frequent," she claimed, and students who have committed sexual assault *typically* have participated in athletics." Dauber provided no evidence for either of these startling assertions, and we are aware of no evidence that would corroborate either claim.[12]

After Judge Aaron Persky ignored her unsolicited advice and gave Turner a six-month sentence that was widely denounced (by us, among others) as too lenient, Dauber became the point person in a campaign to recall the judge, employing a tactic associated almost exclusively with the far right in recent years. This effort drew rebukes from at least two federal judges, from the Santa Clara County Bar Association, from local public defenders, and from the California Judges Association. The latter organization cautioned that "our liberty and fundamental rights will be at risk if judges believe they must be more concerned with public reaction than with the fair and impartial application of the law."[13] But Dauber's efforts attracted substantial political support: the National Organization of Women, four Democratic members of the House, Democratic National Committee interim chair Donna Brazile, and former OCR head Russlynn Ali all publicly demanded that California voters recall Persky.[14]

The general path of events at Stanford typified that at most major institutions, with one exception: at the overwhelming majority of universities, training materials for people who mete out discipline for alleged sexual assault have been kept secret. Middlebury College in Vermont, along with Stanford, is one of the few whose training materials have been leaked. The company that Middlebury hired to train its officials, Margolis Healy, teaches that investigators must "start by believing" the accuser, not by "interrogat[ing]" her, and that a sexual assault investigation is "not the time for 'just the facts.'" It also suggests that a complainant should be called a "victim" or "survivor," never an "accuser."

These training materials, adopted in 2012, counsel that the accused student often is not "who he said he is." They demand that the investigator's report "not include...consensual language," any hint of "mutual participation" or of "inconsistencies with her story," or any conclusion that "the victim's account of the incident is not believable or credible to officers given her actions during and after the encounter with the suspect."[15] The materials mention the subsequently discredited work of "expert" David Lisak eight times.

It's hard to imagine, after reading these materials, how any accused student could ever be found not guilty at Middlebury. After one of us (KC Johnson) wrote about the Middlebury training materials on the blog *Minding the Campus*, they were removed from the Margolis Healy website.

Upon examining Harvard's training material, which is not public, Harvard Law School professor Janet Halley expressed concerns about its fairness. "The OCR insists," she wrote in 2015, "that all participants in the processing of sexual harassment complaints receive training that makes them competent to render prompt and equitable decisions and Harvard complies...PowerPoint slides shown to colleagues at Harvard Law School [show that] their required training...is 100% aimed to convince them to believe complainants, precisely when they seem unreliable and incoherent....Meanwhile, the immense social, cultural, and psychological differences that can affect the credibility and coherence of both parties' accounts do not seem, yet, to warrant any mention. On all of those, cultural incompetence is okay."[16]

Nancy Gertner echoed these concerns in a 2016 contribution to a *Yale Law Journal* forum. Hearing officers, the former federal judge noted, now had been instructed to "take into account the neurobiology of sexual trauma. This means that when an accuser's story is inconsistent, when her memory is fragmented, or when recall is slow or difficult, the hearing officer is supposed to understand that such evidence is consistent with the neurobiological impact of stress and emotional memories. But the opposite is also true: the hearing officer should understand that such characteristics may also be consistent with lack of credibility, evasiveness, and contrivance." Training that conditions the adjudicator to presume the first explanation is true—or training that denies the accused student an opportunity to "test narratives of misconduct [by] questioning the witness and probing for contradictions or improbable accounts"—risks wrongful results.[17]

We obtained the secret training material from a well-known eastern state university and found it similarly one-sided. The chief point of the training seems to be to prompt panelists to consider virtually any accused student guilty and virtually any accuser truthful, no matter the impression each party gives.

The section on accused students, which depends heavily on the discredited research of David Lisak, instructs panelists to discard the "myth" that false claims are common, noting that Lisak determined only 5.9 percent of incidents fell into this category. The training doesn't mention that beyond that total, nearly 60 percent of the cases in Lisak's study had unclear evidence or were unfounded claims (see chapter 2). The material also cites an unnamed "New York judge" in stating that the idea that false reports are common is one of the "false stereotypes applied to sexual assault."

The training material also accepts Lisak's unsupported serial rapist theory, noting that "typical" college rapists "plan and premeditate their attacks." Although they "may have many positive attributes such as talent, charm, and maturity," these students are monsters—"as likely to be serial and multifaceted offenders as incarcerated rapists." And college rapists are everywhere: They "may be popular or not, outgoing or quiet, great athletes or klutzes, top students or slackers." The material cautions panelists that accused students' testimony that they are innocent could actually be among the "subtler forms" of "victim blaming," which should be rejected.

The same training material seems intent on describing any behavior by an accuser—no matter how much it may seem to undermine her claims—as consistent with sexual assault. "Some complainants may have excellent recall of the details of a sexual assault while others may not," the material reminds panelists. Since victims "react in various and different ways," there is "no 'typical' or 'expected' universal pattern." An accuser's having been "impaired by alcohol" is, all by itself, enough to prove a rape charge. Her past sexual history, including with the defendant, is "irrelevant" to determining whether the accuser consented. Panelists in training are also cautioned against interpreting actions such as having "flashed intimate body parts" immediately before participating in sex as a sign of consent. Even an accuser's failure to remember anything at all about the incident might not require a not-guilty finding.

The call for increased training also has included demands for restructured orientation sessions for new students. Donna*, a junior at a small college in the East, gave one of us (Stuart Taylor) a revealing description of what her school's officials taught her and her fellow students.

"Sexual assault is very real and happens all the time," she understood. But she said she did not like the dire picture painted by college officials or the views on gender issues that they instilled in first-year students during several required seminars.

"The way it's presented," she said, "if you're a young woman, you probably have been or will be sexually assaulted. It's a scary thing to hear, and it's not fair.... If he held your hand and you didn't like it, he sexually assaulted you. I've been kissed six or seven times when I didn't expect it and he thought I would like it. Am I supposed to report him for sexual assault? Unconsented hand-holding or a test kiss, it's the nature of romance. It's being a young person. There can't be these barriers to living a human life. We're all adults who make decisions for ourselves every single day." But in the views of college bureaucrats, said Donna, "You can say yes at the time, and maybe four days later change your mind and make sexual assault charges." Her school has a 7,300-word sexual misconduct policy, presided over by a Title IX coordinator. Donna recalled that "the way [the coordinator] presented it, her job is to find boys guilty of sexual assaults."

"Moderates are not acceptable in their crusade," Donna said. "They expect a very blind obedience to this feminist movement. I think it's an anti-feminist movement. They treat women as helpless victims. There is no critical thinking."

As a result of such training and new rules at American universities, guilty findings predictably increased—especially at elite institutions, where the recent procedural changes have had the greatest effect. Cornell University, in Ithaca, New York, the first elite university to fully implement the Obama administration's April 2011 marching orders, created a two-tier disciplinary system that gave students charged with the most serious offense—sexual assault—the weakest procedural protections. When facing charges of plagiarism or petty vandalism, a Cornell student was allowed to cross-examine the person accusing him, and there needed to be "clear and convincing evidence" (roughly a 75 or 80 percent probability) of his guilt. But when facing a sexual assault accusation, the student was not allowed to question his accuser (as Cornell applied OCR's guidance) and might be found guilty so long as the accusation was deemed 50.01 percent true. The university's judicial administrator, a former legal aid attorney named Mary Beth Grant, told *The Cornell Daily Sun* that she hoped more sexual assault complaints would be made.[18]

A contingent of Cornell Law School professors resisted the new procedures. Cynthia Bowman, a specialist in family law and feminist jurisprudence, argued that fairness "requires a rigorous standard of proof and many due process protections." She said, "There is general agreement among faculty at the Law School that the procedures being proposed are Orwellian." Added Kevin Clermont, an expert on litigation procedures: "Not all would characterize the procedure as Orwellian; some have used instead the term Kafkaesque. Across the political spectrum, law professors are in agreement that such an administrative procedure is fundamentally unfair."[19] Other Cornell law professors, sensing danger, kept their heads down as the Cornell administration adopted the new policy.

One of the first students disciplined under the new policy, a Cornell senior named Vito Prasad, sued the school for sex discrimination against him in violation of Title IX. In a February 2016 preliminary ruling, U.S. District Court Judge Thomas McAvoy rejected Cornell's motion to dismiss the case. Expressing concerns much like those of professors Clermont and Bowman, McAvoy said that, based on the limited record before him, an argument could be made that Cornell had "seemingly slanted" the process against Prasad by treating his accuser, Angela

Long,* "more favorably." He skeptically noted Cornell's estimate that the accuser's blood alcohol content might have been as high as a nearly fatal 0.43—even though several witnesses said she had behaved normally at the party at which the two had met. McAvoy also seemed troubled by the investigator's claim that Long's invitation to Prasad to spend the night in her room was due to her family's "sailboat community ideals" and not to a desire to have sex.[20]

Prasad's treatment by Cornell was hardly atypical. In May 2015, Cornell's judicial codes counselor, Amanda Minikus, produced an 80-page report, most of which explained the shortcomings of how Cornell had handled sexual assault allegations during the 2013–2014 academic year. (The office of judicial codes counselor, which is independent of the Cornell administration, provides advice to students accused of disciplinary offenses.) "In its efforts to swiftly revise its procedures and crack down on sexual misconduct," Minikus concluded, "Cornell has implemented policy far beyond what is necessary to comply with OCR's guidance and created a process fraught with inequities." Accused students had no right to remain silent. They had no right to a hearing. They couldn't cross-examine their accuser, even indirectly. They had no right to the evidence gathered by the investigator—on grounds that this constitutes "work product." (After complaints, Cornell agreed to provide accused students with an "edited" version of this critical evidence.) Minikus also worried about the "immediate and severe" effects of pre-adjudication interim punishments, noting that on at least one occasion, Cornell had suspended an accused student because the accuser had said she "disliked" him. Minikus' office discovered that the training Cornell offered to investigators "*assumed* a sexual assault occurred." Finally, Minikus worried about the "troubling" dynamics of a year in which every student accused of sexual assault was male and every investigator was female.[21]

Though it has done nothing to advance fairness, the federal government's assault on due process has served as a jobs program for former OCR officials. The University of North Carolina, for example, created seven full-time positions solely for Title IX compliance. Initially headed by former OCR lawyer Howard Kallem, these new employees earned a collective $541,833 in 2015, with salary hikes expected into the indefinite future.[22] Kallem told the Pope Center's Harry Painter that "we're not getting enough" sexual assault complaints—taking the view that success would consist of "an increase" in complaints.[23]

UNC also paid $160,000 for a consultant to develop a new sexual assault adjudication policy.[24] The recommended changes increased the chance of a guilty finding and seemed designed to neutralize a 2013 North Carolina law requiring institutions to allow accused students to hire lawyers. Under the new rules, an investigator overseen by the Title IX office investigates allegations, interviews witnesses, and drafts a report. The lawyer for the accused can access this material only by viewing it on campus, with no photocopying allowed. A three-person disciplinary panel conducts a hearing that, as required by state law, the accused's lawyer may attend, but UNC rules specify that he or she cannot question or address the accuser. The panel chair also can halt questioning of any other witness if in the chair's view the questioning would be "unduly intimidating or burdensome." The accused can be found guilty of sexual assault even if one of the three panel members dissents. The Dear Colleague letter had specified none of these rules.[25]

The guilt-presuming ideology demonstrated by UNC's new procedures is hardly confined to Chapel Hill. In July 2011, Dartmouth College, in New Hampshire, hired Amanda Childress as its Sexual Assault Awareness Program coordinator. In an address to a February 2014 conference, Childress reasoned: "Why could we not expel a student based on an allegation? It seems to me that we value fair and equitable processes more than we value the safety of our students. And higher education is not a right. Safety is a right. Higher education is a privilege."[26] Between 2010 and 2014, the number of staff members and administrators at Dartmouth increased by 14.6 percent, to 3,503, or 11.6 staffers for every new faculty member. Virtually all these new hires were in "community service, legal, arts, and media occupations" or "student and academic affairs."[27] A similar pattern is evident at many campuses.

Sexual assault allegation staffers are not representative of the university community in terms of gender. In 2013, the National Association of Scholars found that 82.7 percent of Title IX coordinators at 52 colleges and universities were female. At those schools that listed additional Title IX staff, 73.1 percent were female. With Title IX offices now acting as de facto investigatory agencies, the gender disparity is troubling—indeed, if the numbers were reversed, there surely would be Title IX complaints with OCR.[28]

Advocates cite campus safety to justify handling college sexual assault cases administratively on campus. As Senator Gillibrand explained during a 2015 appearance on MSNBC, a rape trial "could take a year or two...or three," forcing a victim to have to face her rapist every day on campus as the judicial process inched forward.[29]

But this claim is false; institutions are free to suspend a student who has been charged with a felony. Nearly all schools currently do so. There is no requirement that suspension await a final ruling of a criminal trial. Consider the following:

- In November 2014, a University of Wyoming graduate student, Jordan McGuire, allegedly raped an incapacitated fellow student at an off-campus party. The accuser complained to police that he thought McGuire had spiked his drink. The police investigated and arrested McGuire a few days later, and the university promptly suspended him.[30] McGuire, who had faced comparable charges in Illinois and Indiana, pleaded guilty to reduced charges after six months in jail awaiting trial.

- In July 2015, a Utah State student told police that she had been raped by a fellow student, Jason Relopez. The police immediately investigated and soon found two other students who said Relopez had also assaulted them. The police arrested Relopez at his fraternity house and charged him with seven counts of rape. The university suspended him. He later pled guilty to two counts and was sentenced to a year in jail.[31]

In September 2015, a University of Georgia student named Bamidele Oluwadare allegedly raped a fellow student, who filed a complaint the next morning and told police that "she repeatedly said no."[32] The Clarke County Sheriff's Office arrested Oluwadare that day. The university promptly barred Oluwadare from its campus.[33]

In October 2015, a SUNY-Oswego student told police she had been sexually assaulted by fellow student Adarsha Budhathoki. Budhathoki was arrested four days later. Oswego State president Deborah Stanley sent a campus-wide email implying that the school had suspended him.[34]

In February 2016, a female Cornell student told police that she had been sexually assaulted at a party hosted by the Psi Upsilon fraternity. The police investigated and arrested the fraternity's president, Wolfgang Ballinger, five days after the party. He was charged with attempted rape, first-degree criminal sexual act, and first-degree sexual abuse. Cornell suspended both Ballinger and the fraternity.[35]

If safety actually were the major concern of politicians like Gillibrand and campus activists, they would encourage students to report crimes to the police. Yet some politicians and campus activists have all but *discouraged* alleged victims of sexual assault from doing so.

As campus activists well understand, involving the police can pose a risk to the preferred narrative. Since the issuance of the Dear Colleague letter, no campus disciplinary process seems ever to have found an accuser guilty of making a false claim. (Yale, the only school to publicly report all sexual assault claims, refused to hear a false sexual assault claim made by a male student). Although criminal prosecutors are generally reluctant to charge accusers with filing a false claim, the fact that they *might* do so provides deterrence. Since 2010, a handful of college students, including two at the University of Arkansas, one at the University of Connecticut, and the University of North Dakota student who falsely accused Caleb Warner, have been charged for filing a false police report.

The most publicized such case came at the University of Wyoming. In April 2013, campus activist Meg Lanker-Simons told police that she had discovered an anonymous Facebook post that said: "I want to hate-fuck Meg Lanker—so hard. That chick that runs her liberal mouth all the time and doesn't care who knows it. I think its hot and it makes me angry. One night with me and she's gonna be a good Republican bitch." A campus "rape culture" protest ensued, with a university administrator thanking the crowd for attending and saying that "sometimes we feel when we challenge rape culture, when we feel like we've been targeted, we feel alone and feel like we're in the minority."[36]

It turned out that Lanker-Simons herself had written the Facebook post. Local police charged her with filing a false complaint, and she pleaded no contest. Rather than criticizing this hoax, a university spokesperson praised Lanker-Simons for sparking "an important discussion reaffirming that the UW community has no tolerance for sexual violence or violence of any type."[37] Lanker-Simons then moved on to attend law school.[38]

UW's indifference to false accusations seems typical. A case at Swarthmore, a suburban Philadelphia liberal arts college, illustrates how some college administrators, especially when panicked by Title IX complaints, react—even when the institution possesses information casting doubt on the accuser's veracity.

In 2013, Swarthmore's preexisting sexual assault policy was even more slanted than most. Accused students were allowed access to the college's evidentiary file only two days before the disciplinary hearing and could read the file only in a dean's office. They were barred from personally asking questions of their accusers. In an especially unusual twist, the college prevented them from sharing information about their cases with journalists *or lawyers* (unless their parents were attorneys).[39]

These policies did not prevent Swarthmore sexual assault accusers Mia Ferguson and Hope Blinn from filing a Title IX complaint against the college in April 2013. The duo informed OCR that Swarthmore administrators had mistreated them and that the college had a "culture of intimidation and silencing" and "a sexually hostile environment" in which "perpetrators of sexual violence, harassment, and intimidation are protected instead of held accountable."[40]

This claim was preposterous on its face. But it nonetheless seemed to terrify Swarthmore's leaders. President Rebecca Chopp announced with a flourish that the school would implement a "zero tolerance" policy—as if admitting the charge. Swarthmore also moved with special zeal to offer up a kind of human sacrifice to OCR by overturning a previous decision in favor of an almost certainly innocent student, Malcolm Burr.*[41]

Burr's case dated back to late April 2011, when he and fellow student Sarah Blatt* kissed, at a time when both were in relationships with people outside Swarthmore. On April 30, they had oral sex. The next day, Blatt confessed to her boyfriend, saying (by his account) that she had "acquiesce[d]" to sex while "drunk." This decision prompted the boyfriend to email Burr later that day.

"You are a worthless, disgusting individual, a narcissistic asshole," the boyfriend wrote, calling the incident "tantamount to rape." The boyfriend added that Burr was "lucky" Blatt had "dissuaded" him from "killing you outright, something which I very seriously considered (I live in Pennsylvania, and characteristically own a gun)." He went on to say that in the hope of "causing you pain," he would tell Burr's girlfriend "all about your little affairs" unless Burr confessed his infidelities.

Understandably rattled by these threats, Burr quickly sent a two-sentence reply, saying that he agreed—without specifying as to what—and had already called his girlfriend. Meanwhile, on learning of her boyfriend's threat, Blatt went to Burr's room to explain, where the two engaged in a conversation that somehow led to consensual sexual intercourse, their second intimate encounter in two days. Blatt asked Burr not to tell anyone what had happened, especially her boyfriend. Burr obliged.

Nineteen months later, in November 2012, when Blatt was studying abroad (and had become engaged to the gun-toting boyfriend) she suddenly filed a complaint against Burr with Swarthmore. She now claimed that her April 2011 kiss and oral sex with Burr—though not the subsequent sexual intercourse—were involuntary on her part. Swarthmore investigated and concluded that charges should not be filed against Burr. The college's Title IX coordinator, Sharmaine LaMar, emailed Burr to thank him for his cooperation.

Then came the April 2013 Ferguson-Blinn Title IX complaint and its negative press. The complaint had nothing to do with Burr. But it seems not to have been a coincidence that, on May 7, Swarthmore told Burr it was reopening his case. By this point, Blatt had changed her story from her November 2012 filing. She now claimed that Burr had used force in their first two encounters—the kiss and the April 30, 2011, oral sex—asserting that he had "attempted" (not "asked") to perform oral sex on her and then "forced" her to perform oral sex on him. Blatt added that the reason she had had sexual intercourse with Burr the next day was that she feared him.

Blatt's revised complaint provided a ready-made opportunity for Swarthmore to show obeisance to the rape-panic zeitgeist. The college convened a hearing after classes had ended, despite guidance that hearings should be held only during the semester. It added a sexual harassment claim two days before the hearing, despite college regulations saying that accused students should be informed of the charges "generally three days in advance." Swarthmore also concealed from

Burr his accuser's revised written statement and thus its conflicts with her earlier one.

Burr asked LaMar, Swarthmore's Title IX coordinator, to serve as his advocate, given her previous thanks to him for his cooperation. A college administrator rejected this request and said LaMar would not attend Burr's hearing. But LaMar did attend—to testify *against Burr*. The panel found Burr guilty, and he was expelled. President Chopp, who received the expected official notice that OCR had opened an investigation into Swarthmore a few days thereafter, rejected Burr's appeal.

Burr sued Swarthmore, and the college settled the case in November 2014. The agreement stated that the panel's finding and Burr's expulsion should be vacated because "additional information became available which both parties believe raises questions" about the disciplinary tribunal's impartiality. In fact, Swarthmore had known about, and apparently approved of, the unfairness of the process all along.

Burr had spent 18 months fighting the charges. He had had to defer his college education and had lost the opportunity to earn a prestigious Swarthmore degree. He transferred to a college in his home state of North Carolina.

Swarthmore and President Chopp learned little from Burr's mistreatment. After the April 2013 Title IX complaint, the college commissioned a review of its sexual misconduct policies by Margolis Healy, the same firm that counseled Middlebury investigators to ignore "inconsistencies with [the accuser's] story." Swarthmore implemented all of the firm's recommendations. As a result, this college of 1,542 students now has on staff a full-time Title IX coordinator, four Title IX deputy coordinators, and a Title IX fellow, who is responsible for helping "with events, resource development, and prevention education." These six administrators' offices occupy an entire building, which Swarthmore informally calls "Title IX House."

Swarthmore also hired a "violence prevention educator and advocate" and an additional public safety investigator. The latter trains other campus safety officials "on how to most effectively and sensitively respond to incidents of sexual misconduct." The office of the dean of students brought aboard an unspecified number of new staffers to provide support for resident advisors in addressing sexual assault and other issues.

Swarthmore must have committed well over half a million dollars a year for the salaries and benefits of the new campus accusers' rights crusaders.[42] It has convened more than 80 training sessions since 2013, including full-day and half-day Title IX sessions for faculty and staff. Additional funds went to a new sexual assault website, which hosts a new, required online course for first-year students, created in consultation with the Title IX coordinator.

Finally, in the aftermath of the Burr case, the college revised its misconduct policies—not to ensure greater fairness, but to better protect itself from lawsuits like Burr's. The 2015–2016 student handbook added a clause affirming that "rules of evidence ordinarily found in legal proceedings shall not be applied, nor shall any deviations from any of these prescribed procedures alone invalidate a decision, unless significant prejudice to a complaint, respondent, or the College may result."[43]

Burr was only the best-known victim of the moral panic that gripped the Swarthmore campus. In the 2013 calendar year alone, 63 rape allegations—up from three in 2010, six in 2011, and eight in 2012—were recorded at this college of fewer than 800 female undergraduates. Unless some accusers reported more than one rape, and assuming no false allegations, around 8 percent of Swarthmore's female undergraduates were rape victims.

A crisis of that magnitude would call for remedies far more drastic than hiring a few new administrators. The 2013 rape rate reported by Swarthmore for women on its suburban Philadelphia campus was more than *four times* the violent crime rate for Detroit, which FBI reports deem the nation's most dangerous city. And the Detroit number includes murders, aggravated assaults, and robberies as well as rapes.[44]

Similar panics have swept through other campuses. At Michigan Tech University, the vice president of student affairs, Les Cook, told the campus newspaper that the school's administration would follow OCR's guidance about Title IX to the letter. Displaying ignorance of the law, he remarked that "[the Constitution] doesn't supersede [Title IX]" and "Title IX is a federal compliance policy [that] supersedes anything else."[45] The University of Southern California required all students to complete a Title IX orientation program before they could register for courses. As part of this program, students had to fill out a questionnaire that grilled them on their sexual history. Program materials advised that any student accused of sexual assault should "admit" to himself that he "may have crossed a boundary," even if he did not think he had done anything wrong.[46]

Heather Mac Donald took a close look at one such orientation program, at Columbia. Called the "Sexual Respect and Community Citizenship Initiative," the program is required for all students. Students are directed to watch a video about "rape culture" or engage in a discussion about masculinity, after which they can "reflect on" profundities such as "the interaction of the constructs of manhood and power dynamics."

Students who identify themselves as "survivors" are channeled toward special "resiliency" sessions. One such session suggests exploring questions like this: "Kalin [a speaker in a video] shares his 'why' for passion around prevention education. What is his why? If you have a passion for prevention, 'what is your why'?"[47] The program does not mention the common role of alcohol in fueling unwise or regretted sex. That information might help students protect themselves—but would no doubt be attacked as "blaming the victim."

Universities have had particular trouble defining how alcohol invalidates consent to sex.[48] As one UNC administrator explained, "It feels to me that we are trying to catch a greased pig, because it comes down to the intent of an individual."[49] Among the alcohol-related policies of *U.S. News and World Report*'s 55 top-ranked universities, 5 avoid the issue, 32 reference incapacitation (the common legal standard), and 18 others brand an accused student a rapist if a disciplinary panel thinks it more likely than not that his *accuser* was "intoxicated," a standard most do not define.[50]

Dartmouth's policy states that "a 'yes' from an individual who is under the influence of alcohol or other drugs may not necessarily mean 'consent,'" since "use of alcohol or other drugs can cloud people's understanding of whether consent has been given (or even sought)."[51] The University of Pennsylvania defines sexual assault as "any physical sexual contact with a person who is unable to consent due to...being under the influence of alcohol."[52] The University of Wisconsin and many other schools essentially tell students that if they fear disciplinary trouble for "improper use of alcohol," they can get a free pass by accusing another student of sexual assault.[53] Conversely, Brown's policy suggests that if an *accused* student consumes any amount of alcohol before sex, even if he is 21 or over, that "will be considered an exacerbating rather than a mitigating circumstance."[54] So consuming alcohol has opposite effects depending on who accuses whom first.

In a 2010 letter to Duke president Richard Brodhead, FIRE explained why equating intoxicated sex with rape was intolerably vague: "On the vast majority of college campuses, a great number of students drink alcohol and then engage in consensual sexual activity. While this circumstance may be lamentable, it is undeniable. By failing to make a distinction between drinking to the point of incapacitation and mere intoxication, [this standard] turns what often is an unwise but ultimately personal decision, for which students should hold themselves responsible, into an episode of sexual misconduct subject to official punishment."[55]

Even NCHERM's Brett Sokolow remarked in April 2015 that "campuses ought to be more honest with their students" and that private schools, at least, could say, "'Our rule is you can't [have] sex if you've been drinking, and if you do, we'll kick you out.'"[56] But given the high percentage of students who drink, Sokolow's suggestion is unrealistic, except at sectarian schools that forbid alcohol based on religious doctrine.

Meanwhile, virtually every university faculty has accepted the assault on due process by the federal government and the universities. The honorable exceptions are a few law professors at Cornell, a group of law professors at Penn, and a striking 28 at Harvard Law School.

Facing a Title IX complaint, in 2014 Harvard University announced new sexual assault procedures and specified a single investigator who would also act as prosecutor, judge, jury, and appeals court—with no disciplinary hearing at all. The federal government has championed this "single investigator-adjudicator" approach, which is ostensibly designed to spare victims the trauma of testifying in disciplinary hearings—even though, before adjudication, it remains unclear which party (if any) is the victim. As U.S. District Judge F. Dennis Saylor noted in March 2016, "The dangers of combining in a single individual the power to investigate, prosecute, and convict, with little effective power of review, are obvious. No matter how well-intentioned, such a person may have preconceptions and biases, may make mistakes, and may reach premature conclusions."[57]

As occurs at most institutions that use the single investigator-adjudicator structure, Harvard's process keeps the alleged perpetrator in the dark by denying him access to the accuser's statement and specific allegations. It gives him one week, and only one chance, to offer his side of the story to the investigator. It limits him to providing "a list of all sources of information (for example, witnesses, correspondence, records, and the like) that the Respondent believes may be relevant to the investigation." But he can only guess at what might be relevant.

The single investigator-adjudicator—sometimes along with a representative from the accusing student's Harvard school, who must be cleared by the Title IX office—separately interviews the accuser, the accused, and other witnesses. The accused receives a redacted version of the evidence to be used against him. The investigator-adjudicator then prepares a document indicating whether he or she believes it more likely than not that the accused is guilty. The accused and the accuser have a week to respond to the written findings, and the accused *might* be allowed to present additional evidence. Then the investigator-adjudicator makes a final determination. If the investigator-adjudicator turns thumbs down, the accused goes before a panel that metes out his punishment; the panel cannot question the investigator's findings.

Most university policies have at least a loose statute of limitations on sexual assault. But Harvard allows a complaint to be filed at any time, even after the alleged victim or the alleged perpetrator or both have graduated. This rule raises a new host of problems for accused students. They might have to find witnesses who have long since graduated, documents likely to be buried in landfills, emails on Harvard accounts that expired after graduation, and text messages from years in the past. Harvard's policy is silent on what penalties the university might impose and whether they could include withdrawing an accused student's degree, banning him from campus, or contacting his employer.[58]

Harvard president Drew Faust lauded the new rules as a process that "will significantly enhance Harvard's ability to address these incidents when they occur."[59]

Twenty-eight current and emeritus members of the Harvard Law School faculty, in a letter in *The Boston Globe* on October 15, 2014, assailed Harvard's new policy as an evisceration of due process. The new rules, they declared, "lack the most basic elements of fairness and due process, are stacked against the accused, and are in no way required by Title IX law or regulation." The rules denied "adequate representation for the accused," especially poorer students; defined sexual harassment too broadly; promulgated arbitrary rules regarding sex while intoxicated; and denied accused students a meaningful right to see the relevant evidence. The law professors urged Harvard to stand up to the Obama administration, noting that if OCR followed through on its threat to withhold federal funds, "Harvard University is positioned as well as any academic institution in the country to stand up for principle in the face of funding threats."[60]

After the letter appeared, a Harvard spokesperson blandly remarked that "some believe the policies and procedures go too far; others believe that they do not go far enough." The document drew sharper criticism from Harvard's Title IX coordinator, Mia Karvonides, a former OCR lawyer, who expressed astonishment that anyone could think that her office's work was anything other than "neutral."[61] As one Law School signatory, Janet Halley, responded, "Karvonides is under immense pressure to increase the number of complaints filed and the number of people held responsible. This is structural. She can be and is a professional and an expert, but she can't undo that structure."[62]

Ultimately a compromise was reached, first with the university and then with OCR. The Law School was allowed to avoid this sprawling bureaucracy and develop its own sexual misconduct policy. As of the 2015–2016 academic year, any law student in the disciplinary process is allowed a lawyer, with the Law School providing counsel for students who can't afford one. An investigator gathers the evidence, and a panel of three people unaffiliated with Harvard hears the case. It is the fairest process adopted by any higher education institution facing OCR pressure, but it still uses the OCR-dictated "more probable than not" standard for adjudicating guilt, and it denies accused students and their lawyers the opportunity to directly cross-examine accusers. Instead, the lawyer must submit all questions for the accuser to the chair of the disciplinary panel, who has limited discretion to reject proposed questions.[63]

Four of the Harvard Law School signatories with strong feminist credentials—Nancy Gertner, Janet Halley, Elizabeth Bartholet, and Jeannie Suk Gersen—have continued to speak out about OCR's crusade.

In January 2015, Gertner wrote in a long article in the liberal *American Prospect* that OCR's demand that colleges use a "more probable than not" standard—coupled with the fact that many colleges concealed relevant evidence while restricting accused students' lawyers—had created "the worst of both worlds, the lowest standard of proof, coupled with the least protective procedures." She feared that the new system "effectively creates a presumption in favor of the woman complainant." Gertner cautioned fellow feminists to "be concerned about fair process, even in private institutions where the law does not require it, because we should be concerned about reliable findings of responsibility. We put our decades-long efforts to stop sexual violence at risk when men come forward and credibly claim they were wrongly accused."[64]

In response, Wendy Murphy—former Massachusetts prosecutor and adjunct professor at the New England School of Law—deemed Gertner "an advocate for accused sex offenders" and demanded that the law professor stop describing herself as a woman.[65] Know Your IX's Alexandra Brodsky sneered that Gertner was like "'men's rights activists' who harass campus survivors on Twitter."[66]

Janet Halley has taught gender and the law and queer theory and has edited volumes on the military's now-defunct anti-gay policy. But in a 2006 book, *Split Decisions*, she also lamented that feminism had "lost a certain power of critical thinking" regarding "what law really does in a complex society." That women were always subordinate to men, once true, is hardly true of today's college campuses, she said.[67] Feminists wield so much power that they led the successful campaign to oust one of the most powerful men in the academy, Harvard president Larry Summers, in 2006.

Commenting on the almost uniform hostility of campus feminists to urging female students to avoid dangerous situations, especially involving alcohol, Halley said she was "really troubled by this trend in which women are helpless and passive and men are the big responsible protectors. That's the ideology of the gilded cage. It's astonishing to see feminists reawakening it uncritically. If young people are going to have a robust role in creating the conditions they want to live in, feminists have to call off this ban on discussing the risks and the moral ambiguities that come up with excessive alcohol use."[68]

Halley played a key role in organizing the Harvard Law faculty's open letter, drafting a 26-page memo critiquing both OCR's policy and the new Harvard University procedures.[69] She added, in February 2015, a trenchant *Harvard Law Review* commentary contending that activists too often pressure schools "to hold students responsible for serious harm even when—precisely when—there can be no certainty about who is to blame for it." Such tactics, she said, "are core to every witch hunt." Noting that in "case after case, both the complainant and the respondent were voluntarily ingesting mind-altering substances," Halley said that Harvard University's policies amounted to "a per se rule in favor of the complainant and an irrebuttable presumption against the respondent." This "steep asymmetry between the consequences of drinking and drug use for the complainant and for the respondent," Halley cautioned, would disproportionately harm innocent students of color, given the criminal justice system's history of bias against black males accused of sex crimes.

There was, Halley acknowledged, a case for "biasing the system to favor women and disfavor men," because "in the campus drinking culture, men have more power than women." But such a policy "is not cost free," Halley warned. "It entails a decision to impose a serious moral stigma and life-altering penalties on men who may well be innocent. Doing this will, in turn, delegitimize the system. And it entails a commitment to the idea that women should not and do not bear any responsibility for the bad things that happen to them when they are voluntarily drunk, stoned, or both. This commitment cuts women off—in theory and in application—from assuming agency about their own lives. Since when was that a *feminist* idea?"[70]

These criticisms notwithstanding, the policy remains in place for all Harvard students other than those attending the Law School. Surveying the scene, FIRE cofounder Harvey Silverglate lamented that the "battle has been lost at the university level at Harvard, and virtually everywhere in academia."[71]

This chapter has portrayed a few examples of how today's universities—including some of the nation's top schools—are handling cases of alleged sexual assault. The motives of some defenders of the current campus disciplinary apparatus, such as Michele Dauber, are deeply troubling. But many administrators, in good faith, contend that colleges must handle questions of sexual misconduct, because their disciplinary system focuses not on whether the accused student is a criminal, but rather on whether his conduct was so dangerous or hurtful to other (mostly female) students that he should be removed from campus. Many administrators see the college system as all the more essential because, they believe, the criminal justice system fails to adequately protect students. In some cases, the victims don't want to subject themselves to the ordeal of a criminal investigation; in some cases, law enforcement does a poor job; and, in some cases, the burden of proving a sex crime beyond a reasonable doubt to a jury is so heavy (as it should be) that dangerous sexual predators cannot be convicted.

As well-intentioned as these views are, they do not justify the current system of campus sexual assault adjudication. First, whether an incident is treated as a crime, a civil tort, or a violation of the campus disciplinary code, the fundamental question remains the same: did student x engage in the alleged sexual aggression against student y? Whatever their faults, the criminal and civil justice systems have critical tools for helping people determine truth: courts can subpoena evidence and require testimony under oath. In addition, courts' decisions are public, and thus we can have some degree of confidence in the findings reached during their proceedings. Colleges and universities have none of these advantages. The case with which we began this book—in which Amherst College's failure to obtain critical text messages produced an unjust outcome—shows the dangers of allowing colleges to make life-altering decisions based on incomplete, and sometimes dramatically incomplete, evidence.

Second, university administrators who in other contexts are extraordinarily sensitive to the dangers of implicit bias seem not to worry about the problem at all when handling sexual assault allegations. Yet aside from some religious institutions, the typical college environment is one-sided—often extremely so—on gender questions. This is especially true of the Title IX, student life, and diversity offices that generally handle campus sexual assault allegations. Can people who seek and obtain such positions put aside their deeply held beliefs on gender issues in order to weigh evidence and make decisions fairly? And, of course, sometimes the bias is far more than implicit. Recall the three Ohio State University officials (in chapter 4) who could not answer "yes" when asked whether they considered it their job to get a correct outcome in sexual assault proceedings.

Third, politicians, the media, friends and colleagues, and employers have come to see the finding by a college that a student was responsible (by a mere preponderance of the evidence) for amorphous "sexual misconduct" as almost indistinguishable from the finding by a judge or jury that he was guilty beyond a reasonable doubt of rape. Campus activists and their media and political allies have convinced much of the nation that campuses are plagued by rampant sexual *assaults*, even though a great many accused students are expelled or disciplined for conduct that is *not* (even though colleges often call it "sexual assault") sexual assault as understood either by the law or in the broader culture.

In this new environment, more and more students judged by their colleges to have engaged in sexual misconduct—often either unproven or noncriminal or both—find themselves unable to transfer to other schools, where officials are understandably reluctant to admit anyone perceived to be a sexual predator. And even those students who can manage to get a degree from another college face life-altering consequences. As U.S. District Court Judge T. S. Ellis III recently observed in reversing a finding of sexual assault by George Mason University, if an accused student "seeks education or employment with institutions or organizations that require disclosure of such records, [his] only options are to forgo opportunities with those institutions or organizations or to authorize the dissemination of records that would likely foreclose [his] ability to pursue such opportunities because of the allegedly defamatory nature of the records."[72] The stakes, in short, have become too high to subject a student to campus discipline for alleged sexual misconduct that has not been proved in a legal process.

Finally, whatever their faults, the criminal and civil justice processes end with decisions by juries and judges who have no financial stake in the outcome of the case. The same can't be said about colleges and universities.[73] Any decision against an accuser can cost them lots of money (as well as generate bad publicity). An accuser's complaint to OCR against her college will at the very least consume years of staffing work (with all the associated costs) for the affected institution and could lead to the loss of millions of dollars in federal funds. By contrast, the worst-case scenario for a college that expels an innocent student for alleged sexual misconduct is a lawsuit leading to a court decision or a settlement two or three years down the road expunging the college's decision.

It's conventional wisdom that colleges and universities act in their own interest. Most of the time, in the current environment, this reality has led schools to establish procedures that favor sexual assault accusers. But in a discrete subset of cases—almost all involving football and basketball stars at universities where those sports bring in vast sums of money—institutions appear to have unfairly favored *accused* students, even in recent years. The next chapter will look at the complicated picture of universities' handling of sexual misconduct allegations against student-athletes.

7

COLLEGE ATHLETES: MYTHS AND REALITIES

Division I intercollegiate athletics often feature preferential treatment, from admitting athletes with poor academic records to relaxing requirements for retention and graduation—especially in the big-money sports, football and men's basketball. Star athletes in the Power Five conferences who are plausibly accused of rape have received unfair support from their colleges. But even some privileged athletes are not immune from being expelled based on dubious allegations.[1]

In 2012, Cincinnati's Xavier University expelled basketball star Dez Wells for, in its view, sexually assaulting a fellow student; yet a contemporaneous criminal investigation convinced the county prosecutor that the allegation was false and Xavier's disciplinary process "fundamentally unfair."

Xavier has one of the nation's top mid-major men's basketball programs. In 2010, the school scored a recruiting coup by signing Wells. He became the first Xavier freshman to start every game in more than a decade. Named conference freshman of the year, he helped lead Xavier to the NCAA Sweet Sixteen in March 2012. College athletic stardom was a heady experience for Wells, who had been raised with his two sisters in modest circumstances by a single mother in Raleigh, North Carolina.

On June 6, 2012, Wells took part in a game of truth or dare with other students, including Mary Grimes*, a resident advisor, in his dorm room. Alcohol flowed, and the game turned raunchy. On a dare, Grimes gave Wells a lap dance. The two also made out in front of the others, which is considered unprofessional behavior for a resident advisor. As the game ended, Grimes invited Wells to her dorm room, and they had sexual intercourse. They returned to his room around 5:15 a.m. to retrieve her cell phone. None of the other students who still were hanging around his room reported any problems.

A few hours later, Grimes went to campus police and claimed that Wells had raped her. Though a medical exam revealed no evidence of trauma, the campus police contacted the Cincinnati police, who referred the case to the office of Hamilton County prosecuting attorney Joseph Deters.

"I had two very veteran investigators and the chief of my criminal division interview her," recalled Deters in a phone interview with Stuart Taylor. "They came to me and said emphatically that there is no way this happened the way she said. They reported to me that she was not credible."

Stressing that the sentence for forcible rape in Ohio is nine years in prison, Deters—who became chief prosecuting attorney in 2004, after 22 years as a prosecutor—said the accuser had been so incredible that "there was . . . discussion of charging her with a crime." He and his staff decided against that option.

Deters reserved his harshest condemnation for the federal government. "Dez had never been in trouble in his life," the prosecutor told us. "What happened [at Xavier] in this case is a complete indictment of what the Department of Education has been doing . . . they are putting a gun to the universities' heads and demanding what amounts to a feminist agenda in which the accuser is always right and the accused is always guilty. . . . The accused are not allowed to be represented by lawyers. All the protections we have in the criminal process they get rid of. Even minimal levels of due process are out the window."

Added Deters: "I am not a defense lawyer. I have gone after bad guys my entire life, and if Dez did rape someone, we would be all over him.

But my job is to seek justice. What these people are doing is incredible. They have a hearing and they tell the accused, 'You can't have a lawyer.' How can this happen in America? It's disgusting."

Deters was also frustrated that Xavier's president, Father Michael Graham, would not talk to him about the case; university lawyers feared that OCR might accuse Xavier of "collusion" with law enforcement. Stressing that he did not blame Father Graham, who "felt that his hands were tied by the Department of Education," Deters said: "This is ridiculous bullshit. I'm the prosecuting attorney, and I can't talk to the president of the university about a law enforcement matter?"

When he finally did get to discuss the case with the university president, Deters recalled, "Father Graham said to me, 'We have to protect our students.' I said to him, 'Dez Wells is a student too.'" Since then, Deters said, Xavier and other nearby schools have agreed to "call us first" before starting the disciplinary process over allegations of rape or other serious crimes on campus.

But in 2012, when Deters asked Xavier to defer action against Wells until his office could complete its inquiry, Xavier refused. The people making the decisions were less concerned with doing justice, Deters said, than with appeasing the federal government, which was bearing down on the school over an unrelated case.

That unrelated case was Xavier's negotiation with OCR to resolve a Title IX complaint: When two female students accused a student named Sean Marron of sexual assaults in 2008 and 2009, an administrator suggested that, to spare all concerned the trouble of going through a hearing, Marron be given the option to simply leave the university. The accusers refused to allow it. In the hearing, Xavier found Marron culpable, and Marron was expelled in 2010. The accusers then complained to OCR about the administrator's suggestion.[2]

Marron's case was ambiguous. The accusers had gone to the police as well as Xavier's Title IX office, but in October 2011 Marron was found not guilty of any crime by a county judge, who cited inconsistencies in the accusers' stories, lack of evidence, and the long delay in the decision to come forward. Despite the outcome of the criminal trial, OCR agreed with the accusers—as it generally does. It presented Xavier with a resolution letter stressing that OCR would not "close the monitoring of this agreement until the university...is in compliance with Title IX."[3] The school signed the letter on July 23, 2012, while the Wells case was pending.

Xavier apparently feared that the federal officials would object if the school took the time necessary to treat Wells fairly, as the county prosecutor had requested. The school rushed ahead with a disciplinary proceeding against the basketball star.

So it was that in August 2012, Wells found himself with his future on the line, facing a five-member, faculty-student University Conduct Board. As in other cases, whether the accused was guilty or innocent, the rules made it hard for him to defend himself. He was not allowed to be represented by anyone with a law degree or even "specialized legal training." The rules also prohibited Wells from cross-examining Grimes.

There was no physical or medical evidence to corroborate Grimes' claim of rape. Xavier's Title IX coordinator, who presented the charges against Wells, told the board that she was "not trained to evaluate" how much doubt the lack of medical evidence might cast on the accuser's story. The hearing transcript shows that "these kids [on the conduct board] are looking at the rape kit and saying, 'I don't know what I'm looking at,'" prosecutor Deters told us with incredulity.

With nothing to go on but the accuser's word, and without even asking to see the evidence that had convinced Deters of Wells' innocence, the board found it more likely than not that Grimes was telling the truth and Wells was "responsible for rape." Xavier denied his appeal and announced publicly that the board had found Wells "responsible for a serious violation of the Code of Student Conduct." Everyone at Xavier, and far beyond, knew what that meant.

A few days after Xavier acted, and after hearing all of Deters' evidence, a grand jury found that there was no probable cause to believe that Wells had committed any crime. Deters then made public his personal view that Wells was not guilty. In a highly unusual move, since prosecutors rarely stand up for people accused of serious crimes, he also stated that Xavier had employed a "fundamentally unfair" procedure to expel Wells, and he urged the school to reconsider. With continued federal oversight looming, the university refused, saying that its disciplinary panel had "heard evidence that may or may not have been heard by the Grand Jury." But Xavier never identified any relevant evidence that Deters had not already considered.

Deters also spoke to the NCAA, prompting it to allow Wells to play immediately after he moved to the University of Maryland. This move was an unprecedented, if implicit, indictment of the unfairness of Xavier's actions. The NCAA habitually defers to colleges' disciplinary actions, and it requires Division I athletes who transfer to wait a year before playing for their new school.

Wells' exoneration by the criminal prosecutor and his vindication by the NCAA could not erase the stain of Xavier's actions. Opposing fans taunted him during road games. When Maryland played at Duke, fans chanted "no means no!" every time Wells touched the basketball.[4] Still, it was fortunate for Wells that Xavier, unlike most colleges, had referred the accusation against him to law enforcement. His exoneration by Deters—like the 2007 exonerations of the Duke lacrosse players by North Carolina Attorney General Roy Cooper—cleared his name in a way that would otherwise have been impossible. He graduated from Maryland in 2015 and is currently playing basketball professionally.

Cases in which star athletes might have gotten away with sexual misconduct have unfolded against a background of pervasive preferential treatment of athletes. Notre Dame football coach Brian Kelly remarked in 2015 that no more than one or two of his team's 100 players was academically qualified to be at Notre Dame without the athletic preference.[5] Harvard's men's basketball team, long a doormat of the Ivy League, flourished after Coach Tommy Amaker broadened Harvard's recruiting base, although the team's "Academic Progress Rate" plunged to the bottom of the league.[6] Following a story broken by the Raleigh *News and Observer* in 2011, it was revealed that the University of North Carolina's Department of African, African-American, and Diaspora Studies had, over a period of 18 years, let 1,500 athletes (along with 1,500 other students) enroll in no-show classes.[7]

Intercollegiate sports are big business. Especially in the Power Five conferences (ACC, SEC, Big Ten, Big XII, and Pac-12), student-athletes in revenue-producing sports often receive perks such as special dorms, lighter punishments, and even, on occasion, preferential disciplinary procedures. Until recently, universities in the South and the West often used teams of "hostesses"—with names such as the Bengal Babes, the Crimson Courters, the Hurricane Honeys, the Texas Angels, the Black-Eyed Susans, and the Tigerettes—to help recruit star football and basketball players. In the early 2000s, recruiting scandals at the University of Colorado and Arizona State University included allegations of rape.

One "hostess" recalled that a high-profile recruit basically demanded she have sex with him, telling her "The girls at Kentucky and Georgia did it."[8] The NCAA cracked down on such conduct in 2004 but still found it necessary to investigate the University of Tennessee in 2009 for using "hostesses" to recruit football players.[9] In 2015, the University of Louisville commenced an investigation into credible allegations that an official on the men's basketball staff hired women to perform exotic dances for and have sex with members of the team, at events held in a special dorm for men's basketball players.[10]

At some universities in the Power Five conferences, the pattern of special treatment, coupled with troubling gender norms, seems to have led administrators to show favoritism when star football and men's basketball players were accused of sexual assault or other violence against women.

- Between 2009 and 2012, five women informed officials at Texas' Baylor University that a defensive end on the football team, Tevin Elliott, had raped them. In one case profiled by ESPN, the victim, whom ESPN identified as "Tanya," was twice raped by Elliott at an off-campus party. Various Baylor officials told her they could do nothing about the allegation, since the incident had not happened on campus. In 2012, the accuser went to police, who arrested Elliott. Elliott was tried, and after deliberating for less than an hour, the jury convicted him of two counts of rape. "I am a great person," Elliott testified, before the jury gave him the maximum sentence: 20 years in prison. Michele Davis, the SANE nurse for Baylor's county, told ESPN that it seemed Baylor had more sexual assaults than other universities and that athletes represented a disproportionate number (between 25 and 50 percent) of the alleged perpetrators. She also said that university officials had known for at least a few years of a much larger problem with sexual assault by student-athletes.[11]

- In 2012, Idaho's Boise State University removed Sam Ukwuachu, a freshman All-American defensive end, from its football team following an incident of domestic violence with his girl-friend. Baylor, a faith-based university, nonetheless admit-ted Ukwuachu, who then joined its football team. (After the verdict, former Boise State coach Chris Peterson said that he "thoroughly apprised Coach [Art] Briles of the circum-stances surrounding Sam's disciplinary record and dismissal"; Briles claimed that Peterson only told him that Ukwuachu had a "rocky relationship with his girlfriend."[12]) In October 2013, a Baylor student-athlete accused Ukwuachu of violently raping her while ignoring her screams of "Stop!" and "No!" A sexual assault nurse's exam found injuries consistent with rape. According to *Texas Monthly*, Baylor's desultory investigation consisted of interviewing the accuser, Ukwuachu, and one friend of each, while ignoring the medical evidence. The Baylor panel found for Ukwuachu. But the accuser also went to the police, and the judge in the criminal case barred Ukwuachu's lawyer from mentioning Baylor's finding, due to what he saw as the flaws in its process. In August 2015, a Waco jury found Ukwuachu guilty of rape but recommended he receive only pro-bation. The judge exercised his discretion to add a sentence of six months in the county jail.[13] In the fallout from these cases, Baylor fired Briles, as well as president and chancellor Kenneth Starr. Athletic Director Ian McCaw resigned. The university has faced multiple lawsuits from students (or groups of students) who say the school ignored or mishandled their sexual assault allegations, and it has promised a $5 million expansion of the Title IX office and related services.[14]
- In 2014, a female University of Tennessee–Knoxville student-athlete accused two football players, A. J. Johnson and Michael Williams, of raping her at a party. She went to law enforcement and underwent a rape exam. Police quickly arrested both Johnson and Williams. A fellow football player, Drae Bowles, later swore in an affidavit that he had encountered the accuser in the park-ing lot after the party and, upon hearing that his teammates had raped her, driven her to the hospital. In a 2016 lawsuit, Bowles

filed an affidavit that football coach Butch Jones had accused him of having "betrayed the team" with this act of basic human decency.[15] In July 2016, the university settled the lawsuit by making a $2.48 million payment to the plaintiffs. The settlement also required creation of an independent commission to consider new sexual assault procedures for all University of Tennessee students—not just the student-athletes who received favorable treatment.[16]

• In 2015, the University of Alabama accepted as a transfer a star defensive lineman named Jonathan Taylor. His previous school, the University of Georgia, had expelled him following his arrest for allegedly punching and choking his girlfriend. After less than a term at Alabama, Taylor was arrested for domestic violence by Tuscaloosa police. Then Alabama, too, expelled him.[17] But the issue of indifference to domestic violence continued to plague SEC football. For the 2016 season, after a video surfaced of Mississippi State University five-star recruit Jeffery Simmons punching a woman to the ground, MSU gave him a token one-game suspension. When asked how he would have felt if the woman in the video had been a member of *his* family, Coach Dan Mullen callously replied, "I don't know that my family would be in that situation, to be honest with you."[18]

• In 2013, Rhode Island's Providence College suspended basketball player Brandon Austin after an allegation of sexual assault for which the police declined to press charges. Austin moved on to play for the University of Oregon, where he was viewed as potentially the best on the team.[19] In March 2014, a female student claimed that Austin and his teammates Dominic Artis and Damyean Dotson had gang-raped her. The school elected not to suspend Artis and Dotson from Pac-12 tournament or NCAA tournament games. (Austin, as a transfer student, was not yet eligible to play.) Only after the season ended did the university bring disciplinary proceedings against the three and expel them. The accuser sued the school and settled out of court for $800,000.[20]

• In 2009, Brendan Gibbons, the placekicker for the University of Michigan, allegedly raped a fellow student in his dorm room.

The evidence—which included the accuser's testimony, Gibbons' semen, and rape kit results indicating nonconsensual activity— seemed strong. The accuser told Ann Arbor police that Taylor Lewan, Gibbons' 309-pound teammate, had threatened to rape her if she pursued criminal charges against Gibbons. She did not, apparently out of fear. Though the accuser reported the allegations promptly, Gibbons' disciplinary proceedings were delayed for several years, which allowed him to stay on the football team until he was expelled with just one game left to play, in December 2013. Lewan was chosen in the first round of the 2014 NFL draft by the Tennessee Titans.[21]

The allegations in these cases were troubling, and the evidence of guilt was powerful in the Baylor and Tennessee cases. But the universities showed more interest in protecting talented male athletes than in punishing alleged sexual offenses.[22] Evidently big-money sports may be the only force that rivals the power of the accusers' rights movement on today's campuses.

The most shocking recent rape allegations against college athletes occurred at Tennessee's Vanderbilt University. The case was solved not by the Title IX office but by law enforcement. Far from confirming the "rape culture" myth, the university behaved appropriately. Here's the story: On June 23, 2013, incoming football player Brandon Vandenburg, together with teammates Cory Batey, Brandon Banks, and Tip McKenzie, carried Vandenburg's passed-out girlfriend to his room. Egged on and videotaped by Vandenburg, who was too high on drugs to get an erection, Batey raped her. Vandenburg texted videos of the rape to two of his friends and sent photos to Chris Boyd, another Vanderbilt football player. Boyd helped clean up the scene and got his teammates to delete all evidence of the incident from their cellphones.

The four athletes might have gotten away with it. But Vanderbilt officials, while examining a dorm video for unrelated reasons, came across images of several men carrying a woman to Vandenburg's room. Instead of calling the university's Title IX coordinator, officials turned the video over to Nashville police. This decision led to a professional investigation that the Title IX office itself could not have conducted, because the victim couldn't recall the incident and the school had no legal authority or forensic tools to subpoena the evidence that proved the rapists' guilt.

The police recovered the deleted rape video from Vandenburg's phone. The local prosecutor entered into a plea bargain with Boyd, who agreed to testify against the others. Confronted with this damning evidence, Vandenburg and Batey defended their actions by citing a campus culture of rampant drinking and random sex. They were both convicted of aggravated rape. Batey was sentenced to 15 years in prison; Vandenburg received a 17-year sentence without the opportunity for parole. The victim praised as "heroes" the "law enforcement officers, prosecutors and victims' advocates who dedicated so many months of their lives to this case [and] made justice possible."[23]

This exemplary case generated almost no interest among campus activists and their media allies. They could have, it seems, used this documented gang rape to dramatize their claims of a campus rape crisis. But doing so would have focused attention on the effective performance of the police and judicial system, undercutting activists' ultimate agenda of discrediting law enforcement as hostile to victims and ensuring that student rape allegations are channeled to campus tribunals.

The New York Times, which ran dozens of staff articles and commentaries on the Duke lacrosse case, covered events at Vanderbilt almost entirely only through wire-service articles. The most substantial article by *Times* staffers focused not on the horrifying crime itself but on what reporters Alan Blinder and Richard Pérez-Peña portrayed as Vanderbilt students' insufficient "sense of urgency" about rape on campus.[24] The usually rape-obsessed *Huffington Post* used wire-service copy only. Know Your IX cofounder Dana Bolger informed Yahoo News that the rapists typified male undergraduates, "particularly [at] 'elite' institutions like Vanderbilt," which "attract some of the most privileged students in the country." She stereotyped male students as having "a certain arrogance and entitlement, whether to a desired grade in the classroom, or to women's bodies."[25] In other words, male students at elite schools feel entitled to rape their classmates.

In some cases, however, the high profiles of college athletes (at least those whose teams don't bring significant revenue for their schools) have produced for them a much worse experience than for typical accused students—who, at the very least, can avoid widespread public knowledge about their fate due to the secrecy of campus tribunals. Because student-athletes are at least somewhat in the public eye, their departure from their team can raise questions among observers. That was certainly the case for Jack Montague, the captain of Yale's 2015–2016 basketball team.

In early 2016, as Yale advanced toward its first NCAA tournament bid since 1962, Montague suddenly stopped playing, without public explanation. He was, as it turned out, facing an allegation of sexual assault, from a female student with whom he had had a brief sexual relationship in the fall 2014 semester. His accuser claimed that her first three instances of sexual contact with Montague had been consensual but her fourth had not—even though it was undisputed that after the allegedly nonconsensual intercourse, she returned to Montague's room and he respected her indication that she didn't want to have sex again; the two still spent the night together in his bed.[26]

The accuser did not go to the police or even file a complaint with Yale. Instead, about a year after the alleged incident, the accuser's roommate mentioned to a Yale Title IX officer, Angela Gleason, that she had heard her roommate had a "bad experience" with Montague. Gleason reached out to the accuser. But a month later, the student was still unwilling to file charges against Montague. So Gleason independently initiated disciplinary proceedings—even though the university's own guidelines indicated that only "exceptionally rare circumstances" (mostly involving potential harm to others in the community) could justify such a decision. The allegations did not come close to meeting this standard; even the accuser never claimed Montague had harassed her in any way after the disputed incident. After a further discussion with the Title IX office, in which she apparently was led to believe that a minor disciplinary infraction from Montague's freshman year had actually been an incident of sexual misconduct, the accuser agreed to testify—to "protect other women," she said—once the hearing commenced.

Yale, for reasons it has never explained, "uses a more expansive definition of [the term] sexual assault" than state or federal criminal law. Like all Yale students accused of sexual assault, Montague went through a process in which he had no right to be given any exculpatory evidence; no right to see the full evidence upon which the university relied to determine his fate; no right to an impartial panel; no right to have a lawyer ask questions or address the panel; and a very limited right to indirect questioning of the accuser by panel members. The accuser stated that she had voluntarily gone to Montague's room, undressed herself, and gone into his bed; she said that she had then communicated her lack of consent during intercourse by having "put her hands up, pressed them against the front of Mr. Montague's shoulders and pushed him, but not very forcefully." The panel found Montague guilty, and Yale expelled him. For reasons it has not explained, Yale kept no audio or video recording of the hearing.

To express solidarity with a teammate going through a difficult time, other members of the men's basketball team wore replicas of Montague's warm-up jersey (bearing his number) before a game. The act recalled the Duke women's lacrosse team, whose members had done something similar a decade before, during the lacrosse case. In that case, the student body was generally supportive of the women's lacrosse team's gesture of support for the accused, and the administration did not silence them. In Montague's case, the campus response was dramatically different.

In protest of the team's show of support, students blanketed the Yale campus with flyers telling the team to "stop supporting a rapist." A column in the campus newspaper criticized Montague's teammates. The Yale Women's Center released a statement in which it questioned the basketball players' attitudes toward sexual assault: "Though we can only speculate as to the intent behind the basketball team's shirt protest, the team's actions appeared to be a dismissal of the very real threat of sexual violence." The next day, citing federal privacy statutes, the Women's Center took down its remarks—but by then, of course, the damage had been done. A Yale dean issued a statement seeming to condemn the basketball players' show of support for Montague but not the other students' labeling him a rapist. The men's basketball team eventually issued a statement—which sounded as if it had been written by a Yale administrator rather than the students themselves—apologizing for having worn a replica of Montague's warm-up jersey.[27]

The willingness of Yale's Title IX administrator to go outside university guidelines and file charges against Montague shows how accusations against athletes have sometimes given universities a perverse incentive to go harder on athletes than they might on a typical student. Montague's lawyer, Max Stern, has plausibly suggested that Yale's Title

IX office chose to initiate the case against Montague to distract from criticism following a campus climate survey suggesting that many unpunished rapes had occurred at Yale.[28]

In June 2016, after the university made clear that it would not revisit its decision, Montague filed suit against Yale. In a statement released to *The Hartford Courant*, Yale spokesperson Tom Conroy remarked that "trained members of the Yale community" had made the decision.[29] Conroy did not respond to a request from one of us for Yale to make public the details of the panelists' training—which the university, thus far, has chosen to keep secret.

Even if Montague prevails, no lawsuit can allow him to get his good name back, as Iowa State University basketball player Bubu Palo discovered after a similar experience. Fellow student Joni Bedell* accused Palo and his friend, Spencer Cruise, of a gang rape in May 2012. Her strongest evidence was a blouse that she said the two had torn. Palo was arrested and suspended from the basketball team. But then police discovered that the blouse had apparently been torn by either the accuser or her mother in an effort to bolster a shaky case. The local prosecutor dropped all charges in January 2013.

But, even though Bedell had graduated by that time, ISU's Title IX office filed a disciplinary complaint against Palo. Soon after, in May 2013, Administrative Law Judge John Priester dismissed the filing, saying that "it is very difficult to reconcile the conflicting versions of events," especially because "the whole evening is covered with a murky fog caused by the consumption of alcohol." This decision would have ended the case had OCR not ordered in 2011 that educational institutions allow all accusers to appeal not-guilty findings. Accordingly, ISU president Steven Leath declared in August 2013—based on no new evidence, but with ample incentive to look tough on sexual assault—that Palo would be removed from the basketball team. School officials refused to comment on the president's rationale, citing a federal privacy law.[30]

It appears that Palo's status as a basketball player had hurt him: publicity surrounding the case made Palo a target for strong discipline. Leath later said: "Everybody involved with the university saw it [the appropriate outcome] in the same way. Interestingly, the only people that saw it differently were people outside the academy who had never worked with our misconduct policy." This comment inadvertently revealed the source of the university's lack of objectivity about the case—corporate groupthink. One of the outsiders who saw it differently was an Iowa state court judge, Steven Oeth, who in January 2014 issued an injunction against Leath's decision. Yet Coach Fred Hoiberg nonetheless refused to let Palo play in any games.[31]

His college basketball career thus affected, Palo filed a defamation suit against Bedell and her mother. *The Ames Tribune* turned to Stanford Law School professor Michele Dauber, who suggested that such lawsuits were "very harassing of sexual assault victims" and denounced Palo's suit as a "stretch." The Bedells' own lawyers apparently disagreed; they settled with Palo, in September 2015.[32]

One question hovering over the case is whether racial motivation infected the university's handling of Palo, a black athlete in an overwhelmingly white community. Other cases raise similar questions, especially when considered in light of a connection suggested by Harvard Law School professor Janet Halley: "American racial history is laced with vendetta-like scandals in which black men are accused of sexually assaulting white women that become reverse scandals when it is revealed that the accused men were not wrongdoers at all," she wrote in a commentary. "Case after case that has come to my attention [at Harvard], including several in which I have played some advocacy or adjudication role, has involved black male respondents, but the institution cannot 'know' this because it has not been thought important enough to monitor for racial bias."[33]

The question of race also hovered over North Carolina's Appalachian State University's handling of accusations by two white female students against black football player Lanston Tanyi and his roommate.

Tanyi's first accuser, Alex Miller, claimed that Tanyi and his roommate had sexually assaulted her after a September 2011 party.[34] During the ensuing investigation, two students who had been at the party and who didn't know Tanyi told a university administrator they had seen Miller invite the football players into her room and heard her imply later that the sex had been consensual. In a move that would have constituted prosecutorial misconduct in a criminal trial, the university concealed these exculpatory witnesses from Tanyi. It also barred Tanyi from calling several other witnesses who he said would back his story. Once the hearing began, the university gave Miller a lawyer to represent her and assigned only a graduate philosophy student to help Tanyi. Even with the deck thus stacked against the accused, Appalachian State could not substantiate Miller's story, and the panel found Tanyi not guilty.

But his ordeal wasn't over. A second accuser, Meaghan Creed, claimed later in September 2011 that Tanyi, the same roommate, and three other men, whom she identified only as "big" and "black," had raped her more than five months before. Creed's case was compromised by her claim that Tanyi, who didn't smoke, had been smoking at the time. He also produced witnesses who said he was with them at the time of the alleged attack. The evidence left the Appalachian State hearing panel no choice but to again find Tanyi not guilty.

Two accusations, two not guilty findings. But Creed appealed and told her fellow accuser Miller about it. Miller in turn posted an item to Facebook accusing the university of coddling rapists. At a result-ing protest rally, more than 100 students wore black tape across their mouths while holding signs that said "Blame Perpetrators, Not Victims" and "End Rape Culture."[35] The rising debate seems to have prompted Appalachian State provost Lori Gonzalez to grant Creed's appeal and order a second hearing.

The initial Creed-Tanyi hearing, Gonzalez said without apparent irony, had "deviated" from a university rule that said the school "must present sufficient witness and/or documentary evidence to establish the violation." So Tanyi's original not-guilty finding was thrown out *because the university conceded it had brought charges against him without sufficient evidence to prove him guilty.*

The university added a sexual harassment charge the night before the second Creed-Tanyi hearing. Tanyi had already designated his witnesses, and the sudden new charge gave him no chance to line up others in response to it. The second panel, like the first, found no evidence of sexual assault. But it found Tanyi guilty of harassment for allegedly laughing at Creed some days after the now-ruled-to-be-unproved assault. The university announced to the news media Tanyi's removal from the football team. He then transferred to Colorado State University, where he played football for a year and earned a graduate degree. He sued Appalachian State, which paid him a $100,000 settle-ment after U.S. District Judge Richard Voorhees refused to dismiss his lawsuit.

Unsatisfied by the chicanery deployed by Appalachian State's administration on her behalf, Creed filed a complaint against the university with the U.S. Department of Education. She claimed that the hearing panels had violated Title IX by finding her rape claim to be, more likely than not, false.[36]

Racial overtones also lingered over a case at the University of Findlay, in Ohio, involving two black student-athletes: Justin Browning, a member of the football team, and Alphonso Baity, who played basketball.[37] In September 2014, Browning and Baity had a party at their house along with their two housemates and several other students, including Molly Kane.* Kane performed oral sex on Browning, and then on Baity, with whom she then slept. She left the house the next morning. Ten days later, she accused the duo of sexual assault in a complaint to Findlay.

Kane's allegation against two black athletes on a campus with fewer than 4 percent black students led to a whirlwind investigation by the university, which in the previous two years had expelled two other black males accused by white female students of sexual assault.

Findlay's designated investigator spoke to the accused but seemed uninterested in hearing from black witnesses who had attended the party. (Reflecting the university's policies, there was no hearing in the case.) The investigator's treatment of one of the white female witnesses prompted a complaint from her mother that the school had retaliated against her daughter for refusing to corroborate Kane's claims. Twenty-four hours after speaking with the investigator, Browning and Baity received notice of their expulsion. The entire process had taken only two days.

Findlay's president announced the expulsions of Browning and Baity by name. The news prompted a dormmate of the accuser to contact her resident advisor and tell her she had heard Kane describe the encounters as consensual. The resident advisor told her to drop the matter because the university had made its decision.

Findlay defended its handling of the matter as an example of "integrity and fairness."[38] Journalists Ashe Schow and Robby Soave, who have written prolifically about such cases, called the university's handling of the complaints one of the worst institutional responses they had seen.[39] Harvard Law School professors Jacob Gersen and Jeannie Suk Gersen detected a broader significance in the Findlay episode, since "racially disproportionate impact is, in a sense, a 'miner's canary' that calls for examination of the workings of the sex bureaucracy."[40]

Accused student-athletes also can lose out by being barred from their teams based on unproven allegations. That's what happened to Corey Mock. A star wrestler at the University of Tennessee–Chattanooga, in 2014 he seemed poised for a strong senior season after being named the most outstanding wrestler at the Southern Conference tournament.[41]

Then he met Molly Morris, a fellow student, through the hookup app Tinder. In March 2014, Morris attended a house party with Mock, arriving after work at 2:00 a.m. Both drank heavily. Feeling sick, Morris went into a bathroom. Mock found her there. They went to Mock's room and woke up in bed together the next morning, unable to remember much. That week, Mock sent Morris a couple of text messages that went unanswered. Finally Morris texted him to ask how things were going in a national wrestling tournament. "Holy crap, you are alive," Mock teasingly replied.

But Morris was not feeling friendly toward Mock when she visited the UTC Women's Center a few days later, on the advice of a friend, and told a staffer that she recalled having intercourse with Mock. It's unclear how the Women's Center staffer responded. Soon thereafter, Morris told Mock that she had not consented. "I was shocked," Mock later recalled. "I didn't even know what to say." He did not speak to Morris again.

Morris never went to the police. But, apparently believing she had been given a date-rape drug, she sent a strand of her hair to a lab for testing. In June 2014, around six weeks after her night with Mock, she filed a disciplinary complaint with UTC. At a hearing, Morris told Administrative Law Judge Joanie Sompayrac that she had not consented to sex and believed she had been drugged; she refused, however, to share the results of the lab test. With no subpoena power, the university could not compel Morris to produce this vital evidence. Mock testified that Morris had clearly consented to sexual intercourse through nonverbal actions. Morris said that she had been too drunk to recall.

Sompayrac found Mock not guilty in August 2014, citing undisputed evidence that Morris "voluntarily drank the alcohol she consumed" and the fact that witnesses had said she had not been incapacitated. Both students had exercised poor judgment, Sompayrac wrote, but "using poor judgment does not necessarily constitute a violation of the UTC Code of Conduct." Although the university needed to respect the rights of accusers and the Obama administration's commands, Sompayrac added, "the rights of the accused must also be ensured," and the university had not proved probable guilt.

High-level campus officials used an appeal by Morris to get the decision reversed. They asked Sompayrac to reconsider her ruling based on an administrator's instructions that Mock must be found guilty "if Ms. Morris was only capacitated [sic] in one sense (i.e., mentally) but not the other (e.g., physically)"—though what that was supposed to mean was far from clear.

Sompayrac got the message. She downplayed her concern for "the rights of the accused" and—with no new evidence—reversed her finding that the university had not proved probable guilt. Chancellor Steve Angle upheld the decision, which would have led to Mock's expulsion, by changing the rules in the middle of his case. Angle now claimed that Mock had failed to prove that his accuser had expressed "affirmative consent" to have sex, a requirement not mentioned in UTC's written policies. The situation reeked of political motivations, as have other interventions by high-level campus officials in comparable appeals.

Mock sued the university. Tennessee Chancery Court Judge Carol McCoy overturned its decision, reinstated Sompayrac's original finding, and ordered UTC to grant Mock his degree. In a scathing 23-page opinion issued in June 2015, McCoy held that UTC's sudden adoption of the new "affirmative consent" standard—after "unrebutted" testimony that the accuser had consented—"erroneously shifted the burden of proof" to require Mock to prove his innocence. This standard "is flawed and untenable if due process is to be afforded to the accused," McCoy wrote. She suggested that, in order to satisfy the university's newly concocted policy, Mock would have needed to go so far as to make a video of the encounter.

McCoy's decision allowed Mock to complete his education. But it did not address his status as a student-athlete, and the university continued to ban the star wrestler from his team. This decision cost him his senior year of intercollegiate competition and his chance to win an NCAA championship. The case also saddled him with $40,000 in attorneys' fees, and the resulting negative publicity may have destroyed his hoped-for career as a wrestling coach.[42]

Corey Mock's treatment also likely played a part in ending his father's job as head wrestling coach at the University of North Carolina. The father, C. D. Mock, started a blog to support his son in December 2014. He also assailed sharply, and sometimes stridently, the system for sexual assault allegations that colleges nationwide have adopted. Coach Mock's blog posts infuriated liberal circles around UNC. Tom Jensen, a prominent figure of North Carolina's Democratic establishment who heads a liberal polling company, chastised Mock for "blasting feminists," assailed him as a champion of "men's rights," and organized a letter-writing campaign to demand his dismissal.[43] Jensen himself wrote to the chancellor and the athletic director to declare that Mock had a "world view that is not acceptable for someone who is supposed to be a leader of young men." When UNC officials responded by citing Mock's freedom of speech, Jensen maintained the pressure: "I understand not wanting to fire him for making inappropriate comments, even though I disagree. So I hope you'll fire him at the end of the season for being a bad wrestling coach instead." Athletic Director Bubba Cunningham reassuringly responded, "I do understand what you are saying in all areas."[44]

Jensen got what he wanted: UNC fired the longtime coach in June 2015, supposedly for performance issues. But although Mock's team's win-loss record had noticeably dipped between 2009 and 2012, it had improved between 2012 and 2015, with three consecutive top-25 finishes in the NCAA championships. And early in his tenure as coach, Mock had twice been named his league's coach of the year. The coach suggested that the move constituted politically motivated retaliation, by a university that is a hotbed of accusers' rights activism, for his outspoken defense of his son.

Tom Jensen's attacks on Coach Mock brought no protest from anyone—at least, no protest from anyone whom UNC's leadership cared about. If a North Carolina *Republican* leader had pressured the state's flagship university to fire, say, the women's swimming coach for championing her daughter's rape claim and assailing campus "rape culture," we have no doubt that academics, politicians, and the media would have ignited a firestorm, and quite appropriately so.

Campus activists are correct that star basketball or football players sometimes receive favorable treatment by schools. Events at Baylor and the University of Tennessee show that. But most college athletes accused of sexual assault are *not* star basketball or football players. Even among this small, highly privileged subset of accused students, the record is ambiguous. As Mock, Palo, Tanyi, Montague, and Wells discovered, in the current collegiate atmosphere, athletes' visibility provides perverse incentives to institutions to rush to find them guilty in order to conform to the preferred narrative, lest the institution be seen as coddling athletes or fostering "rape culture."

8

THE WITCH HUNT INTENSIFIES

When Catherine Lhamon replaced Russlynn Ali as head of the Education Department's OCR in 2013, whatever hope existed that she might slow the evisceration of due process for accused students quickly vanished. Her response to a challenge from widely respected senator Lamar Alexander (R-Tennessee) in a June 2014 oversight hearing provided a taste of her approach.

"What you're doing is writing out detailed guidance for 22 million students on 7,200 campuses, and it's just—it could be your whim, your idea," the Tennessee Republican admonished Lhamon. Holding up a fat file of marching orders issued by OCR to thousands of universities, the former secretary of education added: "We make the law. You don't make the law."

At another point, Alexander asked: "Who gave you the authority" to rewrite Title IX through guidance documents? "Well, with gratitude, you did, when I was confirmed," shot back Lhamon.[1] She thereby suggested that Senate confirmation gave her quasi-dictatorial powers over universities. Or perhaps that the Dear Colleague letter's regulatory commands had been lurking undetected, from 1972 until 2011, between the lines of Title IX's simple ban on sex discrimination.[2] Lhamon had displayed similar disinterest in listening to advocates of due process by rebuffing, as not "useful," FIRE president Greg Lukianoff's request for a meeting when she took office in 2013.[3]

Lhamon's disdain for reasoned disagreements with her actions reflected the attitude of her superiors. In 2013, White House staffers invited five law professors—from Harvard, Penn, Cornell, and the University of Chicago—to discuss the administration's handling of campus sexual assault. According to Geoffrey Stone, the University of Chicago professor, all five expressed concern about the Obama administration's degrading of due process and the inherent unfairness of the procedures it was pressuring universities to use. Asked in a subsequent interview whether the White House staffers appeared to take this concern seriously, Stone replied: "Not really. . . . [T]hey gave us the full opportunity to express our concerns, but they did not really engage them in the way I would have expected in the meeting. The absence of any substantive feedback after the fact left me with the sense that it was at best a fact-finding meeting and was at worst, 'OK, we'll check that off. We did that.'"[4]

The Obama administration ignored not only the reasoned advice of friends such as Stone but also growing criticisms by other defenders of civil liberties, from the ideological left, right, and center.

In February 2015, U.S. Civil Rights Commission members Gail Heriot and Peter Kirsanow questioned OCR's request for a 31 percent budget increase, to $131 million. The nominal justification was a six-fold increase in Title IX complaints, from 391 in 2010—the year before OCR's crusade began in earnest—to 2,354 in 2014, though Catherine Lhamon let slip the phoniness of the 2014 number by telling *The Washington Post* that *two people*, whose identities OCR refused to release, had filed *more than 1,700* of those 2,354 Title IX complaints.[5] Citing "a disturbing pattern of disregard for the rule of law at OCR," Heriot and Kirsanow accused the agency of having "pushed past the limits of its legal authority in addressing sexual assault" on campus. They noted that neither OCR's command to weaken the standard of proof nor its pressure to ban cross-examination of accusers had been authorized "in the text of Title IX or in earlier OCR regulations."[6] The agency wound up with a budget hike of around 6 percent.

A few months later, the nation's oldest law journal, *The Legal Intelligencer*, described the mandates in the Dear Colleague letter as "both unconstitutional and unfair." The editors urged that the document be withdrawn because "higher education institutions are not designed, financed or suited to simultaneously play prosecutor, judge and jury." At the very least, they added, "if schools are to be tasked by the DOE with investigating and adjudicating quasi-criminal accusations, appropriate safeguards must be guaranteed to the accused."[7]

In 2015, the prominent liberal journalist Jonathan Chait, of *New York* magazine, endorsed the penetrating critiques of the administration's—and many universities'—campus sexual assault policies by Harvard Law School professors Nancy Gertner and Janet Halley. Chait questioned the universities' almost unanimous pattern of blaming only the accused "when both partners are too impaired [by alcohol] to give consent." He doubted that "the miscarriages of justice remain a rare or marginal problem in campus sexual assault adjudication" and warned that they could do "real damage to the systems they represent."[8]

Similar sentiments came from the left-of-center editorial page of *The Bangor Daily News*, which cited Emily Yoffe's portrayal of the Drew Sterrett case at the University of Michigan as an example of how colleges mishandle rape allegations. "Sexual assault and attempted sexual assault are crimes," the editors noted. By way of comparison, they added, "It would be hard to imagine a college investigating a murder without bringing in law enforcement help."[9]

Fox News provided the first serious attention by any TV network to the federal government's exploitation of the campus sexual assault frenzy and the proliferation of highly questionable allegations by some female college students. Anchor Megyn Kelly, host of *The Kelly File*, presented three powerful segments on Amherst College's mistreatment of the innocent Michael Cheng and also explored the less-than-credible allegations of the celebrated, mattress-toting Emma Sulkowicz of Columbia University. Kelly, a lawyer turned journalist, asserted that "in an effort to protect alleged victims, [the Department of Education] has completely abolished the rights of defendants, of the accused."[10]

In October 2015, NYU Law School professor Nadine Strossen, former president of the ACLU, argued that "OCR's flawed sexual harassment concept reflects sexist stereotypes that are equally insulting to women and men. For women, it embodies the archaic, infantilizing notion that we're inherently demeaned by any expression with sexual content." Praising the Harvard law professors who had stood up to OCR, Strossen denounced "the current clamor for campus 'safety' [which] seeks protection from exposure to ideas that make one uncomfortable."[11]

In January 2016, Sen. James Lankford (R-Oklahoma) sent a blistering four-page letter to Acting Secretary of Education John King Jr. suggesting that OCR's failure to seek public comment before issuing the Dear Colleague letter had been improper. Citing the 28 Harvard law professors' open letter, Lankford suggested that OCR's interpretation of Title IX contradicted "First and Fourth Amendment protections...that Title IX and its implementing regulations alone have never been said to imperil."[12] Lhamon responded with a canned defense of the agency's actions that was unresponsive to the serious concerns Lankford raised.

Even Obama's former secretary of homeland security, Janet Napolitano, criticized the administration's approach, in a 2015 article in *Yale Law and Policy Review*. She castigated OCR for failing to seek public comment before it "clearly imposed new mandates on schools" in its 2011 and 2014 "guidance" letters. Napolitano stressed that rather than "pushing institutions to become surrogates for the criminal justice system," the government (and campus activists) should explore whether "more work should be done to improve that system's handling and prosecution of sexual assault cases."[13]

The bipartisan hysteria about campus assault drowned out such voices of wisdom. Even after Republicans took control of Congress in the 2014 midterm elections, the vast majority of them—including Tea Party activists who had campaigned on vows to rein in federal abuses of power—did not protest. Several prominent Republican senators even gave a bipartisan veneer to OCR's crusade. The only Senate resistance to the Obama administration's pursuit of injustice came from Lankford and Alexander.

The latter's efforts to limit the damage included extracting from Deputy Assistant Secretary of Education Amy McIntosh a damaging admission in 2015 that "guidance that the Department [of Education] issues [through OCR] does not have the force of law." This admission came after four years of using the Dear Colleague letter to coerce universities across the land as though their "guidance" *did* have the force of law.[14]

In 2015 and 2016, the White House and OCR maintained their approach toward campus due process, as activists, college bureaucrats, consultants, and politicians fanned the mass panic.

OCR issued, and the media sensationalized, press releases naming the colleges and universities it had placed "under investigation," before any meaningful inquiry had occurred. At the same time, these "list of shame" announcements refused to reveal the substance of the Title IX complaints that supposedly gave OCR jurisdiction, and OCR has consistently redacted all information about these complaints in documents made public through Freedom of Information Act requests. A single complaint, plausible or not, from a single accuser could get a school added to "a list of institutions in the OCR queue to be investigated," in the words of Lee Burdette Williams, former dean of Massachusetts' Wheaton College. This approach "baffled us all," she recalled.[15]

It did not baffle the former high-level official of a major university whom we quoted in chapter 1. Some of his words bear repeating here: "[These are] classic bureaucratic responses that one associates with corrupt municipal governments who are out to 'get' a businessman or property owner—namely, a variety of inquiries and worse, designed to remind you who is in charge."

OCR's pattern of stigmatizing before investigating departs from the practice of virtually all other federal agencies. The effect, and the apparent intent, is to put schools under enormous pressure to do whatever OCR demands. It also encourages unhappy students to fan the frenzy by filing more and more Title IX complaints against their schools, at a time when almost all schools are already making frantic efforts to appease campus activists and the government by doing whatever Title IX purportedly requires. Know Your IX official Alyssa Peterson admitted as much in a summer 2016 interview with *The Chronicle of Higher Education*. She explained, "We're seeing the [Title IX] complaints as more of a media strategy"—that is, as a way of creating public pressure for their agenda.[16]

OCR's bureaucratic tactic of choice, a "voluntary" agreement with the targeted university, can impose a host of new mandates beyond those specified in the 2011 Dear Colleague letter. To date, only one university—Tufts, in Massachusetts—has publicly said it would fight OCR's finding that it had violated Title IX. But, buffeted by student protests, the school surrendered within a week: Tufts president Anthony Monaco appeased the protesters by naming some of them to a task force to revise the university's sexual assault policies.[17]

For OCR, as professors Jacob Gersen and Jeannie Suk Gersen observed in a 2016 article, resolution letters allow the agency to achieve "complete compliance with its nonbinding guidance document without ever having to defend its reasoning through public comments or judicial review.... If the agency issued an actual rule requiring disciplinary procedures, unfair aspects could be challenged as a violation of due-process requirements of the federal Constitution or as arbitrary and capricious under the APA. But when a private institution adopts the very same procedures, there is no federal due-process claim because it is not the government acting, nor is there an APA claim to be made.... The off-loading of government responsibility to new mini-bureaucracies inside schools has made it difficult to subject the federal sex bureaucracy to judicial scrutiny."[18]

For a targeted university, a resolution letter avoids the chance of a negative OCR finding and the (however hypothetical) threat of a full withdrawal of federal funds. It also helps minimize bad publicity. Only a university with a massive endowment, such as Harvard, can afford to risk taking on OCR—and so far not even Harvard has chosen to do so.

In "voluntary" resolution agreements in 2013 and 2014, OCR required the State University of New York and Dallas' Southern Methodist University to go far beyond the 2011 Dear Colleague letter's commands. The office ordered the schools to investigate sexual assault accusations even if police found no probable cause to bring charges against the accused. OCR also required interim measures—which always are, in effect, pre-adjudication punishments—against accused students. And it required four SUNY schools (Albany, New Paltz, Buffalo State College, and Morrisville) and Southern Methodist University to reopen numerous cases in which accused students had been found not guilty.[19]

The SUNY schools and SMU weren't the only institutions OCR required to reinvestigate closed cases; Alderson-Broaddus College, Rider University, and Southern Illinois University–Carbondale entered into similar agreements with OCR. In all such cases, as lawyer Stephen

Henrick has recognized, "the school, in essence, signs away the student's rights [in order] to protect itself; because a Title IX administrative complaint is strictly between the government and the college, an accused student is usually not made a party to it or even given notice that it is happening. In these cases, a conviction upon subsequent investigation is all but assured. No risk-averse institution would dare defy OCR's unstated command to convict on the second try."[20]

Even an accuser's mere threat to complain to OCR has prompted at least one college, Vermont's Middlebury College, to act against an accused student who may well have been innocent. In early 2015 a student from another college claimed that a Middlebury student had raped her (while they both were studying abroad) in November 2014. After her claim was heard and rejected by the study-abroad program with which Middlebury was affiliated, the accuser then weaponized Title IX to force Middlebury—a college she had never attended—to retry him.[21]

The details of the case are as follows: After a night of drinking, the Middlebury student, the alleged victim, and a female friend of hers (who was also a former sex partner of his) went to the Middlebury student's room for the night. His roommate was away, so they pushed the two beds together. The Middlebury student got into bed between the two women. After a while, he and the alleged victim began having sexual intercourse, inches from where the friend was lying. The friend then left and went to her own room.

This conduct on the part of the male student was hardly behavior deserving of sympathy. But the incident, which threatened the social equilibrium between the alleged victim and her friend, soon turned uglier, when the female student claimed that the intercourse had been nonconsensual. There is no record that she went to law enforcement. She instead filed a sexual assault claim with the institution that runs Middlebury's study-abroad program: the School for International Training, or SIT. While keeping Middlebury informed of its actions, SIT held a hearing at which all three bedmates testified. The evidence also included contemporaneous text messages. SIT found the male student not guilty. The accuser did not appeal.

She did, however, go to her own college's Title IX coordinator. Then she wrote to a Middlebury administrator that "I am pursuing a complaint with the office of [sic] civil rights." And suddenly Middlebury, which had found no fault with SIT's handling of the case, decided to conduct its own investigation. It set aside SIT's finding based on the *accuser's* "perceptions of SIT's investigation and hearing process," Middlebury associate dean for student affairs Karen Guttentag later testified—with no indication that she had given anyone at SIT a chance to respond to the accuser's unspecified "perceptions."

Middlebury subjected its accused student not only to the campus equivalent of double jeopardy but also to an unfair process. Unlike SIT, Middlebury had adopted the Obama administration's preferred approach of avoiding any hearing and appointing a single investigator to determine the outcome in cases of alleged sexual assault. Middlebury's rules required that the investigator first be "trained" according to the Margolis Healy firm's guilt-presuming guidelines. The investigator's report went to a college administrator, who then interviewed the accused. (Between 2012 and the fall of 2015, every decision of guilt by a Middlebury investigator was upheld by college administrators.)

Middlebury found the accused student guilty the day before he was to begin his senior year, and it ordered him expelled. He sued, asserting that the decision would cost him the job he had been offered after graduation as well as his hope for a Middlebury degree. U.S. District Judge Garvan Murtha, a Clinton appointee, halted the college's decision with a preliminary injunction. Middlebury soon thereafter settled the case. It issued a vague statement that the student would go elsewhere for his senior year, which contained an even vaguer implication that he would ultimately receive a Middlebury degree.

The Obama administration's campaign against due process for students accused of sexual assault was twinned with a related effort to force universities to impose "sexual harassment" rules that violated freedom of speech and academic freedom, as well as any conception of fair process. Civil liberties groups such as FIRE, and academic freedom organizations such as the American Association of University Professors (AAUP), led the campaign against the policy.

The primary target of the latter campaign was a 47-page resolution letter that OCR, in conjunction with the Justice Department, had signed with the University of Montana in May 2013. In what OCR hailed as a "blueprint for colleges and universities throughout the country," the university had pledged to punish as sexual harassment "any unwelcome conduct of a sexual nature"—including "verbal conduct" (that is, speech)—even if it would *not* be offensive to an "objectively reasonable person of the same gender in the same situation." The university was thus poised to punish its students for saying anything that the most hypersensitive person might characterize as offensive. The resolution letter failed to account for free speech or the First Amendment.[22]

Unlike virtually all other OCR actions during the Obama years, the Montana "blueprint" provoked widespread criticism, perhaps because it was such an obvious insult to the First Amendment. FIRE highlighted the blueprint's significance, peppered OCR with questions, and organized a public letter signed by groups including the liberal Electronic Frontier Foundation, the conservative Goldwater Institute, and the Student Press Law Center. (Certain individuals, including one of us, also signed it.) The letter warned that universities "need not—and must not—sacrifice the civil liberties of their students" in their efforts to punish sexual misconduct.[23]

Even the left-leaning Committee on Women in the Academic Profession of the AAUP told OCR that eliminating "the critical standard of 'reasonable speech' . . . may pose a threat to academic freedom in the classroom."[24] Sen. John McCain (R-Arizona) asked U.S. Attorney General Eric Holder what authority OCR had to rewrite Title IX. After months of criticism, OCR backtracked from its "blueprint" boast. In a letter to FIRE, the agency disingenuously suggested that the document was *a* blueprint, not *the* blueprint, and therefore did not represent "OCR or DOJ policy."[25]

But OCR did not post this assurance on its website or send it to other universities. So as far as most administrators could tell, the agency intended to apply the "blueprint" across the board. Some universities— such as Penn State, the University of Connecticut, Clemson, Colorado College, and Georgia Southern—have revised their sexual harassment policies to reflect the blueprint's terms.[26]

The University of Montana fiasco was just one example of threats to academic freedom by OCR and like-minded academics and students. Here are others:

- In late 2014, two graduate students at Yale complained to the Title IX office that a student-run newsletter had published "inappropriate remarks" about them. Without publicly disclosing the remarks, a Yale administrator summoned the student journalists and warned them "regarding appropriate content."[27]

- In December 2014, Harvard Law School professor Jeannie Suk Gersen noted that feminist student organizations were discouraging students from participating in class sessions about rape law lest they be traumatized. She also heard from "about a dozen" criminal law professors who, to avoid complaints, had dropped the subject of rape from their courses. This trend of insisting that "teachers [should] protect them from causing or experiencing discomfort," Suk Gersen noted, was part of "a growing rape exceptionalism, which allows fears of inflicting or re-inflicting trauma to justify foregoing usual procedures and practices of truth-seeking."[28]

- In the summer of 2015, the University of California chancellor's office invited deans and department heads to attend workshops to discuss "microaggressions"—remarks seen by some as slights relating to race, gender, ethnicity, or sexual orientation. The real agenda appeared to be the squelching of disfavored speech. University guidelines prohibited "denying the experiences of students by questioning the credibility/validity of their stories"—including, apparently, accusations of sexual assault and harassment.[29] UCLA Law School professor and First Amendment expert Eugene Volokh denounced the new policy as "a serious blow to academic freedom and to freedom of discourse more generally."[30]

The use of Title IX to threaten academic freedom climaxed at Illinois' Northwestern University. Professor Laura Kipnis, a cultural theorist with impeccable left-wing and feminist credentials, penned an essay in *The Chronicle of Higher Education* mocking regulations discouraging relationships between faculty members and graduate students. She also described a sexual misconduct allegation filed against professor Peter Ludlow at her own school by an unidentified female undergraduate. (Kipnis said she did not know Ludlow.) In addition, the article briefly mentioned that a Northwestern inquiry had found no evidence to support a claim by another woman, this one a graduate student, that Ludlow had coerced her into sex.[31]

Kipnis might well have been too blasé about faculty-student power differentials. But if academic freedom did not protect this essay in a higher-education journal—critiquing a university policy of obvious public concern and related to Kipnis' academic specialty—it will not protect much. Two students nonetheless filed Title IX complaints against Kipnis. One (the graduate student who had accused Ludlow) framed Kipnis' essay as retaliation. A second—who was not mentioned at all in the article—suggested that Kipnis' writing had somehow threatened her safety on campus.

That's worth reading again. A Northwestern student filed a Title IX complaint with the university suggesting that an essay in a higher-education journal that had nothing to do with her somehow threatened her safety. Student protesters, meanwhile, demanded official condemnation of the professor and carried mattresses outside the president's office, mimicking the discredited Columbia sexual assault accuser Emma Sulkowicz. One student called Kipnis' essay "terrifying."

Northwestern sent Kipnis to be interrogated without a lawyer by Northwestern's hired investigators. "The term 'kangaroo court' came to mind," she wrote, in a second article for the *Chronicle*. The investigators said they had "names of students and staff members who'd testify that the essay had chilled them." Kipnis spurned the pressure and penned a third *Chronicle* essay about the Title IX proceeding itself. After Northwestern's conduct provoked a national backlash, it announced that its investigators had cleared Kipnis of the Title IX charges.[32]

"[A]nyone with a grudge, a political agenda, or a desire for attention can quite easily leverage the system," Kipnis concluded. Academics from around the country contacted her as her ordeal progressed. Kipnis said she learned from these exchanges that "when it comes to campus sexual politics . . . the group most constrained from speaking—even those with tenure—is men. No male academic in his right mind would write what I did. Men have been effectively muzzled, as any number of my male correspondents attested."[33]

One prominent male professor who *had* spoken up was sharply attacked for doing so. In November 2014, Yale Law School professor Jeb Rubenfeld penned a *New York Times* op-ed urging universities to focus more on sexual assault prevention, especially by addressing excessive use of alcohol. Far from trivializing the offense, he argued, "sexual assault on campus should mean what it means in the outside world and in courts of law." And he deemed it "critical" to integrate "college rape hearings with law enforcement"—so as to ensure that rapists were appropriately punished.[34]

As a specialist in both constitutional and criminal law, Rubenfeld possessed obvious credentials on the topic. Yet his op-ed triggered a furor on campus. The day after his article appeared, on November 16, Know Your IX's Alexandra Brodsky (@azbrodsky) tweeted her belief that "women at Yale Law School start planning their course selection early so they never have to take criminal law with Rubenfeld." Within two days, 75 Yale law students had joined Brodsky in signing an open letter claiming that Rubenfeld needed to cease offering such "dangerous" remarks and recognize that "campus rape is not an academic puzzle to be parsed."[35] (Again: they were speaking of a specialist in criminal law on the Yale Law School faculty.) In a June 2016 appearance at the Aspen Ideas Forum, Rubenfeld's colleague, Stephen Carter, recalled with amazement that he "had a student in my office talking to me earlier this year because she was upset that another professor at Yale had written a critique arguing that the data on campus rape were flawed. And she was furious. There was a petition at Yale law school objecting to this research, objecting to actually doing research....Those are all ways of trying to pressure and shut down speech."[36]

In early 2016 at Columbia, meanwhile, the University Senate's Academic Affairs Committee asked Columbia president Lee Bollinger to assure them that anonymous complaints in students' course evaluation forms would not be used as a basis for Title IX investigations of faculty members. Such an assurance was necessary, the committee said, lest professors—especially those without tenure—perceive that the only way to protect themselves would be self-censorship, to the detriment of their students' education.

Abby Porter, a member of Columbia's "Coalition against Sexual Violence," countered that the Faculty Senate's proposal "plays into the narrative of 'false reporting is rampant, and false reporting happens all the time, and false reporting is a tactic when someone's trying to be malicious.'" The university administration sided with the student activists against its own faculty. Bollinger even suggested that the Faculty Senate's proposal violated federal law.[37] In part due to concerns like these, the

AAUP in early 2016 issued a report criticizing the tendency of "Title IX administrators from the [Education Department] and within the university [to] overreach and seek to punish protected academic speech."[38]

Just as the healthy but short-lived backlashes against OCR's University of Montana "blueprint" and Northwestern's treatment of Kipnis had little long-term impact on campuses nationwide, so too did they not deter the Obama administration from its efforts to weaken students' due-process rights.

The White House made big headlines in April 2014 by issuing a 20-page task force report adopting the now-familiar tic of referring to complainants as "survivors," rather than as "accusers" or "alleged victims"—as though merely filing an accusation establishes the guilt of the accused. The phrase "due process" did not appear. The report urged colleges to adopt the all-powerful single investigator-adjudicator system for all sexual assault investigations. The guidelines did not address the investigator-adjudicator's inherent conflict of interest: the fact that her continued employment depends on staying in the good graces of the campus Title IX office. The only concession offered to accused students was a mention of "safeguarding an alleged perpetrator's right to notice and to be heard"—meaningless protections in the context of the campus rape panic.[39]

OCR simultaneously issued 46 pages of "guidance," styled as "questions and answers." Moving well beyond the commands in the 2011 Dear Colleague letter, this "guidance" implied that allowing cross-examination of an accuser could, *all by itself*, create a "hostile environment" and put a university in violation of Title IX.[40]

The new OCR document added, "While a criminal investigation is initiated at the discretion of law enforcement authorities, a Title IX investigation is not discretionary; a school has a duty under Title IX to resolve complaints promptly and equitably and to provide a safe and nondiscriminatory environment for all students, free from sexual harassment and sexual violence." This guidance ignored the obvious reality that when an investigation is *mandatory*, due-process protections against arbitrary punishment are all the more vital to any process focused on fairness.

OCR head Catherine Lhamon insisted in a 2015 *Wall Street Journal* interview that the virtually unanimous complaint of advocates of civil liberties that OCR "ignores due process is appalling to me."[41] The evidence for her rebuttal was unpersuasive. Lhamon pointed to an argument in OCR's 2014 guidelines that a student accused of sexual assault before a college tribunal did not deserve the "procedural protections and legal standards" provided by the criminal process, because college discipline "will never result in incarceration." Yet at least one school, New York's Colgate University, stands plausibly accused of incarcerating a student in a campus basement before he even knew the charges against him.[42]

Moreover, the same guidelines suggested that colleges should, with the sexual assault accuser's permission, share with police, who *are* in the incarceration business, the colleges' own interviews, including interviews of the accused. The major effect of this new policy would be to end-run the accused's constitutional right not to be subjected to custodial questioning by police without lawyers. This right protects the innocent as well as the guilty, as the Supreme Court has long stressed.[43]

In 2015, University of Wisconsin chief of police Susan Riseling boasted of a case in which her office had used campus proceedings to gather evidence for subsequent criminal charges against a Wisconsin student. Celebrating her role in circumventing her own student's civil liberties, Riseling proclaimed, "It's Title IX, not *Miranda*. Use what you can."[44]

Reflecting similar impulses, the University of Texas at Austin adopted a new "blueprint" for its campus police. The "blueprint" ordered UT Police, an accredited law enforcement agency, to perform a "victim-centered investigation" when handling sexual assault cases. As part of this new process, officers were required to structure their investigations so as to anticipate defense strategies. Officers should, the university counseled, reduce the "number of reports prepared by investigators" and "avoid writing a detailed report" for follow-up interviews. This kind of investigation, the guidelines maintained, would make it harder for defense lawyers to impeach the accuser in cases that went to trial.[45]

As FIRE's Samantha Harris observed after reading the UT manual, "an investigator who is trying to anticipate and counter defense strategies in the course of his/her investigation is not acting as a neutral fact-finder."[46]

OCR's 2014 guidance also decreed some procedures that dramatize how innocent students facing campus discipline are at far higher risk of being wrongly punished than are criminal defendants. OCR demanded, for example, that all college officials handling sexual assault complaints receive specialized training—which, as the "training" used at institutions from Stanford to Middlebury to Ohio State shows, has often been blatantly one-sided. And although the criminal process allows ample time to prepare a defense, the OCR 60-day limit has made it difficult for accused students to gather the material necessary to prove their innocence, as often is effectively required in the college disciplinary process.

Imagine the different outcome in the Amherst case if Michael Cheng had been given enough time to discover his accuser's self-incriminating text messages. Or in the Miami case if Matthew Sahm had been given enough time to gather statements from all the witnesses who undermined *his* accuser's claims. Or in the Vassar case if Peter Yu had been given enough time to track down witnesses who had seen *his* accuser and him together at the bar.

As if to advertise how little weight OCR gives to due process, its 2014 guidance included a sweeping decree that colleges must "ensure that steps to accord any due process rights do not restrict or unnecessarily delay the protections provided by Title IX to the complainant." This provision suggested that even the *constitutional* protections of accused students must give way to OCR's interpretation of Title IX. The standard also flouts centuries of the Anglo-American legal tradition that due process is the best way both to reach the truth and to protect the innocent.

The White House report did include a suggestion that colleges enter agreements with local police. But the Obama administration later released a model agreement that failed to suggest a greater police presence on campuses—the same campuses that the administration depicted as beset by violent crimes against women.[47]

These continuing efforts to channel rape accusers away from police and into campus proceedings brought a strong complaint from a powerful rape victims' organization, the Rape, Abuse and Incest National Network (RAINN). RAINN urged the federal government "to de-emphasize colleges' internal judicial boards," adding that "it would never occur to anyone to leave the adjudication of a murder in the hands of a school's internal judicial process. Why, then, is it not only common, but expected, for them to do so when it comes to sexual assault?" College disciplinary processes, it added, "were designed to adjudicate charges like plagiarism, not violent felonies. The crime of rape just does not fit the capabilities of such boards."[48] The federal government ignored this advice.

The virtual absence of congressional oversight left only a handful of lawyers and civil libertarians to join RAINN in critically assessing the 2014 White House report. It "continues the apparently inexorable erosion of the rights of the accused on campus," lamented lawyers Matt Kaiser and Justin Dillon, who often represent accused students.[49] The White House effort "reflects a presumption of guilt in sexual assault cases that practically obliterates the due process rights of the accused," said former ACLU national board member Wendy Kaminer.[50] "By continuing to empower campus judiciaries to adjudicate allegations of serious criminal activity, the Task Force's recommendations may ultimately worsen the situation for both victims and the accused," cautioned FIRE president Greg Lukianoff.[51]

The Obama administration's accusers' rights crusade rolled on through the Republican capture of the Senate and retention of the House in the 2014 midterm elections. In April 2015, OCR issued more guidance, suggesting that schools pay for "multiple Title IX coordinators," with "one lead Title IX coordinator who has ultimate oversight responsibility."[52] With this "burgeoning of specified mini-bureaucracies within nongovernmental institutions"—or "bureaucratic sex creep"—"the federal bureaucracy is regulating sex, not merely sexual violence or harassment," Harvard Law School professors Jacob Gersen and Jeannie Suk Gersen have observed. As a result, "nonviolent, nonharassing, voluntary sexual conduct—whether considered normal, idiosyncratic, or perverse—is today regulated by the bureaucracy." And this "sex bureaucracy," which consists of "dedicated offices, employees, and bureaucracies within the regulated institutions," has "managed to plant seeds of its own replication within the parties it regulates, and the plants are blossoming."[53]

The two professors had an opportunity to observe the phenomenon firsthand. Harvard University's Title IX coordinator, Mia Karvonides, oversees a sprawling bureaucracy of 50 Title IX coordinators.[54] The university also employs six staffers in the Office of Sexual Assault Prevention and Response; they, in turn, regulate 33 proctors and tutors living in undergraduate houses.[55] Dedicated to eradicating "rape culture" on the Harvard campus, the office, through its official Harvard website, has expressed concern about how, "in the context of sexual assault, 'innocent until proven guilty' is sometimes invoked to silence survivors."[56]

"This kind of hysteria may be ugly," University of Tennessee Law School professor Glenn Harlan Reynolds observed in late 2014, "but for campus activists and bureaucrats it's a source of power: If there's a 'campus rape crisis,' that means that we need new rules, bigger budgets, and expanded power and self-importance for all involved, with the added advantage of letting you call your political opponents (or anyone who threatens funding) 'pro rape.' If we focus on the truth, however—rapidly declining rape rates already, without any particular 'crisis' programs in place—then voters, taxpayers, and university trustees will probably decide to invest resources elsewhere. So for politicians and activists, a phony crisis beats no crisis."[57]

Under relentless federal pressure, university policies have not only redefined sexual assault but also twisted the meaning of the English language. The University of Georgia, for instance, promises students accused of sexual assault a "hearing"—but then redefines the word to mean "interviews with the investigator."[58] At East Georgia State as well, "Interviews with the Title IX Coordinator constitute the hearing."[59] USC uses the single investigator-adjudicator structure and then adds: "The accused also has the right to appeal the initial findings to a three-member panel. This is a hearing."[60] Such Orwellian abuses of language prompted FIRE's Samantha Harris to tweet, "Calling something a hearing does not actually make it a hearing" (@SamatFIRE, January 21, 2016).

In early 2016, UCLA's Title IX coordinator, Kathleen Salvati, told the campus newspaper that the university's new sexual assault procedure would benefit *accused* students. In fact, since the policy vested almost all power over accused students in a single investigator from the Title IX office, it robbed each accused student of any right to a hearing, to have his accuser cross-examined, or even to see the evidence against him. Yet Salvati enthused that the new policy would "take some of the burden off" of the accused by sparing him any need to prepare for the now-defunct disciplinary hearing—which would have been his best chance of being treated fairly at the university level.[61]

As colleges' rules in cases of alleged sexual assault have become more unfair and at odds with ordinary English usage, the biases of those who administer them have become more egregious. As one Colgate professor told one of us (Stuart Taylor): "The sort of rules that the Office of 'Sex Czar' (our Title IX Coordinator) applies to others—it does not apply to itself. Membership on its Panels hearing claims of sexual assault provide a wonderful example of Old Boy, Old Girl network; she recruits or they volunteer (though technically appointed by the president of the university, it is upon her recommendation); she's responsible for their training...; her colleagues are responsible for the investigation, hearing, and sentencing. And then since the felt obligation of the Office is to ensure that students do not *feel* that they face the risk of sexual harassment, the situation is ripe for indulging [racial and other] stereotypes."

Although attempted murder, armed robbery, and felony assault violate the values of every community, nobody claims to believe—as they do in the case of sexual assault—that if the accused and the accuser happen to be students at the same school, such cases should be handled by academics rather than by law enforcement. That's because the people who investigate felonies need legal and forensic evidence-gathering tools that Title IX offices do not have: search warrants, subpoenas, powers of arrest, legal firearms, the penalty of perjury for false testimony, and so on.

With none of these tools, campus sexual assault investigators will almost always have less evidence and weaker truth-finding abilities than law enforcement. Recall the rape, discussed in chapter 7, of an unconscious female student at Vanderbilt by football players while another made a video. If Vanderbilt's Title IX office, rather than the Nashville Police Department, had handled the investigation, the perpetrators might have gotten away with it. Recall also the accusation by Alice Stanton that got Michael Cheng expelled from Amherst, which any competent law enforcement team would have exposed by obtaining Stanton's cell phone, with its exculpatory text messages.

In the current environment, universities have large financial and reputational incentives to return guilty findings in sexual assault cases (except in the rare cases involving star athletes in revenue-producing sports). By contrast, as lawyer Stephen Henrick has observed, "The civil and criminal courts do not suffer comparable financial incentives to convict innocent people because there is no statute or enforcement mechanism by which a court could forfeit its funding or pay astronomical sanctions based on the outcome of a trial." Colleges and universities know that not-guilty findings can expose them to Title IX complaints by accusers, leading to investigations that almost always bring vast costs and bad publicity. Those risks are structural. Add to that the well-known pro-accuser bias of most college administrators and the current staff at OCR. These conditions, Henrick argued, hang "like a Sword of Damocles over risk-averse administrators as they adjudicate campus sexual assault allegations."[62]

The only risks faced by schools that find all or almost all accused students guilty, on the other hand, are lawsuits. And the record shows that the worst outcome faced by a university in such a lawsuit will almost certainly be nothing more than a court order reversing its decision and perhaps an award of very modest damages.

As universities' rules and processes have grown increasingly unfair, congressional leaders such as Kirsten Gillibrand (D-New York) and Claire McCaskill (D-Missouri) have egged them on. McCaskill, for instance, contended that "the criminal-justice system has been very bad, in fact much worse than . . . college campuses, in terms of addressing victims and supporting victims and pursuing prosecutions."[63] If the senator actually believes this, shouldn't she focus on improving the criminal justice system? McCaskill seems oblivious to the elitism inherent in her almost exclusive preoccupation with allegedly victimized *college* women and *campus* "justice." Indeed, the entire campus accusers' rights movement is "a slap in the face to the millions of Americans who are at a higher risk for sexual assault and who cannot afford college, many of them poor, minority women," as Ashe Schow wrote in *The Washington Examiner*.[64]

Like Senate demagogues of the past, both senators embraced their cause at a time when their political standing was threatened. Elected in the 2006 Democratic wave, McCaskill seemed on her way to losing her 2012 bid for reelection, in part because Missouri was trending Republican. Then Republicans did McCaskill the favor of nominating Representative Todd Akin. After Akin asserted that women needn't worry about getting pregnant from "legitimate rape" because "the female body has ways to try to shut that whole thing down," his campaign appropriately disintegrated.[65]

Gillibrand was first elected to the House in 2006, unseating a scandal-plagued Republican in an upstate New York district. She affiliated with the centrist Blue Dog caucus. But after being appointed by Governor David Patterson to a vacant Senate seat in 2009, Gillibrand pivoted to appeal to the far more liberal statewide constituency she now represented. Expecting possible liberal primary challenges in both the 2010 special election and her 2012 bid for reelection, Gillibrand abandoned her previous hostility to gun control and opposition to marriage for same-sex couples. She also embraced an aggressive feminist agenda, most conspicuously by targeting the military's supposed laxity in policing sexual assault. Gillibrand comes across as a skilled demagogue who reshapes her professed convictions to mirror her political needs.

McCaskill, one of the few former state-level prosecutors in the current Democratic caucus, seems to have internalized the preference of unethical prosecutors for cutting procedural corners in order to get a conviction. Her work "treats the rights of the accused as an afterthought," in the words of Ada Meloy, a former general counsel of the American Council on Education.[66]

In 2014, in a superficial 12-page report based on a survey by her office of college leaders, McCaskill claimed that too many colleges' procedures were "biased or harmful" not to alleged perpetrators (as we have shown in this book) but to alleged *victims* of sexual assault. The bias, she asserted, came from allowing accused students to be tried by disciplinary panels including one or more of their peers—one of the few remaining protections for accused students that OCR had not yet vetoed. The Missouri senator wanted to eliminate student panelists, due to "privacy concerns for survivors who can be forced to divulge intimate and painful details of their experiences to peers that they live and study among." But survivors also live and study among those panel members who are professors or administrators. So why pinpoint students?

McCaskill's real rationale, it appears, was a sense that student panelists might be far less likely than most academics to presume guilt. The Missouri senator displayed her own deep-seated presumption of guilt by describing the parties in a sexual assault proceeding as the "alleged perpetrator" and "the survivor." The absence of "alleged" before "survivor"—before any determination has been made—was no accident.[67]

McCaskill also faulted colleges for allegedly failing to provide "adequate training" for those who hear sexual assault claims, to counteract "pervasive and culturally ingrained misunderstandings of what constitutes sexual assault, such as the prevalence of acquaintance rape versus stranger rape, what constitutes consent, the type of conduct that constitutes rape, and how trauma can impact the survivor's demeanor and memory." It would of course be unconstitutional to put criminal jurors through such guilt-presuming training. And, as we have already shown, the type of training that McCaskill has championed, which more and more universities are utilizing, is unfair to accused students.

Gillibrand has been even more dismissive of accused students' rights. Rejecting the idea of handling campus sexual assaults through the criminal justice system, like all other felonies, she endorsed in late 2015 colleges' "quicker, more streamlined" process. "[I]f there's no evidence," she said, colleges can "make sure a student...doesn't have to be in the same dorm or in the same science class as her assailant." Thus did Gillibrand display in one sentence her prejudice that even in cases with "no evidence," the accused is an "assailant."[68]

Gillibrand enlarged her media image as a champion of victims by inviting a sexual assault accuser who, as discussed in chapter 4, now appears to have not been a victim at all—Columbia's mattress-toting Emma Sulkowicz—as her special guest for President Obama's State of the Union address in January 2015. In a *Huffington Post* essay explaining the invitation, the New York senator expressed solidarity with Sulkowicz, who "carries her mattress everywhere she goes to symbolize the burden she carries every single day as long as her rapist is still on campus."[69]

This statement was both extraordinary and deplorable: a sitting U.S. senator labeling as a "rapist" a presumptively innocent Columbia student living in her own state, based on far-from-credible allegations. As FIRE's Ari Cohn pointed out on Twitter, this senatorial claim that "allegations of rape = guilty of rape" laid bare Gillibrand's "disregard for rights of the accused" (@AriCohn, January 21, 2015). After Sulkowicz's credibility was obliterated by Cathy Young's investigative journalism in February 2015, Gillibrand remained—or at least pretended to remain—a true believer. "I believe Emma" was all she would say, without explaining why.[70]

Both senators' offices did not respond to a request from us for either an interview or written responses to questions regarding their approach to sexual assault and campus due process.

McCaskill and Gillibrand have taken the lead in pushing the benign-sounding Campus Accountability and Safety Act (CASA). The duo sponsored CASA in 2014 and introduced a slightly different version in 2015. After a drafting process that saw the involvement of campus accusers' rights groups such as Know Your IX but not a single civil liberties organization, CASA would require that universities publish data on the outcomes of campus sexual assault cases, which only Yale does at this time. The likely result: Title IX complaints against colleges that find an insufficient number of accused students guilty.[71]

CASA would also require that universities regularly conduct and publish online surveys, known as campus climate surveys, "regarding [students'] experiences with sexual violence and harassment." That sounds reasonable. But experience shows that these campus climate surveys tend to be designed to exaggerate the number of sex crimes. They use the same sorts of overbroad definitions of sexual assault and other gimmicks as the broader surveys by the Association of American Universities and the *Washington Post*–Kaiser Family Foundation poll. And though they purport to poll "campus climate," they never ask about students' attitudes toward the presumption of innocence, the need for fair procedures, or the value of due process—questions that likely would reveal the prevalence of the witch-hunt atmosphere.

In 2014, a White House template suggested that universities survey "perceptions" of "attitudes" among students regarding sexual assault.[72] The document's proposed wording switches between felony sexual assault and unwanted sex as if both could be considered under the rubric of campus sexual assault. Such linguistic looseness, Jacob Gersen and Jeannie Suk Gersen recognized, "contributes to individual and ultimately social understandings that unwanted is the same thing as nonconsensual—that we should feel similarly about unwanted sexual contact and nonconsensual sexual contact.... This conflation of nonconsent and unwantedness matters because many people, both men and women, have consensual sex that is unwanted."[73]

A typical campus climate survey came at the University of Colorado, whose early 2016 offering indicated that 28 percent of female undergraduates had been sexually assaulted. Avoiding such straightforward questions as "Were you sexually assaulted?" the survey's creators instead asked questions such as whether respondents had ever had sex because of "deception, manipulation, or emotional threats" or being caught "off guard"—none of which are crimes or fit the common cultural understanding of sexual assault. A statement from Teresa Wroe, the university's deputy Title IX coordinator, removed any doubt about the university's intentions: "For us, having that number be high means we are doing a good job communicating what the issue is.... When we see that high number I feel like we're doing what we can to try to understand our population."[74]

Some survey data indicate signs of panic that a reasonable administration would seek to soothe, not inflame. The 2016 campus climate survey at the District of Columbia's Georgetown University, for instance, found that almost 40 percent of female undergraduates considered it somewhat, very, or extremely likely that they would experience "sexual assault or sexual misconduct off campus at university-sponsored events." This figure was quite likely higher than the percentage of female undergraduates who would ever *be* "off campus at [a] university-sponsored event" during their time at school, since not many university-sponsored events are held off campus (and few of those that are involve opportunities for sexual contact between students). But even though students' responses on this question were either confused or irrational or both, Georgetown's administration pretended to take them seriously. It promised a host of policy changes, task forces, and other initiatives—each of which doubtless will intensify the panic in time for the next campus climate survey.[75]

In the end, the purpose of these surveys appears to be to confirm activists' preconceived beliefs, rather than to gather new information. Unlike the University of Colorado, in its 2016 campus climate survey Stanford used a definition of sexual assault that more closely conformed to state law. Unsurprisingly, the more accurate definition yielded a far smaller number of alleged victims, with 1.9 percent of Stanford students asserting they had been sexually assaulted. This provoked a furious response from Stanford Law School professor Michele Dauber, and student activists called for a new survey, which would presumably return a higher figure of sexually assaulted students.[76] Sympathetic alumni threatened to withhold financial donations until the university resurveyed the students using questions of the type preferred by Dauber and her fellow campus activists.[77]

If it becomes law, CASA also would order colleges to provide a "confidential advisor" for the "victim," with no comparable help for the accused. The bill presumes guilt by repeatedly referring to students who level unproven allegations as "victim" or "victims," without the critical qualifier "alleged." But Gillibrand defended the 2015 version of CASA by claiming that it "actually has clarified rights for the accused" better than the current system.[78] In fact, the bill's 51 pages contained only two hollow "rights": (1) notice of the charges and (2) enough time—in the unreviewable opinion of the college—to prepare a defense.[79] This book has discussed many cases in which accused students did not receive nearly enough notice or opportunity to prepare a defense, and CASA's toothless wording would have helped none of them.

Though the impetus for unfairness has come from Democrats in both the executive and legislative branches, six Republican senators added momentum to CASA by cosponsoring it. They include Marco Rubio of Florida—the once and perhaps future presidential candidate—Charles Grassley of Iowa, and Kelly Ayotte of New Hampshire.

Rubio has talked a good game—on a statement buried deep in his former presidential campaign website—but his continued sponsorship of CASA indicated the insincerity of his purported embrace of due process. When the enterprising Ashe Schow contacted each sponsor's office to ask how the measure would ensure due process for accused students, a Rubio spokesperson replied, "This bill does not address this issue." When Schow asked who would have the most authority to investigate allegations, the response was, "The victim will have the most authority."[80] This response reflected an astonishing misunderstanding both of the nation's traditions and of the fact that there is no adjudicated "victim" at the investigative stage. An Ayotte spokesperson declined to answer Schow's questions, while justifying CASA through Obama's discredited claim that one in five college women is raped.[81] No Democratic sponsor responded.

A July 30, 2014, tweet by commentator Christina Hoff Sommers (@CHSommers) rang true: "Due process has no lobby. Republicans & Dem[ocrat]s do the bidding of gender warriors. Not a word about falsely accused."

GOP officeholders have challenged what they perceive as OCR overreach—on issues about which they care. In May 2016, OCR issued a guidance document indicating that transgender public school students should be able to use bathrooms that corresponded to their gender identity. The directive generated harsh attacks from numerous Republican governors—each of whom had remained silent about OCR's campaign against the due-process rights of their state universities' students.[82] (Eleven states—all with Republican governors, Republican attorneys general, or both—then sued the Obama administration to prevent Title IX from being used to protect transgender students.) Seventy-three House Republicans signed a public letter likewise challenging OCR's authority for the directive.[83]

Although dozens of Republican officeholders criticized OCR on the rights of transgender teens, only Lamar Alexander, James Lankford, and the trio of House Republicans who cosponsored the Safe Campus Act (see below) have stood up for campus due-process rights. The unusual GOP complicity in the kind of federal overreach that Republicans purport to abhor has multiple origins. Fear of the "war on women" demagoguery greeted any Republican challenge to any Obama administration policy involving gender. Some social conservatives seem to hope that they can exploit the campus rape panic to restore traditional gender roles on campus. In addition, protecting the civil liberties of people accused of violent crimes has never been a priority for most Republicans, who (like most other Americans) remain ignorant of both the mistreatment of innocent students and the true nature of Obama's campus agenda.

A telling example came in a September 2015 House hearing to analyze two legislative proposals: CASA and the Safe Campus Act, a bill with modest due-process protections cosponsored by three House Republicans. Supported by the National District Attorneys Association, the Safe Campus Act would prohibit universities from disciplining students for sex crimes unless the accuser first files a criminal complaint. The schools would still be allowed to provide counseling or any other type of accommodation for the accuser.

The fourth congressional hearing since 2014 focusing on sexual assault on college campuses provided the first occasion on which either the House or the Senate heard from an advocate of due process, FIRE's Joseph Cohn. Cohn questioned the competency of universities to investigate serious felonies and said police were better equipped to do so.[84] As Cohn spoke, Know Your IX activists in the audience held up signs reading "WRONG" and "NOT TRUE."[85] Activist organizer Olivia Ortiz asserted on Twitter that "what FIRE is trying to say is that the police are nicer [than college tribunals] to rich white guys" (@Olivia_A_Ortiz, September 10, 2015).

Cohn's testimony provoked Rep. Jared Polis (D-Colorado) to wonder whether OCR needed to weaken due process even more. Perhaps, he mused, colleges should adopt a "reasonable likelihood" standard, finding accused students guilty even if the probability of innocence is greater than 50 percent. When Cohn objected to this hang-the-innocent-to-get-the-guilty proposal, Polis went even further, noting that if "maybe one or two" of 10 accused students were guilty under this lowered standard, universities should expel all 10, just to be sure. He repeated these sentiments in a post-hearing interview with *Reason's* Robby Soave.[86] Polis' comments generated criticism even in his left-leaning district.[87] A few days later, the congressman issued a halfhearted retraction asserting that he "misspoke" when he urged the expulsion of so many innocent students—while attacking FIRE's expertise on the issue.[88]

OCR's Lhamon, in her own testimony, displayed ignorance of the institutions she regulated by saying that one reason universities should be in charge of campus sex crimes was that they also investigated campus "drug dealing."[89] How any university could conduct a competent drug-dealing investigation Lhamon did not reveal. Senator McCaskill went even further. If universities were required by law to avoid adjudicating sex crimes until they had been reported to police, she warned, "a young woman could be robbed at gunpoint and decide that she wanted to just try to get that person off campus and go to her university and they could take action under Title IX. But if she was raped, she would not be able to do that unless she made the decision to go to the police."[90] McCaskill may have been the first former prosecutor ever to suggest that the way to get an armed robber off of a campus was to go after him with a sex discrimination law.

Know Your IX's Dana Bolger, meanwhile, suggested on Twitter that because "schools respond to all sorts of disciplinary violations," such as plagiarism, they could handle rape (@danabolger, September 10, 2015)—an analogy that trivializes the horror of sex crimes. "Cops Off Campus," screams Know Your IX (@knowyourIX, March 20, 2016), even amid claims that the nation's campuses face an unprecedented wave of violent crime.

Ultimately, the Safe Campus Act got nowhere, because heavy pressure from Gillibrand and McCaskill appeared to intimidate some original supporters—chiefly sorority groups—into abandoning the measure.[91] But defenders of campus due process were heartened by developments in some states, such as Georgia and North Carolina. Cynthia Garrett, a FACE leader, said that after meetings with 67 congressional offices in February and March of 2016, the group was encouraged that House Republican staffers (and a few Democrats) seemed to have become more sensitive to due-process concerns, as well as more fed up with OCR's bureaucratic overreach. And language in the GOP's 2016 platform highlighted the importance of treating sexual assault on campus as a crime.

Civil libertarian Harvey Silverglate, speaking from long experience both with witch hunts and with college discipline, called in February 2015 for a "return to sanity...before more wreckage occurs." In the current "believe-the-accuser" panic, he observed, the unfairness of college tribunals had become "so dire" that civil libertarians were now looking to police and prosecutors—their usual adversaries—to substitute some sanity for campus lunacy. Silverglate added that as with earlier witch hunts, "it is almost certain that the current campus sexual assault madness will burn itself out, leaving in its wake the wreckage of many young lives. My concern is how long it will be before sanity and decency return."[92] Given current trends, this was about as optimistic as it's possible to be for those who think that something more than an accusatory finger is necessary to expel a student as a sexual predator.

9

FROM CAMPUS TO CRIMINAL LAW

I n 1991, Antioch College, the Ohio institution known for its particularly aggressive brand of political correctness, expanded its definition of sexual assault to address what a group called "Womyn of Antioch" contended was a hidden epidemic of rape. Under the new policy, called "Ask First," sexual assault included "any sexual contact or conduct between two or more persons," including "the touching of thighs, genitals, buttocks, or the breast/chest area," if consent "is not expressly obtained in a verbal manner."

The rules stated: "Verbal consent should be obtained with each new level of physical and/or sexual contact/conduct in any given interaction, regardless of who initiates it. Asking 'Do you want to have sex with me?' is not enough. The request for consent must be specific to each act."[1] The only exception allowed for skipping the "verbal" part occurred when the sexual act was "mutually and simultaneously initiated." But the college didn't explain how anyone could ever prove that had happened.

The new policy drew widespread ridicule. A *Saturday Night Live* parody imagined the dialogue that would be required of Antioch students seeking romance:

MALE: May I elevate the level of sexual intimacy by feeling your buttocks?

FEMALE: Yes. You have my permission. [*Male touches Female's buttocks.*]

MALE: May I raise the level yet again, and take my clothes off so that we could have intercourse?

FEMALE: Yes. I am granting your request to have intercourse.[2]

A 1993 *New York Times* editorial criticized the Antioch policy, using reasoning the newspaper soon would abandon. "[A]dolescence, particularly the college years, is a time for experimentation, and experimentation means making mistakes," the *Times* maintained. "No policy will ever be able to protect all young people from those awful mornings-after that are accompanied by the dreadful feeling: 'Oh my God! What have I done?' It's from such moments, accompanied by 'I'll never let that happen again,' that people learn." The editorial went on to underscore the harm the policy could cause by quoting a student who said, "This is a real policy. I can get kicked out over this."[3]

Less than a quarter century later, in 2015, the legislatures in California and New York, two of the nation's most populous states, had *almost unanimously* written slightly less radical versions of Antioch's principles into the laws governing all colleges and universities in their territory. These statutes revolutionized the law for college students—and only college students—by treating common practices as sexual assault for college disciplinary purposes. Activists are currently mounting a potent push, with some success, to similarly redefine rape in the criminal law.

———————

Initially, only a handful of ideologically comparable institutions imitated Antioch's approach. (Pennsylvania's Gettysburg College, for example, required "continuing and active" verbal consent for all "sexual" activity, including "hugging."[4]) But in the past 15 years the Antioch idea—now called "affirmative consent," or "yes means yes"—has gained increasing currency. In 2014, according to the pro–affirmative consent group NCHERM, approximately 800 institutions around the country had voluntarily adopted the standard.[5] By January 2016, that figure had risen to an estimated 1,500 colleges and universities.[6] The mass adoption of such an accuser-friendly standard undermines claims that universities are hostile to accusers' rights and interests in a way that requires federal intervention.

This shift occurred even absent evidence that affirmative-consent regimes such as Antioch's "Ask First" rule had actually done anything to protect women. When asked in 2014 whether her school's standard had made that campus safer, Kristine Herman, an author of the rule, responded, "I don't know...if the numbers have gone down or not."[7] This lack of interest in whether her two-decades-old innovation had served its ostensible objective at all was sadly typical of campus ideologues on the issue.

"Affirmative consent" has a benign ring. But the requirement effectively presumes any student who is accused of sexual assault to be guilty by saddling him with the virtually impossible burden of proving that he obtained the accuser's explicit consent at every step in their encounter—maybe 5, 10, or 20 times—despite her subsequent claim that he did not. Who, in the bias-ridden college disciplinary process, will believe the accused? As Judge Carol McCoy wrote in the Corey Mock case at the University of Tennessee–Chattanooga: "Absent the tape recording of a verbal consent or other independent means to demonstrate that consent was given, the ability of an accused to prove the complaining party's consent strains credulity and is illusory."[8]

Megan McArdle is insightful on the perversity of such a standard: "I'm struggling to know how a man (or a woman) could ever be fully sure that they were not breaking the law. Even affirmative consent can, after all, presumably be withdrawn at any time—without a clear 'no.'...If silence does not signal consent, does it signal consent has been revoked?" In addition, as she points out, "Predators who knowingly violate the law can, after all, always insist that they got that affirmative consent."[9]

By 2014, the affirmative-consent movement had spread from the activist fringe to the legislatures of deep-blue states. In the spring of 2014, California state senators Kevin de León and Hannah-Beth Jackson joined Assemblywoman Bonnie Lowenthal in introducing SB

967, California's affirmative-consent bill. The trio ostensibly acted to counteract what de León called "a rape culture" that was "quite pervasive on our college campuses."[10] (He offered no definition of what this "rape culture" entailed, or on which California campuses it existed.) The measure cleared the California Legislature *unanimously* and was signed into law in October 2015. It requires all universities in California to find a student accused of sexual assault guilty in disciplinary proceedings unless he can prove his accuser gave "affirmative consent," on an ongoing basis, during intercourse.

Although consent can be verbal or nonverbal under this law, the California Legislature left undefined what constitutes nonverbal consent—and cosponsor Bonnie Lowenthal continued to claim that rape occurred unless the female student said "yes."[11] To make things worse, the Legislature also adopted OCR's "more likely than not" standard of proof, meaning that even if a future administration withdraws the "Dear Colleague" letter (or the courts invalidate it for procedural reasons), the document's provisions will remain in effect in California. When asked in June 2014 how an accused student could prove that he had obtained affirmative consent, Lowenthal candidly replied, "Your guess is as good as mine."[12]

The lawmakers also left unexplored the question of why, if affirmative consent is such a good idea, they did not extend it to *all* sexual assault allegations, including accusations against the legislators themselves. Meanwhile, some campus activists imagined that the California Legislature still had not gone far enough. Professor Caroline Heldman, one of the more extreme leaders of the witch hunts at Occidental, wanted a law that would give power to any female student who later claimed that she didn't agree "enthusiastically" to whatever had occurred in sexual intercourse.[13]

In fact, the affirmative-consent champions envisioned a college sexual environment that doesn't exist, as researchers Jason Laker and Erica Boas found in a continuing study of first-year students at an unnamed college in the San Francisco Bay area.[14] In the duo's initial sample, taken in 2012, only one of the 15 students they interviewed said he or she had verbally requested consent prior to sex; most others used vague, nonverbal cues that likely would not satisfy the "yes means yes" requirement. "The answer to this problem, we believe very strongly, is not going to be found in laws and policies, but that's where 95 percent of the efforts are," Laker told *Inside Higher Ed*. "Very often, this is about lawyers making sure universities are not going to get sued. What is that going to do to prevent these problems? We need to give students the tools to help them communicate in a way that fits their own temperament."[15]

In the typical campus case—involving two inebriated sex partners with no eyewitnesses, a pattern that frequently appeared in the Laker/Boas study—"unless the hearing board can show that the consent was offered, [California institutions are] now obligated to treat it as if it was nonconsensual," FIRE's Joe Cohn noted. "That shifts the process dramatically against an accused person."[16] Added journalist Cathy Young, after surveying arguments by the California law's defenders: "In essence, advocates of affirmative consent are admitting that they're not sure what constitutes a violation; they are asking people to trust that the system won't be abused. This is not how the rule of law works."[17]

A case at USC in the 2015–2016 academic year illustrated Young's point. Two students, Will Cranston* and Gwen Douglas,* had a rocky two-month sexual relationship. Their third instance of sexual contact, on the night of October 14, ended badly, but they continued to see each other (and have sexual contact) for more than a month. They eventually broke up when Cranston made clear he wanted to be able to see other women while still sleeping with Douglas.

In dozens of text messages between the two, Douglas interpreted the events of October 14 as nonconsensual. Her descriptions of the incident varied over time, while she also said she wanted to get back together. Cranston, for his part, admitted to having disregarded Douglas' emotional state but repeatedly denied having sexually assaulted her; he also made clear his disinterest in a romantic relationship. By January 2016, Douglas told him she'd file a sexual assault charge with USC unless he moved out of his fraternity. "In a twisted way," she said, "[I] want to gain happiness from knowing you're not doing okay. And I'm frustrated that you're doing way better than I am when I deserve happiness more than you." Though Cranston did as Douglas pressured him to, she still filed a complaint with USC.

USC turned the investigation over to Patrick Noonan, a labor lawyer in the university's Title IX office. He interviewed 19 of Douglas' sorority sisters and friends; they all confirmed that Douglas later had said she was sexually assaulted. But Noonan didn't speak with the only witness who allegedly had firsthand knowledge of the incident: Cranston's roommate, who, Douglas claimed, saw her fleeing Cranston's room in tears on the night of October 14. In his interview with Cranston, Noonan asked what Cranston had done to obtain affirmative consent—using California law effectively to shift the burden to the accused to prove his innocence. And in a case that came down to the parties' credibility, Noonan twice accused Cranston of undermining his credibility by altering the chronological order of text messages he had supplied to the investigator. But if the investigator had asked the student rather than assume a malevolent motive, Noonan would have learned that the app Cranston used to download the texts rearranged them by size. Noonan presented his findings to a body called the Student Equity Review Panel, which recommended expulsion.

To prepare his appeal, Cranston and his lawyer, Mark Hathaway (who had also represented accused students at Occidental and UCSD), convened a conference call with USC officials. Cranston asked for the identities of the panel members who had approved Noonan's recommendation for expulsion; Title IX coordinator Gretchen Means refused to provide them. When the call ended, Hathaway and the accused student stayed on the line to confer with another lawyer from Hathaway's office. Meanwhile, Means and Noonan—evidently believing that Cranston and Hathaway had hung up—continued a conversation between themselves in which they called the accused student and his lawyer "motherfuckers." Means asked, "Does that college motherfucker know who I am?" Cranston cited these comments in his appeal as proof of bias. But the USC appeals panel brushed the "motherfucker" comments aside as not being "new evidence." The panel also rejected Cranston's claim that USC had improperly imposed on him a presumption of guilt. The affirmative-consent law, the USC appeals panel noted, required the accused student to prove he had obtained affirmative consent. It contended that the text messages in which Cranston and Douglas discussed their mutual misunderstandings regarding the October 14 incident showed that the accused student had failed to meet his burden. Only the intervention of a California state court judge, who issued a stay, allowed Cranston to remain enrolled at USC—although the case was then reassigned to another state court judge, who set aside her predecessor's ruling. The matter remains pending in California state court as of this writing (September 2016).[18]

This sort of outcome seemed to be just what the California law's powerful journalistic supporters desired. Ezra Klein, of the news site Vox, abandoned his site's agenda of data-driven journalism to celebrate sacrificing innocents, not merely to identify more of the guilty but also to revolutionize the culture. "Men need to feel a cold spike of fear when they begin a sexual encounter," wrote Klein. In an October 2014 defense of the California statute, Klein conceded that "too much counts as sexual assault" and the law was so "sweeping in its redefinition of acceptable consent" that "two college seniors who've been in a loving relationship since they met during the first week of their freshman years, and who, with the ease of the committed, slip naturally from cuddling to sex, could fail its test." Nonetheless, he continued, "the yes means yes law is a necessarily extreme solution to an extreme problem." Klein hoped that the law would "create a haze of fear and confusion over what counts as consent" by telling male students in "morally ambiguous" situations that "you Better Be Pretty Damn Sure she meant to say yes."[19]

Klein based his conclusions on two statistical claims: (1) that one in five college women was the target of a sexual assault and (2) that "completely false accusations of rape by someone who did offer consent, but now wants to take it back…*happen very, very rarely.*"[20] Klein's citation for the latter assertion was to a column by Cathy Young, who in response claimed that the Vox editor had misrepresented "the whole point of my article[, which] was to rebut the idea that false accusations of rape are so infinitesimally rare that they needn't be a serious factor in deciding whether laws dealing with sexual assault are unfair to the accused."[21]

Jonathan Chait, the liberal commentariat's leading critic of campus political correctness, expressed amazement at Klein's "arguing for false convictions as a conscious strategy in order to strike fear into the innocent," a "conception of justice totally removed from the liberal tradition."[22] Farther to the left, Freddie deBoer echoed Janet Halley by noting that the sacrificial lambs in Klein's affirmative-consent utopia would be disproportionately poor and minority students whose families couldn't hire lawyers.[23] But the punish-the-innocent extremism of Klein captured the zeitgeist among contemporary liberals.

Meanwhile, the affirmative-consent movement spread to other Democratic-dominated states. In New York, Governor Andrew Cuomo led the charge.[24] His December 2014 proposal defined affirmative consent as "a clear, unambiguous, knowing, informed, and voluntary agreement between all participants to engage in sexual activity"—without explaining what constituted an "unambiguous" or "informed" agreement. His proposal dramatically expanded the definition of "incapacitation" to include all "impairment due to drugs or alcohol." That standard would treat as rape many (and perhaps most) consensual sexual encounters between college students.

Cuomo's proposal included a "victim and survivor bill of rights," which guaranteed to every accuser who filed a sexual assault claim with her college the right to be "free from any suggestion that the victim/survivor is at fault when these crimes and violations have occurred, or should have acted in a different manner to avoid such a crime." This language could be construed as ruling out every possible defense, with the exception of mistaken identity. The accused student's claim that his accuser had consented would arguably suggest she was at least partially "at fault"; his claim that she was simply lying would arguably suggest that she "should have acted in a different manner" by telling the truth.

After a brief procedural tussle, in June 2015 legislative leaders supported a redrafted measure, entitled "Enough Is Enough," which made cosmetic changes to Cuomo's proposal while leaving intact its central mission of destroying due process for accused college students.[25] Cuomo cited *The Hunting Ground* when he announced the deal, but he did not mention that his sister, Maria Cuomo Cole, had helped produce the controversial film.[26]

In a reminder that campus due process has no political constituency, the law cleared the Republican-held state Senate and the Democratic-held state Assembly *without a dissenting vote*.

The affirmative-consent bandwagon soon moved to two other deep-blue states, Illinois (which passed its version of an affirmative consent law in August 2015) and Connecticut (whose law was approved in 2016). Lead sponsor Mae Flexer, majority leader of the Connecticut Senate, told *The Hartford Courant* that her bill "will stop the victim blaming" that she purported to believe was rampant in college disciplinary processes. She suggested that mandating affirmative consent was necessary to spare victims from being from being faulted for such things as wearing short skirts. Flexer didn't cite any Connecticut campus sexual assault cases in the previous decade in which the shortness of an accuser's skirt had been raised; we are aware of none in any state in recent years.[27] Flexer also deemed the measure necessary because she could find no evidence of a college student ever having been sent to prison for a rape on campus. We cite many such cases in this book; Flexer could have found any of them—and more—with a brief Internet search.[28]

University of Connecticut student Devin Keehner lamented that the bill's extraordinarily vague definition of affirmative consent brought accused students "one step closer to being presumed guilty until proven innocent." He wondered why legislators had singled out college students to receive a special definition of sexual assault, rather than having the same definition for everyone in the state. (We asked Senator Flexer; her office didn't reply and then blocked one of us—KC Johnson—on Twitter.) At the very least, Keehner cheekily added, in order to subject "officials to the same vague regime that many students already find themselves living under," Connecticut's Legislature should "empower the Office of State Ethics to issue civil penalties against public officials who fail to obtain affirmative consent during sexual intercourse or, for that matter, if their sexual partner is under the influence of alcohol."[29]

Another blue state, Minnesota, stopped short of "affirmative consent" but adopted a sweeping law to regulate how colleges handle sexual assault cases. The law, which went into effect on August 1, 2016, refers to the parties in campus sexual assault cases as "victim" and "alleged perpetrator," and it requires colleges to allow students to file anonymous complaints of sexual assault, which the schools have the option to investigate. The Minnesota law also orders training campus adjudicators in such topics as "the dynamics of sexual assault, neurobiological responses to trauma, and compliance with state and federal laws on sexual assault," by the police or another entity that specializes in investigating sex crimes.[30]

A Minnesota-based company called trainED Solutions, which several private Minnesota colleges employ to conduct their required training, features a module instructing adjudicators to consider conduct that "violates institution's policy" as a yellow light, coming between "acceptable consensual conduct" (green light) and "unlawful" (red light).[31] The clear implication is that Minnesota universities prohibit some vague, unspecified category of *lawful* sexual conduct—which their policies nonetheless describe as "sexual assault."

Even in those states without a legislative mandate, universities have jumped on the bandwagon—sometimes recklessly so. In 2014, the University of Wisconsin's police department launched a new initiative, called "You Can Tell Us," to encourage more reporting of sexual assaults. The new policy promised accusers that they would be "in control of the police investigation," an extraordinary abdication of the department's duty to presume the accused innocent.[32] After the University of Tennessee adopted an "affirmative consent" standard for the 2015–2016 academic year, Assistant Vice Chancellor Jenny Richter conceded, "We had some indication from around the country that this is going to be not looked upon kindly by courts. We know of two court cases at least that are saying, 'That's ridiculous.'" But the university didn't much care, Richter suggested, since judges "don't deal with university students on a regular basis."[33] Richter's stance was mild compared to that of University of Iowa Law School professor Paul Gowder, who teaches classes in constitutional law and professional responsibility. Gowder endorsed the "affirmative consent" standard, saying that it "seems reasonable as a first-pass to me to have an inquisitorial process" instead of an adversarial process in adjudicating campus sexual assault claims.[34]

On the other hand, a few states have moved tentatively to enhance the fairness of college disciplinary proceedings—although there is little evidence that they have succeeded in changing colleges' conduct. In 2013, North Carolina became the first state to approve a law requiring public colleges to allow most accused students to be actively represented by lawyers before disciplinary panels. The measure passed the state House of Representatives 112 to 1, over the strong opposition of most of the state's higher-ed establishment, especially the University of North Carolina. North Dakota followed suit the next year.

Bill Haggard, UNC-Asheville's vice chancellor for student affairs, faulted his state's elected representatives for failing to understand that "a key component of the developmental process of responding to student misconduct is for the student to take responsibility for their [*sic*] own behavior and to learn from the incident." It seemed never to have crossed Haggard's mind that an accused student may have done nothing wrong for which to "take responsibility." He also celebrated accused students having the "learning experience" of defending themselves, without counsel, against accusations that could (be they innocent or guilty) ruin their lives.[35]

The most significant push to protect accused students came in the GOP-dominated Georgia Legislature. State Representative Earl Ehrhart, chairman of the House Appropriations Subcommittee on Higher Education, convened hearings on the question after accused students in two cases filed due-process lawsuits against Georgia Tech. "My concern is due process," Ehrhart told The Atlanta Journal-Constitution. "This is about things that can follow students their entire lives. It can destroy their lives. I cannot in good conscience continue to fund Georgia Tech at the level that it requests without some assurance to parents that there will be due process for their children."[36]

In January 2016, Ehrhart stated that unless Georgia Tech's trustees protected due process, the Legislature would force them to do so.[37] He also called for Georgia Tech president Bud Peterson to resign over his school's denial of due process to accused students.[38] Ehrhart informed university officials, "If you've got a bond project, if you don't protect the students of this state with due process, don't come looking for money. Period." Georgia Tech's leaders made their choice: To avoid protecting the due-process rights of the accused, they temporarily withdrew a request for funds to rehabilitate the university's library. The university eventually backed down, making minor changes to its disciplinary policies that improved the rights of the accused while avoiding the more comprehensive reform that Ehrhart had championed.

The 2016 presidential race also touched on the debate over sexual assault and due process on campus. Hillary Clinton endorsed President Obama's approach, including the move toward a separate college judicial system with far fewer protections for accused students. She appointed to her campaign's digital outreach team Zerlina Maxwell, who had maintained that on college campuses, at least, "we should believe, as a matter of default, what an accuser says," since "false accusations are exceedingly rare, and errors can be undone by an investigation that clears the accused."[39]

Clinton delighted campus activists by proclaiming on Twitter that "every survivor of sexual assault deserves to be heard, believed, and supported" (@HillaryClinton, November 22, 2015). A voter at a New Hampshire town hall asked the candidate whether she would apply this same standard to the many women who had accused her husband of misconduct. "I would say that everyone should be believed at first until they are disbelieved based on evidence," Clinton responded.[40] Yet during President Bill Clinton's time in office, she had resolutely defended him against all charges before hearing any "evidence" about his accusers. In January 2016, one of those accusers, Juanita Broaddrick, tweeted a recollection of her allegations against Bill Clinton. Shortly thereafter, as *BuzzFeed*'s Katie Baker reported, Hillary Clinton's campaign quietly removed from the "campus sexual assault" section of its campaign website a quote from the candidate to accusers: "You have the right to be believed." The Clinton campaign declined comment to Baker on why it had made the change.[41]

Clinton's rival for the nomination, Vermont senator Bernie Sanders, took a quite different approach. Though he unhesitatingly accepted the notion of a rape epidemic on college campuses, Sanders also informed an Iowa audience, "Rape and assault is rape or assault whether it takes place on a campus or a dark street. If a student rapes another student it has got to be understood as a very serious crime, it has to get outside of the school and have a police investigation and that has to take place."[42] For this stance, he was strongly attacked by the media (e.g., *The Huffington Post*) and among activists (e.g., Know Your IX), as well as by people with a financial stake in the status quo (e.g., Brett Sokolow of NCHERM).[43]

The campus sexual assault/due-process issue received almost no attention in the Republican presidential primary. No GOP candidate, including Kentucky senator Rand Paul, who ran on a libertarian platform that emphasized civil liberties and castigated governmental overreach, personally defended campus due process. At a February 2016 forum, Ohio governor John Kasich—whose state's universities had featured some of the most troubling instances of accused students being denied due process—described campus sexual assault as "another thing to worry about."[44] And CASA cosponsor Marco Rubio, who had previously joined forces with enemies of due process, misleadingly defended his work.

After highly critical commentaries about his efforts from columnists George Will and Ashe Schow, Rubio's spokesperson preposterously claimed that the Florida senator had teamed up with Senators Gillibrand and McCaskill to sponsor CASA because "Marco is committed to improving the handling of sexual assault on college campuses while protecting the rights of the accused." The spokesperson continued that, "as president," Rubio would "prioritize stopping the Department of Education's Office [for] Civil Rights from continuing its assault on students' due process rights."[45] Rubio's staff buried on a remote portion of his campaign website—with a URL that ceased to function after he transitioned from the presidential race to a Senate bid—a similar assertion that "those accused of sexual assault should have their due process rights respected." Both statements begged the question of why Rubio had joined the assault on due process by cosponsoring CASA in the first place.[46]

The political and legal allies of the campus accusers' rights movement have every intention of revolutionizing the criminal laws on rape and sexual assault as well. They seek especially to import "affirmative consent"—once a national joke—to make it as difficult as possible for innocent (as well as guilty) men to defend themselves. Gillibrand, for one, said during an MSNBC-hosted panel discussion that the "yes means yes" law "is where our debate needs to go."[47]

It is, of course, hard to imagine people being sent to prison for failing to seek explicit consent before every attempted kiss or fondle. But not long ago it was hard to imagine a student being expelled as a rapist for such conduct or for engaging in alcohol-fueled sex. And if activists continue to have their way, innocent young men such as Michael Cheng, Matthew Sahm, and Dez Wells could be not only kicked out of college but also sent to prison.

According to civil libertarian Harvey Silverglate, if the law criminalizes lack of affirmative consent, "There would be no defense to a rape charge." Thus "the idea that the real world might emulate the campus is very frightening." An influential faction of the American Law Institute (ALI) wants to revise the criminal laws toward this very end.

The ALI is the nation's most prestigious and influential organization that drafts model laws. Its by-invitation-only members include some

4,500 law professors, lawyers, and judges.[48] The current debate focuses on a proposed overhaul of the ALI's "Model Penal Code," which dates to 1962. Although the model code has no legal force of its own, the 1962 version was adopted in whole by a few states and in part by many. It also has influenced judicial interpretations.

There is broad agreement within the ALI that some of the 1962 code's sections on sex crimes are outdated. Examples are provisions that involuntary sex is not rape unless the defendant used force or threats of extreme violence and that no person should be convicted of a sex offense "upon the uncorroborated testimony of the alleged victim."

But an increasingly fierce, if genteel, debate has raged within the ALI since 2013 about other, highly controversial proposals to criminalize many common sexual practices, advanced by New York University Law School professor Stephen Schulhofer. ALI leaders chose Schulhofer to be the powerful "Reporter" in charge of drafting proposed revisions of the Model Penal Code.

Schulhofer, his Associate Reporter and NYU colleague Erin Murphy, and their allies (including Michelle Anderson, who is the president of Brooklyn College, the institution at which author KC Johnson teaches) have pressed for drastic revisions in state criminal laws. They wish to criminalize sexual practices that have always been legal in America and to make felons of many people who reasonably believe that their sex partners consented.[49]

Schulhofer's initial proposals included an affirmative-consent amendment, like the ones that many universities have added in recent years, to the criminal laws.[50] The affirmative-consent proposal would, the National Association of Criminal Defense Lawyers (NACDL) asserted in a March 2016 statement, mean that "the offense would be proved merely upon the proof of a sex act with nothing more. The result is an unconstitutional shifting of the burden of proof requiring the accused to prove that consent was affirmatively given."[51]

Schulhofer and Murphy explained in an introductory note to an early draft that they wanted to change sexual norms by criminalizing "commonplace or seemingly innocuous" behavior in order to reshape "existing social expectations."[52] Columnist Megan McArdle aptly observed that the notion "that somehow these legal changes will change the culture and human nature so that we no longer have gray areas in which two people might have different perspectives on one event" is "asking far too much of the law."[53]

The Schulhofer faction's power reflects the fact that the legal academy, a large and influential bloc of ALI members and leaders, is now ideologically to the left of the vast majority of the nation's population on gender issues. The brilliant—but ideologically extreme—Schulhofer was appointed in 2012, after he circulated a "Prospectus for a Project of Revision" that, critics charge, provided scant notice that he would use as a blueprint the same wish list of radical changes that he had offered in a 1998 book, *Unwanted Sex: The Culture of Intimidation and the Failure of Law*. The project's more than three dozen official advisors have included many academics, such as Catharine MacKinnon, but relatively few trial judges and defense lawyers with experience in rape cases.

Schulhofer has expressed nonchalance about the likelihood that his proposals would ruin the lives of a great many innocent people. It is better, he has said, to risk that "many" men be convicted of rape for initiating sex without first obtaining an expression of "positive agreement" from their partners—even if the evidence shows that their partners in fact wanted sex—than to allow men accused of rape to escape conviction if their accusers had never said no. He has also suggested he wants to coerce guilty pleas by changing the rules in ways that would (in our view) essentially shift the burden to rape defendants *in criminal cases* to prove their innocence, contrary to the rights of all criminal defendants not to be convicted unless proven guilty beyond a reasonable doubt.[54]

At the ALI's 2016 annual meeting, Schulhofer and his allies met with a stinging defeat concerning their proposed definition of "consent." An overwhelming majority of the 1,000 or more members in attendance—energized by strong criticisms of Schulhofer's proposals from more than 100 civil libertarians and other members—rejected Schulhofer's effort to include the equivalent of an affirmative-consent rule.[55] But this voice vote was not necessarily irrevocable; many more proposed radical revisions have not, at the time of this writing, come to a vote; and ALI leaders, including President Roberta Cooper Ramo, have appeared sympathetic to Schulhofer's efforts to push his agenda through one way or another.

The other proposals include provisions that:

- Would make into a "felony of the third degree," punishable by up to 10 years in prison, any inebriated sexual penetration in which the "victim" is "in a state of mental torpor as a result of intoxication." The recommended penalty would include mandatory registration as a sex offender.

  Various dictionaries define "torpor" as including "apathy," "lethargy," and "having very little energy," as professor Laird Kirkpatrick of the George Washington University Law School pointed out in an unpublished letter. So the "torpor" provision would "criminalize a significant percentage of cases where parties who have been drinking subsequently have sexual relations," he wrote. Most jurisdictions currently treat sex with a person under the influence of alcohol as rape only when the accuser is too incapacitated to consent.

- Would make it a felony punishable by up to five years in prison—called "Sexual Penetration without Consent"—if a person "engages in an act of sexual penetration and knows, or consciously disregards a substantial risk, that the other person has not given consent to that act."[56] This change could make a felon of a person who believes that his partner has consented but cannot be sure of it.

- Would make it a crime even for a spouse or intimate partner to initiate sex unless the spouse or partner could prove that he or she "reasonably believed that the complainant would welcome the act."[57] This standard could, critics say, invite further proliferation of the "strategic accusations" of sexual and child abuse that "already plague divorce and child custody matters."[58]

Perhaps the most concise indictment of the overall Schulhofer-Murphy project came from professor Charles Fried, of Harvard Law School, a former Solicitor General of the United States. In a mid-2015 letter to ALI director Richard Revesz, Fried wrote:

"Instead of clarity and reasonableness... ALI [is] proposing a codified standard that will surely be ignored by most, will be subject to general ridicule, celebrated only by a small cadre of ideologues in the grip of a theory, and if enacted would be an invitation to the kind of extortionate, discretionary, discriminatory enforcement that it is a principal aim of a Model Code to prevent.... If the ALI cannot do better than this it has nothing to contribute in this matter."

Fried added, in March 2016: "My preference would be to see the whole project put on a lengthy pause rather than inundating us with drafts at an unusually fast pace.... I have little confidence in these Reporters to produce a useful work by continual tinkering."[59]

Meanwhile, another ALI initiative—the "Project on Sexual and Gender-Based Misconduct on Campus"—is in the works. It is not yet clear how far-reaching it might be.

The push to criminalize sex without affirmative consent is only one example of overkill by the rape-law-reform movement, which has been gaining strength since the mid-1970s. This situation has led to what one scholar calls "a steady erosion in the due process rights of those accused of rape."[60]

The movement to reform state rape laws commendably accomplished a long-overdue overhaul of antiquated common-law rules that had for many centuries of female subordination made a great many forcible rapes legal and many others very difficult to prove.[61] Under now-abandoned laws in many states (as well as the 1962 Model Penal Code), husbands had a legal right to rape their wives. And until the 1970s, most state laws defined rape so narrowly that women had to prove that they had physically resisted by struggling fiercely, even though police advised them to surrender to rapists lest they be further harmed.

In many states, an accuser's testimony, no matter how credible, was not enough to convict a man of rape unless there was also corroborating evidence, such as torn garments or bruises or a witness who had heard screaming; a rape prosecution could proceed only if the woman promptly complained; and at trial, defense lawyers could probe almost without limit into the alleged victim's sex life, including whether she was a virgin or promiscuous, and could suggest that dressing provocatively meant the woman had been "asking for it." All these laws have been revised or repealed almost everywhere, and rightly so.[62] Meanwhile, police, prosecutors, and judges have largely outgrown the sexist attitudes about rape that were fairly common as recently as the 1970s—though, of course, exceptions exist.

States remain divided on some issues. For example, many states will convict a defendant of rape only if it is shown that he used force or overcame "reasonable resistance." On the other hand, almost 20 states have adopted the "no means no" approach of treating as rape any sexual penetration after the alleged victim said or implied "no" and did not take it back.[63] Not unreasonably, the Obama administration and the FBI sided with this "no means no" view in 2012 for purposes of statistical reporting. The new definition deemed rape to be "penetration, no matter how slight, of the vagina or anus with any body part or object, or oral penetration by a sex organ of another person, without the consent of the victim."[64]

These changes increased the number of reported rapes (including attempted rapes) from 85,141 in 2012 to 113,695 in 2013.[65] Despite the increased total, these new figures (which apply to society as a whole) fall far below the 400,000-to-500,000 sexual assaults that the administration has claimed occur annually on college campuses alone.

Some other changes, however, could put many innocent people in prison:

Dispensing with proof of criminal intent. State courts in Massachusetts and Maine have ruled that a man can be convicted of rape even if he had reason to believe from the accuser's words or conduct that she had consented. This position flies in the face of centuries of legal consensus that a person should be convicted of a crime only if he or she intentionally broke the law with a guilty state of mind.[66] Some commentators would convict defendants of rape even in some cases in which the woman herself thought she had consented.[67]

Admitting evidence of the defendant's sexual history. Despite criminal law's long-standing rule that evidence of the defendant's prior crimes may not be introduced to suggest his guilt, Congress changed the Federal Rules of Evidence in 1994 to make an exception for cases involving any form of sexual assault.[68] Prosecutors can introduce not only prior sex-crime convictions but also any other evidence, such as testimony by another woman accusing the same defendant, to show his alleged propensity to commit sex crimes. Although such evidence may indeed be relevant, the traditional rule of inadmissibility reflects a long-standing judgment that the prejudicial impact on the defendant's right to a fair trial outweighs any probative value.

Excluding even highly relevant evidence of the accuser's sexual history. Rape shield laws, at their best, bar defense lawyers from asking questions or introducing evidence of largely irrelevant details of an accuser's sexual history—promiscuity, for example. But at their worst, and even though the Supreme Court has ruled that a trial judge must allow a rape defendant's "cross examination with strong potential to demonstrate the falsity of [the accuser's] testimony," they have been interpreted to require exclusion of highly relevant evidence targeting the accuser's credibility.[69] Such evidence has included (a) prior rape claims by the accuser that proved to be false or that contradicted her current testimony and (b) the accuser's prior and/or subsequent consensual sex with same man she later accused of rape.[70]

Admitting "expert" testimony about rape trauma. Courts from Vermont to New York to Kansas to Colorado have admitted supposedly expert testimony about "rape trauma syndrome" by mental health professionals.[71] Rape, say these experts when hired by prosecutors, causes victims to act in ways that seem inconsistent with having just been raped, such as going about their lives as though nothing had happened and without mentioning the alleged rape to anyone until months later. Such rape-trauma claims may sometimes be true, and rape accusers are entitled to make such claims in their testimony. But as the California Supreme Court held, "permitting a person in the role of an expert to suggest that because the complainant exhibits some of the symptoms of rape trauma syndrome, the victim was therefore raped, unfairly prejudices the appellant by creating an aura of special reliability and trustworthiness."[72]

Putting scarlet letters on people convicted of sex crimes. Congress and every state have created sexual offender registration programs, and many states have also prohibited people convicted of sex offenses from living near a school, park, playground, or day-care center. Such laws are a very serious obstacle to the ability of a person convicted of a sex offense to reenter the community. The premise—that people convicted of sexual assault are likely to be serial predators—is not supported by scientific data. Research suggests that sex offenders, with the exception of pedophiles, are *less* prone to recidivism than people convicted of many other crimes.[73]

Writing "affirmative consent" into the criminal law, as some in the ALI desire, would do more damage than any of these other changes to bedrock constitutional protections for all people accused of crime. It would neuter both the presumption of innocence and the requirement of proof of guilt beyond a reasonable doubt. These constitutional protections are under attack because they allow some rapists (as well as other criminals) to go free and leave many victims feeling humiliated by the legal system. But this is an unavoidable cost of protecting innocent defendants against wrongful conviction for crimes that are often impossible either to prove or to disprove with confidence.

The 17th-century English jurist Sir Matthew Hale wrote that rape "is an accusation easily to be made and hard to be proved, and harder to be defended by the party accused, tho never so innocent."[74] This dictum, though much deplored by accusers' rights activists, reflects a genuine dilemma for rape victims, men falsely accused of rape, and the criminal process alike: In a large percentage of "she said, he said" cases, judges, jurors, and other outsiders can never be confident that the accuser is truly the victim of a horrible crime.

10

A NEW GENERATION'S CONTEMPT FOR CIVIL LIBERTIES

In 2014, *Rolling Stone* reporter Sabrina Rubin Erdely resolved to write an article that would "paint a large picture of what it's like to be on campus now, what the environment is like, where not only rape is so prevalent, but also there's a pervasive culture of sexual harassment/ rape culture."[1]

She began her research not by interviewing college administrators or civil libertarians but by consulting at length with the long-discredited Wendy Murphy and the soon-to-be-discredited David Lisak. According to Erdely's interview notes, Murphy told her that in the college disciplinary process, "the more privileged [the accused student] is, the more violent and the more likely the woman has to die before he's held accountable." Murphy added that S&M was common at MIT because "geeks don't know how to negotiate [sex], they just take knives out." According to Erdely's notes, Lisak, citing his Jewish heritage, indirectly likened the treatment of women on contemporary college campuses to that of Jews in Nazi Germany. Such extremist claims did not dissuade Erdely from seeing Murphy and Lisak as "experts," and her *Rolling Stone* article would adopt their views on sexual assault on college campuses.[2]

For months, Erdely prospected at Ivy League schools and other elite institutions to find the perfect story to prove her thesis. When her search came up dry, Murphy encouraged her to look at the University of Virginia. It was there that a self-described rape victim, campus activist, and recent UVA graduate named Emily Renda provided the key tip. UVA had hired Renda as a sexual assault staffer—a move that might have shaken a thoughtful journalist's assumption that UVA was hostile to rape victims. Renda, in turn, introduced Erdely to Jackie Coakley, whose story Renda herself had once referenced in congressional testimony and who had joined Renda in speaking at campus events to raise awareness of rape. *Rolling Stone* would present the tale as the "single, emblematic college rape case."[3]

Erdely spent much of the summer and early fall of 2014 interviewing Coakley, Renda, and a handful of UVA activists. Though she claimed to be interested in capturing the campus environment, the only male UVA students Erdely seems to have interviewed were people who agreed with her article's planned thesis. Brian Head, 2014–2015 president of One in Four, a UVA all-male peer sexual assault education group, told Erdely of his experience running information sessions for male UVA students. He noted with disappointment that his fellow male students "almost always" raised concerns about the danger of false accusations. A thoughtful reporter might have wondered why—if UVA were awash in a "rape culture" with an administration bent on covering up for sex criminals—so many male students would worry about the risk of being falsely accused.[4]

Erdely didn't explore the issue. By this point, she was focused on Coakley's powerful tale. Coakley claimed that in the fall of 2012, "Drew," a fellow lifeguard at a campus pool, invited her to a party at his fraternity, Phi Kappa Psi. After they arrived, Drew ushered Coakley into a darkened room. Then seven Phi Kappa Psi members—including one student she recognized from her "tiny" anthropology discussion group—brutally raped her, while Drew and another frat brother encouraged them. One attacker assaulted Coakley with a bottle; another raped her atop a glass table—when it shattered, he continued his assault even with "sharp shards digging into her back." Finally the rapists left the room and Coakley fled the frat house, her "dress spattered with blood."

Although spectacular in its details, Coakley's story in many ways resembled the claims of Angie Epifano and Alice Stanton at Amherst and Andrea Pino at the University of North Carolina. The "victim" in these narratives lashed out less at her attacker(s) than at university administrators and/or friends who allegedly behaved with extraordinary callousness in her hour of need. The prime targets in Erdely's *Rolling Stone* article, published on November 19, 2014, were the three friends who had met Coakley after the party, who were portrayed as emblematic of a pervasive campus "rape culture," and UVA dean Nicole Eramo, whom the magazine used to personify college administrators' supposed indifference to rape victims. According to the article, Coakley's friends, after seeing her blood and injuries and hearing her tell of gang rape, urged her not to report the crime, lest their own social standing on campus suffer. Erdely presented one of them as saying, "She's gonna be the girl who cried 'rape,' and we'll never be allowed into any frat party again." Erdely quoted Eramo as expressing fear to Coakley that UVA would be known as a "rape school" if victims reported what had happened to them.[5]

A good investigative journalist would have interviewed the five people with direct knowledge of the events that Coakley alleged to have occurred: Drew, the supposed orchestrator of the gang rape, the three friends who supposedly met Coakley after the attack, and Coakley's mother, who supposedly had seen the blood-spattered dress she wore that night. Erdely had spoken with none of these alleged witnesses. She said that Coakley's mother didn't return her calls. She had accepted Coakley's claim that the three friends didn't wish to speak with *Rolling Stone*, after a feeble effort to reach them. And Erdely had never even tried to contact Drew, since Coakley claimed to be worried he would retaliate against her. It seemed not to have occurred to Erdely that Coakley's professed concern about retaliation had not deterred her from portraying Drew as a monster in a national magazine.[6]

The result was that the article would go to press without its reporter even knowing the *full names* of either Drew or Coakley's three friends. "I wish I had better sourcing on a lot of the Jackie stuff," Erdely conceded in an email to her editor, three weeks before the article was published.[7] As journalist Cathy Young later noted, "Jackie [Coakley]'s story...had more red flags than a Soviet military parade."[8]

Instead of finding witnesses, Erdely had relied on Coakley's fellow campus activists—Emily Renda, Alex Pinkleton, and Sara Surface—who all vouched for their colleague's credibility. Pinkleton said it was "blatantly obvious" that Coakley had been raped. Of course, the trio's belief in Coakley proved nothing but their commitment to the "believe-the-survivor" ideology that credits *all* accusers without question. Indeed, Erdely—and the story's editor, Sean Woods—explained away the inconsistencies in Coakley's story by suggesting that these were to be expected of sexual assault victims.[9] In an Orwellian line, Erdely later explained the contradictions as Coakley having "changed her story to be more truthful."[10]

"A Rape on Campus" was a national sensation. Almost 3 million unique visitors examined the article on *Rolling Stone*'s website, making it the magazine's most trafficked 2014 offering. By the end of December 2014, more than 700 print news stories referenced Erdely's tale, which was mentioned in more than 6,000 television news clips.

Fellow reporters gushed about Erdely's bombshell. Jeffrey Toobin, staff writer at *The New Yorker* and CNN legal analyst, touted this "amazing work" as a "real public service" and "great journalism." Eric Umansky, deputy managing editor at *Pro Publica*, rhapsodized that Erdely had exposed "lawlessness" through "a triumph of investigative storytelling." NBC's Luke Russert hailed Erdely's "extraordinary piece of journalism." David Beard, executive editor for Public Radio International, told Erdely: "You are making change happen. This editor thanks you."[11] Television news programs similarly treated Erdely as an oracle of truth. On her MSNBC talk show, Melissa Harris-Perry gushed that Erdely's piece demonstrated "the unwillingness or inadequacy of colleges and universities to help survivors find justice."[12] Judy Woodruff of *PBS NewsHour* accepted at face value Erdely's description of the alleged gang rape as "very representative of what was going on at American colleges across the country with regard to sexual assault," since "if you dig deep enough really in any campus, this is probably what you will find.... This is the norm."[13]

Erdely's version of events also was accepted as gospel in Charlottesville. Without conducting any investigation, and backed by her university's trustees, UVA president Teresa Sullivan suspended the social activities of not only Phi Kappa Psi but all fraternities. Much like

Richard Brodhead eight years earlier at Duke, Sullivan was ideologically predisposed to believe Erdely's wild tale. "There are individuals in our community who know what happened that night," she declared, "and I am calling on them to come forward to the police to report the facts. Only you can shed light on the truth, and it is your responsibility to do so."[14]

It seems never to have crossed Sullivan's mind that perhaps there was nothing to report. To ensure that "incidents like those described in *Rolling Stone* never happen," she promised "institutional change, cultural change, and legislative change."[15] A few days later, she encouraged the Charlottesville Police Department to enter fraternity houses to monitor students' activities, even if they lacked probable cause to do so—an invitation to strip constitutional protections from many of her university's students.[16]

Sullivan's move against all fraternities, which affected hundreds or thousands of students whom even *Rolling Stone* had not accused of any wrongdoing, earned hearty praise from national journalists. *New York Times* tech policy reporter Celia Kang gave "kudos" to Erdely for spurring the suspension of all UVA fraternities with her "deeply reported" article about only one. *Times* Sunday Styles reporter Katie Rosman declared on Twitter that "THIS is a journalist affecting [sic] change" (@katierosman, November 22, 2014). And *Washington Post* reporter Dan Zak ordered, "Now burn 'em down" (@MrDanZak, November 23, 2014). It would be difficult to imagine any appropriate context for a national reporter to advocate burning down the residence of college students, but how else are we supposed to interpret his remark?

The much maligned Phi Kappa Psi members knew that Coakley was lying. The fraternity had not even held a party on the weekend when she claimed her rape had occurred. And none of the fraternity's members had worked alongside her as a lifeguard. But they sensed that people at UVA did not want to hear the truth. The fraternity house was soon vandalized with such slogans as "UVA Center for Rape Studies" and "Suspend Us!" Protesters armed with chunks of cinder block smashed one fraternity member's bedroom window. Echoing *Post* reporter Dan Zak, a campus protest featured cries to "burn the frat houses down."[17]

UVA's faculty joined the character assault against their own students. Professors from the English, American Studies, and Spanish

Departments participated in a nighttime march, featuring drums and noisemakers, to the Phi Kappa Psi house. The faculty members claimed that the fraternities had created a "rape culture"; according to English professor Susan Fraiman, who organized the event, "We wanted to be out here on the street...to make a statement as faculty."[18] Professor Alison Booth portrayed fraternities as culturally "sick" and as "corrupting the young men."[19] Her English Department colleague, Jahan Ramazani, claimed that fraternities had "been involved for too long in making a safe space for criminal, violent acts."[20]

These voices were not the fringe. UVA's faculty senate demanded revisions in the university's sexual assault policies and debated a lengthier suspension for fraternities; the senate's chair, chair-elect, and former chair asserted that their students had created a campus "culture that allows violence to occur."[21] In the classroom, one UVA professor, departing from the syllabus to discuss Erdely's article, ordered Phi Kappa Psi members in the class to identify themselves.[22]

No evidence exists that any of these faculty members did anything to try to find out whether the allegations against Phi Kappa Psi were true.

Three days after her article appeared, Erdely tweeted that she found this response "heartening" (@SabrinaRErdely, November 22, 2014). But the predictable reaction of an administration and faculty dominated by identity politics, which mirrored the reaction of the Duke faculty and administration to the lacrosse case eight years before, made a mockery of Erdely's thesis that UVA and all elite universities were dominated by a "rape culture."

As the national media hailed *Rolling Stone* for presenting the defining narrative of the campus rape "epidemic," a few journalists departed from the crowd. Five days after Erdely's article appeared, and writing as "a magazine editor who has seen fakes before," *Worth* editor-in-chief Richard Bradley cautioned that the media needed to "be most critical about stories that play into existing biases. And this story nourishes a lot of them," including "pre-existing beliefs about the prevalence—indeed, the existence—of rape culture." He struggled to understand why Erdely had not attempted to contact Coakley's three much-maligned friends or her alleged attackers. The outlandish horror of Coakley's story reminded him of Tawana Brawley's false rape claim in the late 1980s.[23]

Bradley's essay prompted *Reason*'s Robby Soave to wonder whether the entire allegation was a hoax. In a December 1, 2014, column, he described as "perplexing" the fact that after the attack Coakley had not sought medical attention, which she surely would have needed if she had been "basically rolling around in broken glass for hours" with a succession of rapists on top of her. Soave also found Erdely's portrayal of Coakley's friends—casually dismissing her battered and bloodied state and urging her not to go to the hospital—as "almost cartoonishly evil."[24]

These analyses generated a furious backlash. Kat Stoeffel, then at *New York* magazine, mocked Bradley's warnings about Erdely's journalism and shot back that trusting *Rolling Stone* "just means following Erdely in the (still, apparently, radical) move of taking a traumatized young woman at her word."[25] *Jezebel*'s Anna Merlan dismissed Bradley's post as a "piece of shit"; her column's title ridiculed Soave as an "idiot" for even wondering about Coakley's truthfulness.[26] (Much later, she apologized.)

In an unintentional commentary on the lack of professionalism behind the *Rolling Stone* performance, the magazine's fact-checker for the UVA article, Liz Garber-Paul, re-tweeted the *Jezebel* screed.[27] Erdely herself almost taunted her critics, informing *C-VILLE* magazine that "the degradation of women is intrinsically woven into the campus, and on every campus, and frankly in our culture. If people are getting confused by that, I'm sorry to hear that. It's another aspect of their denialism."[28]

Erdely's interviews, however, accelerated her undoing. A turning point came on *Slate*'s "Double X" podcast, when host Hanna Rosin repeatedly asked Erdely (in different ways) whether she had contacted any of the accused students. Erdely clumsily evaded each question while asserting that lots of people on campus would recognize Drew's identity.[29] Subsequent reporting by *The Washington Post*'s T. Rees Shapiro revealed that despite the article's claims, Coakley's three friends would have been willing to talk to Erdely—and would have adamantly denied Coakley's version of what happened after the fraternity party.[30]

In early December 2014, *Rolling Stone* reaffirmed its belief in Coakley's "entirely credible and courageous" tale and "the indifference with which her complaint was met." Behind the scenes, Erdely drafted a rebuttal claiming that Coakley was "being brutalized a second time with strangers questioning if she told the truth," as was "common for rape victims." She planned to defend her "quality journalism" as conducted with "cold, hard diligence" combined with "empathy and humanity."[31]

Others who were ideologically invested in the story likewise tried to prop it up. Professor Booth declared that "if it's a matter of a few facts being incorrect, that won't change the outrage on campus and need to make fundamental changes." Sullivan reaffirmed her commitment to driving out the "evil" that lurked on campus.[32] *The New York Times* even managed to scrounge up two journalism professors who found no ethical or journalistic problems with Erdely not trying to interview any of the accused students.[33]

But on the night of December 4, 2014, the hoax unraveled. By this point, additional reporting by Shapiro and Erik Wemple at *The Washington Post* and Chuck Ross at *The Daily Caller* showed that "Drew," the alleged ringleader of the rape, did not exist. Coakley had identified this invented character to her friends as "Haven Monahan," using a photo that was actually of a high school classmate.[34] When Coakley learned that the fraternity intended to defend itself with a statement, she got in touch with Erdely. In a late-night phone call, she suggested that the attack might have occurred at another fraternity. She was also "evasive," Erdely would later say, when asked about some of the contradictions uncovered by other reporters. Erdely finally had to face the overwhelming evidence that her source had not been truthful. Under the subject heading "our worst nightmare," she emailed her editors, instructing them to retract the article. *Rolling Stone* did so the next day.[35]

Coakley's hoax, it turns out, was a catfishing scheme. She had created "Haven Monahan" in the hope of making jealous a male friend and campus activist to whom she was romantically attracted, Ryan Duffin.[36] She forwarded to Duffin and other friends emails and text messages allegedly from "Haven," cribbing language from the television show *Dawson's Creek* and purporting to discuss concerns about her health. In her own voice, she then explained the fabricated health concerns to Duffin by saying, "Ryan, it means I'm dying." When none of this activity sparked any romantic interest from Duffin, Coakley invented her rape tale.[37]

Erdely could have written a great story, about how a fabulist exploited a campus atmosphere of moral panic and how the UVA administration and professors as well as her fellow activists uncritically accepted her tale. But the *Rolling Stone* reporter was too closed-minded to see through the fantasies and lies.

At UVA, Coakley's former defenders tried to evade the hard questions her false report raised. Campus activist Alex Pinkleton, who privately told Erdely that she still believed something had happened to Coakley, cautioned that "we need to remember that the majority of survivors who come forward are telling the truth."[38] This language implicitly conceded that at least a minority of the people Pinkleton called "survivors" had not, in fact, told the truth. Another of Erdely's sources, UVA activist Sara Surface, admitted to the *Rolling Stone* reporter on the night of December 4–5 that Coakley was no longer credible—but rationalized, "I think trauma has done something to the details."[39]

Rolling Stone commissioned an autopsy by high-ranking administrators at the Columbia Journalism School. *Slate's* Hanna Rosin framed the issue that the autopsy should have explored: whether "this *Rolling Stone* story shows...that maybe we've reached a point where we hold stories about rape to a *lower* standard" of proof and sourcing than all other topics.[40] Instead, *Columbia Journalism Review* writers Steve Coll and Sheila Coronel produced 12,000 words detailing some of *Rolling Stone's* journalistic failures but averted their eyes from the big question: *why* had experienced reporters and editors made such obvious mistakes? They also showed their own guilt-presuming biases by labeling accusers "victims" and labeling accused students "perpetrators."[41]

As Richard Bradley commented, *The Columbia Journalism Review's* analysis failed to comprehend that the entire *Rolling Stone* article was "fashioned on selective presentation of material, the use of bogus or discredited statistics, quotes that are either fabricated or taken out of context, unconfirmed allegations, anonymous sources, the deliberate exclusion of evidence contrary to the author's thesis, and material that is either fabricated or presented in a way that is so profoundly misleading it can only be evidence of incompetence or dishonesty" (emphasis removed).[42]

USA Today's media critic, Michael Wolff, identified—as CJR failed to do—the magazine's economic and cultural incentives to sensationalize Coakley's story. "*Rolling Stone's* editorial vetting procedures may have failed," he noted, but "its editorial positioning was quite on target. It had precisely identified a demographic and brand issue. *Rolling Stone*, journalistically and commercially, is ever trying to position itself in left-leaning, 18-to-35-year-old, socially conscious territory. It would not, we might fairly assume, write the opposite story: a detailed and sympathetic account of the pain and anguish of a male student—a drunken, fraternity lout, let's say—falsely accused of rape. Indeed, *Rolling Stone*'s problem is not really a procedural issue, it's a fog of war issue. There is only one side here, one moral cause, one permissible outcome, hence everything bends to that narrative. And even if it's false, it can at least support the greater, undeniable truth."[43]

As with the collapse of the Duke lacrosse case, *Rolling Stone*'s shame had little effect on rape-culture true believers. A *New York Times* editorial even cited the article's withdrawal as justification for Congress to pass the Gillibrand/McCaskill-sponsored CASA.[44] Gillibrand's own comment on the story's discrediting was "I hope it's just putting more of a spotlight on the problem."[45]

Sullivan, who did not apologize to the members of Phi Kappa Psi, oversaw a redesign of UVA's sexual assault policy. The new procedure, which adopted a single investigator-adjudicator system with minimal procedural rights for the accused, would never have uncovered the evidence discrediting Coakley's version of events.[46]

Most accusers' rights activists turned to portraying Coakley's tale as atypical—though some remained steadfast believers. On April 7, 2015, National Abortion and Reproductive Rights Action League deputy digital director Kate Thomas (@KateThomas) tweeted that she still stood with Coakley, proclaiming, "THE VICTIM BLAMING NEEDS. TO. STOP." The National Organization for Women, in a self-exposing January 2016 open letter, criticized Eramo for seeking Coakley's communications with *Rolling Stone* to help prove the merits of her defamation lawsuit against the magazine and Erdely. The NOW letter claimed that the lawsuit harmed "rape survivors at UVA" by "publicly attacking one such survivor." NOW did not say what possible reason it could have for identifying Coakley—a proven liar—as a "survivor."

The Obama administration displayed similar imperviousness to facts. OCR's Catherine Lhamon granted her ideological ally Erdely a personal interview. (Lhamon did not respond to our own repeated emails requesting first an interview for this book and then written answers to a list of questions.) At their sit-down, the *Rolling Stone* reporter described a UVA Board of Visitors meeting at which, she claimed, a UVA dean "swooped in with a smooth answer" to wrap up a discussion of OCR's investigation of UVA. Lhamon responded by fuming that "nothing annoys me more than a school not taking seriously their review from the federal government about their civil rights obligations."

Later, a video surfaced that contradicted *Rolling Stone's* portrayal of the meeting, but Lhamon refused to apologize. "We continue to stand by the statements Catherine made during her interview with *Rolling Stone*," an OCR spokesperson told *The Daily Caller's* Chuck Ross.[47] Nor did OCR explain how a university that rushed to judgment against (imaginary) alleged rapists could somehow be guilty of discriminating against *women* in violation of Title IX. In September 2015, the office entered into a "voluntary" resolution agreement, in which OCR said it had detected "a basis for a hostile environment" against sexual assault accusers at UVA.[48]

These responses all fit the template of the aftermath of the Duke lacrosse case. But the reaction of one group—undergraduate students—at UVA in 2014 dramatically differed from that at Duke in 2006.

In 2006, Duke's student government took a measured response to the rape allegations until Mike Nifong's abuses became clear, and then it forcefully argued for due process. In 2014, UVA's student government treated Coakley's tale as true both before and after it collapsed. After the hoax was exposed, UVA's student government called for secret trials in all *criminal* prosecutions for rape, which would be unconstitutional; urged the university to provide accusers (but not the accused) access to legal counsel; and suggested requiring all future UVA students to take a course in "Women and Gender Studies."[49] Long after it was clear that Coakley had lied about almost everything, including her friends, the student council president, Jalen Ross, termed it "terrifying" that Coakley's friends had (nonexistently) discouraged her from reporting the (nonexistent) rape.[50]

In 2006, Duke's campus newspaper was fair-minded in its prize-winning editorial and news coverage of the rape allegations against lacrosse players. In 2014, by contrast, the UVA student newspaper, *The Cavalier Daily*, stood aside while Bradley, Soave, *The Washington Post*, and *The Daily Caller* exposed Coakley's lies. Then, as Coakley's story collapsed, *The Cavalier Daily's* executive editor, Katherine Ripley, started sending tweets with the hashtag "IStandWithJackie" about how Coakley's story "resonated with me" (@KatherineRipley, December 13, 2014). Assistant

Managing Editor Julia Horowitz, who would become the paper's editor in the 2015–2016 academic year, wrote an essay for *Politico* warning that "to let fact checking define the narrative would be a huge mistake."[51]

In 2006, nearly 2,000 Duke students registered to vote in the hope of retiring Nifong and electing a more ethical Durham chief prosecutor. In 2014, the most vocal UVA students seemed impervious to facts that contradicted their beliefs. Students Atthar Mirza and Elizabeth Ballou created a video thanking Coakley for coming forward; Mirza remarked, "Even if she made up the story, things like this do happen, and there are sexual assaults that don't get reported, so I meant to bring the focus back to Jackie [Coakley]. Whatever comes of this, we're still behind her and we still think she did something brave by coming forward."[52] *International Business Times* reporter Marisa Alioto found that students wanted to focus on the "conditions that make 'Jackie' plausible even if *Rolling Stone's* version of her story turns out to be false." No student to whom Alioto spoke expressed any sympathy for the falsely accused Phi Kappa Psi members.[53]

In 2014, even UVA students who had personal or institutional reasons to speak up against the mob instead embraced the facts-don't-matter crusade. Tommy Reid, head of UVA's Inter-Fraternity Council, endorsed the student government's proposal for secret rape trials throughout Virginia and claimed that fraternities latently reinforced the "gender norms [that] contribute predominantly to acts of sexual violence."[54] Reid appears to have expressed no concern about the vandalizing of the Phi Kappa Psi house or the false portrayal of fraternity members whose interests he was supposed to represent.

Ryan Duffin, the target of Coakley's catfishing effort, likewise clung to his preconceived beliefs, at least initially. Text messages between Duffin and Coakley, made public by Eramo's lawsuit, showed that Duffin "could find no evidence that Haven [Monahan] was ever at UVA" (@kcjohnson9, January 8, 2016).[55] But rather than showing concern for his falsely accused fellow students, Duffin told the Associated Press, "I still don't really care if what's presented in this article is true or not because I think it's far more important that people focus on the issue of sexual assault as a whole."[56] Eighteen months later, in a deposition for Eramo's lawsuit, Duffin showed greater appreciation of the unhealthy environment he had once occupied. He reflected that "the social setting...was so much that if you tried to speak out against the article, you were immediately shut down." Duffin recalled walking around campus, "constantly...hearing about this thing and hearing people be upset about something I knew was not true without really being able to say anything about it." It was a "very, very hostile environment," he observed, for anyone who suggested that there were two sides to the story.[57]

UVA students' embracing of both Coakley's hoax and the oppressive new disciplinary rules for sexual assault accusations came, tragically, in the wake of an actual rape—and murder—of a UVA student. A second-year student named Hannah Graham had disappeared on September 13, 2014, after getting lost on her way to a party. After her body was found, an intensive police investigation led to the arrest of 32-year-old Jesse Leeroy Matthew, thanks to forensic and video evidence. In short, law enforcement cracked a horrifying case about which campus discipline could have done nothing.[58]

Given how UVA's administration, faculty, and student body responded to Coakley's hoax, it's perhaps fitting that the first major legal challenge to OCR's Dear Colleague letter came from a case at UVA. The broad outline of the case resembled those of many others in this book: In August 2013, two law students had what appeared to be a drunken hookup. More than 18 months later, in March 2015, the female student filed a sexual assault complaint, alleging that she had been too intoxicated to consent. Until the Dear Colleague letter, UVA required "clear and convincing evidence" (around 75 percent certainty) to find a student guilty of sexual assault. But by 2015, UVA had bowed to OCR's demands and reduced the standard of proof to "more likely than not." It also instituted the single investigator-adjudicator model for dealing with sexual assault complaints.

The investigator-adjudicator, albeit reluctantly, found the accused student guilty. It was "very close," a "very difficult case," she wrote. The evidence "slightly" tipped in the accuser's favor, and because OCR's guidance required using "the weakest standard of proof," she said her hands were tied. Her report made clear that the outcome would have differed if she had used the "clear and convincing" standard. Because of her lingering uncertainty about what actually had happened, the investigator-adjudicator recommended a relatively mild punishment—counseling and a lifetime ban from the campus. But because the case delayed his degree, UVA's actions cost the student a promised job and the start of a legal career that came with it.

Instead of suing UVA, the accused student—working with FIRE and lawyer Justin Dillon—sued OCR. He stressed that the guilty finding in his case was directly attributable to the Dear Colleague letter—which UVA had had no choice but to accept, but which OCR had issued without following the requirements of the Administrative Procedure Act. As of September 2016, the suit is pending before the U.S. District Court in the District of Columbia.[59]

The lawsuit enraged accusers' rights activists. "Hell must be empty," scowled Michele Dauber, after she learned of FIRE's idea.[60] Know Your IX already had dismissed the lawsuit's rationale. The organization fantastically argued that the Dear Colleague letter had *benefited* accused students, by guaranteeing them "greater protections than are otherwise provided to them under federal law or policy."[61]

As the *Rolling Stone* drama unfolded at UVA, Phi Kappa Psi's Brown University branch was facing similar charges—and their resolution revealed a similarly troubling, one-sided student body hostility to due process.

The history leading up to Brown's response to Phi Kappa Psi in 2014 shows a pattern of guilt-presuming that predated the Obama administration. In 2006, the daughter of a major Brown donor accused a Brown freshman named William McCormick of sexual assault. The "advocate" whom Brown appointed to help McCormick defend himself was an assistant wrestling coach with no legal training. The key evidence in the case consisted of testimony by a supposedly neutral witness, McCormick's residential advisor. But a subsequent lawsuit by McCormick against Brown and the accuser's father revealed that the residential advisor had exchanged friendly emails and had meetings with the donor about future employment opportunities. Perhaps this conflict of interest led to the settlement of the lawsuit: the donor agreed to pay McCormick a reported $1.05 million—provided that McCormick drop his lawsuit against Brown.[62]

In 2013, Brown vice president Margaret Klawunn, who oversaw the university's handling of sexual assault claims, celebrated the federal government's mandate that schools lower their standard of proof in sexual assault cases. Although she explained to the campus newspaper that accusers often could not prove guilt by clear and convincing evidence, she expressed no concern about the risk of the new policy's erring on the side of expelling innocent students. Klawunn justified the university's weak protections for accused students by saying "We don't want attorneys to start running the University process."[63] "The reason schools don't like lawyers," civil libertarian Harvey Silverglate recognized, "is that they realize lawyers would see the kangaroo nature of the courts."[64]

In another case, which started in 2013, Brown found a student named Daniel Kopin guilty of sexual misconduct, despite the dramatically shifting stories of his accuser and despite what journalist Cathy Young found to be otherwise inconclusive evidence.[65] Brown implicitly confirmed the case's weakness by suspending Kopin rather than expelling him. Egged on by public denunciations by Sen. Kirsten Gillibrand, the Rhode Island school's leaders stood by while student activists hounded Kopin into withdrawing when he returned to school the following year.[66]

Then came the Phi Kappa Psi incident in October 2014. Two female students who had been drinking heavily dropped by the fraternity's party and shared an alcoholic drink provided by a student bartender. One of them later had sex with another student—not a Phi Kappa Psi member—whom she met after the party. She awoke the next morning feeling ill, with only hazy memories of the night before. She went to the campus health clinic, and Brown sent a sample of her urine to a private lab for testing. The lab concluded that the sample contained the date-rape drug GHB. Her friend, who had shared the same drink, did not allege that it had been drugged.

A campus outcry against the fraternity ensued. Brown's sexual assault bureaucracy, headed by Klawunn, charged the student bartender with sexual misconduct. (The fact that the accused student's father was a Brown trustee did him no good.) In a campus-wide email announcing the charges, Klawunn warned all Brown students that "[i]t should also be noted that alcohol is the most common date rape drug."[67] That definition, however, was nowhere to be found in Brown's written sexual assault policies.

Shortly after Klawunn's email, and apparently spurred by the Phi Kappa Psi case, Brown started requiring fraternities to obtain city permits before serving alcoholic beverages.[68] Even though most sexual assaults on college campuses appear to involve excessive drinking by one or both parties, campus activists complained about the new policy. Student Emma Phillips faulted Brown for denying "rape culture" by allegedly not recognizing that "sexual assault can happen independently of alcohol." Student government president Maahika Srinivasan added that the new policy likely would fall wide of the mark because "alcohol is not a root of sexual assault."[69] Blind adherence to a particular type of accusers' rights ideology, it seems, precluded support for a good-faith effort to prevent at least some campus sexual assaults.

Meanwhile, the case against the student bartender fell apart. He obtained a court injunction allowing testing by an independent toxicology expert, whose conclusions forced the private lab to recant its own finding. This elimination of Brown's only evidence, in turn, forced the university to drop the disciplinary proceeding, in February 2015. Klawunn announced the move in the most inflammatory manner possible. She told the campus via email that "a failure to positively identify the presence of exogenous GHB does not prove that GHB or another drug was not ingested."[70]

The Brown case exemplified—as had UVA's Hannah Graham rape-murder case, and the Vanderbilt gang rape case, and others—why the police, and not campus tribunals, should handle sexual assault allegations. If the accuser had taken her allegation of a serious crime to the police, the original lab test likely would have been handled professionally, and the harm done to all concerned by the private lab's error could have been avoided.

The evidence of the student bartender's innocence did not end the controversy. Instead, throughout the spring of 2015, the dismissal of the charge triggered a furious campus backlash, both against the accused student and against the Brown administration for refusing to expel him. Professor J. Timmons Roberts turned the presumption of innocence on its head, saying that "[i]f he is innocent, that should be borne out in a hearing." Undergraduate Jacinta Lomba described Brown's dismissal of charges unsupported by evidence as "an obstruction of justice." Student Ezra Kagan told the campus newspaper that "the priority has to be doing whatever makes women and survivors of sexual assault feel safe on this campus . . . even if that means erring on the side of heavy punishment"—that is, heavy punishment for having done nothing wrong. The student government president complained about the accused student having hired the lawyers who helped prove his innocence.[71]

In short, the Brown student body displayed the same hostility as the UVA student body to basic elements of due process, including the presumption of innocence; the right to counsel; and the right not to be found guilty of life-altering charges unsupported by evidence. Although the protesters' complaints were frivolous, Brown refashioned its policies to increase the likelihood of guilty findings. Since the 2015–2016 academic year, the university has channeled all sexual assault accusations to a "Title IX Committee," chaired by professor Gretchen Schultz, a specialist in gender and sexuality studies. During the 2015–2016 academic year, this committee included 18 specially trained members, three of whom (chosen by Schultz) adjudicate each case. Brown has not revealed the contents of the training, entitled "Title IX and You: Building a Community of Responsibility, Equality, and Safety," that panelists receive.[72]

After interviewing students who applied to be adjudicators, Brown chose eight females and two males for the undergraduate student contingent on the committee. There might have been an outcry had the student membership consisted of eight males and two females. But the gender imbalance seemed to create no comment on campus—except for statements from the two chosen males in which they displayed a predisposition to finding guilt. "When people are doing things that threaten...safety," one said, "it is totally important and natural to have those visceral reactions, otherwise this subject won't be taken as seriously as it should be." The other fretted that a "lot of times people impose their own biases...unfortunately...toward the respondent and to the detriment of the survivor."[73] He cited no evidence of any bias favoring accused students at Brown.

Indeed, a few months after these remarks, U.S. District Court Judge William Smith expressed a strong suspicion that Brown's policies were biased against accused students. The judge allowed an accused student's lawsuit to move forward, in large part because Brown had failed to follow even the weak protections that its written policies promised him: it gave him no opportunity to request disqualification of the panel chair for bias; it rejected his request that the panel consider seemingly exculpatory text messages from his accuser; and it refused to let him see the 80 pages of documentary evidence, including the accuser's medical records, until four days before his hearing, which the judge said gave him too little time to prepare a defense.[74]

In May 2016, Smith issued a temporary injunction in yet another sexual assault case at Brown, after the university ruled that a male student had "manipulated" his accuser into having oral sex. But though the incident occurred in November 2014, Brown did not include "manipulation" as part of its sexual assault definition until the 2015–2016 academic year.

The resulting lawsuit, which produced the first full-fledged trial about campus sexual assault since the Obama administration imposed its 2011 mandates, reflected poorly on the quality of Brown's handling of the issue. Professor Schultz, who chaired both the student's disciplinary hearing panel and his appeals panel, apparently experienced several memory lapses as she testified about how the panels had used the after-the-fact, 2015–2016 definition of consent. Another panelist, Associate Dean Besenia Rodriguez, testified that training from Brown had led her to ignore post-incident texts from the accuser saying she wanted to have sex with the accused. The panel, she implied, looked only for inculpatory material from contemporaneous documentary evidence. And at closing arguments, the judge confessed how he struggled to understand why the investigator assigned to the case, Djuna Perkins, refused to request potentially exculpatory texts between the accuser and a key witness at the hearing.[75]

On September 28, 2016, in an 84-page opinion, Smith held that the myriad procedural problems in the case required Brown to set aside the tribunal's decision. The judge expressed special concern about Brown's utilizing its post-2015 rule that any form of "manipulation" invalidates consent to sex. This, he suggested, meant that the university considered it sexual assault for a man to have sex with a woman after ingratiating himself with "the old school use of presents and flattery." As Smith considered his ruling, a student named Alex Volpicello urged his fellow Brown undergraduates to flood the judge's office with pro-accuser emails; dozens did so.[76] This pressure tactic prompted Smith to write, in the most passionate section of his opinion, that federal courts "cannot be swayed by public opinion." He emphasized that "an organized campaign to influence the outcome" had "no place in the judicial process," adding, "This is basic civics, and one would think students and others affiliated with a prestigious Ivy League institution would know this. Moreover, having read a few of the emails, it is abundantly clear that the writers, while passionate, were woefully ignorant about the issues before the Court. Hopefully, they will read this decision and be educated." Yet the decision seemed not to influence in any way the witch-hunt atmosphere that had come to dominate at Brown.

The Brown student body ignored the lessons of both cases before Judge Smith. And Brown students' newfound hostility to due process is mirrored at other campuses, especially elite ones. Here are some examples:

- In May 2013, *The Daily Princetonian* praised the Princeton administration's lowering the standard of proof in sexual assault cases from "clear and persuasive" to "preponderance of evidence." The editorial argued that the difficulty of finding clear and persuasive evidence to prove a sexual assault accusation called for making it *easier* to find a student guilty of the *most serious charge* he could face than to find him guilty of lesser, non-sex offenses.[77]

- In September 2013, *The Yale Daily News* concluded that "the interests of survivors"—not the interests of justice—should guide all aspects of Yale's policy. The paper did not mention due process or the presumption of innocence.[78]

- In July 2014, even as Harvard's new sexual assault policy generated the protest letter from 28 Harvard Law School faculty members (see chapter 6), the student president and the vice president of the Undergraduate Council demanded that Harvard adopt an affirmative-consent requirement. No student leader expressed concern about the new policy's denial of due process for accused students.[79]

- In April 2015, Penn State's *Daily Collegian* expressed outrage that members of UVA's Phi Kappa Psi fraternity had sued *Rolling Stone* for libel. The editors wrote that the lawsuit would "show anyone who may have something to say against a fraternity that they have the power, they can sue and they will essentially always win." *The Daily Collegian* maintained, curiously, that "the most important thing to come out of this failed journalism is the

concept that sexual assault is a huge problem on college campuses, and false accusations are extremely unlikely."[80]

- In a September 2015 editorial, *The Middlebury Campus* castigated a federal court ruling that had prevented the college from
  expelling a student for sexual assault after he already had been
  investigated and cleared by his study-abroad program (covered in
  chapter 6). Campus editors assailed the lawyers for the accused as
  people who "find legal loopholes without having to contend with
  their clients' guilt." They especially railed against "outside individuals like [Harvey] Silverglate," people "with axes to grind."[81]

- The following month, Boston University's student newspaper,
  The Daily Free Press, urged BU to adopt an "affirmative consent"
  standard—even though "it seems near impossible to prove that
  there was affirmative consent in a sexual encounter." The likelihood that "some of [the] men who are accused of sexual assault
  aren't guilty," the editors indicated, would not "make us change
  our minds." The editors concluded that they "would rather see
  someone falsely accused than see someone avoid coming forward
  for fear of retribution for wrongly accusing someone."[82]

Individual student op-eds have been even more extreme. Writing
in *The Yale Daily News*, Adriana Miele described her mealtime routine:
she went to the dining hall, she paid for her food, and "then I count the
amount of rapists in the room." Student rapists, for Miele, were everywhere—"in our suites...in our seminars and lecture halls...with our
classmates...with us at lunch...at a party. Sometimes they are friends.
Sometimes they're Republican, and sometimes they're die-hard feminist
Democrats"—all the while victimizing, she maintained, a majority of
Yale's around 2,700 undergraduate females.[83] A group of self-described
"senior girls" at Colby College, in Waterville, Maine, penned an op-ed
implying an equivalence between rape and "vulgar name-calling," citing
both as examples of the "sexual misconduct" that the college needed
to address.[84]

Students' reactions to criminal allegations of rape against fellow
students were equally skewed. In early 2016, after the arrest of Wolfgang
Ballinger at Cornell (see chapter 6), student Yana Lysenko implied that
Ballinger was particularly "dangerous"—because he was "a good-looking

guy...and generally popular." Citing Ballinger's leadership of a fraternity, student George Tsourounakis added that he was "happy" to hear of
the charges, because he had "yet to meet any non-cis[gender] individuals
that participate in Greek life.... This overtly heteronormative system
just enforces an environment of oppression."[85]

Amid a campus consensus that the evil of sexual assault requires
an erosion of due process, it should come as little surprise that a 2015
Washington Post–Kaiser Family Foundation poll found that respondents
saw the prospect of a "person who commits sexual assault getting away
with it" as "MORE unfair" than that of an "innocent person getting
kicked out," by a margin of 7 percent.[86]

Reflecting a broader hostility to basic civil liberties on campus, a
spring 2015 Pew Global Attitudes survey revealed that 40 percent of
millennials (ages 18 through 29) thought the government should have
the power to censor speech that is offensive to minority groups. This
percentage far exceeded the figure for any other age group.[87] A spring
2016 Gallup Poll, conducted at the behest of the Knight Foundation,
indicated that 27 percent of all college students (with black students,
at 41 percent, the highest subgroup) endorsed restricting expression
of "political views" that groups on campus found "upsetting." Forty-
nine percent (including two-thirds of black students, again the highest
subgroup) favored giving campus protesters authority to restrict media
coverage of their public events if the protesters believed the reporters
would cover them unfairly.[88]

Students' hostility both to unpopular views and to due process has
led to several high-profile efforts to muffle visiting speakers who challenged the conventional wisdom about sexual assault on college campuses. A particularly egregious example came at Brown. In November
2014, amid the Phi Kappa Psi controversy, student organization the
Janus Forum, which "seeks to inspire open-minded debate on relevant,
political, social, and economic issues," scheduled a debate about "rape
culture." Jessica Valenti, a *Guardian* columnist known for her dogmatic
embrace of accusers, would face off against Wendy McElroy, who had
penned an essay earlier in the year denouncing the "rape culture" concept as a "big lie."

The mere idea of allowing McElroy to set foot on campus produced
a strong backlash. Student government president Srinivasan complained

that "having this event now might seem like backtracking from the forward direction that we've been moving in." Katherine Byron, a student member of the university's Task Force on Sexual Assault, worried that the event could be "triggering" or "really hurtful" to activists. So she teamed with Srinivasan, university vice president Margaret Klawunn, and others to plan a competing event—featuring a "researcher" on "rape culture"—to divert attention and attendance from the Valenti-McElroy debate.[89]

Christina Paxson, Brown's president, then sent a campus-wide email explicitly disagreeing with McElroy's critique of the "rape culture" concept and effectively endorsing the alternative event, which she said would supply "research and facts" about "the role that community norms and values play in sexual assault."[90] FIRE's Samantha Miller observed that Paxson's email made sense only "if you assume the real goal is to provide an intellectual cocoon for students—an effort to create a[n] ideological bubble on campus in which students' beliefs will be free from challenge."[91]

The dueling events occurred as planned, though at the Janus Forum debate, Valenti seemed disinterested in an exchange of ideas. ("I'm tired of talking about rape culture in a context that assumes the existence of rape culture is up for debate," she groused.[92]) In addition to the Paxson-blessed alternative event, several students organized the "BWell Safe Space" for undergraduates who might be "triggered" by discussion of sexual assault.

Journalist Judith Shulevitz discovered that the "Safe Space," which received around two dozen visitors, was filled "with cookies, coloring books, bubbles, Play-Doh, calming music, pillows, blankets and a video of frolicking puppies, as well as students and staff members trained to deal with trauma." Student Emma Hall briefly left the "Safe Space," which she had helped organize, to watch a bit of the Valenti-McElroy debate. But she soon had to retreat, she later told Shulevitz, because "I was feeling bombarded by a lot of viewpoints that really go against my dearly and closely held beliefs."[93] As Cathy Young subsequently observed, the entire affair "could have been an episode in a sharp and outrageous satire of political correctness gone mad."[94]

Some single-speaker events, especially when the speaker was a female supporter of due process—such as Emily Yoffe, Cathy Young, or Christina Hoff Sommers—have encountered even stronger resistance. At Georgetown, after Sommers challenged the validity of surveys claiming that one in five college women will be sexually assaulted, the university had to provide her with protection by undercover police (@ CHSommers, April 16, 2015). In an editorial charging that Sommers' speech "encourages rape denialism," *The Georgetown Hoya* did not challenge any of Sommers' arguments but nonetheless concluded that "conversations that focus on whether or not the problem is 'overstated,' rather than on how the problem can be solved, are an insult to Georgetown's survivors."[95]

Before Sommers addressed a crowd at Ohio's Oberlin College, dozens of students published a "love letter to ourselves," accusing Sommers of being a "rape denialist." Imitating Brown's effort to evade exposure to views that disagreed with their beliefs, activists scheduled a competing event at the time same as Sommers' address, which—through engaging "in some radical, beautiful community care, support and love"—would "make [Sommers'] talk irrelevant in the face of our love, passion and power."[96] Two campus police officers had to escort Sommers from the lecture hall after her address.[97]

In February 2015, one of us (KC Johnson) seemed on the verge of being prevented from presenting his views by protesters at Ohio University, until university police threatened to arrest them. As he began his address at the school—which had a reported sexual assault rate of 0.06 percent over the three previous years—some 20 members of a group calling itself "F*ckRapeCulture" stood as one across the first three rows of the room, holding up signs to prevent audience members from seeing his PowerPoint presentation. Only police intervention prevented the heckler's veto from succeeding.

The protesters' actions suggested a lack of confidence that their ideas could prevail in an open exchange. During Johnson's talk, a female protester alleged that the odds of being falsely accused of rape are "2.7 million to one"; when Johnson requested a source for this nonexistent statistic, another protester accused him of committing a "micro-aggression." Ohio professor Thomas Costello took the floor to argue that "young men on campus" didn't know what it meant to "be a man." The idea that college professors—of all people—are qualified how to teach fellow adults how to "be a man" appeared lost on Costello. Nor did he seem aware of how bizarre most people would find the opposite, a professor publicly proclaiming that "young women on campus" didn't know what it means to "be a woman."[98]

All these events are scenes from a revolution in students' attitudes about campus civil liberties. FIRE president Greg Lukianoff told *The Los Angeles Times* in November 2015 that for most of his organization's 16 years in existence, students had been its most reliable allies. But no more. "It's disheartening to see how they are now using freedom of speech to demand there be less freedom of speech," he said.[99]

Attacks on free speech have proliferated in tandem with attacks on due process for accused students. In the fall of 2015, angry and disruptive campus protests spread across the nation. Rather than standing up for civil discourse, university leaders seemed inclined to appease the protesters.[100]

Protesters at Guilford College, in Greensboro, North Carolina, suggested "that every week a faculty member come forward and publicly admit their participation in racism" in the college paper. Wesleyan protesters wanted "an anonymous student reporting system for cases of bias, including microaggressions, perpetrated by faculty and staff." At the University of North Carolina, protesters wanted to discourage "white professors...from leading and teaching departments about demographics and societies colonized, massacred, or enslaved under white supremacy," along with "mandatory programming [on] ways in which racial capitalism, settler colonialism, and cisheteropatriarchy [i.e., the dominance of heterosexual, non-transgender males] structure our world." UCLA protesters demanded official "consequences" for law professor Richard Sander, who (with Stuart Taylor, an author of this book) authored *Mismatch*, a book that laid out a wealth of evidence that large racial admissions preferences—by creating large racial gaps in college academic performance—harm many of the minority students that universities claim to be helping.[101]

Many of these vague demands seemed almost reflexive, as extremists at one school after another joined the crowd. But with the exception of the University of Missouri, the most visible early protests all came at institutions that in the previous half-decade had also decimated accused students' due-process rights:

- At Yale, protests erupted after (of all things) dueling emails over Halloween costumes. The university's "Intercultural Affairs Council" emailed students to urge them to avoid costume choices "that threaten our sense of community or disrespects, alienates or ridicules [sic] segments of our population based on race, nationality, religious belief or gender expression."[102] Associate master of Yale's Silliman College, Erika Christakis, a lecturer in childhood development issues, responded with a temperate email defending students' right to self-expression and lamenting how American campuses "have become places of censure and prohibition."[103] Furious protests attracted national attention when a group of students confronted Christakis' husband, Nicholas, on the campus quad and a female student shrieked at him, "Who the fuck hired you?" His job, she continued, was "not about creating an intellectual space" but "creating a home."[104] Yale president Peter Salovey did not quite bow to the protesters' demands to fire the Christakises (who nonetheless left their roles at Silliman College at the end of the academic year) but offered them no moral support and otherwise capitulated to the protesters' demands: he promised to spend another $50 million—enough money to lower every Yale undergraduate's tuition fees by more than $9,000 for a year—on more diversity hires.

• At Amherst, "Amherst Uprising" protesters claimed that censoring students' speech was necessary to combat pervasive racism on campus. They demanded that President Biddy Martin issue a statement condemning an antiabortion "All Lives Matter" poster and a "Free Speech" poster defending student journalists who had been mobbed at the University of Missouri. They also demanded that Amherst warn the students who had created the posters that the college "may require them to go through the Disciplinary Process [and] to attend extensive training for racial and cultural competency."[105] Seventeen Amherst academic departments issued letters expressing varying degrees of support for the protesters.[106] The whole show culminated in an occupation of the campus library. Martin responded by promising to devise a new campus speech policy based on the same tenets of the school's sexual assault policy—which had eviscerated the rights of accused students.

- At Dartmouth, protesters' 59 demands included calls for racial quotas for undergraduate admissions, graduate admissions, and new faculty. Professors would "be required to be trained in not only cultural competency but also the importance of social justice in their day-to-day work." Some 150 protesters stormed the library, where they screamed at students who were trying to study. Tsion Abera, the vice president of the campus NAACP, proclaimed that "[w]hatever discomfort that many white students felt in that library is a fraction of the discomfort that many Natives, blacks, Latina and LGBTQ people feel frequently."[107] A Dartmouth administrator responded by apologizing *to the protesters*, calling their effort a "wonderful, beautiful thing." She also dismissed critics as "a whole conservative world out there that's not being very nice."[108]

As Laura Kipnis discovered in her Title IX fight at Northwestern, the war against students' liberties will inevitably degrade faculties' liberties. In a November 2015 public forum, the most extreme manifestation of this trend of which we are aware was revealed—at Duke, the university that began the assault on accused students' civil liberties 10 years earlier.

At the forum, Dean Valerie Ashby revealed that the university had adopted a (previously nonpublic) policy on tenure review. Now, Ashby told the assembled students, untenured faculty received a simple message from the administration: "You can't be a great scholar and be intolerant. *You have to go*." Upon receiving this news—that Duke would no longer respect academic freedom for its faculty—the crowd burst into applause.[109]

In this environment, any student questioning the conventional wisdom needed considerable courage. In February 2015, after Cathy Young's article undermined Emma Sulkowicz's credibility, Daniel Garisto, the 2013–2015 opinion page editor of the Columbia *Spectator*, penned a column in which he reconsidered his role hyping Sulkowicz's tale. He confessed that the paper had "failed specifically with Sulkowicz's story by not being thorough and impartial." The reason, he said, was that "[c]ampus media's goal to promote discussion about sexual assault and to support survivors became conflated with a fear of rigorous reporting. Personally, I felt that if I covered the existence of a different perspective—say, that due process should be respected—not only would I have been excoriated, but many would have said that I was harming survivors and the fight against sexual assault."

Garisto added that—for admitting that his newspaper should have stuck to journalistic principles even when covering an alleged sexual assault—he anticipated an enormous backlash against his column. Perhaps that explains why he also stuck to his view that Nungesser was "probably guilty," even "statistically guilty"—an opinion against the clear weight of the evidence and for which he offered no specific reason.[110]

Some of Garisto's successors at the Columbia *Spectator* took his confession of failure to heart. In September 2015, *Spectator* op-ed columnist Josh Kolb condemned the excessively broad definition of sexual assault in the Association of American Universities survey. He also worried that the "current system of adjudication for these crimes" had compounded the problem by turning "colleges into police, court, and jury." Channeling the issue to the criminal justice system, Kolb concluded, represented the better approach.[111]

Toni Airaksinen offered a more sweeping indictment of the AAU survey in another *Spectator* op-ed, in February 2016. The survey's wording "paternalistically decides whether women have been victims," she wrote. "When I hear the term 'sexual assault,' I think of rape"—not an unwanted kiss. Airaksinen added that "many of the sexual acts the survey classifies as assault are simply what my friends and I would call 'bad sex' caused by alcohol, communication issues, or mutual sexual desire." She also worried that "when a heavily charged word like 'assault' is used to describe relatively banal occurrences, the word loses its power." Airaksinen concluded, "As undergraduates at one of the most elite universities in the country, it seems like we have to prove that we are exceptional in every way, from our academic prowess, to how sexually victimized we are."[112]

Though not alone, it seems that the two Columbia students were members of a forlorn minority.

In the spring of 2016, Tufts student Jake Goldberg organized a letter signed by 336 undergraduates nationwide that excoriated OCR's demand for increased funding. He then sent it to the chairs and ranking members of the relevant U.S. Senate subcommittees. "We believe," the letter maintained, "that no further funding should be provided to this department until OCR revises its illegal and immoral guidance to our colleges and universities," the best example of which was the Dear Colleague letter, which "forced our schools to enact policies which effectively deny us of our due process rights when we are accused of violating sexual harassment policies and face disciplinary proceedings." The signatories promised, "We will not go away; we will no longer be silent; we will always be monitoring OCR's actions."[113]

Perhaps the most perceptive student op-ed on OCR's commands came from Yale's Isaac Cohen in February 2015. He reasoned that campus sexual assault was better handled by police than by colleges. The structural weaknesses of the campus system made it too easy, he wrote, "to get the wrong answer in cases of campus sexual assault, where he-said-she-said accounts, lubricated with copious amounts of alcohol, abound." Cohen elaborated: "[F]ew of the protections found in the criminal law are present on campus today. Instead, inexperienced and inexpert campus tribunals are asked to apply standards for 'sexual misconduct' that are protean and ill-defined, and that too often serve as a Rorschach test for administrators' prejudices and presuppositions about ideal male-female relations. Under many campus codes, non-consent alone—regardless of whether and how that state of mind is communicated to the accused—is enough to ground misconduct. This situation is an invitation to error, arbitrariness, inconsistency and injustice."[114]

Kolb, Airaksinen, Goldberg, and Cohen are lonely voices on contemporary campuses. But they provide a reminder that even in these dark times, some students are willing to defend principles of fairness, dispassionate evaluation of evidence, and due process.

CONCLUSION

This book has told a pessimistic tale, and the atmosphere of moral panic that we have described shows no sign of abating. As a result, unfair treatment of students accused of sexual assault doubtless will increase. And because of the secrecy of college disciplinary processes, many of the worst miscarriages of justice will remain shielded from public view. Current college disciplinary systems are so arbitrary that the same conduct that can have no repercussions 99 times out of 100—when neither sex partner would dream of complaining to authorities—can lead to a life-altering expulsion. Such a situation invites selective enforcement and the abuses of power that are documented in this book.

We conclude with several "how-to" lists aimed at helping parents, students, media, judges, and politicians navigate this campus environment.

Parents

College education is perhaps the only product in the United States for which consumers spend hundreds of thousands of dollars without any clear sense of what they are purchasing.

Parents know institutions by reputation, of course, and millions of parents peruse college websites, admissions materials, and *U.S. News* and *Princeton Review* rankings. But how many closely examine colleges' hiring patterns, to get a sense of the ideological and pedagogical diversity among faculties? How many check out the public statements of a university's leaders to get a sense of whether they have any respect for due process or freedom of speech?

Finally, how many parents look closely at college disciplinary policies? There's a surprising amount of variation in this regard. Students' rights can depend on the state, for one thing. New York and California, for example, have adopted laws that make guilty findings likely even for students who are probably or even almost certainly innocent. North Carolina and North Dakota, on the other hand, have laws requiring at least a modicum of due process.

Students' rights also can depend on the institution. Contrast, for example, Harvard University's single investigator-adjudicator system, which denies to an accused student even a hearing, with the exception carved out by Harvard Law School. The law school guarantees legal assistance, access to exculpatory information, and at least some form of cross-examination. Given the gravity of a sexual assault finding—likely expulsion or a lengthy suspension, with life-altering financial and employment consequences—parents owe it to their children to examine a college's disciplinary policies before committing to it.

Parents should strongly caution college-bound children (of both genders) against heavy use of alcohol. Although such advice might well be futile, most of the cases we profile in this book feature both parties having consumed alcohol, often in significant amounts; in the current campus environment, the combination of sex and alcohol can endanger both students. Moreover, as journalist Emily Yoffe has pointed out, excessive use of alcohol can place a student in a harmful situation that she otherwise would have avoided.[1]

As for parents of college-bound sons, one of us (Stuart Taylor) would also tell a son (if he had one):

You should of course treat women with respect; avoid making unwanted sexual overtures; and be quick to help the victim of any apparent assault, sexual or otherwise. What may be less obvious is that—just as women in college face grave dangers from rapists and other sexual predators—men like you face grave dangers from false accusers and—even more—from other young women who have been misled by colleges and activists. They have been propagandized and lobbied to believe that they should make claims against you whenever they end up unhappy about sexual contact, even if it was clearly consensual. You also face danger from egregiously unfair disciplinary processes and from campus sex bureaucrats who are, in many cases, extremely biased against males. For this reason, be aware that any fellow student with whom you have sexual contact may have the power to get you expelled for sexual assault if she feels regret or becomes angry with you an hour, a day, a month, a year, or even two years later. Casual sex with women you barely know is especially dangerous.

Finally, parents should consider donating to an organization such as FIRE, which stands up for the rights and liberties of all students against overwhelming odds.

Students

Undergraduates should read stories like the ones in this book about accused students at Amherst and Occidental. Only real cases can drive home the lesson that sometimes even overwhelming evidence of innocence isn't enough to avoid a guilty finding by a campus tribunal.

The overwhelming majority of the cases in this book involved behavior that is considered sexual assault only on contemporary college campuses, on the pages of publications like *The New York Times* and *The Huffington Post*, and among some powerful government officials. Students such as those accused at Amherst and Occidental doubtless believe—and correctly so—that they did not commit sexual assault. Yet their colleges branded them rapists anyway.

The only two theoretically foolproof ways to avoid a false accusation, students should understand, are both likely to be nonstarters. One is celibacy, a defense strategy that few will find appealing. The other is videotaping all sexual encounters, including foreplay—an immoral practice that would violate college procedures and quite possibly state law at most campuses.

Otherwise, the best way to avoid campus tribunals is to avoid sexual relations with fellow students from the same institution. It's true that in a handful of cases (one each at Middlebury and George Mason; two at Yale), schools have disciplined students accused of sexual assault even though the accusers did not attend the same school. But most universities process sexual assault accusations only if they involve two students at that institution.

Like their parents, students need to understand their institution's disciplinary process. It's our sense that few of them do. Apart from cursory (and often biased) discussion of discipline during freshman orientation sessions, universities tell their students very little about the disciplinary process. Very, very few students seem to search out the procedures that are detailed at considerable length on their institution's website. And sometimes universities, such as Duke, announce new policies that are not publicly specified in writing anywhere. It might, at least subconsciously, influence your on-campus behavior if you understand how few rights you actually have.

Finally, if you find yourself facing college sexual assault charges: get a lawyer immediately! Although most colleges go out of their way to minimize the role that a lawyer can play in the process, there is still much that a lawyer can do, and the stakes are enormous. A guilty finding will likely lead to your expulsion or a lengthy suspension, as well as brand you a rapist. The financial damage it does to you could be hundreds of thousands or even millions of dollars in reduced earnings over your lifetime; for example, it forecloses any career that requires a background check. Most employers are, understandably, reluctant to hire people who have been branded by their colleges as rapists.

The repeated assertions by figures like Senator Gillibrand that robust procedural protections aren't necessary in college tribunals "because you're not throwing someone in jail" are nonsense.[2] Indeed, accused students who defend themselves in campus proceedings could wind up in criminal jeopardy. Law enforcement always has the option of subpoenaing college investigative files. And even when they don't do so, recall the University of Wisconsin's police chief boasting about using Title IX to get around *Miranda* protections.

Media

Most people in the mainstream media appear to be biased beyond any hope of redemption on the campus sexual assault issue. Buying into an ideologically preferred storyline that also facilitates profitable sensationalism, they have, with only a handful of exceptions, turned a blind eye to bureaucrats' efforts to weaken the civil liberties of our nation's college students. This poor performance makes the invaluable work of Emily Yoffe, Richard Dorment (on the Occidental case), Cathy Young, James Taranto, Robby Soave, and Ashe Schow stand out all the more.

It is unlikely that we will see responsible coverage of sexual assault on college campuses from many major news organizations unless and until they employ a better brand of journalist. And one of us (Stuart Taylor), who wrote happily for *The New York Times* from 1980 to 1988 and for *Newsweek* from 1998 to 2010, among other publications, believes that it would be impossible for him to succeed at any major newspaper or magazine today because he still holds views about gender and racial issues that were common in the 1980s but have become unfashionable in the major news media as well as the universities. Among these views are that males are no more dishonest than females and should be presumed innocent until proven guilty of alleged sex crimes; that the freedom of speech is more important than protecting people from exposure to views that they don't want to hear; and that our educational and governmental institutions should not embrace racial preferences indefinitely. In the current journalistic climate, he would be better off practicing law, as he did from 1977 to 1980.

Even for those journalists who uncritically accept the widespread claim that hundreds of thousands of female undergraduates are sexually assaulted each year, there should be two obvious items on the "how-to" list for approaching articles on the topic. First, seek evidence from both sides, and work extra hard at getting it from accused students, who are understandably media-shy. In covering the case of mattress-toting Emma Sulkowicz, for example, the *Times* and others not only uncritically accepted Sulkowicz's story but seem not even to have tried to seek evidence from accused student Paul Nungesser. When one reporter, Cathy Young, functioned as a real journalist rather than an advocate, speaking not only to Sulkowicz but also to Nungesser and—importantly—Nungesser's "advocate" in the disciplinary hearing, the "mattress girl's" narrative collapsed.

Obtaining this evidence can often be difficult, given the opacity of campus courts. But reporters can be alert to the difference in credibility when one side is willing to share all the evidence and the other is not. Harvard Law School student Brandon Winston, for example, went a long way toward proving his innocence by showing his evidence to any solid reporter who bothered to ask for it.

Second, reporters should recognize their obligation—which almost all have failed to fulfill—to describe in detail the college disciplinary process. A nation familiar with police procedurals such as *Law & Order* has a basic understanding of the criminal justice process. Most people probably assume the campus judiciary works in roughly the same way. But it does not. There's scant reason to believe, for example, that the typical reader of most of the *Times'* frenzied articles about campus rape understands that most campus processes are run by people with strong institutional and ideological biases against accused students. Or that the process severely restricts (or outright prohibits) accused students and their lawyers from cross-examining their accusers; usually bars their lawyers from participating in any meaningful way; denies them access to exculpatory evidence; and uses an accuser-friendly "more likely than not" standard of proof.

One reason why Yoffe and Dorment so excelled is that these two journalists, unlike most of their peers, described the processes (at the University of Michigan and Occidental, respectively) that ensnared the wrongfully accused students.

Judges

The courts traditionally have deferred to colleges' disciplinary judgments, not unreasonably concluding that academics can best evaluate matters such as what constitutes plagiarism. But academics—and bureaucrats hired by academics—deserve no deference in determining when a sexual assault has occurred, or in understanding appropriate procedures for making such a determination. In addition, the consequences of being expelled (as a rapist) dwarf those of being disciplined for stealing an MP3 player or plagiarizing a paper. As long as academic institutions facilitate the current witch hunt, the judiciary must ensure that students, including those accused of serious offenses, receive a process fair enough to determine the truth. With scores of lawsuits by accused students advancing through the legal system, both state and federal judges will have many opportunities to act.

So far, state court judges in California and Tennessee have properly invalidated the procedurally indefensible judgments against accused students by powerful public universities in their states. A handful of federal judges, most notably F. Dennis Saylor (Brandeis), William Lawrence (DePauw), William Smith (Brown), and T. S. Ellis III (George Mason), have issued similarly courageous decisions. But it's hard to respect the reasoning of many federal judges who have sided with universities, even after describing snap hearings, biased investigators, and tactics irreconcilable with fundamental fairness. Perhaps the most troubling such decision, in which U.S. District Court Judge Ronnie Abrams deferred to a guilty ruling by Vassar, found nothing "inherently inadequate" about a rushed, less-than-10-day investigation and hearing process in which the accused student, without counsel and with his family thousands of miles away, frantically sought exculpatory evidence about an incident that had happened more than a year earlier. Absent a consistent judicial check, unfairness will persist at universities.

Judges also should take a close look at how best to evaluate claims by accused students that their universities discriminated against them based on their gender in violation of Title IX. The courts should not hide behind the gender-neutral language of OCR and university rules, given that the effect of denial of due process falls almost entirely on accused male students. The 2016 ruling from the 2nd Circuit (see chapter 4) provides a model to follow in such cases.

Politicians

Few politicians whose priority is short-term electoral gain are likely to stand up for campus due process, which has no political constituency. But with the exception of demagogues such as Gillibrand, most politicians are concerned with their legacies—and history tends to look poorly on craven political figures who bowed to the mob and overrode civil liberties. To avoid staining their reputations through history, legislators should look more to the common good and see how they can help ensure basic fairness in college disciplinary proceedings.

The best proposal in Congress on the campus rape due-process issue, the Safe Campus Act, has no chance of passage. But Congress could take a small step in the right direction by mandating far more openness at colleges. Although a conversation about sexual assault on college campuses has been going on for more than five years, fewer than a dozen actual *transcripts* of campus hearings have entered the public domain. This secrecy, for which colleges cite the requirements of FERPA, has played a key role in impoverishing legislative debate about how the campus kangaroo courts actually operate.

Congress could ensure greater transparency in other ways. It should require schools to release the materials that they use to train disciplinary panels, exposing the bias and hostility to basic fairness that pervade this training. It also should clarify the Clery Act's 2014 amendments in two ways. First, Congress should require schools to distinguish alleged sex crimes from alleged noncriminal violations of the often absurdly broad college disciplinary codes. The way to do that is to replace the confusing categories that schools are now required to use in their reports— "rape" and "fondling"—with criminal rape, criminal sexual assault, and noncriminal sexual behavior. Second, Congress should require schools to report how many sexual assault allegations were deemed unfounded. Instead, current guidelines lump together unfounded claims of all campus offenses (there were 1,452 of them in 2014), without allowing anyone to see what percentage of them were alleged sexual assaults.[3]

The legislative response to the Obama administration's campus sexual assault policy was a textbook example of failed congressional oversight. Obama's two OCR heads, Russlynn Ali and Catherine Lhamon, faced only around six minutes—*combined*—of challenging questions in Senate oversight hearings. The questions came from Lamar Alexander.[4] Only Alexander and James Lankford pressed OCR in writing to justify its policies.

Oversight committees also should demand documents regarding the origins of the "Dear Colleague" letter. How much was the White House involved? Did anyone in the process worry about the certainty that a great many innocent as well as guilty accused students would be expelled as rapists? What did the document's earlier drafts say? Why did the Obama administration subsequently tell universities they can't require alleged victims of sexual assault to report their complaints to police? Do any other federal agencies discourage reporting felony offenses to law enforcement? Why is the focus almost exclusively on alleged victims at elite colleges and not on the far more numerous less privileged women for whom police are the only recourse? These are obvious questions that Congress refused to present to the Obama administration.

These questions almost certainly will remain important for future administrations. A principled Republican president should deem it necessary to at least withdraw the Dear Colleague letter, given the document's constitutional infirmities. Whether he or she would have the political will to do so, however, is an open question. If the executive branch remains cautious about (or opposed to) reform, congressional action is necessary. In an encouraging sign, shortly after the 2016 election, James Lankford indicated that as the Education Department had "used Dear Colleague letters and guidance documents to mandate policies for schools without adhering to legally required regulatory processes," he would "push our new Republican-led Washington to put a stop to this abuse and restore proper regulatory and guidance proceses to the federal government."[5]

In an ideal world, OCR would recognize the limitations of universities' ability to adjudicate these complex matters and would require schools to adjust their punishments accordingly. As long as schools retain the pretense of an educational—as opposed to a criminal justice—mission, they should focus on resolving sexual assault complaints through the tools they possess, which are primarily counseling and conflict resolution. Kent State University professor Mary Koss has championed "restorative justice," which CUNY's Barry Latzer likewise recently endorsed.[6] Latzer noted that colleges providing "professional counseling for students, male or female, who claim that they were sexually assaulted," coupled with diverting "these cases to victim-offender mediation programs," would "help the victim cope with her trauma and refocus on her academic work, and it could be provided faster and more anonymously than campus misconduct hearings."[7]

Academics

All universities should strive to imitate Harvard Law School and CUNY, which allow lawyers for accused students to participate fully in the disciplinary process. They should reject the single investigator-adjudicator model, under which it is nearly impossible to discover whether the accuser is telling the truth. They should provide accused students with all evidence uncovered by their investigations, not merely summary reports. They should stop using interim restrictions to punish accused students based on mere unproven accusations. They should stop training their sexual assault adjudicators to presume guilt.

Let's return to the case with which we started this book, that of Alice Stanton and Michael Cheng at Amherst. Amherst's procedures, which are by no means atypical, ensured that even a fair inquiry would never uncover the truth. Yet Amherst administrators seemed not to care. Indeed, when the truth *was* discovered, by the exposure of Stanton's text messages, they told the student whom they had expelled after wrongly branding him a rapist that they could not be bothered to reverse their position.

The distinctive place of colleges and universities in American society resides in a commitment to the pursuit of truth. But in the crusade to eradicate campus sexual assault, schools have rushed to use processes that seem at best indifferent to not only truth but also facts, evidence, and logic. Politicians, judges, members of the media, academics, and—perhaps most important—students need to join together to help higher education find its way back to a pursuit of truth.

ACKNOWLEDGMENTS

Our research benefited from insights from many people (on all sides of the issue) who for personal or career reasons need to remain anonymous. We express our gratitude to them. Samantha Harris, Linda LeFauve, Chris Halkides, Margaret King, and Harvey Silverglate each offered detailed comments on drafts of the manuscript; so too did several readers who need to remain anonymous. Guidance from Jonathan Rauch, Brad Bannon, Robert Shibley, Greg Lukianoff, John Leo, and Stephen Henrick proved helpful at various stages of the project.

Without timely assistance from Dorothy Rabinowitz, this project never would have been launched. Our agents, Glen Hartley and Lynn Chu, provided unfailing advice; Lynn's detailed edits went well beyond the call of duty and immeasurably improved the final product. The careful, professional editing of Will DeRooy helped us clarify our argument, tighten our prose, and avoid pitfalls in presentation. We are grateful to Encounter Books for giving this book a home, and especially to Roger Kimball and Katherine Wong for their work bringing the book to fruition.

From Stuart Taylor Jr.: My special thanks to Kate Stith, David Rudovsky, Justin Dillon, Ron Henry, Ed Bartlett, and Paul Larkin for their expert insights; to Jon Gordon, who provided valuable research as well as detailed comments on the manuscript; and to Shelly Dempsey, Sherry Warner-Seefeld, and Cynthia Purcell Garrett for their understanding of the human toll taken by wrongful accusations.

From KC Johnson: My thanks to Matthew Hennessy and Zach Wood, of the Uncomfortable Learning program at Williams College; Robert Ingram, of the George Washington Forum at Ohio University; and Philip Hamburger, of the Center on Law and Liberty at Columbia University. Invitations from each of these people for a lecture on this topic prompted me to think about the subject more broadly, leading to the proposal for this book. The programs they are involved with demonstrate the need for outside donors to step in when academic leadership proves unwilling or unable to foster an intellectually diverse environment on campus.

The latter stages of this project benefited from a grant from the Kurz Undergraduate Research Assistant Program at Brooklyn College and the excellent work of Ben Cohn as a research assistant. Timely legal help from Patrick Strawbridge allowed me to continue writing on this topic. And assistance from Lorraine Greenfield and Ann Ciarlo in the Brooklyn College History Department office allows me to better manage a sometimes chaotic schedule. I remain grateful to my father, J. Robert Johnson; my sister, Kathleen Johnson; and my brother-in-law, Mike Sardo.

NOTES

Introduction

1 Throughout this book, we have used parties' real names when the parties previously identified themselves, by giving interviews or filing a lawsuit. In one additional case (University of Virginia), multiple media outlets reported the accuser's identity, which subsequent legal filings confirmed. In all other cases, the use of an asterisk indicates a pseudonym.

2 Except as noted, all quotes regarding the case at Amherst come from *John Doe v. Amherst College*, U.S. District Court for the District of Massachusetts, Case No. 3:15-cv-30097 (documents available at https://kc-johnson.com).

3 Angie Epifano, "An Account of Sexual Assault at Amherst College" (opinion), *Amherst Student*, October 17, 2012, http://amherststudent.amherst.edu/?q=article/2012/10/17/account-sexual-assault-amherst-college.

4 Rosemary Kelly and Shaina Mishkin, "Angie Epifano Profile: How One Former Amherst Student Sparked a Movement against Sexual Assault," *Huffington Post*, June 2, 2013, http://www.huffingtonpost.com/2013/06/02/angie-epifano-profile_n_3353941.html.

5 "President Martin's Statement on Sexual Assault," Amherst College, October 18, 2012, https://www.amherst.edu/campuslife/letters_president/node/436469.

6 The Special Oversight Committee on Sexual Misconduct, Amherst College, *Toward a Culture of Respect: The Problem of Sexual Misconduct at Amherst College*, January 2013, https://www.amherst.edu/media/view/452118/original/Toward_a_Culture_of_Respect_Title_IX.pdf.

7 "Amherst College Sexual Misconduct and Harassment Policy," Amherst College, n.d., https://www.amherst.edu/campuslife/health-safety-wellness/sexual-respect/sexual-misconduct-and-harassment-policy/node/497976.

8 "About Me," Eric Hamako, http://erichamako.com/about; "Equity and Social Justice Faculty: Rachel David," Shoreline Community College, https://www.shoreline.edu/esj/faculty.aspx.

9 "Student Rights and Policies," Amherst College, https://www.amherst.edu/offices/student-affairs/handbook/studentrights%23appendixb#StmtConsent.

10 Colleges use words such as "culpable" and "responsible" instead of "guilty." On this issue, some also use words such as "sexual misconduct" instead of "sexual assault." Here we often use the colloquial "guilty" and words that best describe the specific alleged acts that become known to fellow students and others familiar with their cases.

11 Tyler Kingkade, "Amherst College Sexual Assault Policies Treat Alleged Rapists Better Than Laptop Thieves," *Huffington Post*, December 15, 2013, http://www.huffingtonpost.com/2013/12/15/amherst-college-sexual-assault-policies_n_4402315.html.

12 KC Johnson, "Amherst Update," *Academic Wonderland* (blog), May 27, 2016, https://academicwonderland.com/2016/05/27/amherst-update.

13 Andrew Berger, "Brandeis and the History of Transparency," Sunlight Foundation blog, May 26, 2009, https://sunlightfoundation.com/blog/2009/05/26/brandeis-and-the-history-of-transparency.

14 David G. Savage and Timothy M. Phelps, "How a Little-Known Education Office Has Forced Far-Reaching Changes to Campus Sex Assault Investigations," *Los Angeles Times*, August 17, 2015, http://www.latimes.com/nation/la-na-campus-sexual-assault-20150817-story.html.

15 Ashe Schow, "Lady Gaga Pushes 'One in Five' Campus Sex Assault Myth at the Oscars," *Washington Examiner*, February 29, 2016, http://www.washingtonexaminer.com/article/2584509.

16 "Effects of Sexual Violence," RAINN (Rape, Abuse and Incest National Network), https://rainn.org/get-information/effects-of-sexual-assault.

17 "Rape: Weapon of War," United Nations Human Rights Office of the High Commissioner, http://www.ohchr.org/en/newsevents/pages/rapeweaponwar.aspx.

18 Although universities' policies are gender-neutral, the most recent data available indicate that "nearly all" (99 percent) of accused students are male. United Educators, "Confronting Campus Sexual Assault: An Examination of Higher Education Claims," https://www.ue.org/uploadedFiles/Confronting%20Campus%20Sexual%20Assault.pdf.

19 Sabrina Rubin Erdely, "A Rape on Campus: A Brutal Assault and Struggle for Justice at UVA," *Rolling Stone*, November 19, 2014, http://web.archive.org/web/20141119200349/http://www.rollingstone.com/culture/features/a-rape-on-campus-20141119.

20 KC Johnson and Stuart Taylor Jr., "U-Va. Reaction to Rape Claim: Worse Than at Duke?" *RealClearPolitics*, January 2, 2015, http://www.realclearpolitics.com/articles/2015/01/02/u-va_reaction_to_rape_claim_worse_than_at_duke.html.

21 KC Johnson and Stuart Taylor Jr., "Stanford Sex Assault Case: The Sentence Was Too Short but the System Worked," *Washington Post*, June 8, 2016, https://www.washingtonpost.com/opinions/stanford-case-shows-why-the-justice-system-should-handle-campus-sexual-assault/2016/06/08/38a6af24-2cf2-11e6-9b37-42985f6a265c_story.html.

22 Michele Landis Dauber to Judge Aaron Persky, May 24, 2016, https://assets.documentcloud.org/documents/2852617/Dauber-Letter-On-Brock-Turner-Sentencing.pdf.

23 Dorothy Rabinowitz, "From the Mouths of Babes to a Jail Cell," *Harper's*, May 1990, http://harpers.org/archive/1990/05/from-the-mouths-of-babes-to-a-jail-cell.

24 Stuart Taylor Jr., email interview with David Rudovsky, January 22, 2015.

25 *John Doe v. Brandeis University*, U.S. District Court for the District of Massachusetts, 2016 U.S. Dist. LEXIS 43499 (available at https://kc-johnson.com).

26 Jonathan Haidt, "The Yale Problem Begins in High School," Heterodox Academy, November 24, 2015, http://heterodoxacademy.org/2015/11/24/the-yale-problem-begins-in-high-school.

27 A term popularized by, among others, Valerie Jarrett, President Obama's most influential advisor.

28 Valerie Jarrett, "Taking On Sexual Assault: Here Are Four Questions Parents Can Ask When Choosing a College," *U.S. News and World Report*, October 27, 2015, http://www.usnews.com/news/the-report/articles/2015/10/27/how-to-protect-college-students-from-sexual-assaults.

29 This claim is odd in an era in which 58 percent of the nation's undergraduate students are female. "Table 310. Degrees Conferred by Degree-Granting Institutions, by Level of Degree and Sex of Student: Selected Years, 1869–70 through 2021–22," National Center for Education Statistics, June 2012, https://nces.ed.gov/programs/digest/d12/tables/dt12_310.asp.

30 Sandy Hingston, "The New Rules of College Sex," *Philadelphia*, August 22, 2011, http://www.phillymag.com/articles/the_new_rules_of_college_sex/page2.

31 *Questions and Answers on Title IX and Sexual Violence* (Washington, D.C.: U.S. Dept. of Education, 2014), http://www2.ed.gov/about/offices/list/ocr/docs/qa-201404-title-ix.pdf.

32 Jeannie Suk Gersen, "Shutting Down Conversations about Rape at Harvard Law," *New Yorker*, December 11, 2015, http://www.newyorker.com/news/news-desk/argument-sexual-assault-race-harvard-law-school.

33 Alexander Volokh, "Aside: n Guilty Men," *University of Pennsylvania Law Review* 146 (1997), 173–216, http://scholarship.law.upenn.edu/cgi/viewcontent.cgi?article=3427&context=penn_law_review.

34 Robby Soave, "Rep. Jared Polis Thinks Colleges Should Be Able to Expel Students When They're Only 20% Sure a Rape Happened," *Hit and Run* (blog), Reason.com, September 10, 2015, https://reason.com/blog/2015/09/10/rep-jared-polis-thinks-colleges-should-b.

Chapter 1 – The Foundations of the Panic

1 "NO Excuse for Sexual Assault," Facebook, https://www.facebook.com/NoexcuseMSU.

2 *Michigan State University Annual Fire and Safety Report*, October 1, 2015, p. 23, http://police.msu.edu/wp-content/uploads/2015/09/asfsreport2015.pdf.

3 Michigan Penal Code, Section 750.320b, http://www.legislature.mi.gov/(S(00d0xxa005kk43tph10l3y3h))/mileg.aspx?page=getObject&objectName=mcl-750-520b.

4 U.S. Dept. of Education, Office for Civil Rights, Region XV, "Re: OCR Docket # 15-11-2098 and #15-14-2113" (letter to Kristine Zayko, deputy general counsel, Michigan State University), September 1, 2015, http://www2.ed.gov/documents/press-releases/michigan-state-letter.pdf.

5 20 U.S.C. § 1681.

6 *A Matter of Simple Justice: The Report of the President's Task Force on Women's Rights and Responsibilities* (Washington, D.C.: Government Printing Office, April 1970), https://www.libraries.psu.edu/content/dam/psul/up/digital/afgw/AMatterofSimpleJustice.pdf.

7 John David Skrentny, *The Minority Rights Revolution* (Cambridge: Belknap Press, 2004), p. 235; Susan Tolchin, *Women in Congress* (Washington, D.C.: Government Printing Office, 1976), p. 32.

8 Sara Evans, *Tidal Wave: How Women Changed America at Century's End* (New York: Free Press, 2010), p. 61.

9 Skrentny, *The Minority Rights Revolution*, pp. 246–47.

10 "Against Our Will," Susanbrownmiller.com, http://www.susanbrownmiller.com/susanbrownmiller/html/against_our_will.html.

11 *Alexander v. Yale*, 459 F. Supp. 1, 5 (D. Conn. 1977); *Alexander v. Yale*, 631 F.2d 178 (2d Cir. 1980) (affirming decision of District Court).

12 Catherine MacKinnon, "A Rally against Rape (1981)," in MacKinnon, *Feminism Unmodified: Discourses on Life and Law* (Cambridge, MA: Harvard University Press, 1987), p. 82.

13 Catharine MacKinnon, *Toward a Feminist Theory of the State* (Cambridge, MA: Harvard University Press, 1989), p. 146.

14 Catharine MacKinnon, "Feminism, Marxism, Method, and the State: Toward Feminist Jurisprudence," *Signs* 8 (1983), p. 647.

15 Ariel Levy, "The Prisoner of Sex," *New York*, n.d., http://nymag.com/nymetro/news/people/features/11907.

16 Andrea Dworkin, *Letters from a War Zone: Writings, 1976–1989* (New York: E.P. Dutton, 1989), p. 14.

17 *American Booksellers v. Hudnut*, 771 F.2d 323, 324, quoting *Police Department v. Mosley*, 408 U.S. 92 (1972).

18 Nadine Strossen, "Censuring the Censors of Free Speech," *Chicago Tribune*, September 2, 1993, http://articles.chicagotribune.com/1993-09-02/news/9309020012_1_feminists-censorship-law-students-and-professors.

19 Amelia Thomson-Deveaux, "A New Form of Justice for Rape Survivors," *National Journal*, May 1, 2015.

20 Ibid.

21 Institute of Education Sciences, National Center for Education Statistics, "Table 303.10. Total fall enrollment in degree-granting postsecondary institutions, by attendance status, sex of student, and control of institution: Selected years, 1947 through 2023," *Digest of Education Statistics*, July 2014, http://nces.ed.gov/programs/digest/d13/tables/dt13_303.10.asp.

22 Neil Gilbert, "The Phantom Epidemic of Sexual Assault," *Public Interest* 103 (1991), pp. 54–65.

23 Katie Roiphe, "Date Rape's Other Victim," *New York Times Magazine*, June 13, 1993, http://www.nytimes.com/1993/06/13/magazine/date-rape-s-other-victim.html.

24 Richard Cohen, "Surveying Rape," *Washington Post*, May 19, 1991, https://www.washingtonpost.com/archive/lifestyle/magazine/1991/05/19/surveying-rape/8ce36ef2-9018-4c7c-bec2-96a6c645e6ec. See also Camille Paglia, *Sex, Art, and American Culture: Essays* (New York: Vintage Books, 1992), p. 57.

25 Barbara Raffel Price, "Female Police Officers in the United States," in *Policing in Central and Eastern Europe: Comparing Firsthand Knowledge with Experience from the West*, ed. Milan Pagon (Slovenia: College of Police and Security Studies, 1996), https://www.ncjrs.gov/policing/fem635.htm; Lynn Langton, *Crime Data Brief: Women in Law Enforcement, 1987–2008* (Washington, D.C.: U.S. Dept. of Justice, Office of Justice Programs, Bureau of Justice Statistics, June 2010), http://www.bjs.gov/content/pub/pdf/wle8708.pdf.

26 Katherine Bouton, "Linda Fairstein vs. Rape," *New York Times Magazine*, February 25, 1990, http://www.nytimes.com/1990/02/25/magazine/ linda-fairstein-vs-rape.html; Robert D. McFadden, "Fairstein Is to Retire as Prosecutor of Sex Crimes," *New York Times*, December 18, 2001, http://www.nytimes.com/2001/12/18/nyregion/fairstein-is-to-retire-as-prosecutor-of-sex-crimes.html.

27 Human Rights Watch, *Improving Police Response to Sexual Assault* (N.p.: Author, 2013), https://www.hrw.org/sites/default/files/reports/ improvingSAInvest_0.pdf.

28 American Prosecutors Research Institute, *State Rape Statutes* (Alexandria, VA: Author, n.d.), http://www.arte-sana.com/articles/rape_ statutes.pdf.

29 American Forensic Nurses, "FAQ," http://amrn.com/faq.html; International Association of Forensic Nurses, "SANE Program Listing," http://www.forensicnurses.org/?page=a5; Shefali Luthra and K. K. Rebecca Lai, "More Hospitals to Collect Sexual Assault Evidence," *Texas Tribune*, August 13, 2013, http://www.texastribune.org/2013/08/13/ er-staff-must-be-able-gather-sexual-assault-eviden.

30 Alex Campbell and Katie J. M. Baker, "Police Pledge 'Fresh Look' at Rape Cases after BuzzFeed News Investigation," BuzzFeed, September 9, 2016, https://www.buzzfeed.com/alexcampbell/ police-pledge-fresh-look-at-rape-cases-after-buzzfeed-news-i.

31 "For Baltimore Rape Victims, Added Pain" (editorial), *Washington Post*, August 13, 2016, https://www.washingtonpost.com/opinions/for-baltimore-rape-victims-added-pain/2016/08/13/dc8243ea-60c5-11e6-9d2f-b1a3564181a1_story.html.

32 Joseph Cohn, "Senate Committee Conducts Hearing on Campus Sexual Assault," December 9, 2014, https://www.thefire.org/ senate-committee-conducts-hearing-campus-sexual-assault.

33 Richard Pérez-Peña, "College Groups Connect to Fight Sexual Assault," *New York Times*, March 19, 2013, http://www.nytimes.com/2013/03/20/ education/activists-at-colleges-network-to-fight-sexual-assault.html.

34 Nancy Gertner, "Sex, Lies and Justice: Can We Reconcile the Belated Attention to Rape on Campus with Due Process?" *American Prospect*, January 12, 2015, http://prospect.org/article/sex-lies-and-justice.

35 *Commonwealth v. Jonathan Stockhammer*, 409 Mass. 867 (1991).

36 OCR Policy Memorandum from Antonio J. Califa, Director of Litigation, Enforcement, and Policy Service, to Regional Civil Rights Directors (Aug. 31, 1981), cited in Stephen Henrick, "A Hostile Environment for Student Defendants: Title IX and Sexual Assault on College Campuses," *Northern Kentucky Law Review* 40 (2013), p. 51.

37 David Wilezol, "How the Education Department Warped Title IX," *Minding the Campus* (blog), October 22, 2014, http://www. mindingthecampus.org/2014/10/how-the-education-department-warped-title-ix.

38 Public Law 101-542, 101st Congress, November 8, 1990, http://www.gpo. gov/fdsys/pkg/STATUTE-104/pdf/STATUTE-104-Pg2381.pdf; Beverly Beyette, "Campus Crime Crusade: Howard and Connie Clery Lost Their Daughter to a Crazed Thief; Now They're Angry and Fighting Back," *Los Angeles Times*, August 10, 1989, http://articles.latimes.com/1989-08-10/ news/vw-301_1_campus-crime-statistics.

39 102nd Congress, S. 1150 (102nd): Higher Education Amendments of 1992, https://web.archive.org/web/20150510065915/https://www. govtrack.us/congress/bills/102/s1150#summary.

40 Lauren Germain, *Campus Sexual Assault: College Women Respond* (Baltimore: Johns Hopkins University Press, 2016), pp. 1–2.

41 Deirdre Carmody, "Increasing Rapes on Campus Spur Colleges to Fight Back," *New York Times*, January 1, 1989, http://www.nytimes. com/1989/01/01/us/increasing-rapes-on-campus-spur-colleges-to-fight-back.html.

42 Nancy Gibbs, "Cover Stories Behavior: When Is It RAPE?" *Time*, June 24, 2001, https://web.archive.org/web/20150510020122/http://content. time.com/time/magazine/article/0,9171,157165,00.html.

43 Anonymous, "Catherine Comins: The Bigot of Vassar College" (editorial), *Vassar Spectator*, September 1, 1991, http:// newspaperarchives.vassar.edu/cgi-bin/vassar?a=d&d=vcsp ec19910901-01.2.32.

44 Alan Charles Kors and Harvey Silverglate, *The Shadow University: The Betrayal of Liberty on America's Campuses* (New York: Free Press, 1998).

45 Ibid., p. 289.

46 Ibid., pp. 154–55, 158, 178–79.

47 Donald P. Russo, "Campus 'Courts' Deny Basic Rights to Students Congress Can Step In and Assure That the Constitution Applies on College Campuses, Too," Philly.com, January 3, 1994, http://articles. philly.com/1994-01-03/news/25822029_1_student-private-liberal-arts-colleges-hearsay.

48 Kors and Silverglate, *Shadow University*, pp. 312–13.

49 For early examples of such policies, *see UWM Post, Inc. v. Board of Regents of the Univ. of Wis. Sys.*, 774 F. Supp. 1163 (E.D. Wis. 1991); *Doe v. Univ. of Mich.*, 721 F. Supp. 852 (D. Mich. 1989).

50 *Rowinsky v. Bryan Independent School District*, 80 F.3d 1006, 1016 (5th Cir., 1996).

51 Eugene Volokh, "Freedom of Speech, Cyberspace, Harassment Law, and the Clinton Administration," *Law and Contemporary Problems* 63 (2000), pp. 299, 315.

52 Henrick, "A Hostile Environment for Student Defendants," p. 70.

53 U.S. Dept. of Education, Office for Civil Rights, *Sexual Harassment Guidance: Harassment of Students by School Employees, Other Students, or Third Parties* (March 1997), http://www2.ed.gov/about/offices/list/ocr/docs/sexhar01.html.

54 *But see* Stuart Taylor Jr., "Opening Argument – Harassment by Kids: Are More Lawsuits the Answer?" http://www.stuarttaylorjr.com/?p=16352#more-16352.

55 *Davis v. Monroe County Bd. of Educ.*, 526 U.S. 629, 650 (1999).

56 U.S. Dept. of Education, Office for Civil Rights, *Revised Sexual Harassment Guidance: Harassment of Students by School Employees, Other Students, or Third Parties* (January 19, 2001), http://www2.ed.gov/about/offices/list/ocr/docs/shguide.pdf.

57 Sandra Stephens, Compliance Team Leader, Office for Civil Rights, Region VI, to David Schmidly, President, Oklahoma State University, Re: Case No. 06-03-2054, 10 June 2004, https://www.ncherm.org/documents/114-OklahomaStateUniversity--06032054.pdf.

58 John F. Carroll, Compliance Team Leader, Office for Civil Rights, Region II, to Muriel A. Howard, President, Buffalo State College, State Univ. of N.Y., Re: Case No. 02-05-2008, 30 Aug. 2005, cited in Jacob Gersen and Jeannie Suk Gersen, "The Sex Bureaucracy," *California Law Review* 104, no. 4 (2016), pp. 881–948, http://scholarship.law.berkeley.edu/californialawreview/vol104/iss4/2.

59 Except as noted, all quotes regarding the case at Yale come from *Kathryn Kelly v. Yale University*, U.S. District Court for the District of Connecticut, 2003 U.S. Dist. LEXIS 4543 (documents available at https://kc-johnson.com).

60 *Davis v. Monroe County Bd. of Educ.*

61 *Kelly v. Yale University* (2003), http://www.ctd.uscourts.gov/sites/default/files/opinions/032603.JCH_.Kelly_.pdf.

62 *Simpson v. University of Colorado Boulder*, 500 F.3d 1171, 1173 (10th Cir. 2007); *Williams v. Board of Regents of the University System of Georgia*, 477 F.3d 1282 (11th Cir. 2007); *J.K. v. Ariz. Bd. of Regents*, 2008 WL 4446712 (D. Ariz. Sept. 30, 2008).

63 American Civil Liberties Union, "Re: Campus Sexual Assault: The Role of Title IX (Roundtable)" (letter to Hon. Claire McCaskill and Hon. Ron Johnson), June 2, 2014, https://www.aclu.org/sites/default/files/assets/aclu_statement_for_roundtable_on_campus_sexual_assault_and_the_role_of_title_ix_on_letterhead_final_6.2.14.pdf; American

Civil Liberties Union, "Re: Hearing on Sexual Assault on Campus – Working to Ensure Student Safety" (letter to Hon. Tom Harkin and Hon. Lamar Alexander), June 26, 2014, https://www.aclu.org/sites/default/files/assets/campus_sexual_assault-help_committee_hearing-aclu_statement-6-25-14.pdf.

64 *Williams v. Board of Regents of the University System of Georgia*, 477 F.3d 1282 (11th Cir. 2007).

65 Anonymous, *Barack Obama on Women's Rights*, n.d., http://obama.3cdn.net/4ad874dbd8e8eaff7d_71m6btc7j.pdf.

66 Lara Setrakian, "Obama: Investigate Duke Lacrosse DA Nifong," ABC News, March 25, 2007, http://abcnews.go.com/Politics/LegalCenter/story?id=2980582.

67 "Agenda: Women," Change.gov, http://change.gov/agenda/women_agenda.

68 Sofi Sinozich and Lynn Langton, *Special Report: Rape and Sexual Assault Victimization among College-Age Females, 1995–2013* (N.p.: U.S. Dept. of Justice, Office of Justice Programs, Bureau of Justice Statistics, December 2014), http://www.bjs.gov/content/pub/pdf/rsavcaf9513.pdf; Joseph Shapiro, "Campus Rape Victims: A Struggle For Justice," *Morning Edition*, NPR, February 24, 2010, http://www.npr.org/templates/story/story.php?storyId=124001493; for significant discrepancies in the coverage's central vignette, that of former Wisconsin student Laura Dunn, see Christina Hoff Sommers, "The Media Is Making College Rape Culture Worse," *Daily Beast*, January 23, 2015, http://www.thedailybeast.com/articles/2015/01/23/the-media-is-making-college-rape-culture-worse.html; Anonymous, "NPR, Center for Public Integrity Ignored Details in University of Wisconsin Alleged Rape Case," *Lust for Life* (blog), n.d., http://derekrose.com/wp/?p=1717.

69 Jackie Jones, "Freedom from Assault: Colleges Act after Office for Civil Rights Warns That Title IX Requires Protections against Sexual Violence," *Convergence: Diversity and Inclusion*, March 8, 2013, http://mydigimag.rrd.com/display_article.php?id=1323531.

70 Shapiro, "Campus Rape Victims."

71 "Who We Are," Education Trust, https://edtrust.org/who-we-are.

72 "Archived Online Trainings," National Center for Higher Education Risk Management, https://www.ncherm.org/online-trainings/archived-online-trainings.

73 "Sexual Assault on Campus," Center for Public Integrity, http://www.publicintegrity.org/investigations/campus_assault/articles/entry/1947.

74 For background on the incident, see "FIRE letter to Yale President Richard C. Levin, June 17, 2011," https://www.thefire.org/fire-letter-to-yale-president-richard-c-levin-june-17-2011.

75 "Voluntary Resolution Agreement: Yale University," Complaint No. 01-11-2027, June 11, 2012, https://www2.ed.gov/about/offices/list/ocr/docs/investigations/01112027-b.pdf.

76 Ronald Brownstein, "The Democrats' White Flight," *Atlantic*, January 7, 2011, http://www.theatlantic.com/politics/archive/2011/01/the-democrats-white-flight/69047.

77 Michael Riley, "Buck's Remarks on Homosexuality Loom after Meet the Press Debate," *Denver Post*, October 17, 2010, http://www.denverpost.com/ci_16362834; Allison Sherry, "Gender Divide Plays Big Role in Buck vs. Bennet," *Denver Post*, October 27, 2010, http://www.denverpost.com/campaign/ci_16453030.

78 Stuart Taylor Jr. and KC Johnson, "The New Standard for Campus Sexual Assault: Guilty until Proven Innocent," *National Review*, December 7, 2015, http://www.nationalreview.com/article/428910/campus-rape-courts-republicans-resisting.

79 U.S. Dept of Education, Office for Civil Rights, Dear Colleague Letter on Sexual Violence (April 4, 2011), http://www2.ed.gov/about/offices/list/ocr/letters/colleague-201104.pdf.

80 Catherine Lhamon, "Dept. of Education Response to Lankford Letter," February 17, 2016, http://chronicle.com/items/biz/pdf/DEPT.%20of%20EDUCATION%20RESPONSE%20TO%20LANKFORD%20LETTER%202-17-16.pdf.

81 Sheralyn Goldbecker, Compliance Team Leader, Office for Civil Rights, Region III, to John DeGioia, President, Georgetown University, Re: Case No. 11-03-2017, 5 May 2004, https://www.ncherm.org/documents/199-GeorgetownUniversity--11032017.pdf.

82 "Law Professors' Open Letter regarding Campus Free Speech and Sexual Assault," *Wall Street Journal*, May 16, 2016, http://online.wsj.com/public/resources/documents/Law-Professor-Open-Letter-May-16-2016.pdf; see Jacob Gershman, "Dershowitz and Other Professors Decry 'Pervasive and Severe Infringement' of Student Rights," *Law Blog*, *Wall Street Journal*, May 18, 2016, http://blogs.wsj.com/law/2016/05/18/dershowitz-and-other-professors-decry-pervasive-and-severe-infringement-of-student-rights.

83 Hans Bader, "Education Department Illegally Ordered Colleges to Reduce Due-Process Safeguards," Examiner.com, September 21, 2012, http://www.examiner.com/article/education-department-illegally-ordered-colleges-to-reduce-due-process-safeguards.

84 Cynthia Gordy, "The Root: The Far-Reaching Teachings of Russlynn Ali," NPR.org, April 20, 2011, http://www.npr.org/2011/04/20/135568364/the-root-the-far-reaching-teachings-of-russlynn-ali.

85 Anonymous, "An Open Letter to OCR," *Inside Higher Ed*, October
    28, 2011, https://www.insidehighered.com/views/2011/10/28/
    essay-ocr-guidelines-sexual-assault-hurt-colleges-and-students.

86 Lee Burdette Williams, "The Dean of Sexual Assault" (opinion),
    Inside Higher Ed, August 7, 2015, https://www.insidehighered.com/
    views/2015/08/07/how-sexual-assault-campaign-drove-one-student-
    affairs-administrator-her-job-essay.

87 Sandy Hingston, "The New Rules of College Sex: How the Federal
    Government and a Malvern Lawyer Are Rewriting the Rules on
    Campus Hookups—and Tagging Young Men as Dangerous Predators,"
    Philadelphia, August 22, 2011, http://www.phillymag.com/articles/
    the-new-rules-of-college-sex/#DzO22ZQA7gQ4ogEb.99.

88 Adam Goldstein, "Rape Is a Crime, Treat It as Such" (opinion), *Room for
    Debate* (blog), *New York Times*, March 12, 2013, http://www.nytimes.com/
    roomfordebate/2013/03/12/why-should-colleges-judge-rape-accusations/
    rape-is-a-crime-treat-it-as-such.

89 Conor Friedersdorf, "What Should the Standard of Proof Be in Campus
    Rape Cases?" *Atlantic*, June 17, 2016, http://www.theatlantic.com/
    politics/archive/2016/06/campuses-sexual-misconduct/487505.

90 Tamara Rice Lave, "Campus Sexual Assault Adjudication: Why
    Universities Should Reject the Dear Colleague Letter," *University of
    Kansas Law Review* 64 (2016), pp. 913–59.

91 Jacob E. Gersen, "How the Feds Use Title IX to Bully Universities"
    (commentary), *Wall Street Journal*, January 24, 2016, http://www.wsj.com/
    articles/how-the-feds-use-title-ix-to-bully-universities-1453669725.

92 Samantha Harris and Greg Lukianoff, "Executive Branch Overreach and
    the Accelerating Threats to Due Process and Free Speech on Campus,"
    in *Liberty's Nemesis: The Unchecked Expansion of the State*, ed. Dean
    Reuter and John Yoo (New York: Encounter Books, 2016), pp. 169–80.

93 S.Amdt.141 to S.Amdt.2, 114th Congress (2015–2016), https://www.
    congress.gov/amendment/114th-congress/senate-amendment/141/text.

94 Letter from Sen. James Lankford to John King Jr., Acting Secretary of
    Education, March 4, 2016, copy in authors' possession.

95 *Mathew v. Eldridge*, 424 U.S. 319, 335 (1976).

96 Jeannie Suk Gersen, "St. Paul's School and a New Definition of Rape,"
    New Yorker, November 3, 2015, http://www.newyorker.com/news/
    news-desk/st-pauls-school-and-a-new-definition-of-rape.

97 Joe Palazzolo, "Harvard Law Professor: Feds' Position on Sexual-Assault
    Policies Is 'Madness,'" *Law Blog, Wall Street Journal*, December 31, 2014,
    http://blogs.wsj.com/law/2014/12/31/harvard-law-professor-feds-position-
    on-sexual-assault-policies-is-madness.

Chapter 2 – Misleading through Statistics

1　Sofi Sinozich and Lynn Langton, *Special Report: Rape and Sexual Assault Victimization among College-Age Females, 1995–2013* (N.p.: U.S. Dept. of Justice, Office of Justice Programs, Bureau of Justice Statistics, December 2014).

2　Office of the Press Secretary, The White House, "Remarks by the President at 'It's On Us' Campaign Rollout" (press release), September 19, 2014, https://www.whitehouse.gov/the-press-office/2014/09/19/remarks-president-its-us-campaign-rollout.

3　Monica Alba, "Clinton Pushes Crackdown on 'Epidemic' of Campus Sexual Assault," NBC News, September 14, 2015, http://www.nbcnews.com/politics/2016-election/clinton-roll-out-plan-combat-sexual-assault-colleges-n427016.

4　David G. Savage and Timothy M. Phelps, "How a Little-Known Education Office Has Forced Far-Reaching Changes to Campus Sex Assault Investigations," *Los Angeles Times*, August 17, 2015, http://www.latimes.com/nation/la-na-campus-sexual-assault-20150817-story.html.

5　Sinozich and Langton, *Special Report: Rape and Sexual Assault Victimization.*

6　David Cantor, Bonnie Fisher, Susan Chibnall, Reanne Townsend, Hyunshik Lee, Carol Bruce, and Gail Thomas, *Report on the AAU Campus Climate Survey on Sexual Assault and Sexual Misconduct* (Rockville, MD: Westat, 2015), http://www.aau.edu/uploadedFiles/AAU_Publications/AAU_Reports/Sexual_Assault_Campus_Survey/AAU_Campus_Climate_Survey_12_14_15.pdf (table 6.1).

7　Institute of Education Sciences, National Center for Education Statistics, "Table 303.70. Total undergraduate fall enrollment in degree-granting postsecondary institutions, by attendance status, sex of student, and control and level of institution: Selected years, 1970 through 2024," *Digest of Education Statistics*, March 2015, http://nces.ed.gov/programs/digest/d14/tables/dt14_303.70.asp.

8　Sinozich and Langton, *Special Report: Rape and Sexual Assault Victimization*, p. 11.

9　Candace Kruttschnitt, William D. Kalsbeek, and Carol C. House (eds.), *Estimating the Incidence of Rape and Sexual Assault* (Washington, D.C.: National Academies Press, 2014), p. 154. Available at http://www.nap.edu/catalog/18605/estimating-the-incidence-of-rape-and-sexual-assault.

10　Ibid.

11　Sinozich and Langton, *Special Report: Rape and Sexual Assault Victimization*, p. 12.

12　U.S. Dept. of Justice, Federal Bureau of Investigation, "Table 1: Crime in the United States by Volume and Rate per 100,000 Inhabitants, 1995–2014," https://www.fbi.gov/about-us/cjis/ucr/crime-in-the-u.s/2014/ crime-in-the-u.s.-2014/tables/table-1.

13 For report data, see U.S. Dept. of Education, Office of Postsecondary Education, http://ope.ed.gov/campussafety.

14 The victims' rights group Rape, Abuse & Incest National Network (RAINN) has cited various government data to claim that only 32 percent of all rapes are reported. See https://rainn.org/get-information/ statistics/reporting-rates.

15 White House Council on Women and Girls and Office of the Vice President, *Rape and Sexual Assault: A Renewed Call to Action* (Washington, D.C.: White House, 2014), https://www.whitehouse.gov/ sites/default/files/docs/sexual_assault_report_1-21-14.pdf, p. 14.

16 The low end of recent Clery Act reports (4,558) divided by 500,000 is 0.9 percent; the high end (5,335) divided by 400,000 is 1.3 percent.

17 Matt Rocheleau, "Sexual Assault Reports Climb at Area Colleges: N.E. Schools' Data Tied to a Greater Awareness," *Boston Globe*, October 6, 2014, http://www.bostonglobe.com/metro/2014/10/05/ reports-sexual-assaults-area-college-campuses-rise-sharply/ FoRoBoigySPVOaWn5YXeDI/story.html.

18 U.S. Dept. of Justice, Federal Bureau of Investigation, "Table 1: Crime in the United States by Volume and Rate per 100,000 Inhabitants, 1994–2013," https://www.fbi.gov/about-us/cjis/ucr/crime-in-the-u.s/2013/crime-in-the-u.s.-2013/tables/1tabledatadecoverviewpdf/ table_1_crime_in_the_united_states_by_volume_and_rate_per_100000_ inhabitants_1994-2013.xls#overview; U.S. Dept. of Justice, Office of Justice Programs, Bureau of Justice Statistics, "Over 60 Percent Decline in Sexual Violence against Females from 1995 to 2010" (press release), http://www.bjs.gov/content/pub/press/fvsv9410pr.cfm.

19 Office of the President, Dartmouth, "Moving Dartmouth Forward: The President's Plan," last updated January 29, 2015, http://www.dartmouth. edu/~president/forward/plan.html.

20 For details of the disparity in reports between non-elite and elite schools, see the tables at https://kc-johnson.com.

21 *Occidental College Annual Fire Safety and Security Report*, p. 57, http://cache.oxy.edu/sites/default/files/assets/Campus_Safety/ AFSSR_10-2-15_LR.pdf.

22 Christopher P. Krebs, Christine H. Lindquist, Tara D. Warner, Bonnie S. Fisher, and Sandra L. Martin, *The Campus Sexual Assault (CSA) Study* (Washington, D.C.: National Institute of Justice, 2007), https://www. ncjrs.gov/pdffiles1/nij/grants/221153.pdf.

23   James Alan Fox and Richard Moran, "Sex Assault Surveys Not the Answer: Column," *USA Today*, August 10, 2014, http://www.usatoday.com/story/opinion/2014/08/10/sexual-assault-rape-survey-college-campus-column/13864551.

24   Justin Lehmiller, "America Has a College Rape Problem, but We Need the Right Data to Address It," *Playboy*, August 31, 2015, http://www.playboy.com/articles/college-sexual-assaults.

25   Scott H. Greenfield, "As the Definitions of Rape Slide down the Slippery Slope," *Simple Justice* (blog), n.d., http://blog.simplejustice.us/2014/10/13/as-the-definitions-of-rape-slides-down-the-slippery-slope.

26   Emily Yoffe, "The College Rape Overcorrection," *Slate*, December 7, 2014, http://www.slate.com/articles/double_x/doublex/2014/12/college_rape_campus_sexual_assault_is_a_serious_problem_but_the_efforts.html.

27   For other studies, see Alexandra Sifferlin, "Rape Is Common among Female College Freshmen, Study Shows," *Time*, May 20, 2015, http://time.com/3891039/college-campus-rape-freshmen; Kate B. Carey, Sarah E. Durney, Robyn L. Shepardson, and Michael P. Carey, "Incapacitated and Forcible Rape of College Women: Prevalence across the First Year," *Journal of Adolescent Health* 56, no. 6 (2015), pp. 678–80; Ashe Schow, "Replicating a Flawed Campus Sexual Assault Study Doesn't Make It True," *Washington Examiner*, May 20, 2015, http://www.washingtonexaminer.com/replicating-a-flawed-campus-sexual-assault-study-doesnt-make-it-true/article/2564786; Brown University, "A Statistical Study of First-Year College Rape" (press release), May 20, 2015, http://www.eurekalert.org/pub_releases/2015-05/bu-ass051515.php; Stacy Teicher Khadaroo, "Preventing College Rape: Why Freshman Year Is Key, Especially for Past Victims," *Christian Science Monitor*, May 20, 2015, http://www.csmonitor.com/USA/Education/2015/0520/Preventing-college-rape-why-freshman-year-is-key-especially-for-past-victims.

28   Cantor et al., *Report on the AAU Campus Climate Survey*, p. xv. Individual data of the 27 are here: https://www.washingtonpost.com/news/grade-point/wp/2015/09/21/what-a-massive-sexual-assault-survey-showed-about-27-top-u-s-universities.

29   For an unconvincing argument that victims were underrepresented in the survey, see Jennifer J. Freyd, "Examining Denial Tactics: Were Victims Overrepresented in the AAU Survey of Sexual Violence on College Campuses?" *Huffington Post*, September 29, 2015, http://www.huffingtonpost.com/jennifer-j-freyd/examining-denial-tactics-were-victims-overrepresented-in-the-aau-survey-of-sexual-violence-on-college-campuses_b_8216008.html.

30   Stuart S. Taylor Jr., "The Latest Big Sexual Assault Survey Is (Like

Others) More Hype Than Science," *Grade Point* (blog), *Washington Post*, September 23, 2015, https://www.washingtonpost.com/news/grade-point/wp/2015/09/23/the-latest-big-sexual-assault-survey-is-like-others-more-hype-than-science.

31 Cantor et al., *Report on the AAU Campus Climate Survey*, tables 3-2 and 6.1.

32 Victims who did not report their sexual assaults to campus authorities don't affect the validity of this calculation. That's because none of them (assuming honesty) were among the 2.17 percent who told the surveyors that they had so reported. And all of those 2.17 percent should show up in the Clery Act submissions.

33 Greg Piper, "The Massive New Campus Sexual-Assault Survey Has One Giant Design Flaw," *College Fix*, September 22, 2015, http://www.thecollegefix.com/post/24320.

34 Cantor et al., *Report on the AAU Campus Climate Survey*, p. xv. Individual data of the 27 institutions are here: https://www.washingtonpost.com/news/grade-point/wp/2015/09/21/what-a-massive-sexual-assault-survey-showed-about-27-top-u-s-universities.

35 Heather Mac Donald, "An Assault on Common Sense: The Phony Campus Rape Crisis," *Weekly Standard*, November 2, 2015, http://www.weeklystandard.com/an-assault-on-common-sense/article/1051200.

36 Ibid.

37 Emily Yoffe, "The Problem with Campus Sexual Assault Surveys: Why the Grim Portrait Painted by the New AAU Study Does Not Reflect Reality," *Slate*, September 24, 2015, http://www.slate.com/articles/double_x/doublex/2015/09/aau_campus_sexual_assault_survey_why_such_surveys_don_t_paint_an_accurate.2.html.

38 Nick Anderson and Scott Clement, "Kaiser Poll Shows That 20 Percent of Women Sexually Assaulted [*sic*] in College," *Washington Post*, June 12, 2015, http://www.washingtonpost.com/sf/local/2015/06/12/1-in-5-women-say-they-were-violated; "Poll: One in 5 Women Say They Have Been Sexually Assaulted in College," *Washington Post*, June 12, 2015, http://www.washingtonpost.com/graphics/local/sexual-assault-poll; Emma Brown, Nick Anderson, Susan Svrluga, and Steve Hendrix, "Survivor Stories Show How Campus Sexual Assault Is Common, Life-Altering," *Washington Post*, June 12, 2015, http://www.washingtonpost.com/sf/local/2015/06/12/sex-assault-during-college-is-common-and-life-altering.

39 Scott Clement, "How Was Sexual Assault Measured?" *Washington Post*, June 12, 2015, https://www.washingtonpost.com/local/education/how-was-sexual-assault-measured/2015/06/11/db542664-08ab-11e5-a7ad-b430fc1d3f5c_story.html.

40 Sinozich and Langton, *Special Report: Rape and Sexual Assault Victimization*.

41 Brown et al., "Survivor Stories."

42 Rachel Beck, "Sako Gets 8-Year Term for Rape," *Corvallis Gazette-Times*, May 20, 2009, http://www.gazettetimes.com/news/local/sako-gets--year-term-for-rape/article_18d714d8-2aaf-58fd-9724-10f5977502ce.html.

43 Fred Contrada, "UMass Gang Rape Victim Files Civil Suits against 4 Defendants, University," MassLive, October 14, 2015, http://www.masslive.com/news/index.ssf/2015/10/victim_in_umass_rape_case_file.html.

44 Kmarko, "Text from Wisconsin Student Arrested for Sexual Assault: 'Sorry for Literally Raping You,'" April 15 [no year], Barstool Sports, http://www.barstoolsports.com/barstoolu/text-from-wisconsin-student-arrested-for-sexual-assault-sorry-for-literally-raping-you.

45 Steve Schering, "Kenilworth Man Sentenced to Probation for Wisconsin Sexual Assault," *Chicago Tribune*, April 13, 2015, http://www.chicagotribune.com/suburbs/winnetka/news/ct-wtk-douglas-gill-tl-0416-20150413-story.html.

46 Sam Ruland, "Former Penn State Student Sentenced to Jail for Sexual Assault," *Daily Collegian*, May 20, 2016, http://www.collegian.psu.edu/news/crime_courts/article_37434b74-1edd-11e6-a305-2bdf4e0750b3.html.

47 Emily Welker, "Suspended MSUM Wrestler to Get Four Months for Dorm Rape," Inforum, May 18, 2015, http://www.inforum.com/news/3747635-suspended-msum-wrestler-get-four-months-dorm-rape.

48 KC Johnson and Stuart Taylor Jr., "Stanford Sex Assault Case: The Sentence Was Too Short—But the System Worked" (opinion), *Washington Post*, June 9, 2016, https://www.washingtonpost.com/opinions/stanford-case-shows-why-the-justice-system-should-handle-campus-sexual-assault/2016/06/08/38a6af24-2cf2-11e6-9b37-42985f6a265c_story.html.

49 Morgan Baskin, "Q&A: Sen. Bob Casey on His Campus Sexual Assault Bill," *USA Today College*, October 16, 2015, http://college.usatoday.com/2015/10/16/qa-sen-bob-casey-on-his-campus-sexual-assault-bill.

50 Sinozich and Langton, *Special Report: Rape and Sexual Assault Victimization*, p. 17.

51 Kirsten Gillibrand, "Kirsten Gillibrand: 'We Will Not Allow These Crimes to Be Swept under the Rug Any Longer,'" *Time*, May 15, 2014, http://time.com/100144/kirsten-gillibrand-campus-sexual-assault.

52 Sinozich and Langton, *Special Report: Rape and Sexual Assault Victimization*.

53 Ibid.

54 Suzanna Bobadilla and Kate Sim, "Dealing with Activist Burn-out and Self-Care," Know Your IX, http://knowyourix.org/dealing-with/dealing-with-activist-burn-out-and-self-care.

55 Callie Marie Rennison, "Privilege, among Rape Victims: Who Suffers Most from Rape and Sexual Assault in America?" (op-ed), *New York Times,* December 21, 2014, http://www.nytimes.com/2014/12/22/opinion/who-suffers-most-from-rape-and-sexual-assault-in-america.html.

56 Delece Smith-Barrow, "10 National Universities Where Students Usually Live on Campus," *U.S. News & World Report,* March 3, 2015, http://www.usnews.com/education/best-colleges/the-short-list-college/articles/2015/03/03/10-national-universities-where-students-usually-live-on-campus.

57 Institute of Education Sciences, National Center for Education Statistics, "Table 303.70. Total undergraduate fall enrollment in degree-granting postsecondary institutions," nces.ed.gov/programs/coe/indicator_cha.asp.

58 David Lisak and Paul M. Miller, "Repeat Rape and Multiple Offending among Undetected Rapists," *Violence and Victims* 17, no. 1 (2002), pp. 73–84. Available at http://www.davidlisak.com/wp-content/uploads/pdf/RepeatRapeinUndetectedRapists.pdf.

59 Amelia Thomson-DeVeaux, "What If Most Campus Rapes Aren't Committed by Serial Rapists?" FiveThirtyEight, July 13, 2015, http://fivethirtyeight.com/features/what-if-most-campus-rapes-arent-committed-by-serial-rapists.

60 Linda M. LeFauve, "Campus Rape Expert Can't Answer Basic Questions about His Sources: The Problem with David Lisak's Serial Predator Theory of Campus Sexual Assault," *Reason,* July 28, 2015, http://reason.com/archives/2015/07/28/campus-rape-statistics-lisak-problem; see also Robby Soave, "How an Influential Campus Rape Study Skewed the Debate: Widely Cited Study Relies on Surveys That Don't Actually Have Anything to Do with On-Campus Sexual Assaults," *Hit & Run* (blog), *Reason,* July 28, 2015, https://reason.com/blog/2015/07/28/campus-rape-stats-lisak-study-wrong.

61 Soave, "How an Influential Campus Rape Study Skewed the Debate" (exclamation mark in original).

62 Linda M. LeFauve, "The Misleading Video Interview with a Rapist at the Heart of the Campus Sexual Assault Freakout: How Influential Sexual Assault Expert David Lisak Used a Misleadingly Edited Video to Sell His Serial Predator Theory of Campus Rape," *Reason,* November 20, 2015, https://reason.com/archives/2015/11/20/lisak-frank-interview-problem-rape.

63 Jon Krakauer, *Missoula: Rape and the Justice System in a College Town* (New York: Doubleday, 2015), p. 121.

64 Kevin M. Swartout, Mary P. Koss, Jacquelyn W. White, Martie P. Thompson, Antonia Abbey, and Alexandra L. Bellis, "Trajectory Analysis of the Campus Serial Rapist Assumption," *JAMA Pediatrics* 169, no. 12 (2015), pp. 1148–54, http://archpedi.jamanetwork.com/article.aspx?articleid=2375127; Robby Soave, "Campus Rape Expert Who Misrepresented His Work Faces Powerful New Criticism," *Hit & Run* (blog), *Reason*, August 11, 2015, http://reason.com/blog/2015/08/11/campus-rape-expert-who-misrepresented-hi.

65 Robby Soave, "Adherents of Junk Campus Rape Science Are Retaliating against Critics," *Reason*, February 2016, https://reason.com/reasontv/2016/02/09/adherents-of-junk-campus-rape-science-ar.

66 White House Council on Women and Girls and Office of the Vice President, *Rape and Sexual Assault*.

67 Kimberly Lonsway, Joanne Archambault, and David Lisak, "False Reports: Moving beyond the Issue to Successfully Investigate and Prosecute Non-Stranger Sexual Assault," *Voice* 3, no. 1 (n.d.), pp. 1–11, http://ndaa.org/pdf/the_voice_vol_3_no_1_2009.pdf.

68 David Lisak, Lori Gardinier, Sarah C. Nicksa, and Ashley M. Cote, "False Allegations of Sexual Assualt [sic]: An Analysis of Ten Years of Reported Cases," *Violence against Women* 16, no. 12 (2010), p. 1328, http://www.icdv.idaho.gov/conference/handouts/False-Allegations.pdf; End Violence against Women International, "The Making a Difference (MAD) Project: Basic Research Design," http://www.evawintl.org/mad.aspx?subpage=5.

69 Heather Mac Donald, "The Campus Rape Myth," *City Journal*, Winter 2008, http://www.city-journal.org/2008/18_1_campus_rape.html.

70 Taylor and Johnson, *Until Proven Innocent*, pp. 301–355.

71 End Violence against Women International, "The Making a Difference (MAD) Project." For a general survey of earlier false rape-rate surveys, see Philip Rumney, "False Allegations of Rape," *Cambridge Law Journal*, 65 (2006), pp. 128–58.

72 Kimberly A. Lonsway, Joanne Archambault, and Alan Berkowitz, *False Reports: Moving Beyond the Issue to Successfully Investigate and Prosecute Non-Stranger Sexual Assault* (Addy, WA: End Violence against Women International, 2007), https://www.evawintl.org/Library/DocumentLibraryHandler.ashx?id=38.

73 Francis Walker, "How to Lie and Mislead with Rape Statistics: Part 2," *Data Gone Odd* (blog), January 27, 2015, http://www.datagoneodd.com/blog/2015/01/27/how-to-lie-and-mislead-with-rape-statistics-part-2.

74 Candida Saunders, "The Truth, the Half-Truth, and Nothing Like the Truth: Reconceptualizing False Allegations of Rape," *British Journal of Criminology* 52 (2012), p. 1169.

75 Benjamin Baughman, "A Study of Rape Investigation Files Involving Female Survivors: A Comparison of Allegations Deemed False and Genuine," Ph.D. thesis, University of Huddersfield (UK), 2016, http://eprints.hud.ac.uk/27856/1/PhDFinalEdition12Jan2016.pdf.

76 Report of the Response Systems to Adult Sexual Assault Crimes Panel, Figure 13, p. 127. See http://140.185.104.231/Public/docs/Reports/00_Final/RSP_Report_Final_20140627.pdf.

77 John Roman, Kelly Walsh, Pamela Lachman, and Jennifer Yahner, "Post-Conviction DNA Testing and Wrongful Conviction," Urban Institute, June 18, 2012, http://www.urban.org/research/publication/post-conviction-dna-testing-and-wrongful-conviction.

78 Eugene J. Kanin, "False Rape Allegations," *Archives of Sexual Behavior* 23, no. 1 (1994), pp. 81–92.

79 Garrett, citing Robby Soave, "Student Accused of Rape by 'Mattress Girl' Sues Columbia U., Publishes Dozens of Damning Texts," *Reason*, April 24, 2015, http://reason.com/blog/2015/04/24/student-accused-of-rape-by-mattress-girl.

80 Shaunna Murphy, "'The Hunting Ground' Team Tells Us Why Campus Rapes Are Being Covered Up: Kirby Dick and Amy Ziering Weigh In," MTV News, March 3, 2015, http://www.mtv.com/news/2094808/hunting-ground-campus-rape-interview.

81 Jon Krakauer, April 7, 2015, "The Bungled *Rolling Stone* Rape Article Doesn't Change the Fact That Sexual Assault Is the Most Under-reported Crime in the U.S.," *Women in the World*, http://nytlive.nytimes.com/womenintheworld/2015/04/07/the-bungled-rolling-stone-rape-article-doesnt-change-the-fact-that-sexual-assault-is-the-most-under-reported-crime-in-the-us.

82 Daniel Roberts, "Jameis Winston Is Not a Victim," Deadspin, December 4, 2014, http://deadspin.com/jameis-winston-is-not-a-victim-1666874524.

83 Dylan Matthews, "The Saddest Graph You'll See Today," *Wonkblog*, *Washington Post*, January 7, 2013, https://www.washingtonpost.com/news/wonk/wp/2013/01/07/the-saddest-graph-youll-see-today.

84 The Enliven Project, http://theenlivenproject.com.

85 Anonymous, "num.drinks," n.d., http://www.nyu.edu/projects/england/ocsls/codebook/num.drinks.html.

86 Except as noted, all quotes regarding the case at Miami come from *Matthew Sahm v. Miami University, et al.*, U.S. District Court for the

Southern District of Ohio, 110 F. Supp. 3d 774 (documents available at https://kc-johnson.com).

87   Caitlin Dickson, "As Activists Graduate, Campus Sexual Assault Remains in the Spotlight," Yahoo News, June 15, 2015, http://news. yahoo.com/as-activists-graduate--the-debate-over-campus-sexual-assault-continues-011335638.html.

88   Miami University, *Annual Security and Fire Safety Report*, 2013, https:// web.archive.org/web/20140816202314/http://www.miamioh.edu/_files/ documents/campus-safety/Annual_Security_Fire_Safety_Report.pdf, p. 3.

89   Miami University, *Final Report of the Task Force for the Prevention of Sexual Assault*, https://www.miamioh.edu/_files/documents/campus-safety/ Task_Force_Final_Report.pdf.

Chapter 3 - The Realities of "Rape Culture"

1   "What Is Rape Culture?" Carrying the Weight Together, https://web. archive.org/web/20141030040057/http://www.carryingtheweighttogether. com/what_is_rape_culture.

2   "Rape Culture, Victim Blaming, and the Facts," Southern Connecticut State University, https://www.southernct.edu/sexual-misconduct/facts. html.

3   Cathy Young, "Guilty until Proven Innocent: How the Government Encourages Kangaroo Courts for Sex Crimes on Campus," *Reason*, December 17, 2014, http://reason.com/archives/2013/12/17/guilty-until-proven-innocent.

4   The White House, Office of the Press Secretary, "Remarks by the President and Vice President at an Event for the Council on Women and Girls" (press release), January 22, 2014, https://www.whitehouse. gov/the-press-office/2014/01/22/remarks-president-and-vice-president-event-council-women-and-girls.

5   Kendall Foley, "McCaskill Talks about Campus Rape Culture and Legislation," *Missourian*, October 7, 2014, http://www. columbiamissourian.com/news/local/mccaskill-talks-about-campus-rape-culture-and-legislation/article_d29cdfd3-b331-500a-8250-690b86db110f. html.

6   Student Affairs Administrators in Higher Education, "NASPA Asks Student Affairs Professionals to Take Pledge: #SAPledge Campaign Supports #ItsOnUs to Prevent Sexual Assault on Campuses" (news release), September 19, 2014, http://www.naspa.org/images/uploads/main/ NASPA_Press_Release_-_SA_Pledge_-_final.pdf.

7   Stacy Teicher Khadaroo, "'Rape Culture' on Campus: Why Harvard's New Policy Is 'Really Important' (+Video)," *Christian Science Monitor*, July 2, 2014, http://www.csmonitor.com/USA/Education/2014/0702/

Rape-culture-on-campus-why-Harvard-s-new-policy-is-really-important-video.

8 Jennifer Steinhauer, "UVA Furor Sparks Debate over Existence of 'Rape Culture,'" *New York Times*, December 8, 2014, http://www.nytimes.com/2014/12/09/us/fraternity-and-sorority-groups-call-for-uva-to-lift-ban-on-greek-life.html.

9 Young, "Guilty until Proven Innocent."

10 Janel Davis and Shannon McCaffrey, "Wrongly Accused of Rape? Students Question Their Expulsions from Tech," *Atlanta Journal-Constitution*, January 16, 2016, http://www.myajc.com/news/news/local/wrongly-accused-of-rape-students-question-their-ex/np59z.

11 Tyler Kingkade, "Alleged American University Frat Emails Discuss Rape, Assault and Substance Abuse," *Huffington Post*, April 19, 2014, http://www.huffingtonpost.com/2014/04/19/american-university-frat-emails_n_5174130.html.

12 Tom McKay, "These Disturbing 'First Day of School' Banners Reveal Fraternity Rape Culture at Its Worst," Mic, August 24, 2015, http://mic.com/articles/124331/these-disturbing-first-day-of-school-banners-reveal-fraternity-rape-culture-at-its-worst#.RSeNsNiOq.

13 Caitlin Flanagan, "Stand-Up Comics Have to Censor Their Jokes on College Campuses," *Atlantic*, September 2015, http://www.theatlantic.com/magazine/archive/2015/09/thats-not-funny/399335.

14 Material in the above four paragraphs comes from Stuart Taylor Jr. and KC Johnson, *Until Proven Innocent: Political Correctness and the Shameful Injustices of the Duke Lacrosse Rape Case* (New York: St. Martin's, 2007), chapters 1–6.

15 Authors' interview with Stefanie Sparks, March 24, 2007.

16 "Reaction to Rape Charges at Duke" (recording), available at http://www.ibiblio.org/wunc_archives/sot/?cat=15&paged=3.

17 "Provost Responds to Faculty Letter Regarding Lacrosse," Duke News & Communications, April 3, 2006, http://today.duke.edu/showcase/mmedia/features/lacrosse_incident/lange_baker.html.

18 Taylor and Johnson, *Until Proven Innocent*, chapters 6–8.

19 Photo at https://web.archive.org/web/20070216040413/http://img20.imageshack.us/img20/2912/potbangerrallyafo.jpg.

20 KC Johnson, "When the Potbangers Were Riding High," *Durham-in-Wonderland* (blog), February 14, 2007, http://durhamwonderland.blogspot.com/2007/02/when-potbangers-were-riding-high.html.

21 Selena Roberts, "When Peer Pressure, Not a Conscience, Is Your Guide," *New York Times*, March 31, 2006, http://query.nytimes.com/gst/fullpage.html?res=9D04E0DC1230F932A05750C0A9609C8B63.

22 "Letter to the Community from President Brodhead," *Duke Today*, April 5, 2006, http://m.today.duke.edu/2006/04/rhbletter.html.

23 KC Johnson, "Two E-Mail Chains; or R. Brodhead, Movie Critic," *Durham-in-Wonderland* (blog), February 4, 2012, http://durhamwonderland.blogspot.com/2012/02/two-e-mail-chains-or-r-brodhead-movie.html.

24 For a copy of the ad, see http://photos1.blogger.com/x/blogger/2862/372/1600/99636/Listening_Statement_b.jpg.

25 Dan Bowens, "Lacrosse Publicity 'Unwished' For Duke, Durham, Brodhead Says," WRAL.com, April 20, 2006, http://www.wral.com/news/local/story/157148.

26 Gautam Hathi, "'I Am Certainly at Ease in My Conscience': Brodhead on 10-Year Anniversary of the Lacrosse Case," *Chronicle*, March 10, 2016, http://www.dukechronicle.com/article/2016/03/i-am-certainly-at-ease-in-my-conscience.

27 Sociology professors and students, letter to Campus Culture Initiative, May 1, 2006, copy in authors' possession.

28 Rachel Smolkin, "Justice Delayed," *American Journalism Review*, August/September 2007, http://ajrarchive.org/Article.asp?id=4379.

29 Harvey Araton, "At Duke, Freedom of Speech Seems Selective," *New York Times*, May 26, 2006, http://www.nytimes.com/2006/05/26/sports/othersports/26araton.html.

30 Duff Wilson and Jonathan D. Glater, "Files from Duke Rape Case Give Details but No Answers," *New York Times*, August 25, 2006, http://www.nytimes.com/2006/08/25/us/25duke.html.

31 Jeff D. Gorman, "No Relief for Tech Fired in Duke Lacrosse Bungle," Courthouse News Service, August 10, 2011, http://www.courthousenews.com/2011/08/10/38878.htm.

32 "N.C. Attorney General: Duke Players 'Innocent,'" CNN, April 11, 2007, http://www.cnn.com/2007/LAW/04/11/cooper.transcript/index.html.

33 Office of News & Communications, "Duke President Shares Lessons Learned, Regrets about Lacrosse Case," *Duke Today*, September 29, 2007, https://today.duke.edu/2007/09/rhb_lawconf.html.

34 Cathy N. Davidson, "In the Aftermath of a Social Disaster" (op-ed), *News and Observer*, January 5, 2007, https://web.archive.org/web/20070110232732/http://www.newsobserver.com/559/story/528708.html.

35 Office of News & Communications, "McClain Appointed Dean of Graduate School," *Duke Today*, May 8, 2012, https://today.duke.edu/2012/05/mcclaindean.

36 Stuart Taylor Jr., "The Rot at Duke—And Beyond," *National Journal*, December 19, 2009.

37 Global National, "Rape Scandal at Elite U.S. Campus Unraveling," April 14, 2006, http://www.canada.com/story_print. html?id=227fd347-b0ba-4a42-a8c8-1160d5f85a78.

38 Christian Red, "After the Scandal, Duke Lacrosse Starts Over," *New York Daily News*, February 25, 2007.

39 KC Johnson, "Reflections on the Lisker Appointment," *Durham-in-Wonderland* (blog), October 22, 2007, http://durhamwonderland. blogspot.com/2007/10/reflections-on-lisker-appointment.html.

40 Donna Lisker email message to KC Johnson (author), October 18, 2007.

41 Shreya Rao, "Lisker to Fill Undergrad Admin Post," *Chronicle*, October 17, 2007, https://issuu.com/dukechronicleprintarchives/docs/ the_chronicle_2007-10-17_sm.

42 KC Johnson, "Regarding Dr. Kimmel," *Durham-in-Wonderland* (blog), May 20, 2010, http://durhamwonderland.blogspot.com/2010/05/ regarding-dr-kimmel.html.

43 Melissa Harris-Perry, *Sister Citizen: Shame, Stereotypes, and Black Women in America* (New Haven: Yale University Press, 2011), p. 173.

44 Angela Hattery, "Rape in High School and College Athletics: Why Do We Settle for the Explanation That Boys Will Simply Be Boys?" (op-ed), January 23, 2013, http://www.opednews.com/articles/Rape-in-High-School-and-Co-by-Angela-Hattery-130122-689.html?show=votes# allcomments.

45 KC Johnson, "Cohan & Mangum's Credibility," *Durham-in-Wonderland* (blog), April 23, 2014, http://durhamwonderland.blogspot.com/2014/04/ cohan-mangums-credibility.html.

46 "Author on Duke Lacrosse Scandal: There's a Lot of Evidence 'Something Untoward Happened That Night,'" May 16, 2014, *The Lead with Jake Tapper* (blog), http://thelead.blogs.cnn.com/2014/05/16/ duke-durham-lacrosse-scandal.

47 Radley Balko, "The Attempted Rehabilitation of Mike Nifong," *Watch* (blog), *Washington Post*, April 21, 2014, https:// www.washingtonpost.com/news/the-watch/wp/2014/04/21/ the-attempted-rehabilitation-of-mike-nifong.

48 As noted above, Duke, like other schools, typically does not use the word "rape" when it finds a student responsible for initiating intercourse without his partner's consent.

49 Lindsey Rupp, "Rape Policy Mandates Reporting," *Chronicle*, August 28, 2009, http://www.dukechronicle.com/article/2009/08/ rape-policy-mandates-reporting.

50 Ada Gregory, "Comment on Rape Policy Not Aimed at All Students," *Chronicle*, August 31, 2009, http://www.dukechronicle.com/article/2009/08/comment-rape-policy-not-aimed-all-students.

51 KC Johnson, "Simply Extraordinary," *Durham-in-Wonderland* (blog), September 1, 2009, http://durhamwonderland.blogspot.com/2009/09/simply-extraordinary.html.

52 Rupp, "Rape Policy Mandates Reporting."

53 Julian Spector, "An Exploration of Duke's Sexual Misconduct System," *Chronicle*, April 22, 2014, http://www.dukechronicle.com/articles/2014/04/22/exploration-dukes-sexual-misconduct-system#.Vb6BF_lVgSU.

54 Rupp, "Rape Policy Mandates Reporting."

55 Neelesh Morthy, "Experts Explain Title IX Lawsuit, Note Plaintiff's Burden of Proof," *Chronicle*, August 19, 2016, http://www.dukechronicle.com/article/2016/08/experts-explain-plaintiffs-evidentiary-burden-in-recently-filed-title-ix-lawsuit.

56 Spector, "An Exploration of Duke's Sexual Misconduct System."

57 Quotes in the above paragraphs are from KC Johnson, "Simply Extraordinary," *Durham-in-Wonderland* (blog), September 1, 2009, http://durhamwonderland.blogspot.com/2009/09/simply-extraordinary.html.

58 Editorial Board, "Reconsidering How We Try Sexual Assault," *Chronicle*, September 1, 2014, http://www.dukechronicle.com/articles/2014/09/01/reconsidering-how-we-try-sexual-assault#.VbO5IvlVgSV.

59 Except as noted, all quotes regarding the case at Duke come from *Lewis McLeod v. Duke University*, No. 14-CVS-3075, 2014-WL-8843115, N.C. Superior Court (documents available at https://kc-johnson.com).

60 "Dr. Celia Irvine, Psychologist, Chapel Hill, NC 27514," *Psychology Today*, https://therapists.psychologytoday.com/rms/name/Celia_Irvine_PhD_Chapel+Hill_North+Carolina_73526.

61 AICPA Forensic and Valuation Services Section, *Conducting Effective Interviews* (N.p.: Author, n.d.), http://www.aicpa.org/InterestAreas/ForensicAndValuation/Resources/PractAidsGuidance/DownloadableDocuments/10834-378_interview%20whiite%20paper-FINAL-v1.pdf, especially pp. 9–11.

62 Spector, "An Exploration of Duke's Sexual Misconduct System."

63 John H. Tucker, "A Duke Senior Sues the University after Being Expelled over Allegations of Sexual Misconduct," *Indy Week*, May 28, 2014, http://www.indyweek.com/indyweek/a-duke-senior-sues-the-university-after-being-expelled-over-allegations-of-sexual-misconduct/Content?oid=4171302.

64 Valerie Bauerlein, "In Campus Rape Tribunals, Some Men See Injustice," *Wall Street Journal*, April 10, 2015, http://www.wsj.com/articles/in-campus-rape-tribunals-some-men-see-injustice-1428684187.

Chapter 4 – Denying Due Process

1 Except as noted, all quotes regarding the case at Brandeis come from *John Doe v. Brandeis University*, U.S. District Court for the District of Massachusetts, 2016 U.S. Dist. LEXIS 43499 (documents available at https://kc-johnson.com).

2 Fred Thys, "Brandeis Case Reveals Complexity of Disciplining Students for Sexual Assault," WBUR News, September 26, 2014, http://www.wbur.org/2014/09/26/brandeis-sexual-assault-case.

3 Tyler Kingkade, "Brandeis University Punishes Sexual Assault with Sensitivity Training," *Huffington Post*, June 12, 2014, http://www.huffingtonpost.com/2014/06/11/brandeis-sexual-assault_n_5476508.html.

4 Abigail Bessler, "Universities Keep Failing to Actually Punish Rapists," ThinkProgress, June 13, 2014, https://thinkprogress.org/universities-keep-failing-to-actually-punish-rapists-36052882805.

5 Judith Shulevitz, "Accused College Rapists Have Rights, Too," *New Republic*, October 11, 2014, https://newrepublic.com/article/119778/college-sexual-assault-rules-trample-rights-accused-campus-rapists.

6 Except as noted, all quotes regarding the case at Vassar come from *Peter Yu v. Vassar College*, U.S. District Court for the Southern District of New York, 97 F. Supp. 3d 448 (documents available at https://kc-johnson.com).

7 "Judge Sandra S. Beckwith," http://www.ohsd.uscourts.gov/BioBeckwith.

8 *John Doe I and John Doe II v. University of Cincinnati, et al.*, U.S. District Court for the Southern District of Ohio, 2016 U.S. Dist. LEXIS 37924 (documents available at https://kc-johnson.com).

9 *DeBoer v. Snyder*, 772 F.3d 434 (6th Cir. 2014).

10 "Court Audio," 16-3334 *John Doe 1 v Daniel Cummins et al.*, September 29, 2016, http://www.opn.ca6.uscourts.gov/internet/court_audio/save/09-29-2016%20-%20Thursday/16-3334%20John%20Doe%201%20v%20Daniel%20Cummins%20et%20al.zip.

11 *SJU Adult Student Handbook 2013–2014*, http://www.sju.edu/int/studentlife/adult/docs/AdultStudentHandbook.pdf.

12 *Brian Harris v. St. Joseph's University, et al.*, U.S. District Court for the Eastern District of Pennsylvania, 2014 U.S. Dist. LEXIS 65452 (documents available at https://kc-johnson.com).

13 Unless otherwise noted, all information in this section comes from *John Doe v. Columbia University*, U.S. District Court of the Southern District of New York, 2015 U.S. Dist. LEXIS 52370 (documents available at https://kc-johnson.com).

14 Kate Taylor, "List of Names in Sex Assaults Roils Columbia," *New York Times*, May 13, 2014, http://www.nytimes.com/2014/05/14/nyregion/list-of-names-in-sex-assaults-roils-columbia.html.

15 *John Doe v. Pennsylvania State University, et al.*, U.S. District Court for

the Middle District of Pennsylvania, Case 4:15-cv-02072 (documents available at https://kc-johnson.com).

16   Archivist, "Brett Sokolow: Colleges Now Are Expelling and Suspending People They Shouldn't for Sexual Assault," *Community of the Wrongly Accused* (blog), April 18, 2012, http://www.cotwa.info/2012/04/brett-sokolow-colleges-now-are.html.

17   Brett A. Sokolow, "Tip of the Week: Sex and Booze," April 24, 2014, https://atixa.org/wordpress/wp-content/uploads/2012/01/ATIXA-Tip-of-the-Week-04_24_141.pdf.

18   "An Open Letter to Higher Education about Sexual Violence from Brett A. Sokolow, Esq. and The NCHERM Group Partners," May 27, 2014, https://www.ncherm.org/wordpress/wp-content/uploads/2012/01/An-Open-Letter-from-The-NCHERM-Group.pdf.

19   Emily Shire, "Columbia Student Joins the Men Fighting Back in Campus Rape Cases," *Daily Beast*, April 24, 2015, http://www.thedailybeast.com/articles/2015/04/24/columbia-student-joins-the-men-fighting-back-in-campus-rape-cases.html.

20   Katherine Mangan, "2 High-Profile Cases Offer Glimpse of Future Trends in Campus Sexual Assaults," *Chronicle of Higher Education*, June 19, 2016.

21   Craig Wood, Josh Whitlock, Melissa Nelson, Tyler Laughinghouse, and Jillian Nyhof, "Between a Rock and a Hard Place: A Discussion of Issues That Frequently Arise in Sexual Misconduct-Related Litigation against Colleges and Universities," *NACUA Notes*, May 18, 2016, http://counsel.cua.edu/res/docs/titleixlitigation.pdf.

22   Susan Kruth, "Senators McCaskill and Blumenthal Lead Third Roundtable on Campus Sexual Assault," FIRE, June 25, 2014, https://www.thefire.org/senators-mccaskill-and-blumenthal-lead-third-roundtable-on-campus-sexual-assault.

23   Katie J. M. Baker, "The Accused," BuzzFeed News, November 20, 2014, http://www.buzzfeed.com/katiejmbaker/accused-men-say-the-system-hurting-college-sexual-assault-su.

24   For two accounts of such stories, see Emily Shire, "Sexual Assault: The Accused Speak Out," *Daily Beast*, January 27, 2016, http://www.thedailybeast.com/articles/2016/01/28/sexual-assault-the-accused-speak-out.html; Baker, "The Accused."

25   "Can Colleges Handle Sexual Assault Cases Fairly?" (editorial), *Los Angeles Times*, July 17, 2015, http://www.latimes.com/opinion/editorials/la-ed-sexual-assault-uc-san-diego-case-20150717-story.html.

26   KC Johnson, "More Shenanigans from GA Tech," *Academic Wonderland* (blog), December 18, 2015, http://academicwonderland.com/2015/12/18/more-shenanigans-from-ga-tech.

27 *Nolan Youngmun v. University of Alaska*, Case 3AN-16-7798, Third
    Judicial District, Alaska Superior Court (documents available at https://
    kc-johnson.com).

28 Peter Berkowitz, "Lawsuit Casts Harsh Light on Due Process at Colgate,"
    Real Clear Politics, October 3, 2014, http://www.realclearpolitics.com/
    articles/2014/10/03/lawsuit_casts_harsh_light_on_due_process_at_
    colgate__124167.html.

29 Anonymous, "Is Our Response to Title IX Racist?" *Colgate AAUP Issues*
    (blog), February 26, 2015, http://colgateaaup.blogspot.com/2015/02/
    is-our-response-to-title-ix-racist.html.

30 Concerned Minority Faculty, "Colgate to "Crow-Gate": A Report
    from the Diversity Front," *Colgate AAUP Issues* (blog), December 8,
    2014, http://colgateaaup.blogspot.com/2014/12/colgate-to-crow-gate-
    reportfrom.html.

31 Erin Alberty, "BYU Student Who Reported Sex Assault Says Her
    Honor Code File Shows School Saw Her as a 'Suspect,'" *Salt Lake
    Tribune*, April 22, 2016, http://www.sltrib.com/news/3808891-155/
    byu-student-who-reported-sex-assault.

32 Erin Alberty, "Students: BYU Honor Code Leaves LGBT Victims of
    Sexual Assault Vulnerable and Alone,'" *Salt Lake Tribune*, August 16,
    2016, http://www.sltrib.com/home/4186603-155/students-byu-honor-
    code-leaves-lgbt.

33 Paula Lavigne and Mark Schlabach, "Police Records Detail Several
    More Violence Allegations against Baylor Football Players," ESPN, May
    19, 2016, http://espn.go.com/espn/otl/story/_/id/15562625/waco-police-
    records-reveal-additional-violence-allegations-baylor-football-players.

34 See, for example, OCR data request to Rider University, OCR
    Docket #02-16-2156, April 4, 2016, https://www.documentcloud.org/
    documents/2892868-Education-Department-Letter-to-Rider-University.
    html.

35 C-ville Writers, "Burden of Proof: UVA's Sexual Assault Policy under
    Fire," *C-ville*, November 20, 2012, http://www.c-ville.com/burden-of-
    proof-uvas-sexual-assault-policy-under-fire.

36 Andrea Pino, "Rape, Betrayal, and Reclaiming Title IX," *Huffington Post*,
    January 13, 2014, http://www.huffingtonpost.com/andrea-pino/more-that-
    a-teal-ribbon_b_3165293.html.

37 KC Johnson, "The Hunting Ground and UNC," *Academic Wonderland*
    (blog), November 22, 2015, http://academicwonderland.com/2015/11/22/
    the-hunting-ground-and-unc.

38 *McClatchy-Tribune*, "Federal Complaint Claims UNC Violated Assault
    Victims' Rights," *Winston-Salem Journal*, January 21, 2013, http://

www.journalnow.com/news/state_region/federal-complaint-claims-unc-violated-assault-victims-rights/article_785c7fc4-6435-11e2-9181-0019bb30f31a.html.

39　Sophie Murguia, "Expulsion Draws Focus to New Title IX Policies," *Amherst Student*, January 29, 2014, http://amherststudent.amherst. edu/?q=article/2014/01/29/expulsion-draws-focus-new-title-ix-policies.

40　Emily Bazelon, "The Return of the Sex Wars: The Decades-Old Intellectual Debate Simmering beneath the Current Conversation over Sexual Assault on Campus," *New York Times Magazine*, September 10, 2015, http://www.nytimes.com/2015/09/13/magazine/the-return-of-the-sex-wars.html.

41　Dana Bolger, "Colleges Help Rape Survivors Where Courts Fail," *New York Times*, March 12, 2013, http://www.nytimes.com/roomfordebate/2013/03/12/why-should-colleges-judge-rape-accusations/colleges-help-rape-survivors-where-courts-fail.

42　*Education Summit 2016* (video), AtlanticLIVE, May 19, 2016, https://www.youtube.com/watch?list=PLwj46yNDLyTWnTelABDMgdAlQukcE956N&time_continue=514&v=R-byeOjrkoI.

43　Alyssa Peterson, "Campus Policy Guide," Know Your IX, http://knowyourix.org/campus-policy-guide.

44　Ashe Schow, "'Dateline' Highlights Campus Sexual Assault and the Difficulties for College Adjudication," *Washington Examiner*, June 22, 2015, http://www.washingtonexaminer.com/dateline-highlights-campus-sexual-assault-and-the-difficulties-for-college-adjudication/article/2566773.

45　Emma Kerr, "Investigational Equity: Student Challenges University Sexual Assault Policies," *Michigan Daily*, April 7, 2015, https://www.michigandaily.com/article/investigational-equity-student-challenges-university-sexual-assault-policies.

46　Taylor Malmsheimer, "Department of Education Launches Title IX Probe against College," *Dartmouth*, July 23, 2013, http://thedartmouth.com/2013/07/23/department-of-education-launches-title-ix-probe-against-college.

47　Tyler Kingkade, "Sexual Assaults Mishandled at Dartmouth, Swarthmore, USC, Complaints Say," *Huffington Post*, May 23, 2013, http://www.huffingtonpost.com/2013/05/23/sexual-assaults-mishandled-dartmouth-swarthmore_n_3321939.html.

48　Claire Ballentine, "Duke Faces Federal Title IX Investigation," *Chronicle*, January 19, 2016, http://www.dukechronicle.com/article/2016/01/duke-faces-federal-title-ix-investigation.

49　Juliet Eilperin, "Biden and Obama Rewrite the Rulebook on College Sexual Assaults," *Washington Post*, July 3, 2016, https://www.

washingtonpost.com/politics/biden-and-obama-rewrite-the-rulebook-on-college-sexual-assaults/2016/07/03/0773302e-3654-11e6-a254-2b336e293a3c_story.html.

50 Robin Wilson, "Colleges under Investigation for Sexual Assault Wonder What Getting It Right Looks Like," *Chronicle of Higher Education*, August 11, 2015, http://chronicle.com/article/Colleges-Under-Investigation/232205; Robin Wilson, "As Federal Investigations of Sex Assault Get Tougher, Some Ask if That's Progress," *Chronicle of Higher Education*, October 8, 2015, http://chronicle.com/article/As-Federal-Investigations-of/233698.

51 Except as noted, all quotes regarding the case at Ohio State come from *John Doe v. Ohio State University*, U.S. District Court for the Southern District of Ohio, Eastern Division, 2016 U.S. Dist. LEXIS 21064 (documents available at https://kc-johnson.com).

52 Resolution Agreement, Ohio State University, OCR Docket #15-10-6002, September 8, 2014, https://www2.ed.gov/documents/press-releases/ohio-state-agreement.pdf.

53 Erdely-Lhamon interview transcript, attached to Sabrina Rubin Erdely affidavit, June 30, 2016, in *Nicole Eramo v. Rolling Stone, LLC, et al.*, U.S. District Court for the Western District of Virginia, 2016 U.S. Dist. LEXIS 80794 (available at https://kc-johnson.com).

54 Janet Halley, "Trading the Microphone for the Gavel in Title IX Enforcement," *Harvard Law Review*, February 18, 2015, http://harvardlawreview.org/2015/02/trading-the-megaphone-for-the-gavel-in-title-ix-enforcement-2.

55 Radley Balko, "Why Do High-Profile Campus Rape Stories Keep Falling Apart?" *Watch* (blog), *Washington Post*, June 2, 2015, https://www.washingtonpost.com/news/the-watch/wp/2015/06/02/why-do-high-profile-campus-rape-stories-keep-falling-apart.

56 Cathy Young, "Campus Sexual Assault and a Modern American 'Crucible,'" *Real Clear Politics*, October 22, 2015, http://www.realclearpolitics.com/articles/2015/10/22/campus_sexual_assault_and_a_modern_crucible_128508.html.

57 Katie Van Syckle, "Emma Sulkowicz Was 'Let Down' by Obama SOTU Speech," *Daily Intelligencer*, New York, January 21, 2015, http://nymag.com/daily/intelligencer/2015/01/sulkowicz-was-let-down-by-state-of-the-union.html.

58 Cathy Young, "Columbia Student: I Didn't Rape Her," *Daily Beast*, February 3, 2015, http://www.thedailybeast.com/articles/2015/02/03/columbia-student-i-didn-t-rape-her.html.

59 Cathy Young, "The Mattress Story under More Fire," *Minding the Campus*

(blog), February 10, 2015, http://www.mindingthecampus.org/2015/02/
the-mattress-story-under-more-fire.

Chapter 5 – Media Malpractice

1 "Talk to the Newsroom: Sports Editor Tom Jolly," *New York Times*, February 11, 2008, http://www.nytimes.com/2008/02/11/business/media/11asktheeditors.html.

2 Jeannie Suk Gersen, "Shutting Down Conversations about Rape at Harvard Law," *New Yorker*, December 11, 2015, http://www.newyorker.com/news/news-desk/argument-sexual-assault-race-harvard-law-school.

3 Richard Pérez-Peña, "At Yale, the Collapse of a Rhodes Scholar Candidacy," January 26, 2012, http://www.nytimes.com/2012/01/27/sports/ncaafootball/at-yale-the-collapse-of-a-rhodes-scholar-candidacy.html.

4 Richard Bradley, "Where Did You Go, Richard Perez-Pena?" *Shots in the Dark* (blog), January 31, 2012, http://www.richardbradley.net/shotsinthedark/2012/01/31/where-did-you-go-richard-perez-pena.

5 Arthur S. Brisbane, "The Quarterback's Tangled Saga," *New York Times Sunday Review*, February 4, 2012, http://www.nytimes.com/2012/02/05/opinion/sunday/the-quarterbacks-tangled-saga.html.

6 Patrick Witt, "A Sexual Harassment Policy That Very Nearly Ruined My Life" (opinion), *Boston Globe*, November 3, 2014, https://www.bostonglobe.com/opinion/2014/11/03/sexual-harassment-policy-that-nearly-ruined-life/hY3XrZrOdXjvX2SSvuciPN/story.html.

7 Richard Pérez-Peña, "Student's Account Has Rape in Spotlight," *New York Times*, October 26, 2012, http://www.nytimes.com/2012/10/27/education/amherst-account-of-rape-brings-tension-to-forefront.html.

8 Richard Pérez-Peña, "Sexual Assaults Roil Amherst, and College President Welcomes the Controversy," *New York Times*, November 11, 2012, http://www.nytimes.com/2012/11/12/us/amherst-president-tackles-sexual-assault-crisis.html.

9 "Comparing: College Groups Connect to Fight Sexual Assault," http://www.newsdiffs.org/diff/185019/185187/www.nytimes.com/2013/03/20/education/activists-at-colleges-network-to-fight-sexual-assault.html.

10 Richard Pérez-Peña and Kate Taylor, "Fight against Sexual Assaults Holds Colleges to Account," *New York Times*, May 3, 2014, http://www.nytimes.com/2014/05/04/us/fight-against-sex-crimes-holds-colleges-to-account.html.

11 Megan Jula, "Bogdanich to Discuss Reporting on Campus Rape," March 4, 2015, Indiana University Media School, http://mediaschool.indiana.edu/news/bogdanich-to-discuss-reporting-on-campus-rape.

12 Laken Litman, "Bobby Bowden: Jameis Winston was an 'embarrassment' to FSU," *USA Today*, May 12, 2015, http://ftw.usatoday.com/2015/05/bobby-bowden-jameis-winston-embarrassment-florida-state.

13 Walt Bogdanich, "A Star Player Accused, and a Flawed Rape Investigation," *New York Times*, April 16, 2014, http://www.nytimes.com/interactive/2014/04/16/sports/errors-in-inquiry-on-rape-allegations-against-fsu-jameis-winston.html.

14 Stuart Taylor Jr., "Is New York Times Smearing Jameis Winston?" *Real Clear Sports* (blog), February 17, 2015, http://www.realclearsports.com/articles/2015/02/17/new_york_times_and_jameis_winston_98148.html.

15 Matthew Purdy, "New York Times Responds to Winston Article," *Real Clear Sports* (blog), February 19, 2015, http://www.realclearsports.com/articles/2015/02/19/new_york_times_responds_to_winston_article_98151.html.

16 The Pulitzer Prizes, "Finalist: Walt Bogdanich and Mike McIntire of *The New York Times*," http://www.pulitzer.org/finalists/walt-bogdanich-and-mike-mcintire.

17 Walt Bogdanich, "Reporting Rape, and Wishing She Hadn't: How One College Handled a Sexual Assault Complaint," *New York Times*, July 12, 2014, http://www.nytimes.com/2014/07/13/us/how-one-college-handled-a-sexual-assault-complaint.html.

18 Mike Hibbard, "DA Says No Basis for Sexual Assault Charge in HWS Case," *Finger Lakes Times*, July 20, 2014, http://www.fltimes.com/news/article_7f181016-0fc0-11e4-9637-0014abcf887a.html.

19 "Note from Mark and Dean," PressRun, October 7, 2015, http://www.nytco.com/note-from-mark-and-dean.

20 "Arthur Gregg Sulzberger Named Associate Editor," PressRun, July 30, 2015, http://www.nytco.com/arthur-gregg-sulzberger-named-associate-editor.

21 Sabrina Rubin Erdely affidavit, June 30, 2016, in *Nicole Eramo v. Rolling Stone, LLC, et al.*, U.S. District Court for the Western District of Virginia, 2016 U.S. Dist. LEXIS 80794 (available at https://kc-johnson.com).

22 osacoalition, "Nine Facts about Sexual Assault and Title IX: Please Share," *OXY Sexual Assault Coalition* (blog), June 10, 2013, https://oxysexualassaultcoalition.wordpress.com.

23 KC Johnson, "A College with Strange Sex Misconduct Hearings ('No' Means 'No,' and 'Yes' Can Mean 'No' Too)," *Minding the Campus* (blog), March 29, 2013, http://www.mindingthecampus.org/2013/03/a_college_with_strange_sex_mis.

24 Jason Felch, "Occidental College Flooded with Fake Reports of Sexual

Assault," *Los Angeles Times*, December 19, 2013, http://www.latimes.com/
local/la-me-occidental-abuse-hotline-20131220-story.html.

25 Ibid.

26 Editor's note, *Los Angeles Times*, March 14, 2014, http://www.latimes.
com/local/la-me-editors-note-20140315-story.html.

27 Kate Bloomgarden-Smoke, "Katie J.M. Baker Is Going to BuzzFeed,"
Observer, February 19, 2014, http://observer.com/2014/02/katie-j-m-
baker-is-going-to-buzzfeed.

28 Jessica Testa, "Inside the Sexual Assault Civil War at Occidental
College," BuzzFeed News, March 26, 2014, http://www.buzzfeed.com/jtes/
inside-the-sexual-assault-civil-war-at-occidental-college.

29 Vanessa Grigoriadis, "Meet the College Women Who Are Starting a
Revolution against Campus Sexual Assault," *Cut, New York*, http://
nymag.com/thecut/2014/09/emma-sulkowicz-campus-sexual-assault-
activism.html.

30 Sheila Coronel, Steve Coll, and Derek Kravitz, "*Rolling Stone* and
UVA: The Columbia University Graduate School of Journalism
Report," April 5, 2015, http://www.rollingstone.com/culture/
features/a-rape-on-campus-what-went-wrong-20150405.

31 Poynter Institute, "About US: Kelly McBride," http://about.poynter.org/
about-us/our-people/kelly-mcbride; Kelly McBride, "*Yale Daily News,
New York Times* Both Make Wrong Call on Patrick Witt Sexual Assault
Complaint Coverage," Poynter, January 30, 2012, http://www.poynter.
org/news/mediawire/161151/yale-daily-news-new-york-times-both-make-
wrong-call-on-patrick-witt-sexual-assault-story.

32 KC Johnson, "Poynter & The Serial Fabricator," *Durham-in-Wonderland*
(blog), February 7, 2012, http://durhamwonderland.blogspot.
com/2012/02/poynter-serial-fabricator.html.

33 Alex Pareene, "Why Cable News Never Punishes Liars," *Salon*, August
12, 2010, http://www.salon.com/news/politics/war_room/2010/08/12/
wendy_murphy_cable_news_liar.

34 Keila Szpaller, "Marketers: Krakauer's Book Will Tarnish Missoula's
Reputation," *Missoulian*, February 10, 2015, http://missoulian.com/news/
local/marketers-krakauer-s-book-will-tarnish-missoula-s-reputation/
article_05b83184-4454-5a75-8add-5c8fcf975fa8.html.

35 Linda M. LeFauve, "Campus Rape Expert Can't Answer Basic Questions
about His Sources: The Problem with David Lisak's Serial Predator
Theory of Campus Sexual Assault," *Reason*, July 28, 2015, http://reason.
com/archives/2015/07/28/campus-rape-statistics-lisak-problem.

36 Dillon Kato, "Montana to Pay $245K to Settle with Ex-Quarterback over
Rape Case," *Billings Gazette*, February 16, 2016, http://billingsgazette.

com/news/state-and-regional/montana/montana-to-pay-k-to-settle-with-ex-quarterback-over/article_b0f6c135-5eea-51eb-9c85-6a7b2ac10e91.html.

37 *John Doe v. University of Montana*, U.S. District Court for the District of Montana, 2012 U.S. Dist. LEXIS 88519 (available at https://kc-johnson.com).

38 Dillon Kato, "Montana to Pay Former Griz QB Jordan Johnson $245K in Settlement," *Missoulian*, February 16, 2016, http://missoulian.com/news/local/montana-to-pay-former-griz-qb-jordan-johnson-k-in/article_a3881f4e-d522-11e5-8b82-73598bda98c4.html.

39 Jon Krakauer, *Missoula: Rape and the Justice System in a College Town* (New York: Doubleday, 2015), pp. 97–98.

40 Ibid., p. 113.

41 Stuart Taylor Jr., "A Smoking-Gun E-mail Exposes the Bias of *The Hunting Ground*," *National Review*, November 16, 2015, http://www.nationalreview.com/article/427166/smoking-gun-e-mail-exposes-bias-hunting-ground.

42 *The Hunting Ground - Q&A* (video), Landmark Theatres, https://www.youtube.com/watch?v=yrmXBMG74s8.

43 Taylor, "Is New York Times Smearing Jameis Winston?"

44 Emily Yoffe, "How *The Hunting Ground* Blurs the Truth," *Slate*, June 1, 2015, http://www.slate.com/articles/news_and_politics/doublex/2015/06/the_hunting_ground_a_closer_look_at_the_influential_documentary_reveals.html.

45 Robert Scheer, "Scheer Intelligence: Discussing 'The Hunting Ground' with Director Kirby Dick and Producer Amy Ziering," *Huffington Post*, December 26, 2015, http://www.huffingtonpost.com/robert-scheer/scheer-intelligence-rober_b_8879950.html.

46 See https://twitter.com/janet_halley/status/685125934328987650; Kirby Dick and Amy Ziering, "How Harvard Law Professors Retaliated against an Assault Survivor," *Huffington Post*, January 5, 2016, http://www.huffingtonpost.com/kirby-dick/how-harvard-law-professor_b_8916026.html.

47 *Variety* Staff, "*Variety* Critics Pick Their Least Favorite Films of 2015," *Variety*, December 31, 2015, http://variety.com/2015/film/columns/variety-critics-least-favorite-films-of-2015-1201669690.

48 Emily Yoffe, "College Women: Stop Getting Drunk," *Slate*, October 15, 2013, http://www.slate.com/articles/double_x/doublex/2013/10/sexual_assault_and_drinking_teach_women_the_connection.html.

49 Except as noted, all discussion of the Michigan case comes from Emily Yoffe, "The College Rape Overcorrection," *Slate*, December 7, 2014, http://www.slate.com/articles/double_x/doublex/2014/12/

college_rape_campus_sexual_assault_is_a_serious_problem_but_the_
efforts.html.

50 Yoffe, "The College Rape Overcorrection."

51 Except as noted, all discussion about the Occidental case comes from
Richard Dorment, "Occidental Justice: The Disastrous Fallout When
Drunk Sex Meets Academic Bureaucracy," *Esquire*, March 25, 2015,
http://www.esquire.com/news-politics/a33751/occidental-justice-case.

52 Susan Kruth, "Former Occidental Student Files Title IX Complaint after
Being Denied Fair Hearing," FIRE, October 29, 2014, https://www.thefire.
org/former-occidental-student-files-title-ix-complaint-denied-fair-hearing.

53 Resolution Agreement, Occidental College, OCR Docket #09-13-
2264, June 9, 2016, http://www2.ed.gov/about/offices/list/ocr/docs/
investigations/more/09132264-a.pdf.

54 Susan Kruth, "OCR's Occidental Findings Letter Accepts Reduced
Sanctions as Attempt at Due Process," FIRE, June 13, 2016,
https://www.thefire.org/ocrs-occidental-findings-letter-accepts-
reduced-sanctions-as-attempt-at-due-process.

55 James Taranto, "Taranto: An Education in College Justice"
(commentary), *Wall Street Journal*, December 6, 2013, http://www.wsj.
com/articles/SB10001424052702303615304579157900127017212.

56 KC Johnson, "Journalism, Campus Procedure, and Biases," *Minding the
Campus* (blog), December 19, 2013, http://www.mindingthecampus.
org/2013/12/journalism_campus_procedure_an.

57 Mensah M. Dean, "Former Temple Football Player Preparing to
Challenge Rape Charge in Court," Philly.com, September 30, 2013,
http://articles.philly.com/2013-09-30/news/42505055_1_funt-martin-
oguike-temple-university; http://articles.philly.com/2013-10-08/
news/42797796_1_temple-football-player-praise-martin-oguike-text-
messages.

58 Maura Lerner and Liz Sawyer, "University of Minnesota Police No
Longer Believe Student Was Raped at Knifepoint," *Star Tribune*, May
8, 2015, http://www.startribune.com/u-police-don-t-think-student-was-
victim-of-armed-assault/303006671; Taylor Nachtigal, "Police: Sanford
Rape No Longer a Threat," *Minnesota Daily*, May 6, 2015, http://
www.mndaily.com/news/campus/2015/05/06/police-sanford-rape-no-
longer-threat; Ethan Nelson, "Woman Raped in Sanford," *Minnesota
Daily*, May 6, 2015, http://www.mndaily.com/news/campus/2015/05/06/
woman-raped-sanford.

59 Eric Adelson, "Exonerated of Rape, Brian Banks Now Realizing NFL
Dream – in Different Capacity," Yahoo Sports, January 26, 2015, http://

sports.yahoo.com/news/exonerated-of-rape--brian-banks-realizing-nfl-dream-%E2%80%93-in-different-capacity-005927279-nfl.html.

60 Nicholas Kristof, "When the Rapist Doesn't See It as Rape," *New York Times Sunday Review*, May 23, 2015, http://www.nytimes.com/2015/05/24/opinion/sunday/nicholas-kristof-when-the-rapist-doesnt-see-it-as-rape.html.

61 Stuart Taylor, Jr. interview with Sherry Warner-Seefeld, March 2016.

62 "Re: Warner Rehearing" (letter from Julie Ann Evans to Robert Shibley [vice president, FIRE]), May 20, 2011, https://d28htnjz2elwuj.cloudfront.net/pdfs/9eefe8126a6e152dc3d9cb9b54f8d08a.pdf.

63 Justin Pope, "On College Campuses, Title IX Transforms Response to Rape — but Not without Critics," *Bangor Daily News*, April 21, 2012, http://bangordailynews.com/2012/04/21/news/on-college-campuses-title-ix-transforms-response-to-rape-but-not-without-critics.

64 Stuart Taylor, Jr. interview with Sherry Warner-Seefeld, March 2016.

65 "Cases: University of North Dakota: Accuser Is Criminally Charged with Lying to Police, but School Refuses to Reopen Misconduct Case," FIRE, https://www.thefire.org/cases/university-of-north-dakota-accuser-is-criminally-charged-with-lying-to-police-but-school-refuses-to-reopen-misconduct-case.

Chapter 6 – The Witch-Hunt Mentality

1 Except as noted, all quotes regarding the case at UCSD come from *Doe v. Regents of the University of California, San Diego*, Superior Court of the State of California, Case 37-2015-00010549-CU-WM-CTL (documents available at https://kc-johnson.com).

2 Scott Greenfield, "Judge Joel Pressman to UC San Diego: I Got a Digit for You," *Simple Justice* (blog), July 14, 2015, http://blog.simplejustice.us/2015/07/14/judge-joel-pressman-to-uc-san-diego-i-got-a-digit-for-you.

3 U.S. Senate, Committee on Health, Educational, Labor, and Pensions, *Hearings, Reauthorizing the Higher Education Act: Combating Campus Sexual Assault*, July 29, 2015, http://www.help.senate.gov/hearings/reauthorizing-the-higher-education-act-combating-campus-sexual-assault (exchange at 2:25:00).

4 Katy Murphy, "Rape at Colleges: Victims Challenge Policies Favoring Attackers," *San Jose Mercury News*, January 25, 2014, http://www.mercurynews.com/education/ci_24993247/rape-at-colleges-victims-challenge-policies-favoring-attackers.

5 Kathleen Sullivan, "Senate Approves New Student Disciplinary Process for Sexual Assault and Harassment Cases," *Stanford Report*, May 3, 2013, http://news.stanford.edu/news/2013/may/faculty-senate-two-030313.html.

6 Ibid.

7 KC Johnson, "Stanford: Guilty Even if Innocent," *Minding the Campus* (blog), July 20, 2011, http://www.mindingthecampus. org/2011/07/stanford_guilty_even_if_innoce/; Preexisting policy: Stanford University, *Administrative Guide Memo 23.3: Sexual Assault*, December 15, 2009, https://d28htnjz2elwuj.cloudfront.net/pdfs/ b6c0fa0511ba6bd299a0c17b60d41a56.pdf.

8 The Abusive Man in the World, https://d28htnjz2elwuj.cloudfront. net/pdfs/bb4ff4c3aff9d3b2450c44e9ec2f28f1.pdf; Nicole Baran, "Stanford Drops the Ball on Sexual Assault Case" (opinion), *Stanford Daily*, June 21, 2014, http://www.stanforddaily.com/2014/06/21/ stanford-drops-the-ball-on-sexual-assault-case.

9 This material is from the notes of KC Johnson (who also testified against the ARP) from the meeting.

10 Tyler Kingkade, "Stanford Punishes Rapist with Forced 'Gap Year,' as Students Demand Tougher Sanctions," *Huffington Post*, June 5, 2014, http://www.huffingtonpost.com/2014/06/05/stanford-sexual-assault-sanctions-gap-year_n_5454189.html.

11 Sarah Ortlip-Sommers, "Five Professors Release Letter Outlining Concerns with New Title IX Process," *Stanford Daily*, January 14, 2016, http://www.stanforddaily.com/2016/01/14/five-professors-release-letter-outlining-concerns-with-new-title-ix-process.

12 KC Johnson, "More on the Turner Case," *Academic Wonderland* (blog), June 8, 2016, https://academicwonderland.com/2016/06/08/ more-on-the-turner-case.

13 California Judges Association, press release, June 22, 2016, http:// www.caljudges.org/docs/PDF/Press%20Release%20%20Judiciary%20 Independence%20Statement.pdf.

14 "Endorsements," Recall Judge Aaron Persky, http://www. recallaaronpersky.com/endorsements.

15 Margolis Healy, "Gender & Sexual Violence Investigation Program," PowerPoint presentation in authors' possession.

16 Janet Halley, "Trading the Megaphone for the Gavel in Title IX Enforcement: Backing off the Hype in Title IX Enforcement" (commentary), *Harvard Law Review*, February 18, 2015, http:// harvardlawreview.org/2015/02/trading-the-megaphone-for-the-gavel-in-title-ix-enforcement-2.

17 Nancy Gertner, "Complicated Process," *Yale Law Journal* forum, March 22, 2016, http://www.yalelawjournal.org/forum/complicated-process.

18 Danielle Sochaczevski, "Skorton Seals Changes to Sexual Assault Policy," *Cornell Daily Sun*, April 26, 2012, https://web.archive.

org/web/20140829005414/http://cornellsun.com/blog/2012/04/26/
skorton-seals-changes-to-sexual-assault-policy.

19   Michael Linhorst, "Law Professors: 'Dear Colleague Letter' Creates
Procedures That Are 'Orwellian,' 'Kafkaesque,' and 'Fundamentally
Unfair,'" *Cornell Daily Sun*, April 4, 2012, http://www.cotwa.
info/2012/04/law-professors-dear-colleague.html.

20   *Vito Prasad v. Cornell University*, U.S. District Court for the District
of Northern District of New York, Case 5:15-cv-00322 (documents
available at https://kc-johnson.com).

21   "Annual Report of the Judicial Codes Counselor: Academic Year 2013-
2014," May 31, 2015, in *John Doe v. Cornell University*, Supreme Court
of the State of New York, County of Thompkins, Case EF2016-0069
(documents available at https://kc-johnson.com).

22   "UNC System Salaries," *News & Observer*, http://www.newsobserver.
com/news/databases/public-salaries.

23   Harry Painter, "Title IX Compliance and Then Some," John William
Pope Center, April 4, 2014, http://www.popecenter.org/commentaries/
article.html?id=2992%23.uowkba1duoc.

24   Caitlin McCabe, "The Cost of a Scandal," https://synapse.atavist.com/
scandal.

25   *Procedures for Reporting and Responding to Complaints of Discrimination,
Harassment, and Related Misconduct Involving a Student as the
Responding Party*, University of North Carolina at Chapel Hill, http://
sexualassaultanddiscriminationpolicy.unc.edu/files/2014/08/UNCCH_
Procedures_for_Students_as_the_Responding_Party1.pdf.

26   Allie Grasgreen, "Classrooms, Courts or Neither? Students,
Administrators and Lawyers Argue over Whether and How
Colleges Should Adjudicate Campus Assault Cases at U. of Virginia
Conference on Sexual Misconduct," *Inside Higher Ed*, February
12, 2014, https://www.insidehighered.com/news/2014/02/12/
disagreement-campus-judicial-systems.

27   Joseph Asch, "Ready, Aim, Hire: +60 Staffers in 2014," *Dartblog* (blog),
April 6, 2015, http://www.dartblog.com/data/2015/04/011999.php.

28   Peter Wood, "Gender Inequity among the Gender Equity Enforcers,"
National Association of Scholars, June 12, 2013, https://www.nas.org/
articles/gender_inequity_among_the_gender_equity_enforcers.

29   Ashe Schow, "Kirsten Gillibrand's Assault on Reality," *Washington
Examiner*, June 25, 2015, http://www.washingtonexaminer.com/
kirsten-gillibrands-assault-on-reality/article/2566958.

30   Lillian Schrock, "University of Wyoming Student Charged with Raping
Man at Party," *Missoulian*, December 12, 2014, http://missoulian.com/

news/state-and-regional/university-of-wyoming-student-charged-with-raping-man-at-party/article_3c8b0a65-6cc0-5956-b19f-1495dc534392.html.

31 Anonymous, "USU Student Arrested for 7 Counts of Rape," Good4Utah.com, July 22, 2015, http://www.good4utah.com/news/local-utah-state-news-/usu-student-arrested-for-7-counts-of-rape.

32 Joe Johnson, "UGA Student Charged with Raping Coed in East Campus Dorm Room," Online Athens, September 29, 2015, http://onlineathens.com/mobile/2015-09-28/uga-student-charged-raping-coed-east-campus-dorm-room.

33 Christopher Seward, "UGA Student Held in Dorm Rape," *Atlanta Journal-Constitution*, September 29, 2015, http://www.ajc.com/news/news/local/athens-man-charged-in-uga-dorm-rape/nnqJn.

34 Ken Sturtz, "SUNY Oswego Student Charged with Raping Woman in Campus Dorm Room," Syracuse.com, October 29, 2015, http://www.syracuse.com/crime/index.ssf/2015/10/suny_oswego_student_charged_with_raping_woman.html.

35 Stephanie Yan, "Psi Upsilon President Pleads Not Guilty to Sexual Assault Charges," *Cornell Daily Sun*, February 6, 2016, http://cornellsun.com/2016/02/06/police-charge-student-with-sexual-assault-at-psi-upsilon-fraternity.

36 Eric Owens, "Police Say 28-Year-Old Undergrad Threatened Herself with Rape in Facebook Hoax," *Daily Caller*, May 1, 2013, http://dailycaller.com/2013/05/01/police-say-28-year-old-undergrad-threatened-herself-with-rape-in-facebook-hoax.

37 Kyle Roerink, "University of Wyoming Police: Rape Threat Came from Alleged Target," *Casper Star-Tribune*, May 1, 2013, http://trib.com/news/local/crime-and-courts/university-of-wyoming-police-rape-threat-came-from-alleged-target/article_f412613b-e144-5fb5-bbfb-2178bbd68821.html.

38 David Lat, "Law Student of the Day: Alleged Social Media Hoaxer," *Above the Law* (blog), October 14, 2013, http://abovethelaw.com/2013/10/law-student-of-the-day-alleged-social-media-hoaxer.

39 KC Johnson, "Swarthmore, Occidental and Their Kangaroo Courts," *Minding the Campus* (blog), April 25, 2013, http://www.mindingthecampus.org/2013/04/swarthmore_occidental_and_thei.

40 Gil Spencer, "Swarthmore College Finds Itself in Crosshairs," Delaware County *Daily Times*, April 27, 2013, http://www.delcotimes.com/article/DC/20130427/NEWS/304279942.

41 Except as noted, all quotes regarding the case at Swarthmore come from *John Doe v. Swarthmore College*, U.S. District Court for the Eastern

District of Pennsylvania, Case 2:14-cv-00532 (documents available at https://kc-johnson.com).

42 "History (College Action Steps)," Swarthmore College, http://www. swarthmore.edu/share/history-college-action-steps.

43 Swarthmore College, "Procedures for Resolutions of Complaints against Students," http://www.swarthmore.edu/share/procedures-resolution-complaints-against-students.

44 Swarthmore College, *Annual Fire Safety and Security Report 2015*, http://www.swarthmore.edu/sites/default/files/assets/documents/public-safety/DPSAnnualReport2015.pdf.

45 Dan Roblee, "Tech Censures Satire Sheet: Sex Assault Article Oversteps Administration's Bounds," *Daily Mining Gazette*, December 4, 2015, http://www.mininggazette.com/page/content.detail/id/549703/Tech-censures-satire-sheet.html?nav=5006.

46 Ashe Schow, "USC Asks Students to Detail Sexual History," January 12, 2016, http://www.washingtonexaminer.com/usc-asks-students-to-detail-sexual-history/article/2580227; for the 1990s antecedents of this movement, see Alan Charles Kors, "Thought Reform 101," FIRE, March 1, 2000, https://www.thefire.org/thought-reform-101.

47 Heather Mac Donald, "The Fainting Couch at Columbia: A New 'Sexual-Respect Initiative' Puts Another Stake into the Heart of Academic Seriousness," *Commentary*, September 1, 2015, https://www.commentarymagazine.com/articles/fainting-couch-columbia.

48 J. Guillermo Villalobos, Deborah Davis, and Richard A. Leo, "His Story, Her Story: Sexual Miscommunication, Motivated Remembering, and Intoxication as Pathways to Honest False Testimony Regarding Sexual Consent," in Ros Burnett, ed., *Wrongful Allegations of Sexual and Child Abuse* (New York: Oxford University Press, 2016), chapter 10.

49 Bradley Saacks, "Sexual Assault Task Force Votes on Policy Draft," *Daily Tar Heel*, June 16, 2014, http://www.dailytarheel.com/article/2014/06/sexual-assault-task-force-votes-on-policy-draft.

50 KC Johnson, "If She Had Drinks, You May Be a Rapist," *Minding the Campus* (blog), June 18, 2014, http://www.mindingthecampus.org/2014/06/if-she-had-drinks-you-may-be-a-rapist.

51 Dartmouth College, *Annual Security and Fire Safety Report: October 1, 2013*, https://dartmouthspcsa.files.wordpress.com/2013/10/dartmouth-clery-2012.pdf.

52 University of Pennsylvania, *Penn Violence Prevention Resource Guide*, January 2016, https://secure.www.upenn.edu/vpul/pvp/files/Updates_2016_PVP_Resource_Guide_FINAL_with_bleeds.pdf.

53 University of Wisconsin–Madison, University Health Services, *Options*

for Victims of Sexual Assault, Dating Violence, Domestic Violence, and Stalking (pamphlet), http://www.uhs.wisc.edu/assault/documents/sadv.pdf.

54 Brown University, *Sexual Harassment Policy: Revised May 2013*, https:// www.brown.edu/about/administration/institutional-diversity/sites/ brown.edu.about.administration.institutional-diversity/files/uploads/ SexualHarassmentPolicy_Feb2014.pdf.

55 Admin, "FIRE Letter to Duke University President Richard H. Brodhead Regarding Duke's Sexual Misconduct Policy," FIRE, March 4, 2010, https://www.thefire.org/fire-letter-to-duke-university-president-richard-h-brodhead-regarding-dukes-sexual-misconduct-policy.

56 Tyler Kingkade, "Judge Dismisses Lawsuit against Vassar College Filed by Student Expelled for Sexual Assault," *Huffington Post*, April 15, 2015, http://www.huffingtonpost.com/2015/04/15/vassar-lawsuit-gender_n_7071694.html.

57 *John Doe v. Brandeis University*, U.S. District Court for the District of Massachusetts, 2016 U.S. Dist. LEXIS 43499 (available at https:// kc-johnson.com).

58 Harvard University, *Procedures for Handling Complaints Involving Students Pursuant to the Sexual and Gender-Based Harassment Policy*, http://titleix. harvard.edu/files/title-ix/files/harvard_student_sexual_harassmnt_ procedures.pdf.

59 Matthew Q. Clarida and Madeline R. Conway, "Univ. Announces New Sexual Assault Policy Including Central Office, 'Preponderance of the Evidence' Standard," *Harvard Crimson*, July 3, 2014, http://www. thecrimson.com/article/2014/7/3/new-sexual-assault-policies.

60 28 members of the Harvard Law School faculty, "Rethink Harvard's Sexual Harassment Policy" (opinion), *Boston Globe*, October 15, 2014, http://www.bostonglobe.com/opinion/2014/10/14/rethink-harvard-sexual-harassment-policy/HFDDiZN7nU2UwuUuWMnqbM/story.html.

61 Andrew M. Duehren and Emma K. Talkoff, "Seeking Trust: Navigating Harvard's Sexual Assault Policies," *Harvard Crimson*, March 10, 2016, http://www.thecrimson.com/article/2016/3/10/ harvard-sexual-assault-policies.

62 Steven S. Lee and Dev A. Patel, "Karvonides Assures Neutrality after Law School Op-Ed," *Harvard Crimson*, October 21, 2014, https://www. thecrimson.com/article/2014/10/21/karvonides-neutrality-op-ed.

63 Theodore R. Delwiche and Andrew M. Duehren, "New Law School Sexual Harassment Procedures Break from University Framework," *Harvard Crimson*, January 3, 2015, http://www.thecrimson.com/ article/2015/1/3/pending-procedures-law-school-title-ix.

64 Nancy Gertner, "Sex, Lies and Justice: Can We Reconcile the Belated

Attention to Rape on Campus with Due Process?" *American Prospect*, January 12, 2015, http://prospect.org/article/sex-lies-and-justice.

65 Wendy Murphy, "An Open Letter to Harvard Law Professor Nancy Gertner," *Title IX on Campus* (blog), February 2, 2015, http://title9.us/an-open-letter-to-nancy-gertner/#.VckPmCZVgSU.

66 Alexandra Brodsky, "Fair Process, not Criminal Process, Is the Right Way to Address Campus Sexual Assault," *American Prospect*, January 21, 2015, http://prospect.org/article/fair-process-not-criminal-process-right-way-address-campus-sexual-assault.

67 John Sutherland, "The Ideas Interview: Janet Halley," *Guardian*, August 8, 2006, http://www.theguardian.com/world/2006/aug/08/gender.academicexperts.

68 Emily Bazelon, "The Return of the Sex Wars: The Decades-Old Intellectual Debate Simmering beneath the Current Conversation over Sexual Assault on Campus," *New York Times Magazine*, September 10, 2015, http://www.nytimes.com/2015/09/13/magazine/the-return-of-the-sex-wars.html.

69 Janet Halley, "A Call to Reform the New Harvard University Sexual Harassment Policy and Procedures," October 28, 2014, http://orgs.law.harvard.edu/acs/files/2014/10/ACSPost.014.pdf.

70 Janet Halley, "Trading the Microphone for the Gavel in Title IX Enforcement," *Harvard Law Review*, February 18, 2015, http://harvardlawreview.org/2015/02/trading-the-megaphone-for-the-gavel-in-title-ix-enforcement-2.

71 Harvey Silverglate, "The New Panic: Campus Sex Assaults," *Boston Globe*, February 20, 2015, https://www.bostonglobe.com/opinion/2015/02/20/the-new-panic-campus-sex-assaults/oXoa9RoCySmrLUMFQ73kWM/story.html.

72 *John Doe v. The Rectors and Visitors of George Mason University, et al.*, U.S. District Court for the Eastern District of Virginia, 149 F. Supp. 3d 602.

73 Stephen Henrick, "A Hostile Environment for Student Defendents: Title IX and Sexual Assault on College Campuses," *Northern Kentucky Law Review* 40 (2013), p. 81.

Chapter 7 – College Athletes: Myths and Realities

1 Except as noted, all quotes regarding the case at Xavier come from *Dezmine Wells v. Xavier College and Fr. Michael Graham*, U.S. District Court for the Southern District of Ohio, 7 F. Supp. 3d 746 (documents available at https://kc-johnson.com) or from Stuart Taylor Jr.'s interview with Joseph Deters.

2   KC Johnson, "The OCR's Newest Target: Xavier University," *Minding the Campus* (blog), August 2, 2012, http://www.mindingthecampus. org/2012/08/the_ocrs_newest_target_xavier_.

3   "Resolution Agreement, Xavier University, OCR Docket Number 15-12-2048," https://atixa.org/documents/Xavier%20Resolution%20 Agreement.pdf.

4   Jeff Barker, "At Maryland, Dez Wells Has Put Stressful Past behind Him," *Baltimore Sun*, March 12, 2013, http://articles.baltimoresun.com/2013- 03-12/sports/bs-sp-terps-dez-wells-0313-20130312_1_dez-wells-levelle- moton-mark-turgeon.

5   Steven Godfrey and Bud Elliott, "Notre Dame's Coach Said Something Jarring (and Refreshing) about Player Academics," SB Nation, June 11, 2015, http://www.sbnation.com/college-football/2015/6/11/8761689/ notre-dame-football-academics-brian-kelly.

6   "2013–2014 NCAA Division I Academic Progress Rate Public Report— Institution: Harvard University," May 26, 2015, https://web1.ncaa.org/ app_data/apr2014/275_2014_apr.pdf; "NCAA—Academic Progress Rate," http://web1.ncaa.org/maps/aprRelease.jsp.

7   Dan Kane, "Austin's UNC Transcript Raises Questions," *News & Observer*, August 21, 2011, http://www.newsobserver.com/news/local/ education/unc-scandal/article10349711.html; "UNC Scandal News," *News & Observer*, http://www.newsobserver.com/news/local/education/ unc-scandal.

8   Dashiell Bennett, "A Brief History of Campus Recruiting Hostesses," Deadspin, December 9, 2009, http://deadspin.com/5422547/a-brief- history-of-campus-recruiting-hostesses.

9   Pete Thamel and Thayer Evans, "N.C.A.A. Puts Tennessee's Recruiting Under Scrutiny," *New York Times*, December 8, 2009, http://www. nytimes.com/2009/12/09/sports/ncaafootball/09tennessee.html; Michael Rand, "College Recruits and 'Hostesses': Where Is the Line Drawn?" *RandBall* (blog), *Star Tribune*, December 9, 2009, http://www.startribune. com/college-recruits-and-hostesses-where-is-the-line-drawn/78884262.

10   Pat Forde, "Louisville Investigating New Book's Damaging Sexual Allegations Involving Basketball Team," Yahoo Sports, October 2, 2015, http://sports.yahoo.com/news/new-book-makes-damaging-sexual- allegations-involving-louisville-basketball-202333537.html.

11   Paula Lavigne, "Baylor Faces Accusations of Ignoring Assault Victims," ESPN, February 2, 2016, http://espn.go.com/espn/otl/story/_/ id/14675790/baylor-officials-accused-failing-investigate-sexual-assaults- fully-adequately-providing-support-alleged-victims.

12   Staff and Wire Reports, "Chris Peterson, Art Briles in a Battle of Words

over Sam Ukwuachu Case," *Idaho Statesman*, August 21, 2015, http://www.idahostatesman.com/sports/college/mountain-west/boise-state-university/boise-state-football/article41565330.html.

13 Jessica Luther and Dan Solomon, "Silence at Baylor," *Texas Monthly*, August 20, 2015, http://www.texasmonthly.com/article/silence-at-baylor.

14 Kalyn Story, "Tumultuous Summer Unfolds for Administration, Lawsuits Filed against Baylor," *Baylor Lariat*, August 19, 2016, http://baylorlariat.com/2016/08/20/tumultuous-summer-unfolds-for-administration-lawsuits-filed-against-baylor.

15 *Jane Doe, et al. v. University of Tennessee*, U.S. District Court for the Middle District of Tennessee, Case 3:16-cv-09999; Nate Rau and Matt Slovin, "Lawsuit: Tennessee Player Assaulted by Teammates for Helping Rape Victim," *Tennessean*, February 24, 2016, http://www.tennessean.com/story/sports/college/ut/2016/02/10/lawsuit-tennessee-player-put-hit-teammate-helping-rape-victim/80170032.

16 Nate Rau and Anita Wadhwani, "Tennessee Settles Sexual Assault Lawsuit for $2.48 Million," *Tennesseean*, July 6, 2016, http://www.tennessean.com/story/news/crime/2016/07/05/tennessee-settles-sexual-assault-suit-248-million/86708442.

17 ESPN.com News Services, "Jonathan Taylor Dismissed by Bama," ESPN, March 29, 2015, http://espn.go.com/college-football/story/_/id/12581466/jonathan-taylor-dismissed-alabama-crimson-tide-following-arrest.

18 Bruce Feldman, "Mississippi State's Mullen Botches Domestic Violence Issue at SEC Meetings," FoxSports.com, July 12, 2016, http://www.foxsports.com/college-football/story/mississippi-state-s-mullen-botches-domestic-violence-issue-at-sec-meetings-071216.

19 Jon Rothstein, "Humbled by Past Mistakes, Brandon Austin Seeks Another Chance," CBS Sports, May 29, 2015, http://www.cbssports.com/collegebasketball/eye-on-college-basketball/25199618/humbled-by-past-mistakes-brandon-austin-seeks-another-chance.

20 Steven J. Gaither, "Oregon Reaches Settlement with Woman in Sexual Assault Lawsuit," Sporting News, August 4, 2015, http://www.sportingnews.com/ncaa-basketball/story/2015-08-04/oregon-lawsuit-sexual-assault-title-ix-dana-altman-basketball.

21 Tom Ley, "Former Michigan Kicker Expelled for Sexual Misconduct," Deadspin, January 29, 2014, http://deadspin.com/former-michigan-kicker-expelled-for-sexual-misconduct-1511488287.

22 Tom Farrey and Nicole Noren, "Mizzou Did Not Pursue Alleged Assault," ESPN, February 12, 2015, http://espn.go.com/espn/otl/story/_/id/10323102/university-missouri-officials-did-not-pursue-rape-case-lines-investigation-finds. See, more generally, if in a one-sided fashion,

Jessica Luther, *Unsportsmanlike Conduct: College Football and the Politics of Rape* (Brooklyn: Edge of Sports, Akashic Books, 2016). But also see Robby Soave, "Female Student Admits to Incredible Lie That Got Auburn Football Player Kicked Off Team," *Hit and Run* (blog), Reason.com, September 9, 2016, https://reason.com/blog/2016/09/09/female-student-admits-to-incredible-lie.

23 Joey Garrison, "Vanderbilt Rape Victim Speaks Out after Verdict," *Tennessean*, January 27, 2015, http://www.tennessean.com/story/news/2015/01/27/vanderbilt-rape-survivor-statement/22434833.

24 Alan Blinder and Richard Pérez-Peña, "Vanderbilt Rape Convictions Stir Dismay and Denial," *New York Times*, January 28, 2015, http://www.nytimes.com/2015/01/29/us/vanderbilt-rape-trial-didnt-stir-students-on-campus.html.

25 Yahoo Health, "What's Really behind College 'Rape Culture'?" January 28, 2015, https://www.yahoo.com/health/whats-really-behind-college-rape-culture-109414596787.html.

26 Except as noted, all quotes regarding the case at Yale come from *Jack Montague v. Yale University*, U.S. District Court for Connecticut, Case 3:16-cv-00885 (documents available at https://kc-johnson.com).

27 KC Johnson, "The Montague Case," *Academic Wonderland* (blog), March 5, 2016, http://academicwonderland.com/2016/03/05/the-montague-case.

28 Susan Svrluga, "Expelled Yale Basketball Captain: Alleged Sexual Misconduct Was Consensual," *Grade Point* (blog), *Washington Post*, March 14, 2016, https://www.washingtonpost.com/news/grade-point/wp/2016/03/14/expelled-yale-basketball-captain-alleged-sexual-misconduct-was-consensual.

29 Kathleen Megan, "Former Yale Basketball Captain Files Complaint over Assault Allegation," *Hartford Courant*, June 9, 2016, http://www.courant.com/education/hc-yale-montague-complaint-20160609-story.html.

30 Beau Berkley, "New Documents Show Contrast in Bubu Palo Rulings," *Iowa State Daily*, September 19, 2014, http://www.iowastatedaily.com/news/article_cb565986-3f7e-11e4-aa73-731dc303d9f2.html; Alex Halsted, "Bubu Palo Dropped from ISU Men's Basketball Team," *Iowa State Daily*, September 1, 2013, http://www.iowastatedaily.com/sports/mens_basketball/article_c97ce362-128b-11e3-8518-001a4bcf887a.html; Anonymous, "It's Final: Bubu Palo Didn't Rape Hunter Elizabeth Breshears," *Cityview*, September 9, 2015, http://www.dmcityview.com/featured-story/2015/09/09/its-final-bubu-palo-didnt-rape-hunter-elizabeth-breshears.

31 Alex Halsted, "ISU President Steven Leath Talks Bubu Palo as Appeal Continues," *Iowa State Daily*, January 25, 2014, http://www.

iowastatedaily.com/sports/mens_basketball/article_882347b6-85f5-11e3-8732-001a4bcf887a.html.

32 Gavin Aronsen, "Palo Civil Suit 'Seems Like a Stretch'," *Ames Tribune*, June 21, 2014, http://amestrib.com/news/palo-civil-suit-seems-stretch.

33 Halley, "Trading the Megaphone for the Gavel."

34 Except as noted, all quotes regarding the case at Appalachian State come from *Lanston Tanyi v. Appalachian State University*, U.S. District Court for the Western District of North Carolina, 2015 U.S. Dist. LEXIS 95577 (documents available at https://kc-johnson.com).

35 Monte Mitchell, "Students Rally at Appalachian State," *Winston-Salem Journal*, March 3, 2012, http://www.journalnow.com/news/local/students-rally-at-appalachian-state/article_0f7eafa9-7601-593c-8c3a-15276cece4ac.html.

36 David Forbes, "Shut Up and Pay," *NSFWCORP*, April 9, 2013, https://www.nsfwcorp.com/dispatch/shut-up-and-pay/545f5d4f5b9dbb4b189976a0f9bb7b216d694768.

37 Except as noted, all quotes regarding the case at Findlay come from *Justin Browning and Alphonso Baity v. University of Findlay, et al.*, U.S. District Court for the Northern District of Ohio, Case 3-15-CV-02687 (documents available at https://kc-johnson.com).

38 Ashe Schow, "University Accused of Racism in Campus Sexual Assault Lawsuit," *Washington Examiner*, January 6, 2016, http://www.washingtonexaminer.com/university-accused-of-racism-in-campus-sexual-assault-lawsuit/article/2579741.

39 Robby Soave, "Is This the Most Unfair Campus Rape Investigation Ever?" (opinion), *Newsweek*, January 13, 2016, http://www.newsweek.com/university-findlay-campus-rape-investigation-415331.

40 Jacob Gersen and Jeannie Suk Gersen, "The Sex Bureaucracy," *California Law Review* 104, no. 4 (2016) pp. 881–948, http://scholarship.law.berkley.edu/californialawreview/vol104/iss4/2.

41 Except as noted, all quotes regarding the case at UTC come from *Corey Mock v. University of Tennessee, Chattanooga*, Chancery Court of Davidson County, Tennessee, Case 14-1687 II (documents available at https://kc-johnson.com).

42 Jessica Luther, "The Wrestler and the Rape Victim," Vice Sports, December 15, 2014, https://sports.vice.com/en_us/article/the-wrestler-and-the-rape-victim.

43 Brooke Pryor, "Former UNC Wrestling Coach 'Blown Away' by His Firing," *Herald-Sun*, June 17, 2015, http://www.heraldsun.com/sports/colleges/x110773679/Former-UNC-wrestling-coach-blown-away-by-his-firing.

44 Tom Jensen to Carol Folt and Bubba Cunningham, January 8, 2015, January 16, 2015; Cunningham to Jensen, January 21, 2015; emails in authors' possession.

Chapter 8 – The Witch Hunt Intensifies

1 S.Amdt.141 to S.Amdt.2, 114th Congress (2015–2016), https://www. congress.gov/amendment/114th-congress/senate-amendment/141/text.

2 "Sexual Assault College Campuses" (video and transcript), C-SPAN, June 26, 2014, http://www.c-span.org/video/?320167-1/ sexual-assault-college-campuses.

3 "Letter from Department of Education Office for Civil Rights Assistant Secretary Catherine E. Lhamon to FIRE," FIRE, December 3, 2013, https://www.thefire.org/letter-from-department-of-education-office-for-civil-rights-assistant-secretary-catherine-e-lhamon-to-fire.

4 Becky Beaupre Gillespie, "We Can Contribute to the Larger Society Precisely Because We Are Scholars," *Record*, Fall 2015, http://www. law.uchicago.edu/alumni/magazine/fall15/geoffrey-stone-advising-intelligence-community-white-house-supreme-court.

5 Lyndsey Layton, "Civil Rights Complaints to U.S. Department of Education Reach a Record High," *Washington Post*, March 18, 2015, http://www.washingtonpost.com/news/local/wp/2015/03/18/civil-rights-complaints-to-u-s-department-of-education-reach-a-record-high.

6 Letter from Gail Heriot and Peter Kirsanow (U.S. Commission on Civil Rights) to members of Congress, February 26, 2016, https://kcjohnson. files.wordpress.com/2013/08/ocr-budget-ltr2.pdf.

7 "2011 Update to Title IX: The Pendulum Has Swung Too Far," *Legal Intelligencer,* June 16, 2015.

8 Jonathan Chait, "Feminists Criticizing Campus Sexual Assault Rules," *Daily Intelligencer, New York*, February 24, 2015, http://nymag.com/daily/ intelligencer/2015/02/feminists-criticizing-campus-sex-assault-rules.html.

9 The BDN Editorial Board, "Campus Rape: Confusion and Misperceptions Blur Problem of Sexual Violence" (op-ed), *Bangor Daily News*, December 18, 2014, http://bangordailynews.com/2014/12/18/ opinion/campus-rape-confusion-and-misperceptions-blur-problem-of-sexual-violence.

10 Ashe Schow, "Megyn Kelly Lashes Out at Amherst College Again," *Washington Examiner*, June 17, 2015, http://www.washingtonexaminer. com/megyn-kelly-lashes-out-at-amherst-college-again/article/2566431.

11 Conor Friedersdorf, "How Sexual-Harassment Policies Are Diminishing Academic Freedom," *Atlantic*, October 20, 2015, http://www.theatlantic.com/politics/archive/2015/10/ sexual-harassment-academic-freedom/411427.

12 Letter from Sen. James Lankford to Hon. John B. King Jr., January 7,
    2016, http://bloximages.newyork1.vip.townnews.com/tulsaworld.com/
    content/tncms/assets/v3/editorial/5/eb/5eb92d5f-8986-58c0-82c7-
    9d5b44a62c62/568d9fbc56239.pdf.pdf; "Academics and Legal Experts
    Agree with Senator Lankford: Dept. of Education Actions Are Clearly
    Executive Overreach" (press release), February 25, 2016, https://www.
    lankford.senate.gov/news/press-releases/academics-journalists-and-legal-
    experts-agree-with-senator-lankford-dept-of-education-actions-are-
    clearly-executive-overreach.

13 Janet Napolitano, "'Only Yes Means Yes': An Essay on University
    Policies Regarding Sexual Violence and Sexual Assault," *Yale Law Review*
    33 (2015), pp. 387–402, http://ylpr.yale.edu/sites/default/files/YLPR/33.2_
    policy_essay_-_napolitano_final.pdf.

14 Joseph Cohn, "Second Department of Education Official in Eight Days
    Tells Congress Guidance Is Not Binding," FIRE, October 2, 2015, https://
    www.thefire.org/second-department-of-education-official-in-eight-days-
    tells-congress-guidance-is-not-binding.

15 Lee Burdette Williams, "The Dean of Sexual Assault" (opinion),
    Inside Higher Ed, August 7, 2015, https://www.insidehighered.com/
    views/2015/08/07/how-sexual-assault-campaign-drove-one-student-
    affairs-administrator-her-job-essay.

16 Sara Lipka, "What the Future Holds for the Crackdown on Campus
    Sexual Assault," *Chronicle of Higher Education*, July 31, 2016, http://
    chronicle.com/article/What-the-Future-Holds-for-the/237320.

17 Tyler Kingkade, "Tufts University Backs Down on Standoff with Feds
    over Sexual Assault Policies," *Huffington Post*, May 9, 2014, http://www.
    huffingtonpost.com/entry/tufts-sexual-assault-title-ix_n_5297535.

18 Jacob Gersen and Jeannie Suk Gersen, "The Sex Bureaucracy," *California
    Law Review* 104, no. 4 (2016), pp. 881–948, http://scholarship.law.
    berkley.edu/californialawreview/vol104/iss4/2.

19 For recent OCR resolution letters, see http://www2.ed.gov/about/offices/
    list/ocr/docs/investigations/index.html?exp=2#title9rev.

20 Stephen Henrick, "A Hostile Environment for Student Defendants: Title
    IX and Sexual Assault on College Campuses," *Northern Kentucky Law
    Review* 40 (2013), p. 71.

21 Except as noted, all quotes regarding the case at Middlebury come from
    John Doe v. Middlebury College, U.S. District Court for the District of
    Vermont, 2015 U.S. Dist. LEXIS 124540 (documents available at https://
    kc-johnson.com).

22 "Re: DOJ Case No. DJ 169-44-9, OCR Case No. 10126001" (Letter
    from Anurima Bhargava and Gary Jackson to Royce Engstrom and Lucy

France), May 9, 2013, http://www.justice.gov/sites/default/files/opa/legacy/2013/05/09/um-ltr-findings.pdf.

23 "FIRE Coalition Letter to Departments of Education and Justice," FIRE, July 16, 2013, https://www.thefire.org/fire-coalition-letter-to-departments-of-education-and-justice.

24 Letter from Ann Green and Donna Potts to Thomas E. Perez and Russlynn Ali, June 6, 2013, http://www.aaup.org/file/AAUP_June_2013_Letter_to_DOJ_and_OCR.pdf.

25 "Letter from Department of Education Office for Civil Rights Assistant Secretary Catherine E. Lhamon to FIRE."

26 Samantha Harris and Greg Lukianoff, "Executive Branch Overreach and the Accelerating Threats to Due Process and Free Speech on Campus," in *Liberty's Nemesis: The Unchecked Expansion of the State*, ed. Dean Reuter and John Yoo (New York: Encounter Books, 2016), pp. 169–80.

27 Yale University, *Report of Complaints of Sexual Misconduct Brought forward from July 1, 2014 through December 31, 2014*, n.d., http://provost.yale.edu/sites/default/files/files/Final_Jan2015_Report.pdf.

28 Jeannie Suk Gersen, "The Trouble with Teaching Rape Law," *New Yorker*, December 15, 2014, http://www.newyorker.com/news/news-desk/trouble-teaching-rape-law.

29 "Tool: Recognizing Microaggressions and the Messages They Send," adapted from Derald Wing Sue, *Microaggressions in Everyday Life: Race, Gender and Sexual Orientation* (Hoboken, NJ: Wiley & Sons, 2010), https://web.archive.org/web/20150414025830/http://ucop.edu/academic-personnel-programs/_files/seminars/Tool_Recognizing_Microaggressions.pdf.

30 Eugene Volokh, "UC Teaching Faculty Members Not to Criticize Race-Based Affirmative Action, Call America 'Melting Pot,' and More," *Volokh Conspiracy* (blog), *Washington Post*, June 16, 2015, https://www.washingtonpost.com/news/volokh-conspiracy/wp/2015/06/16/uc-teaching-faculty-members-not-to-criticize-race-based-affirmative-action-call-america-melting-pot-and-more.

31 Laura Kipnis, "Sexual Paranoia Strikes Academe," *Chronicle of Higher Education*, February 27, 2015, http://chronicle.com/article/Sexual-Paranoia/190351; Colleen Flaherty, "The Case for Student Shields," *Inside Higher Ed*, November 5, 2014, https://www.insidehighered.com/news/2014/11/05/unusual-sexual-harassment-case-northwestern-u-brings-out-advocates-student.

32 Tyler Kingkade, "How Laura Kipnis' 'Sexual Paranoia' Essay Caused a Frenzy at Northwestern University," *Huffington Post*, May 31, 2015, http://www.huffingtonpost.com/2015/05/31/laura-kipnis-essay-northwestern-title-ix_n_7470046.html.

33 Laura Kipnis, "My Title IX Inquisition," *Chronicle of Higher Education, Chronicle Review*, May 29, 2015, http://laurakipnis.com/wp-content/uploads/2010/08/My-Title-IX-Inquisition-The-Chronicle-Review-.pdf.

34 Jeb Rubenfeld, "Mishandling Rape" (op-ed), *New York Times*, November 15, 2014, http://www.nytimes.com/2014/11/16/opinion/sunday/mishandling-rape.html.

35 Tyler Kingkade, "Yale Law Students: Professor's Campus Rape Op-Ed Gets It Wrong," November 17, 2014, http://www.huffingtonpost.com/2014/11/17/yale-law-students-campus-rape_n_6172410.html.

36 Conor Friedersdorf, "Should Any Ideas Be 'Off the Table' in Campus Debates?" *Atlantic*, June 30, 2016, http://www.theatlantic.com/politics/archive/2016/06/should-any-ideas-be-off-the-table-in-campus-debates/489710.

37 Hana Kateman, "Debate Brews over Role of Anonymous Title IX-Related Complaints in Course Evaluations," *Columbia Spectator*, January 20, 2016, http://columbiaspectator.com/news/2016/01/20/anonymous-title-ix-complaints.

38 Colleen Flaherty, "Title IX as a Threat to Academic Freedom," *Inside Higher Ed*, March 24, 2016, https://www.insidehighered.com/news/2016/03/24/aaup-critiques-education-department-crackdown-sexual-assault-and-harassment.

39 *Not Alone: The First Report of the White House Task Force to Protect Students From Sexual Assault*, April 2014, http://www.whitehouse.gov/sites/default/files/docs/report_0.pdf.

40 OCR, *Questions and Answers on Title IX and Sexual Violence*, April 29, 2014, http://www2.ed.gov/about/offices/list/ocr/docs/qa-201404-title-ix.pdf.

41 Valerie Bauerlein, "In Campus Rape Tribunals, Some Men See Injustice," *Wall Street Journal*, April 10, 2015, http://www.wsj.com/articles/in-campus-rape-tribunals-some-men-see-injustice-1428684187.

42 Peter Berkowitz, "Lawsuit Casts Harsh Light on Due Process at Colgate," *Real Clear Politics*, October 3, 2014, http://www.realclearpolitics.com/articles/2014/10/03/lawsuit_casts_harsh_light_on_due_process_at_colgate__124167.html.

43 *Edwards v. Arizona*, 451 U.S. 477 (1981); see, e.g., *Gideon v. Wainwright*, 372 U.S. 335, 345 (1963). ("He lacks both the skill and knowledge adequately to prepare his defense, even though he have a perfect one. He requires the guiding hand of counsel at every step in the proceedings against him. Without it, though he be not guilty, he faces the danger of conviction because he does not know how to establish his innocence.")

44 Jake New, "Making Title IX Work," *Inside Higher Ed*, July 6, 2015, https://www.insidehighered.com/news/2015/07/06/

college-law-enforcement-administrators-hear-approach-make-title-ix-more-effective.

45　The University of Texas at Austin, School of Social Work, Institute on Domestic Violence and Sexual Assault, *The Blueprint for Campus Police: Responding to Sexual Assault* (2016), https://utexas.app.box.com/blueprintforcampuspolice.

46　Samantha Harris, "University of Texas 'Blueprint' for Campus Police Raises Fairness Concerns," FIRE, March 11, 2016, https://www.thefire.org/university-of-texas-blueprint-for-campus-police-raises-fairness-concerns.

47　The White House Task Force to Protect Students from Sexual Assault, *Building Partnerships among Law Enforcement Agencies, Colleges and Universities*, n.d., https://www.whitehouse.gov/sites/default/files/docs/white_house_task_force_law_enforcement_mou.pdf.

48　Anonymous, "RAINN Urges White House Task Force to Overhaul Colleges' Treatment of Rape," Rape, Abuse and Incest National Network, March 6, 2014, https://rainn.org/news-room/rainn-urges-white-house-task-force-to-overhaul-colleges-treatment-of-rape.

49　Matt Kaiser and Justin Dillon, "The White House Flunks a Test on Sexual Assault" (commentary), *Wall Street Journal*, May 5, 2014, http://www.wsj.com/articles/SB10001424052702304831304579541970401038080.

50　Wendy Kaminer, "Victimizing the Accused? Obama's Campus Sexual Assault Guidelines Raise Concerns," *Cognoscenti*, May 5, 2014, http://cognoscenti.wbur.org/2014/05/05/due-process-and-sexual-assault-wendy-kaminer#.U2e3BQt-bz4.twitter.

51　"FIRE Responds to White House Task Force's First Report on Campus Sexual Assault," FIRE, April 29, 2014, https://www.thefire.org/fire-responds-to-white-house-task-forces-first-report-on-campus-sexual-assault.

52　Letter from Catherine Lhamon to "Colleague," April 24, 2015, http://www2.ed.gov/about/offices/list/ocr/letters/colleague-201504-title-ix-coordinators.pdf.

53　Jacob Gersen and Jeannie Suk Gersen, "The Sex Bureaucracy."

54　Andrew M. Duehren and Emma K. Talkoff, "Seeking Trust: Navigating Harvard's Sexual Assault Policies," *Harvard Crimson*, March 10, 2016, http://www.thecrimson.com/article/2016/3/10/harvard-sexual-assault-policies.

55　"People," Office of Sexual Prevention and Response, http://osapr.harvard.edu/people-0.

56　"Vocabulary," Office of Sexual Prevention and Response, http://osapr.harvard.edu/pages/vocabulary.

57 Glenn Harlan Reynolds, "The Great Campus Rape Hoax," *USA Today*, December 15, 2014, http://www.usatoday.com/story/opinion/2014/12/14/campus-rape-uva-crisis-rolling-stone-politicscolumn/20397277.

58 "Non-Discrimination and Anti-Harassment Policy," University of Georgia Equal Opportunity Office, https://eoo.uga.edu/policies/non-discrimination-anti-harassment-policy.

59 Robert Shibley, "FIRE Testifies before Georgia House of Representatives on Campus Due Process (VIDEO)," FIRE, January 26, 2016, https://www.thefire.org/fire-testifies-before-georgia-house-of-representatives-on-campus-due-process.

60 Ruling in *John Doe v. University of Southern California*, California Court of Appeal, 2nd Appellate District, April 5, 2016, http://www.courts.ca.gov/opinions/documents/B262917.PDF.

61 Kat Bocanegra Speed, "Q&A: UCLA Title IX Officer Talks New Model to Investigate Sexual Assault Reports," *Daily Bruin*, January 11, 2016, http://dailybruin.com/2016/01/11/qa-ucla-title-ix-officer-talks-new-model-to-investigate-sexual-assault-reports.

62 Stephen Henrick, "A Hostile Environment for Student Defendants," pp. 75, 84.

63 Joseph Cohn, "Senate Committee Conducts Hearing on Campus Sexual Assault," FIRE, December 9, 2014, https://www.thefire.org/senate-committee-conducts-hearing-campus-sexual-assault.

64 Ashe Schow, "More Evidence That 1 in 5 College Women Have Not Been Sexually Assaulted," December 11, 2014, http://www.washingtonexaminer.com/more-evidence-that-1-in-5-college-women-have-not-been-sexually-assaulted/article/2557262.

65 David Cohen, "Earlier: Akin: 'Legitimate Rape' Rarely Leads to Pregnancy," *Politico*, August 19, 2012, http://www.politico.com/story/2012/08/akin-legitimate-rape-victims-dont-get-pregnant-079864.

66 Chuck Raasch, "McCaskill Criticizes Colleges and Universities on Sexual Assault," *St. Louis Post-Dispatch*, July 9, 2014, http://www.stltoday.com/news/local/crime-and-courts/mccaskill-criticizes-colleges-and-universities-on-sex-assault/article_318798fd-2244-56c5-a5bd-5e46cfa4f278.html.

67 U.S. Senate Subcommittee on Financial and Contracting Oversight, *Sexual Violence on Campus* (2014), http://www.mccaskill.senate.gov/SurveyReportwithAppendix.pdf.

68 Jessica Grose, "The Lenny Interview: Kirsten Gillibrand," *Lenny* (blog), November 6, 2015, http://www.lennyletter.com/politics/interviews/a149/the-lenny-interview-kirsten-gillibrand.

69 Kirsten Gillibrand, "Carrying Their Weight: Giving Voice to Survivors of Campus Sexual Assault," *Huffington Post*, January 21, 2015, http://

www.huffingtonpost.com/rep-kirsten-gillibrand/carrying-their-weight-giv_b_6516630.html.

70   Daniel Flatley, "Sen. Gillibrand Presses President Obama on Campus Sexual Assault; Reforms Would Apply to 2- and 4-year Schools Alike," *Watertown Daily Times*, January 21, 2015, http://www.watertowndailytimes.com/article/20150121/NEWS03/150129750.

71   Caroline Kitchens, "One-Sided Campus-Rape Bill," *National Review*, August 7, 2014, http://www.nationalreview.com/article/384779/one-sided-campus-rape-bill-caroline-kitchens.

72   Not Alone, *Climate Surveys: Useful Tools to Help Colleges and Universities in Their Efforts to Reduce and Prevent Sexual Assault*, https://www.notalone.gov/assets/ovw-climate-survey.pdf.

73   Jacob Gersen and Jeannie Suk Gersen, "The Sex Bureaucracy."

74   Kitchens, "One-Sided Campus-Rape Bill."

75   "Tabulations of the Georgetown University Sexual Assault and Misconduct Climate Survey," June 16, 2016, https://georgetown.app.box.com/s/7pbb03fzqi86v8onp5gylabhz9c6pghm.

76   Ariel Liu, "Campus Climate Survey Ballot Initiative," *Stanford Daily*, April 8, 2016, http://www.stanforddaily.com/2016/04/08/campus-climate-survey-ballot-initiative.

77   "Alumni Letter—Stanford Campus Climate Survey," April 16, 2016, https://www.scribd.com/doc/308656799/Alumni-Letter-Stanford-Campus-Climate-Survey.

78   "CASA One Pager," http://www.scribd.com/doc/235449362/CASA-One-Pager.

79   Joseph Cohn, "Senators Introduce New Version of CASA," FIRE, February 27, 2015, http://www.thefire.org/senators-introduce-new-version-casa.

80   Ashe Schow, "Marco Rubio Spokesman Answers Questions on Campus Sexual Assault Bill," *Washington Examiner*, July 31, 2014, http://washingtonexaminer.com/marco-rubios-office-responds-to-questions-about-campus-sexual-assault-bill/article/2551518.

81   Ashe Schow, "Kelly Ayotte's Spokeswoman Answers Questions about Campus Sexual Assault Bill," August 13, 2014, http://www.washingtonexaminer.com/kelly-ayottes-spokeswoman-answers-questions-about-campus-sexual-assault-bill/article/2551987.

82   KC Johnson, "GOP Officeholders Discover OCR Overreach," *Academic Wonderland* (blog), May 16, 2016, https://academicwonderland.com/2016/05/16/gop-officeholders-discover-ocr-overreach.

83   Nico Lang, "73 Republican Congressmen Challenge Obama's Trans Bathroom Policy," *Advocate*, May 19, 2016, http://www.advocate.com/transgender/2016/5/19/73-republican-congressmen-challenge-obamas-trans-bathroom-policy.

84 Nikki Eastman, "FIRE Written Testimony House Education Committee — With Attachments," FIRE, September 8, 2015, https://www.thefire. org/fire-written-testimony-house-education-committee-with-attachments.

85 Tyler Kingkade, "Activists, College Officials Protest Controversial Campus Rape Bill," *Huffington Post*, September 10, 2015, http://www. huffingtonpost.com/entry/safe-campus-act-opposition_55f1d303e4b0378 4e2787013.

86 Robby Soave, "Rep. Jared Polis Thinks Colleges Should Be Able to Expel Students When They're Only 20% Sure a Rape Happened," *Hit and Run* (blog), Reason.com, September 10, 2015, https://reason.com/ blog/2015/09/10/rep-jared-polis-thinks-colleges-should-b.

87 Stan Garnett, "Stan Garnett: 'Shadow' Campus System Is No Solution" (opinion), *Daily Camera*, September 18, 2015, http://www.dailycamera. com/guest-opinions/ci_28837636/stan-garnett-shadow-campus-system-is-no-solution.

88 Jared Polis, "Jared Polis: Colleges Should Handle Sex Assault Cases" (opinion), *Daily Camera*, September 15, 2015, http://www.dailycamera. com/guest-opinions/ci_28818663/jared-polis-colleges-should-handle-sex-assault-cases.

89 Koran Addo, "SLU Case Highlights the Gray Areas of Campus Sex Assault Investigations," *St. Louis Post-Dispatch*, October 12, 2015, http:// www.stltoday.com/news/local/education/article_160c1a40-03c7-5db7-bb9d-ab23b1ca858e.html.

90 Christina Cauterucci, "Senators Gillibrand and McCaskill Slam Fraternities That Lobby for Sexual Assault Bill," *XX Factor* (blog), *Slate*, October 29, 2015, http://www.slate.com/blogs/xx_factor/2015/10/29/ senators_gillibrand_and_mccaskill_slam_fraternity_organizations_that_ lobby.html.

91 Tyler Kingkade, "Safe Campus Act Continues to Lose Support," *Huffington Post*, November 17, 2015, http://www.huffingtonpost.com/ entry/safe-campus-act-opposition_us_564b4f1be4b08cda348a9a02.

92 Harvey Silverglate, "The New Panic: Campus Sex Assaults" (opinion), *Boston Globe*, February 20, 2015, http://www.bostonglobe.com/opinion/ 2015/02/20/the-new-panic-campus-sex-assaults/ 0X0a9RoCySmrLUMFQ73kWM/story.html.

Chapter 9 – From Campus to Criminal Law

1 J. M. Bishop, "Revisiting Antioch's 'Ask First' Policy 23 Years Later," *Powder Room* (blog), October 5, 2014, http://powderroom.kinja.com/ over-20-years-ago-antioch-college-was-pilloried-nation-1642728042.

2 Anonymous, "Is It Date Rape," SNL Transcripts, http://snltranscripts. jt.org/93/93bdaterape.phtml.

3 Anonymous, "'Ask First' at Antioch" (opinion), *New York Times*,

October 11, 1993, http://www.nytimes.com/1993/10/11/opinion/ask-first-at-antioch.html.

4 Anonymous, "Gettysburg College: Hug at Your Own Risk," FIRE, May 11, 2006, https://www.thefire.org/gettysburg-college-hug-at-your-own-risk.

5 NCHERM Group, "The NCHERM Group Continues to Advocate for Affirmative Consent Policies in Colleges and Schools across the Nation" (news release), October 10, 2014, http://www.prnewswire.com/news-releases/the-ncherm-group-continues-to-advocate-for-affirmative-consent-policies-in-colleges-and-schools-across-the-nation-278778841.html.

6 Jessica Bennett, "Campus Sex…with a Syllabus," January 9, 2016, http://mobile.nytimes.com/2016/01/10/fashion/sexual-consent-assault-college-campuses.html.

7 "The History Behind Sexual Consent Policies" (interview with Kristine Herman), *All Things Considered*, NPR, October 5, 2014, http://www.npr.org/2014/10/05/353922015/the-history-behind-sexual-consent-policies.

8 Kendi A. Rainwater, "Judge Rules Former UTC Wrestler Accused of Rape Shouldn't Have Been Expelled," *Times Free Press*, August 12, 2015, http://www.timesfreepress.com/news/local/story/2015/aug/12/judge-rules-favor-utc-student-accused-rape/319413.

9 Megan McArdle, "'Affirmative Consent' Will Make Rape Laws Worse," *Bloomberg View*, July 1, 2015, http://www.bloombergview.com/articles/2015-07-01/-affirmative-consent-will-make-rape-laws-worse.

10 Patrick McGreevy and Melanie Mason, "Lawmakers OK Bill Setting Standards for Campus Sexual Assault Policies," *Los Angeles Times*, August 28, 2014, http://www.latimes.com/local/politics/la-me-pol-bills-legislature-20140829-story.html.

11 Josh Dulaney, "Students Question 'Affirmative Consent' Bill Designed to Combat Sexual Assaults," *San Gabriel Valley Tribune*, June 8, 2014, http://www.sgvtribune.com/government-and-politics/20140608/students-question-affirmative-consent-bill-designed-to-combat-sexual-assaults.

12 Ibid.

13 Michele Kort, "California Takes On Campus Rape — And So Does Ms.," *Ms.* magazine blog, February 11, 2014, http://msmagazine.com/blog/2014/02/11/california-takes-on-campus-rape-and-so-does-ms.

14 See Jason Laker and Erica Boas' website, Consent Stories, at http://www.consentstories.org.

15 Jake New, "'It Just Happened,'" *Inside Higher Ed*, August 2, 2016, https://www.insidehighered.com/news/2016/08/02/researchers-argue-affirmative-consent-policies-out-touch-reality.

16 Susan Kruth, "California SB 967 Supporters Ignore Due Process Concerns," FIRE, August 15, 2014, https://www.thefire.org/california-sb-967-supporters-ignore-due-process-concerns.

17 Cathy Young, "Campus Rape: The Problem with 'Yes Means Yes'" (opinion), *Time*, August 29, 2014, http://time.com/3222176/campus-rape-the-problem-with-yes-means-yes.

18 All quotes regarding the case at USC come from *John Doe v. Ainsley Carry, et al.*, Superior Court of the State of California, County of Los Angeles, Case BS163736 (documents available at https://kc-johnson.com).

19 Ezra Klein, "'Yes Means Yes' Is a Terrible Law, and I Completely Support It," Vox.com, October 13, 2014, http://www.vox.com/2014/10/13/6966847/yes-means-yes-is-a-terrible-bill-and-i-completely-support-it.

20 Paul O'Donnell, "Ezra Klein Finds Conversations about the Future of Journalism 'Tiresome,'" *Washingtonian*, August 11, 2015, http://www.washingtonian.com/blogs/capitalcomment/media/ezra-klein-finds-conversations-about-the-future-of-journalism-tiresome.php.

21 Cathy Young, "The Argument against Affirmative Consent Laws Gets Voxjacked," *Hit and Run* (blog), Reason.com, October 15, 2014, https://reason.com/blog/2014/10/15/the-argument-against-affirmative-consent.

22 Jonathan Chait, "Liberals Get Illiberal on Campus Rape," Daily Intelligencer, *New York*, October 14, 2014, http://nymag.com/daily/intelligencer/2014/10/does-liberalism-have-an-answer-to-campus-rape.html.

23 Freddie, "The Burden of Expanding the Police State's Power to Prosecute Sex Crimes Will Fall on the Poor and the Black," *Interfaces of the Word – Fredrik deBoer* (blog), October 13, 2014, http://fredrikdeboer.com/2014/10/13/the-burden-of-expanding-the-police-states-power-to-prosecute-sex-crimes-will-fall-on-the-poor-and-the-black.

24 Governor Andrew M. Cuomo, "Governor Cuomo Announces SUNY Adopts a Comprehensive System-Wide Uniform Sexual Assault Policy For All 64 Campuses" (press release), December 2, 2014, https://www.governor.ny.gov/news/governor-cuomo-announces-suny-adopts-comprehensive-system-wide-uniform-sexual-assault-policy.

25 "Enough Is Enough: Combating Sexual Assault on College Campuses," New York State, https://www.ny.gov/programs/enough-enough-combating-sexual-assault-college-campuses.

26 ISDA Staff, "Her Mother's Daughter" (profile of Maria Cuomo Cole), Italian Sons and Daughters of America, July 30, 2015, https://www.orderisda.org/culture/women/her-mothers-daughter.

27 Kathleen Megan, "Senate Passes 'Yes Means Yes' Bill Targeting Sexual

Assault," *Hartford Courant*, May 20, 2015, http://www.courant.com/politics/hc-affirmative-consent-0321-20150520-story.html.

28 Noah Daponte-Smith, "Yale Students Push for Affirmative Consent," *Yale Daily News*, March 4, 2016, http://yaledailynews.com/blog/2016/03/04/yale-students-push-for-affirmative-consent.

29 Devin Keehner, "Why Legislate Sexual Consent for College Students Only?" *Hartford Courant*, February 17, 2015, http://www.courant.com/opinion/op-ed/hc-op-fresh-talk-keehner-sexual-affirmative-consent-0218-20150217-story.html.

30 2015 Minnesota Statutes, Chapter 135A, Sexual Harassment and Violence Policy, https://www.revisor.mn.gov/statutes/?id=135A.15.

31 *trainED Introduction: Student Training and Compliance Requirements* (video), trainED, https://www.youtube.com/watch?v=5tgcj9q_PgM.

32 "Sexual Assaults: TELL US," UW–Madison Police Department, https://uwpd.wisc.edu/tellus.

33 "New UT Sexual Misconduct Policy Goes into Effect Next Week," WBIR.com, http://downtown.wbir.com/news/news/660642-new-ut-sexual-misconduct-policy-goes-effect-next-week.

34 Paul Gowder, September 3, 2015 (12:49 p.m.), comment on Tamara Rice Lave, "Affirmative Consent and Switching the Burden of Proof," *Prawfsblawg* (blog), September 3, 2015, http://prawfsblawg.blogs.com/prawfsblawg/2015/09/affirmative-consent-and-switching-the-burden-of-proof.html.

35 Allie Grasgreen, "Students Lawyer Up," *Inside Higher Ed*, August 26, 2013, https://www.insidehighered.com/news/2013/08/26/north-carolina-becomes-first-state-guarantee-students-option-lawyer-disciplinary.

36 Janel Davis and Shannon McCaffrey, "Wrongly Accused of Rape? Students Question Their Expulsion from Tech," *Atlanta Journal-Constitution*, January 16, 2016, http://www.myajc.com/news/news/local/wrongly-accused-of-rape-students-question-their-ex/np59z.

37 Glenn Harlan Reynolds, "Glenn Reynolds: Turning Tide in War on College Men?" (opinion), *USA Today*, January 28, 2016, http://www.usatoday.com/story/opinion/2016/01/28/glenn-reynolds-turning-tide-war-college-men-georgia-tech-sexual-assault-column/79417496.

38 Greg Bluestein and Jim Galloway, "Powerful State Lawmaker Calls for Georgia Tech President's Ouster," *Political Insider* (blog), *Atlanta Journal-Constitution*, March 7, 2016, http://politics.blog.ajc.com/2016/03/07/powerful-state-lawmaker-calls-for-georgia-tech-presidents-ouster.

39 Jonah Goldberg, "Hillary Clinton's Awkward New Hire," *National Review*, February 11, 2016, http://www.nationalreview.com/corner/431208/clintons-awkward-hire.

40 Daniel Halper, "Hillary Asked Whether Juanita Broaddrick, Kathleen

Willey, and Paula Jones Have Right to Be Believed," *Weekly Standard*, December 3, 2015, http://www.weeklystandard.com/hillary-asked-whether-juanita-broaddrick-kathleen-willey-and-paula-jones-have-right-to-be-believed/article/2000062.

41 Katie Baker, "Juanita Broaddrick Wants to Be Believed," BuzzFeed, August 14, 2016, https://www.buzzfeed.com/katiejmbaker/juanita-broaddrick-wants-to-be-believed.

42 Ben Kamisar, "Sanders: Law Enforcement Should Handle Campus Rape," *Hill*, January 11, 2016, http://thehill.com/blogs/ballot-box/dem-primaries/265515-sanders-law-enforcement-should-handle-campus-rape.

43 Tyler Kingkade, "Bernie Sanders Comments on Campus Rape, and Totally Drops the Ball," *Huffington Post*, January 12, 2016, http://www.huffingtonpost.com/entry/bernie-sanders-campus-rape_us_5695431ee4b086bc1cd5616e; Brett Sokolow, "Bernie Is Wrong about Rape," *Huffington Post, Blog* (blog), January 13, 2016, http://www.huffingtonpost.com/brett-a-sokolow/bernie-is-wrong-about-rape_b_8965772.html.

44 Noah Rothman, "More Compassion Than Conservative," *Commentary*, February 19, 2016, https://www.commentarymagazine.com/politics-ideas/campaigns-elections/john-kasich-more-compassion-conservative.

45 Ashe Schow, "Rubio Should Follow Sanders' Lead on Campus Sexual Assault," *Washington Examiner*, January 14, 2016, http://www.washingtonexaminer.com/rubio-should-follow-sanders-lead-on-campus-sexual-assault/article/2580472.

46 "Marco Rubio: Sexual Assault on Campus Must Be Confronted," Marco Rubio, n.d., https://web.archive.org/web/20160216093704/https://marcorubio.com/news/marco-rubio-campus-sexual-assault-bill-due-process.

47 Conor Skelding, "Weingarten: *Rolling Stone* 'Retraction' Made Her 'Stand Up,'" *Politico*, December 15, 2014, http://www.capitalnewyork.com/article/city-hall/2014/12/8558535/weingarten-emrolling-stoneem-retraction-made-her-stand.

48 "Project on Sexual and Gender-Based Misconduct on Campus: Procedural Frameworks and Analysis," American Law Institute, https://www.ali.org/meetings/show/project-sexual-and-gender-based-misconduct-campus-procedural-frameworks-and-analysis-advisers-meeting; Stuart Taylor Jr., "Legal Group Weighs Radical Expansion of Sex Crimes," *Real Clear Politics*, May 14, 2016, http://www.realclearpolitics.com/articles/2016/05/14/legal_group_weighs_radical_expansion_of_sex_crimes_130557.html.

49 Richard Klein, "An Analysis of Thirty-Five Years of Rape Reform: A Frustrating Search for Fundamental Fairness," *Akron Law Review*

41 (2008), pp. 981–1058, http://digitalcommons.tourolaw.edu/cgi/
viewcontent.cgi?article=1075&context=scholarlyworks.

50 See generally The American Law Institute, Model Penal Code: Sexual
Assault and Related Offenses, Tentative Draft No. 2 (April 15, 2016),
sections 213.0, 213.3.

51 Norman Reimer to ALI Director, Deputy Director, Project Reporters,
Council, and Members, March 22, 2016, https://www.nacdl.org/
comments_mpc_sexual_assault.

52 Stuart Taylor Jr., "Legal Group Weighs Radical Expansion of Sex
Crimes," *Real Clear Politics*, May 14, 2016, http://www.realclearpolitics.
com/articles/2016/05/14/legal_group_weighs_radical_expansion_of_sex_
crimes_130557.html.

53 McArdle, "'Affirmative Consent' Will Make Rape Laws Worse."

54 Stuart Taylor Jr., "Legal Group Weighs Radical Expansion"; ALI Model
Penal Code: Sexual Assault and Related Offenses, *Preliminary Draft No.
5* (September 8, 2015), pp. 68–69.

55 Ashe Schow, "'A Mess': Law Group Rejects Affirmative Consent,"
Washington Examiner, May 18, 2016, http://www.washingtonexaminer.
com/a-mess-law-group-rejects-affirmative-consent/article/2591692.

56 Tentative Draft No. 2, section 213.2.

57 Tentative Draft No. 2, Section 213.9(b).

58 Larry Catá Backer, "Sexual Assualt [*sic*] at the American Law Institute—
Controversy over the Criminalization of Sexual Contact in the Proposed
Revision of the Model Penal Code," *Law at the End of the Day* (blog),
May 14, 2015, http://lcbackerblog.blogspot.com/2015/05/sexual-assualt-
at-american-law.html.

59 Email to Stuart Taylor, March 20–21, 2016.

60 Klein, "Thirty-Five Years of Rape Reform," p. 982.

61 Stacy Futter and Walter Mebane Jr., "The Effects of Rape Law Reform
on Rape Case Processing," *Berkeley Women's Law Journal* 16 (2001), pp.
72–111; Cassia Spohn and Julie Horney, *Rape Law Reform: A Grassroots
Revolution and Its Impact* (New York: Plenum Press, 1992), p. 160; Ronet
Bachman and Raymond Paternoster, "A Contemporary Look at the
Effects of Rape Law Reform: How Far Have We Really Come?" *Journal of
Criminal Law and Criminology* 84 (1993), pp. 554–74.

62 Klein, "Thirty-Five Years of Rape Reform," p. 985.

63 Emily Bazelon, "The St. Paul's Rape Case Shows Why Sexual-Assault
Laws Must Change," *New York Times Magazine*, August 26, 2015, http://
www.nytimes.com/2015/08/26/magazine/the-st-pauls-rape-case-shows-
why-sexual-assault-laws-must-change.html; Deborah Tuerkheimer, "Rape
on and off Campus" (abstract), *Emory Law Journal* 65 (2015), http://

papers.ssrn.com/sol3/papers.cfm?abstract_id=2515905; *Model Penal Code Article 213, Rape and Related Offenses, Prospectus for a Project of Revision*, May 14, 2012, http://jpp.whs.mil/Public/docs/04-Meetings/sub-20150409/09_Prospectus_for_Revision_MPC213.pdf; ALI, *Preliminary Draft No. 5*, p. 45.j.

64 "Crime in the United States 2013: Rape," FBI.gov, https://www.fbi.gov/about-us/cjis/ucr/crime-in-the-u.s/2013/crime-in-the-u.s.-2013/violent-crime/rape.

65 "Crime in the United States by Volume and Rate per 100,000 Inhabitants, 1995–2014," FBI.gov, https://www.fbi.gov/about-us/cjis/ucr/crime-in-the-u.s/2014/crime-in-the-u.s.-2014/tables/table-1.

66 *Commonwealth v. Kenny Lopez*, 745 N.E. 2d 961, 966 (Mass. 2001) (citing *State in the Interest of M.T.S.*, 609 A.2d 1266 (N.J. 1992); *Commonwealth v. Simcock*, 575 N.E. 2d 1137, 1141 (Mass. App. Ct. 1991); *State v. Glenn Reid*, 479 A.2d 1291, 1296 (Me. 1984).

67 Nicholas Little, "From No Means No to Only Yes Means Yes: The Rational Results of an Affirmative Consent Standard in Rape Law," *Vanderbilt Law Review* 58 (2005), pp. 1321, 1324, 1358; Martin D. Schwartz and Walter Dekeseredy, *Sexual Assault on the College Campus: The Role of Male Peer Support* (New York: SAGE Publications, 1997), p. 23; Robin Warshaw, *I Never Called It Rape: The Ms. Report on Recognizing, Fighting and Surviving Date and Acquaintance Rape* (New York: Harper Perennial, reprint edition, 1994), pp. 63–64.

68 Fed. R. Evid. 413(a).

69 *Olden v. Kentucky*, 488 U.S. 227, 231-232 (1988); for a troubling lower-court interpretation, see *Wood v. Alaska*, 957 F.2d 1544 (9th Cir. 1992).

70 Klein, "Thirty-Five Years of Rape Reform," pp. 1021–24.

71 E.g., *State v. Marks*, 647 P.2d 1292, 1299 (Kan. 1982); *State v. Kinney*, 762 A.2d 833 (Vt. 2000); *People v. Baenziger*, 97 P.3d 271, 275 (Colo. App. 2004); *People v. Nelson*, 22 A.D.3d 769, 770 (N.Y. App. Div. 2005). Other states, however, have excluded this testimony; see *People v. Bledsoe*, 681 P.2d 291, 300 (Cal. 1984); *State v. Black*, 745 P.2d 12, 19 (Wash. 1987).

72 Quoting *State v. Saldana*, 324 N.W.2d 227, 230 (Minn. 1982).

73 See Jill Levenson et al., "Sex Offender Residence Restrictions: Sensible Crime Policy or Flawed Logic?" *Federal Probation* 71, no. 3 (2007).

74 Matthew Hale, *Historia Placitorum Coronae: The History of the Pleas of the Crown*, Volume 1 (Philadelphia: Robert H. Small, 1847), p. 635, https://books.google.com/books?id=FhseAAAAMAAJ&pg=PA635#v=onepage&q&f=false.

Chapter 10 – A New Generation's Contempt for Civil Liberties

1 Sheila Coronel, Steve Coll, and Derek Kravitz, "*Rolling Stone* and UVA: The Columbia University Graduate School of Journalism Report," April 5, 2015, http://www.rollingstone.com/culture/features/a-rape-on-campus-what-went-wrong-20150405.

2 Sabrina Rubin Erdely reporting notes, attached to Sabrina Rubin Erdely affidavit, June 30, 2016, in *Nicole Eramo v. Rolling Stone, LLC, et al.*, U.S. District Court for the Western District of Virginia, 2016 U.S. Dist. LEXIS 80794 (available at https://kc-johnson.com).

3 Coronel, Coll, and Kravitz, "*Rolling Stone* and UVA."

4 Sabrina Rubin Erdely reporting notes, attached to Sabrina Rubin Erdely affidavit, June 30, 2016, in *Nicole Eramo v. Rolling Stone, LLC, et al.*

5 Sabrina Rubin Erdely, "A Rape on Campus," http://web.archive.org/web/20141119200349/http://www.rollingstone.com/culture/features/a-rape-on-campus-20141119.

6 Sabrina Rubin Erdely reporting notes, attached to Sabrina Rubin Erdely affidavit, June 30, 2016, in *Nicole Eramo v. Rolling Stone, LLC, et al.*

7 Sabrina Rubin Erdely to Sean Woods, email, October 25, 2014, in Nicole Eramo, "Counter-statement of Facts," July 22, 2016, in *Nicole Eramo v. Rolling Stone, LLC, et al.* (available at https://kc-johnson.com).

8 Cathy Young, "Jackie's UVA Fake Rape Story Had More Red Flags Than a Soviet Military Parade," HeatStreet, July 7, 2016, https://heatst.com/culture-wars/jackies-uva-fake-rape-story-had-more-red-flags-than-a-soviet-military-parade.

9 Sabrina Rubin Erdely affidavit, June 30, 2016; Sean Woods affidavit, June 30, 2016; in *Nicole Eramo v. Rolling Stone, LLC, et al.* (available at https://kc-johnson.com).

10 Sabrina Rubin Erdely deposition, in *Nicole Eramo v. Rolling Stone, LLC, et al.* (available at https://kc-johnson.com); Coronel, Coll, and Kravitz, "*Rolling Stone* and UVA."

11 KC Johnson, "Celebrating Erdely as a Journalist," *Academic Wonderland* (blog), https://academicwonderland.com/2016/07/07/celebrating-erdely-as-a-journalist.

12 Transcript of *The Melissa Harris-Perry Show* for November 29, 2014, NBCNews.com, http://www.nbcnews.com/id/56533906/ns/msnbc/t/melissa-harris-perry-show-saturday-november-th/g.

13 "Article on Brutal Sexual Assault Provokes Investigation" (interview with Sabrina Erdely), *PBS NewsHour*, November 21, 2014, http://www.pbs.org/newshour/bb/article-brutal-sexual-assault-provokes-investigation-university-virginia.

14 "A Message from President Sullivan Regarding Sexual Violence,"

UVA Today, November 22, 2014, https://news.virginia.edu/content/message-president-sullivan-regarding-sexual-violence.

15 "Statement from U-Va. President Teresa Sullivan on Sexual Assault Allegations," *Washington Post*, November 22, 2014, https://www.washingtonpost.com/local/education/statement-from-u-va-president-teresa-sullivan-on-sexual-assault-allegations/2014/11/22/342d40ec-728c-11e4-8808-afaa1e3a33ef_story.html.

16 Michael McDonald and Allyson Versprille, "UVA Faculty Propose Extending Frat Ban through School Year," Bloomberg, December 3, 2014, http://www.bloomberg.com/news/articles/2014-12-03/uva-faculty-propose-longer-frat-ban-as-alleged-rape-investigated.

17 Jeffrey Scott Shapiro, "Unpunished Vandalism Rampage Inspired by *Rolling Stone*'s U.Va. Rape Story," *Washington Times*, December 21, 2014, http://www.washingtontimes.com/news/2014/dec/21/rolling-stone-university-of-virginia-rape-story-sp/?page=all.

18 Thrisha Potluri, "Faculty Host 'Take Back the Party' Protest on Beta Bridge, Corner," *Cavalier Daily*, November 23, 2014, http://www.cavalierdaily.com/article/2014/11/faculty-host-take-back-the-party-protest-on-beta-bridge.

19 McDonald and Versprille, "UVA Faculty Propose Extending Frat Ban."

20 Sandy Hausman, "Magazine Sheds Light on Allegations of Rape Culture at UVA," *Morning Edition*, NPR, November 25, 2014, http://www.npr.org/2014/11/25/366504641/university-of-virginia-investigates-rape-allegations.

21 Anna Higgins, Lee Williams, and Madeline Nagy, "University Faculty Respond to *Rolling Stone* Article Released Wednesday," *Cavalier Daily*, November 25, 2014, http://www.cavalierdaily.com/article/2014/11/university-faculty-respond-to-rolling-stone-article-released-wednesday.

22 Chuck Ross, "Phi Kappa Psi Lawsuit against *Rolling Stone*," http://www.scribd.com/doc/289602946/Phi-Kappa-Psi-lawsuit-against-Rolling-Stone.

23 Richard Bradley, "Is the *Rolling Stone* Story True?" *Shots in the Dark* (blog), November 24, 2014, http://www.richardbradley.net/shotsinthedark/2014/11/24/is-the-rolling-stone-story-true.

24 Robby Soave, "Is the UVA Rape Story a Gigantic Hoax?" *Hit and Run* (blog), Reason.com, December 1, 2014, https://reason.com/blog/2014/12/01/is-the-uva-rape-story-a-gigantic-hoax.

25 Kat Stoeffel, "The UVA Gang Rape Backlash Is a Trap for Feminists," *New York*, December 3, 2014, http://nymag.com/thecut/2014/12/doubting-uvas-gang-rape-victim-is-a-trap.html.

26 Anna Merlan, "'Is the UVA Rape Story a Gigantic Hoax?' Asks Idiot," *Jezebel*, December 1, 2014, http://jezebel.com/is-the-uva-rape-story-a-gigantic-hoax-asks-idiot-1665233387.

27 https://twitter.com/nero/status/584870076697935872 (account suspended).

28 Graelyn Brashear, "UVA Activists, Author of *Rolling Stone* Article Speak," *C-VILLE*, November 26, 2014, http://www.c-ville.com/uva-activists-author-rolling-stone-article-speak.

29 Hanna Rosin, June Thomas, and Katy Waldman, "DoubleX Gabfest: The Butch Goddess Edition" (*Slate* podcast), November 27, 2014, http://www.slate.com/articles/podcasts/doublex_gabfest/2014/11/the_double_x_gabfest_on_uva_frats_and_rape_in_rolling_stone_husbands_hurting.html.

30 T. Rees Shapiro, "U-Va. Students Challenge *Rolling Stone* Account of Alleged Sexual Assault," *Washington Post*, December 10, 2014, https://www.washingtonpost.com/local/education/u-va-students-challenge-rolling-stone-account-of-attack/2014/12/10/ef345e42-7fcb-11e4-81fd-8c4814dfa9d7_story.html.

31 Sabrina Rubin Erdely reporting notes, attached to Sabrina Rubin Erdely affidavit, June 30, 2016, in *Nicole Eramo v. Rolling Stone, LLC, et al.*

32 McDonald and Versprille, "UVA Faculty Propose Extending Frat Ban"; Karin Kapsidelis, "As Calls Mount from Lawmakers, U.Va. to Address How It Handles Assault," *Richmond Times-Dispatch*, December 1, 2014, http://www.timesdispatch.com/news/sullivan-uva-too-good-to-allow-evil-to-reside/article_9e6c3480-3ab3-5896-84c2-feffdad5ecao.html.

33 Ravi Somaiya, "Magazine's Account of Gang Rape on Virginia Campus Comes under Scrutiny," *New York Times*, December 2, 2014, http://www.nytimes.com/2014/12/03/us/magazines-account-of-gang-rape-on-virginia-campus-comes-under-scrutiny.html.

34 Shapiro, "U-Va. Students Challenge *Rolling Stone* Account."

35 Sabrina Rubin Erdely affidavit, June 30, 2016, in *Nicole Eramo v. Rolling Stone, LLC, et al.*

36 Chuck Ross, "Did UVA Student Plagiarize 'Dawson's Creek' in Love Letter to Friend?" *Daily Caller*, December 18, 2014, http://dailycaller.com/2014/12/18/did-uva-student-plagiarize-dawsons-creek-in-love-letter-to-friend.

37 Nicole Eramo motion, January 6, 2016, in *Nicole Eramo v. Rolling Stone, LLC, et al.* (available at https://kc-johnson.com).

38 T. Rees Shapiro, "Key Elements of *Rolling Stone*'s U-Va. Gang Rape Allegations in Doubt," *Washington Post*, December 5, 2014, http://wapo.st/1vnF3ed.

39 Sabrina Rubin Erdely reporting notes, attached to Sabrina Rubin Erdely affidavit, June 30, 2016, in *Nicole Eramo v. Rolling Stone, LLC, et al.*

40 Hanna Rosin, "Blame *Rolling Stone*," *Slate*, December 5, 2014, http://www.slate.com/articles/double_x/doublex/2014/12/rolling_stone_backs_away_from_its_uva_gang_rape_story.2.html.

41 Coronel, Coll, and Kravitz, "*Rolling Stone* and UVA"; see also KC Johnson, "It Could Have Been True, So Why Not Print It?" *Minding the Campus* (blog), April 6, 2015, http://www.mindingthecampus. org/2015/04/it-could-have-been-true-so-why-not-print-it.

42 Richard Bradley, "In the End, It's All about Rape Culture—or the Lack Thereof," *Shots in the Dark* (blog), April 7, 2015, http://www. richardbradley.net/shotsinthedark/2015/04/07/in-the-end-its-all-about-rape-culture-or-the-lack-thereof (emphasis removed).

43 Michael Wolff, "Wolff: At *Rolling Stone*, 'Rape Culture' Stopped Questions," *USA Today*, April 9, 2015, http://www.usatoday.com/ story/money/columnist/wolff/2015/04/08/rolling-stone-story-and-rape-culture/25464501.

44 "*Rolling Stone* and Rape on Campus" (editorial), *New York Times*, December 8, 2014, http://www.nytimes.com/2014/12/09/opinion/rolling-stone-and-rape-on-campus.html.

45 *Sen. Kirsten Gillibrand Targets the Rape Epidemic on College Campuses* (video), Women in the World, April 24, 2015, https://youtu.be/ yqRz_znYgQw.

46 KC Johnson, "Jackie's Story and UVA's Stalinist Rules," *Minding the Campus* (blog), December 16, 2014, http://www.mindingthecampus. com/2014/12/jackies-story-and-uvas-stalinist-rules.

47 Chuck Ross, "Department of Education Still Standing by Comments Official Made in Debunked *Rolling Stone* Article," *Daily Caller*, July 2, 2015, http://dailycaller.com/2015/07/02/department-of-education-still-standing-by-comments-official-made-in-debunked-rolling-stone-article.

48 Letter from Alice B. Wender (OCR) to Teresa A. Sullivan (UVA), September 21, 2015, https://www2.ed.gov/documents/press-releases/ university-virginia-letter.pdf.

49 *Taking Action on Sexual Assault: A Student Perspective*, http://media.cav. s3.amazonaws.com/10072_studentssexualassaultsolutionso.pdf.

50 Marissa Daisy Alioto, "Life after *Rolling Stone*: UVA Students See 'Jackie' as Opportunity to Reform Sexist Greek System," *International Business Times*, December 12, 2014, http://www.ibtimes.com/life-after-rolling-stone-uva-students-see-jackie-opportunity-reform-sexist-greek-1749631.

51 Julia Horowitz, "Why We Believed Jackie's Rape Story," *Politico*, December 6, 2014, http://www.politico.com/magazine/story/2014/12/why-we-believed-jackies-story-113365.html.

52 Kelly Kaler, "Student-Produced Video Thanks Jackie for 'Pulling Back the Curtain' on Rape," *Cavalier Daily*, December 11, 2014, http://www. cavalierdaily.com/article/2014/12/students-produce-video-thanking-jackie.

53 Alioto, "Life after *Rolling Stone*."

54 Kelly Kaler, "Sullivan Requests Phi Kappa Psi Investigation," *Cavalier*

Daily, November 21, 2014, http://www.cavalierdaily.com/article/2014/11/sullivan-requests-phi-psi-investigation.

55 https://twitter.com/kcjohnson9/statuses/685597371431010304.

56 Associated Press, "Correction: UVa Fraternity–*Rolling Stone* story," December 15, 2014, http://bigstory.ap.org/article/0559772b9bdb44b0b6d05a034c3d8bb2/friends-say-they-pushed-uva-jackie-call-cops.

57 Ryan Duffin deposition, in *Nicole Eramo v. Rolling Stone, LLC, et al.* (available at https://kc-johnson.com).

58 Catherine E. Shoichet, "Hannah Graham Case: Jesse Matthew Charged with Capital Murder," CNN, May 5, 2015, http://www.cnn.com/2015/05/05/us/jesse-matthew-hannah-graham-capital-murder.

59 FIRE, "Complaint in '*Doe v. Lhamon*,'" https://www.thefire.org/complaint-doe-v-lhamon.

60 Dauber screenshot, at https://twitter.com/kcjohnson9/status/743573070875615232.

61 Know Your IX to Chairman King, Ranking Member Cohen, and Members of the Executive Overreach Task Force, May 24, 2016, http://knowyourix.org/wp-content/uploads/Letter-to-House-Judiciary-Cmte-Task-Force-on-Executive-Overreach.pdf.

62 KC Johnson, "More on the Rape Accusation at Brown," *Minding the Campus* (blog), June 12, 2012, http://www.mindingthecampus.org/2012/06/more_on_the_rape_accusation_at_brown/#more-8367.

63 Katherine Cusumano and Tonya Riley, "Sexual Misconduct Process Alienates Accused," *Brown Daily Herald*, April 24, 2013, http://www.browndailyherald.com/2013/04/24/sexual-misconduct-disciplinary-process-alienates-accused.

64 Harvey Silverglate, authors' interview.

65 David Duncan to Office for Civil Rights, June 11, 2014, copy in *John Doe v. Brown University*, U.S. District Court for the District of Rhode Island, 2016 U.S. Dist. LEXIS 21027 (available at https://kc-johnson.com).

66 Cathy Young, "Exclusive: Brown University Student Speaks Out on What It's Like to Be Accused of Rape," *Daily Beast*, June 7, 2014, http://www.thedailybeast.com/articles/2014/06/08/exclusive-brown-university-student-speaks-out-on-what-it-s-like-to-be-accused-of-rape.html.

67 "Safety Information: Suspected Use of Date Rape Drugs," Vice President for Campus Life and Student Services, Brown University, October 25, 2014, http://www.brown.edu/about/administration/vp-campus-life/news/2014-10/safety-information-suspected-use-date-rape-drugs.

68 Duncan Gallagher and Kate Talerico, "Email Clarifies Interim Alcohol Policy Changes," *Brown Daily Herald*, January 30, 2015, http://www.browndailyherald.com/2015/01/30/email-clarifies-interim-alcohol-policy-changes.

69 Emma Harris, "Undergrads Question New Alcohol Policy," *Brown Daily Herald*, January 22, 2015, http://www.browndailyherald.com/2015/01/22/ undergrads-question-new-alcohol-policy.

70 Greg Piper, "After Lab Recants Date-Rape Drug Finding, Brown Stands by Its Punishment of Frat," *College Fix*, March 4, 2015, http://www. thecollegefix.com/post/21503.

71 Shavon Bell and Aleksandra Lifshits, "Campus Reacts to New Details in Phi Psi Case," *Brown Daily Herald*, March 5, 2015, http://www. browndailyherald.com/2015/03/05/campus-reacts-new-details-phi- psi-case.

72 "Gretchen Schultz | French Studies," Brown University, http://www. brown.edu/academics/french-studies/gretchen-schultz.

73 Kate Talerico, "Students Appointed to Title IX Council, Oversight Board," *Brown Daily Herald*, September 21, 2015, http://www. browndailyherald.com/2015/09/21/students-appointed-to-title-ix- council-oversight-board.

74 *John Doe v. Brown University*, U.S. District Court for the District of Rhode Island, 2016 U.S. Dist. LEXIS 21027 (documents available at https://kc-johnson.com).

75 *John Doe v. Brown University*, U.S. District Court for the District of Rhode Island, Case 1:16-cv-00077 (documents available at https:// kc-johnson.com).

76 Alex Volpicello, "Why We Need to Stop the Student Convicted of Sexual Assault from Coming Back to Brown," *The Tab*, September 1, 2016, http://thetab.com/us/brown/2016/09/01/why-we-need-to-stop-the- student-convicted-of-sexual-assault-coming-back-to-brown-3077.

77 "Editorial: On-Campus Discipline for Sexual Assault," *Daily Princetonian*, May 6, 2013, http://dailyprincetonian.com/opinion/2013/05/ editorial-on-campus-discipline-for-sexual-assault.

78 "'News' View: Punishing Sexual Violence," *Yale Daily News*, September 6, 2013, http://yaledailynews.com/blog/2013/09/06/ punishing-sexual-violence.

79 Ivan B. K. Levingston and Tyler S. B. Olkowski, "Sexual Assault Policy Changes Met with Mixed Reactions from Student Leaders, Activists," *Harvard Crimson*, July 28, 2014, http://www.thecrimson.com/ article/2014/7/28/sexual-assault-reform-reactions.

80 "U.Va. Fraternity Lawsuit Is Harmful" (editorial), *Daily Collegian*, April 9, 2015, http://www.collegian.psu.edu/opinion/editorials/article_ eaec4bc8-de3b-11e4-b593-7b278b3005da.html.

81 "Zero Tolerance: Here or Anywhere," *Middlebury Campus*, http:// middleburycampus.com/article/zero-tolerance-here-or-anywhere.

82 "Editorial: Sexual Assault 'Yes Means Yes' Legislation Necessary in

Understanding Consent and the Accused," *Daily Free Press*, October 19, 2015, http://dailyfreepress.com/2015/10/19/editorial-sexual-assault-yes-means-yes-legislation-necessary-in-understanding-consent-and-the-accused.

83 Adriana Miele, "Miele: The Brunch Problem," *Yale Daily News*, February 4, 2016, http://yaledailynews.com/blog/2016/02/04/miele-the-brunch-problem/#pq=ulbyw7.

84 Dylan Alles et al., "Sexual Healing: Senior Girls Want Action," *Colby Echo*, November 19, 2015, http://colbyechonews.com/sexual-healing-senior-girls-want-action.

85 Mary Jarvis, "Cornell Students' Emotional Reactions to Alleged Sexual Assault," *USA Today College*, February 9, 2016, http://college.usatoday.com/2016/02/09/cornell-students-emotional-reactions-to-alleged-sexual-assault.

86 "Washington Post-Kaiser Family Foundation Survey of College Students on Sexual Assault," http://apps.washingtonpost.com/g/page/national/washington-post-kaiser-family-foundation-survey-of-college-students-on-sexual-assault/1726 (page 13).

87 Jacob Poushter, "40% of Millennials OK with Limiting Speech Offensive to Minorities," Pew Research Center, November 20, 2015, http://www.pewresearch.org/fact-tank/2015/11/20/40-of-millennials-ok-with-limiting-speech-offensive-to-minorities.

88 *Free Expression on Campus: A Survey of U.S. College Students and U.S. Adults* (Washington, D.C.: Gallup, Inc., 2016), http://www.knightfoundation.org/media/uploads/publication_pdfs/FreeSpeech_campus.pdf.

89 Camilla Brandfield-Harvey and Caroline Kelly, "Janus Forum Sexual Assault Event Sparks Controversy," *Brown Daily Herald*, November 17, 2014, http://www.browndailyherald.com/2014/11/17/janus-forum-sexual-assault-event-sparks-controversy.

90 "Email from President Christina Paxson to the Brown Community," FIRE, November 14, 2014, https://www.thefire.org/email-president-christina-paxson-brown-community.

91 Samantha Miller, "Brown University's Two-Faced Attitude toward Free Speech," FIRE, November 18, 2014, https://www.thefire.org/brown-universitys-two-faced-attitude-toward-free-speech.

92 Noah Fitzgerel, "[Liveblog] How Should Colleges Handle Sexual Assault?" *Brown Political Review*, November 18, 2014, http://www.brownpoliticalreview.org/2014/11/liveblog-how-should-colleges-handle-sexual-assault.

93 Judith Shulevitz, "In College and Hiding from Scary Ideas," *New York Times Sunday Review*, March 21, 2015, http://www.nytimes.

com/2015/03/22/opinion/sunday/judith-shulevitz-hiding-from-scary-ideas.html.

94 Cathy Young, "The Debate at Brown," *Minding the Campus* (blog), November 24, 2014, http://www.mindingthecampus.com/2014/11/the-debate-at-brown.

95 "No More Distractions" (editorial), *Hoya*, April 21, 2015, http://www.thehoya.com/no-more-distractions.

96 Oberlin community members, "In Response to Sommers' Talk: A Love Letter to Ourselves" (letter), *Oberlin Review*, April 18, 2015, http://oberlinreview.org/8032/opinions/in-response-to-sommers-talk-a-love-letter-to-ourselves.

97 *Victims, Victims Everywhere: Trigger Warnings, Liberty, and the Academy* (video), Hillsdale College, May 28, 2015, https://youtu.be/WW5j3TtIV7U?t=564.

98 *George Washington Forum 16 FEB 2015* (video), CreMedia Productions, February 19, 2015, https://www.youtube.com/watch?v=KH26HU7JldA.

99 Teresa Watanabe, "Sharp Divisions Emerge on Campuses as Some Criticize Activists' Tactics as Intimidation," *Los Angeles Times*, November 20, 2015, http://www.latimes.com/local/education/la-me-campus-dissent-20151121-story.html.

100 Jonathan V. Last, "It's All About 'Muscle: Understanding the Campus Unrest,'" *Weekly Standard*, December 14, 2015, http://www.weeklystandard.com/its-all-about-muscle/article/2000074.

101 See "the demands," http://www.thedemands.org.

102 "Email from the Intercultural Affairs Committee," FIRE, October 27, 2015, https://www.thefire.org/email-from-intercultural-affairs.

103 "Email from Erika Christakis: 'Dressing Yourselves,' Email to Silliman College (Yale) Students on Halloween Costumes," FIRE, October 30, 2015, https://www.thefire.org/email-from-erika-christakis-dressing-yourselves-email-to-silliman-college-yale-students-on-halloween-costumes.

104 Haley Hudler, "Yale Students Demand Resignations from Faculty Members over Halloween Email," FIRE, November 6, 2015, https://www.thefire.org/yale-students-demand-resignations-from-faculty-members-over-halloween-email.

105 http://www.thedemands.org.

106 "Letters of Solidarity," http://amherstuprising.com/letters.html.

107 Rachel Favors, "College Sees No Official Reports of Violence at Protest, Despite Rumors," *Dartmouth*, November 17, 2015, http://thedartmouth.com/2015/11/17/college-sees-no-official-reports-of-violence-at-protest-despite-rumors.

108 Blake Neff, "Dartmouth Admin APOLOGIZES to Protesters Who

Menaced Students," *Daily Caller*, November 17, 2015, http://dailycaller.com/2015/11/17/dartmouth-admin-apologizes-to-protesters-who-menaced-students.

109 KC Johnson, "At Duke, 'Intolerance' Can Cost You Tenure," *Minding the Campus* (blog), November 21, 2015, http://www.mindingthecampus.org/2015/11/at-duke-intolerance-can-cost-you-tenure.

110 Daniel Garisto, "Better Media Coverage of Sexual Assault for Survivors" (opinion), *Columbia Daily Spectator*, February 3, 2015, http://columbiaspectator.com/opinion/2015/02/03/better-media-coverage-sexual-assault-survivors.

111 Josh Kolb, "The Trivialization of Sexual Assault" (opinion), *Columbia Daily Spectator*, September 30, 2015, http://columbiaspectator.com/opinion/2015/09/30/trivialization-sexual-assault.

112 Toni Airaksinen, "Rape Culture and the Problem with the 1 in 5 Sexual Assault Statistic" (opinion), *Columbia Daily Spectator*, February 24, 2016, http://columbiaspectator.com/opinion/2016/02/24/rape-culture-and-problem-1-5-sexual-assault-statistic.

113 Jake Goldberg, et al., to Office for Civil Rights, April 15, 2016 (copy in authors' possession).

114 Isaac Cohen, "Cohen: Leave Rape to Courts," *Yale Daily News*, February 27, 2015, http://yaledailynews.com/blog/2015/02/27/leave-rape-to-courts.

Conclusion

1 Emily Yoffe, "College Women: Stop Getting Drunk," *Slate*, October 15, 2013, http://www.slate.com/articles/double_x/doublex/2013/10/sexual_assault_and_drinking_teach_women_the_connection.html.

2 Ashe Schow, "Kirsten Gillibrand Claims Her Bill Gives Equal Rights to Accusers and Accused, but It Doesn't," *Washington Examiner*, June 17, 2015, http://www.washingtonexaminer.com/kirsten-gillibrand-claims-her-bill-gives-equal-rights-to-accusers-and-accused-but-it-doesnt/article/2566469.

3 "How Many Unfounded Crimes Were Reported?" U.S. Dept. of Education, Campus Safety and Security, http://ope.ed.gov/campussafety/Trend/public/#/answer/5/501/main?row=-1&column=-1.

4 *Sen. Alexander Oversight* (video), KC Johnson, May 2, 2015, https://www.youtube.com/watch?v=BEJSKwKBgLM.

5 Jake New, "Campus Sexual Assault in a Trump Era," *Inside Higher Ed*, November 10, 2016, https://www.insidehighered.com/news/2016/11/10/trump-and-gop-likely-try-scale-back-title-ix-enforcement-sexual-assault.

6 Robby Soave, "Campus Rape Expert Who Misrepresented His Work Faces Powerful New Criticism," *Hit & Run* (blog),

Reason, August 11, 2015, http://reason.com/blog/2015/08/11/
campus-rape-expert-who-misrepresented-hi.

7 Barry Latzer, "Rape and Retribution: Jon Krakauer's Compelling but
Misguided *Missoula*" (book review), *City Journal*, January 28, 2016, http://
www.city-journal.org/html/rape-and-retribution-14166.html.

INDEX

The use of a * behind a name denotes a pseudonym.